WHOM FORTUNE FAVOURS

Whom Fortune Favours

THE BANK OF MONTREAL AND THE RISE OF NORTH AMERICAN FINANCE

Volume One: A Dominion of Capital, 1817–1945

LAURENCE B. MUSSIO

Foreword by Niall Ferguson

McGill-Queen's University Press
Montreal & Kingston | London | Chicago

© McGill-Queen's University Press 2020

ISBN 978-0-2280-0068-6 (cloth)
ISBN 978-0-2280-0069-3 (ePDF)

Legal deposit first quarter 2020
Bibliothèque nationale du Québec

Printed in Canada on acid-free paper

Funded by the   Financé par le
Government   gouvernement      Canada Council   Conseil des arts
of Canada   du Canada   for the Arts   du Canada

We acknowledge the support of the Canada Council for the Arts.
Nous remercions le Conseil des arts du Canada de son soutien.

Library and Archives Canada Cataloguing in Publication

Title: Whom fortune favours : the Bank of Montreal and the rise of North American
   finance / Laurence B. Mussio ; foreword by Niall Ferguson.
Names: Mussio, Laurence B., author.
Description: Includes bibliographical references and index. | Contents: Volume I.
   A dominion of capital, 1817–1945.
Identifiers: Canadiana (print) 2019013304X | Canadiana (ebook) 20190133376
   | ISBN 9780228000686 (set ; cloth) | ISBN 9780228000693 (set ; ePDF)
Subjects: LCSH: Bank of Montreal—History. | LCSH: Banks and
   banking—Canada—History.
Classification: LCC HG2710.M63 B328 2020 | DDC 332.1/20971—dc23

Set in 11/14 Sina Nova by Sayre Street Books
Book design by Garet Markvoort, zijn digital

The author dedicates this book to the four living leaders
of the Bank of Montreal, past and present:

W. Darryl White
William A. Downe
F. Anthony Comper
Matthew W. Barrett

Each in their time
assumed the burden and privilege
of inheriting a remarkable past,
responding to the grand challenges and opportunities of the present,
and renewing their institution for the future that awaits

CONTENTS

VOLUME ONE: A DOMINION OF CAPITAL, 1817–1945

A Note to Readers by Darryl White   xi

Foreword by Niall Ferguson   xiii

Acknowledgments   xix

Tables and Figures   xxiii

General Introduction   xxv

Part One | In the Beginning, 1760–1817   1

1   An Unchartered Territory   3

Part Two | Forging Canadian Finance, 1817–1870   19

Introduction   20

2   Canada's Reputational Capitalists   27

3   Style, Strategy, Stability   42

4   Legislator, Lord, Banker   56

5   Risk, Return, Reward   81

Part Three | Fortune's Faithful Disciples, 1870–1918   103

Introduction   104

6   Players and Performance: Strategy and Organization   113

7   Bankers and Nation Builders   143

8   Capital Unshackled: Bankers, Mergers, Trade,
    and the Expansionist Spirit   164

Part Four | A Changeful Fortune, 1918–1945   183

Introduction   184

9   The Boreal Winds   191

10   The Montreal Banker's Paradox   221

11   No Banker's Dominion: Montreal Bankers and the
     Financial Fate of Newfoundland   241

12   Winners, Losers, and Bankers: The Making of the Bank of Canada   253

13   Building Canada's Financial Arsenal   287

Notes   303

VOLUME TWO: TERRITORIES OF TRANSFORMATION, 1946–2017

Tables and Figures   xi

Preface   xiii

Part Five | A Magnificent Facade, 1946–1974   1

Introduction   2

14   *Les Trente Glorieuses?* 1946–1973   6

15   Remaking the Bank of Montreal in an Era of Transformation,
     1965–1974   48

16   The [Digital] Conversion of St James [Street]   66

Part Six | The Road of Return, 1974–1989   93

Introduction   94

17   The Saviour General and the Two-Front War, 1975–1989   98

18   The Day the BMO Universe Changed   152

19   The Far Journey: The Bank in the World   172

Part Seven | A Time to Every Purpose, 1990–2017   207

Introduction   208

20   The Great Regeneration, 1990–1997   212

21   Trajectories, 1998–2017   231

Section 1: The Icarus Trap   231

Section 2: The Phoenix Protocol   246

Epilogue | One Past, Many Possible Futures   265

Afterword for Academic Readers   271

Notes   275

Bibliography   309

Index   337

A NOTE TO READERS

Darryl White
CEO, *BMO Financial Group*

Being the subject of an academic volume of history is like hearing a recording of your own voice for the first time, or catching a glimpse of yourself in a photo: we're usually surprised at the voice – do I really sound like that? – and, because a camera does not lie, we gain a new perspective.

For those of us who have had the honour to work at the Bank of Montreal, reading *Whom Fortune Favours* is bound to have a similar effect. Dr Laurence Mussio's comprehensive and definitive history sheds new light on the institution we know and love, and on the generations of bankers who have shaped what it is today.

I have the privilege to serve as the first CEO of BMO's third century of business. My tenure began on the eve of the Bank's bicentennial celebration on 3 November 2017. So, naturally, these pages tell the story of the leaders who preceded me.

Two of them – my friends Bill Downe and Tony Comper – were the individuals who conceived the project. It was Tony who first engaged Laurence Mussio to capture an oral history of the Bank by interviewing its top leaders, and it was Bill who invited Laurence to write the book. He did so on condition that he bring a historian's discipline to the project, and that he have the independence and freedom to produce a careful examination of the Bank worthy of review by his academic peers.

Our interest and willingness to participate hinged on our belief that critical self-examination helps inform future action. We need the next generation of bankers to learn from the experience of those who came before them.

Both conditions have been met – and exceeded.

Laurence's careful research relied, in part, on original files from the BMO Archives not available to outside researchers, but it went far beyond the archival record at the Bank. *Whom Fortune Favours* is a detailed accounting not only of BMO's growth over time but also of the Bank's place in the evolution of Canada's economy and global financial services. Decision-makers of today will quickly recognize that their predecessors faced similar situations in their time; in many ways, the driving forces in 2020 of adapting to technological change, growing through economic cycles, serving clients, and beating the competition were also at work in 1817.

What also remains the same – and shines through in this history – are the values shared by ten generations of BMO bankers which motivated their actions. Today, we define them as Integrity, Empathy, Diversity, and Responsibility – but, whatever labels are used, they form the foundation that inspires us to help businesses and individuals to succeed and, by doing so, to make our nation and society more prosperous and purposeful. Or, as Laurence puts it, "there is a BMO way, a BMO personality, a solidarity, an approach to people and projects, an earned reputation of standing by clients and getting through tough times together."

I recommend this book to anyone who wants to understand how organizations thrive and evolve over time, or who wants to gain new insights into the economic forces that brought Canada into being, or who simply wants to learn more about the financial-services industry – and to anyone who enjoys a good story, well told, because Laurence's storytelling skills are superb. In particular, I recommend it to my colleagues at Bank of Montreal who share my pride in being part of Canada's First Bank and now have the chance to know it better!

I trust you'll enjoy this history of our Bank that skilfully chronicles the trials and triumphs of those who came before us. As for the generation of bankers serving BMO's customers in 2020?

We're just getting started.

FOREWORD

Niall Ferguson

Books about bankers do not generally attract as wide a readership as books about kings and queens, emperors and generals, presidents and princesses. This is a pity. Most of us interact much more frequently with the financial system than with the political system. We go to the ATM far more often than to the polling booth. If we are prudent, we read our bank statement as attentively as the front page of the newspaper. To be ignorant of financial history is thus to be ignorant of an indispensable part of modern economic life.

In many respects, the United States and Canada are similar. Indeed, if you dropped the average Briton in Toronto or Vancouver, she might take some time to work out that she was not in fact in Chicago or Seattle. To European ears, there is just one generic North American accent. When I first visited Canada as a boy in the 1970s, what struck me most was how much more it resembled the glitzy United States I had seen on television than grim old Scotland.

Yet, in a number of very important ways, Canada and the United States are different, despite their superficial resemblances, and perhaps no difference is more pronounced than the one between their financial systems. To read Laurence B. Mussio's deeply researched and insightful history of the Bank of Montreal is to appreciate the depth of that difference. It is true today that the Bank of Montreal is a North American bank – and one of the top ten. However, for roughly the first century and a half of its existence it was much more a British bank – and indeed a Scottish one.

When the Articles of Association of the Montreal Bank were posted on 19 May 1817, less than two years had elapsed since Napoleon's defeat at Waterloo. Only five years before, US troops had launched an abortive invasion of Britain's remaining North American colonies. Beginning in the 1770s, the population of what was to become Canada had received a substantial boost from Loyalists – up to half a million people who had opted to remain faithful to the crown by emigrating northward from the thirteen rebellious colonies.

Scots were overrepresented in the British Empire. By the end of the nineteenth century, around three-quarters of the population of Great Britain lived in England, compared with a tenth in Scotland and a tenth in Ireland. But in the Empire the English accounted for barely half of colonists. Scots constituted around 21 per cent of the British-born population in Canada; around the same proportion was of Irish origin. The Bank of Montreal reflected this. Among the nine founders of the Bank, there was one French Canadian, Augustin (Austin) Cuvillier, and one Massachusetts man, Horatio Gates. But most were Scots. John Richardson consciously modelled the Bank on the half-Scottish Alexander Hamilton's First Bank of the United States. Other founders included the Presbyterian George Garden and Peter McGill, "perhaps the most popular Scotchman that has ever lived in Montreal." McGill's successor as president, Thomas B. Anderson, had been born in Edinburgh in 1796. John Redpath, vice-president of the Bank between 1860 and 1869, was born in Earlston in Berwickshire the same year.

In the later nineteenth century, too, the Bank of Montreal was in many respects an institution run by expatriate Scots. David Torrance was the son of a Lowland Scot. George Stephen was born in Banffshire. Richard Bladworth Angus hailed from Bathgate. Sir George Alexander Drummond started life in Edinburgh. The best known of them was Donald Alexander Smith, 1st Baron Strathcona and Mount Royal, who first saw the light of day in Forres on the Moray coast in 1820. It is not surprising that the building that housed the Bank's headquarters from 1848 was a neo-classical near-replica of the Edinburgh head office of the Commercial Bank of Scotland.

None of this was unusual. To an extent that still tends to be underestimated, the British Empire, though it was sometimes depicted as an elaborate English hierarchy extending downward from the Queen-Empress Victoria, was in reality run by a network of Scottish professionals: not only bankers but also engineers, physicians, teachers, and clergymen.

This strong Scottish influence helps explain not only the architecture of the Bank of Montreal but also the major difference in financial regulation between Canada and the United States. As Laurence Mussio explains:

> The Canadian branch-banking system was based on a British system. It had its roots in Scotland, and it was the prominent Anglo-Canadian businessman Alexander Tilloch Galt who, as finance minister in 1860, proposed that the Canadian banking system should expand across the

country "through the extension of branch networks of the existing banks rather than through the creation of new banks." This approach was in sharp contrast with the United States, which adopted a banking system based on "unit banks," established under federal or state jurisdiction. The American system famously veered away from branch banking after the National Banking Act of 1864. Individual states passed banking statutes that controlled banks founded with state charters.

The very different system that evolved in the United States led to formation of hundreds of banks – there were 849 by 1839 – and later thousands. By contrast (and as also happened in Scotland), a small number of big banks emerged in Canada. The nineteenth-century rivalry between the Bank of Montreal and the Royal Bank of Canada had its counterpart in that between the Bank of Scotland and the Royal Bank of Scotland. By 1856, the Bank of Montreal operated twenty-one branches and three subagencies. In the United States it would have been two dozen separate institutions.

Given its proximity to and inexorably growing economic interaction with the United States, Canada was exposed to the numerous financial crises – "panics" – that were a feature of the decentralized US system, notably in 1837, 1857, and 1907. Yet its continuing integration into the Empire meant that British crises also made themselves felt: 1847–48 and 1878, in particular.

Nevertheless, the principal roles played by the Bank of Montreal, from its creation until the 1930s, were in the management and development of the Canadian economy. It was, Mussio tells us, "the coordinator-in-chief of the Canadian chartered banks before the establishment of the Bank of Canada." It also led the way in the financing of major projects such as the Lachine Canal (1821), the Magnetic Telegraph Company, which built the first telegraph line between Montreal and Toronto in 1847, and the Canadian Pacific Railway. Large though London still loomed in the lives of the Bank's senior executives, the coming of responsible government in 1849 and Confederation in 1867 meant that by the end of the nineteenth century it was primarily a Canadian rather than British imperial entity.

Or was it? By 1912, the Bank of Montreal had 167 offices across Canada. But it also had "branches in Great Britain, the United States, and Mexico, and affiliate branches in major cities in Asia, Europe, Australia, New Zealand, Argentina, Bolivia, Brazil, Chile, Peru, and British Guiana." Between 1870 and 1947, key decisions about the placing of Dominion government and business loans in the city of London were taken on the spot by the London committee, for many years under the direction of Sir John Rose.

With the coming of "the war of the world" – the two great conflicts that threatened the very existence of the British Empire between 1914 and 1945

– the Bank of Montreal's fundamental Britishness was violently reasserted. While Americans could watch and wait – until 1917 – Canadians fought alongside Britons from the outset of the First World War, and there were no exemptions for bank managers or bank clerks. Those who "made the last great sacrifice in the cause of liberty and civilization" were commemorated by the nine-foot-tall bronze soldier by the American sculptor James Earl Fraser that has stood outside the Bank's Winnipeg branch since December 1923. The Bank itself was drawn deeply into the Dominion's wartime finances, a role that was more patriotic than it was profitable.

Yet the centre of the world's financial gravity was shifting from London to New York. Though the United States remained neutral until April 1917, Wall Street lent its assistance to the so-called Entente Powers from the earliest stages of the war. The pull of Canada's now much larger southern neighbour was one that the Bank of Montreal resisted. To the generation of Sir Charles Blair Gordon, the Canadian system remained manifestly superior to the American. True, it was not perfect, as the failure of the Home Bank of Canada in 1923 revealed. But the Canadians were not wrong to argue that their much more concentrated system had no need of a public central bank like the Federal Reserve. Historians have long agreed that the Federal Reserve disastrously mismanaged the aftermath of the 1929 stock-market crash, pursuing contractionary policies that led to the failures of nearly five thousand US banks. In Canada there was no central bank – and no bank failures during the Depression, despite the fact that the magnitude of the macroeconomic shock was roughly as big as that suffered by the United States.

The problem was that this argument cut less and less ice with a new generation of Canadian politicians, who viewed with suspicion the oligopoly of big banks that dominated their country's financial system. As prime minister, William Lyon Mackenzie King remarked that he had "no desire to see them [the Bank of Montreal] monopolize Govt. business." In the eyes of an Ontarian, there were good reasons to be wary of the "Montreal interests." Despite sustained opposition from the Bank of Montreal's senior management, the Bank of Canada was established in 1935 – though it was modelled on the Bank of England, not the Fed.

The best justification for challenging the Bank of Montreal–Royal Bank duopoly was, however, commercial rather than political. The reality, as Mussio shows, was that by the 1940s, prolonged predominance had bred an unhealthy culture. All successful enterprises must at some point become bureaucratic – especially those, like the Bank of Montreal, with hierarchical structures that centralize decision making at headquarters and treat branch employees as little more than functionaries. However, there comes a point at which the benefits of rational organization are outweighed by the costs. In

Mussio's words, because of its "hierarchical structure, its size ... and the necessity for a regulations-based order, the Bank tended toward a conservative approach and outlook in the functioning of its organization as much as in the conduct of its affairs. The Bank also often resembled a military organization in its approach to people and resources." In the words of one senior executive of the post-war era: "You served your time and then you moved up the ranks." Add to this the clubbish culture of the time – in particular, the lengthy and bibulous lunches – and one sees how far the Bank had drifted from the hard-driving, hard-nosed ethos of its Scottish founders. The business consequences were predictable. With the understatement so beloved of the old officer class, the Bank's economic adviser W.T.G. Hackett summed the problem up politely: "A preponderance of big accounts, borrowing little, does tend to have an adverse effect on interest earnings."

Lagging behind newer competitors, the Bank of Montreal was ill prepared for the combined shocks of stagflation, new information technology, and aggressive American competition, all of which battered it in the 1970s. Yet there proved to be a way out of the hole. It was not so much the advice of the McKinsey consultants as the abrasive leadership of William David Mulholland Jr that pulled the Bank of Montreal back from the brink. A native of Albany, NY, a US Army war hero, and a graduate of Harvard and Harvard Business School, Mulholland administered long-overdue shock therapy. Another Bank official recalled the changed atmosphere: "We're a bank. We're not a social club."

Mussio calls Mulholland a "saviour general." Not everyone recognized him as the Bank's armed messiah. By 1989, he had become "legendary for public humiliations of even the most senior executives." His overseas forays into Brazil, Mexico, and the Caribbean were largely unsuccessful. Yet Mulholland turned the Bank of Montreal around. His own work ethic was quickly adopted by those beneath him, for those who failed to match his punishingly long hours were soon gone. He saw with great clarity that developing Canada's natural resources – especially the energy sector – offered the best way out of economic malaise. And he also grasped that it was better for the Bank of Montreal to get into the United States than to worry about keeping the US banks out of Canada – hence the acquisition of the Harris Bank of Chicago in 1984, the beginning of a prolonged and successful expansion into the American Midwest.

It is not the role of a foreword to be a spoiler for the book it precedes. Suffice to say here that the Bank's "great regeneration" in the 1990s – despite the over-ambitious launch of "mbanx" and the failed merger with Royal Bank – offers a case study in survival and renewal in an era that saw the disappearance of many venerable banking names on both sides of the Atlantic. Readers will also come away with a greater appreciation of the skill with which chief executive Bill Downe navigated the storm of the global financial crisis, which offered fresh proof of the resilience of Canada's financial system.

Today, the Bank of Montreal is the fourth-largest Canadian bank by market capitalization and the thirteenth-largest in North America. But it is one of very few of the world's top forty banks to have celebrated its 200th birthday. Bicentennials are rare in financial history. Often, the firms that celebrate them turn out to be banks that have made a point of learning from financial history as well as making it. At around the time of the Bank of Montreal's bicentenary, a journalist asked Bill Downe what kind of conversations he was having with his successor, Darryl White. "The conversation that we have been having now," he replied, "is that history matters, because there are analogs that you can look to."

It is in this spirit that Laurence Mussio has written this exemplary history of the Bank of Montreal. History does indeed matter – and Canadian financial history turns out to matter a good deal more than most people suppose.

Stanford University
September 2019

ACKNOWLEDGMENTS

Three years ago, I was privileged to acknowledge those who helped me in the publication of *A Vision Greater than Themselves: The Making of the Bank of Montreal, 1817–2017*. I now have the honour to extend my thanks again, this time for the work you have before you.

Whom Fortune Favours: The Bank of Montreal and the Rise of North American Finance (WFF) has been a complex, massive, and all-absorbing undertaking. The long-run experience of the Bank has been at the centre of most of my professional thoughts and conversations for almost a decade. The challenge was to produce a work that was equal to BMO's unique role in Canada's and North America's economic and financial life. Yet, if the historian must ultimately find himself alone with his thoughts, judgments, analysis, and evidence, many share the burden, and thus the achievement. In some way, to borrow a term from Niall Ferguson, if networks did not literally make this book possible (that honour belongs to William A. Downe), then they certainly made this book much, much better and a hell of a lot more fun to write. If you mapped the WFF network – the many hundreds of connections that lit up the book's pathways to completion – you would bear witness to a remarkable and, in some ways, surprising set of connections. The network would include many senior executives, bank directors, and managers. At least 150 such connections from the BMO's past were interviewed, constituting key nodes in that network. Multiple lines would also be drawn from colleagues, scholars, and friends in the field to the project's engine room, where insights and conceptual frameworks across a two-century-wide stretch of North Atlantic history were assembled. Other network connections included those who worked closely in helping to gather and sort through hundreds of thousands of documents. Yet other nodes included multiple personal and professional contacts – people who provided strategic or practical advice in the navigation of complex bureaucratic structures. Some nodes were intensely local, while others were national and extended across the North Atlantic world. The informal ones, involving close friends and kin, mattered more to the making of the book than the subject matter might suggest. Put all together, the architecture of the WFF network, in itself, constituted a remarkably productive and resilient entity, underwritten by both an idea and a passion. The idea was a belief in the relevance of analyzing and sharing the long-run experience of institutions like Bank of Montreal. For many in BMO, the passion that fuelled their participation was grounded in their unique position in the financial history of a country and a continent. It was also motivated by an impatience to write the next chapter of that history in the twenty-first century.

For my work to have been at the centre of this purpose-driven network has been one of the highlights of my professional career. I could scarcely have imagined, a few short years ago, the potential this project had to create not only a history (that's been done before) but also a network of people inside the Bank and beyond who have rallied round the idea of the contemporary relevance of properly mobilizing historical context. The internationally active Long Run Initiative (LRI), which I co-founded in 2018 with Michael Aldous and John Turner at Queen's University, Belfast, is one of the many initiatives, both inside the Bank of Montreal and in the wider world, that can trace at least part of its genesis to the desire to apply insight from hindsight to contemporary challenges. Bill Downe, Dr Kevin G. Lynch, and Mona Malone, all governors of the LRI, represent a measure of their personal commitment to the idea.

I have more people to thank than space available. My first debt of gratitude is to William A. Downe, who commissioned this work and foresaw the uses it could serve. The difference between Bill and me is that, while we are both students of history, he also makes it. Miada Neklawi was the executive overseeing the administrative and financial aspects of the project, a task not to be underestimated. Brian J. Smith was deputized to lead a review committee and to handle the many administrative details leading to publication, assisted by Ron Taylor. David J. Montgomery, Maurice Hudon, Peter E. Scott, and Yolaine Toussaint reviewed early drafts. The Art and Archives Committee of the Bank, under the chairship first of Anthony Comper and then of Catherine Roche, were very supportive of the project throughout. You all have my heartfelt thanks.

This book would simply not have been possible without the vital support of the Bank of Montreal Corporate Archives – in particular, I pay tribute to Yolaine Toussaint, now former archivist, Shawna Satz, senior associate archivist, and Shannon Mooney, associate archivist. I consider them comrades-in-arms! I also take this opportunity to thank John D. Stoneman for his friendship and outstanding commitment to the success of this project, and for acting as a superb quartermaster. Rick Kuwayti provided a sounding board as well as delivering a shrewd set of insights into the past and present state of a Bank he has served with exceptional creativity and distinction. My thanks are also due to Mark B.P. Ryan, my oldest friend, who bore my frequent updates on the progress of the work with genuine interest and great patience.

I had the privilege of superb research assistants in this project: Dr Brittany Gataveckas was the first, and she helped to lay the foundations of a massive project. Dr Tim Müller was the second, who was involved both with *A Vision Greater than Themselves* and with *Whom Fortune Favours*. Tim and I worked very closely, almost every day, for about five years. Though he left well before the present work's completion, it is hard to imagine publication of the same work without him. In return, I hope that Dr Müller feels that that his work on the project constituted a unique apprenticeship for the future. Dr Ruud Huyskamp, a superb young historian, brought to bear his professional, scholarly, and diplomatic talents to the project in the latter years to see it through to the end.

With this volume, McGill-Queen's University Press is publishing my fifth book, all under the creative direction of Executive Director Philip J. Cercone. Philip and I have now been friends for almost a quarter-century, and it has been an adventure. MQUP is a Canadian literary institution thanks to his leadership; long may it be so. I also extend my thanks to my copy editors, Curtis Fahey and Eleanor Gasparik, the anonymous peer reviewers of this work, and all those at McGill-Queen's who worked to make this very large book a success. My thanks are also extended to the translator of this work into the French, Michel Buttiens.

I would like to offer my sincere thanks as well to Darryl White, chief executive officer of BMO Financial Group, for his kind words at the beginning of this work. Darryl has shared his predecessor's passion for gaining insight from hindsight – especially in this age of disruption. I also extend my heartfelt appreciation to Niall Ferguson for writing such a remarkable foreword. I admire both these extraordinary men for their courage, their drive, and their passion to serve the wider world in different but substantial ways. Each of them is an inspiration. To have these two friends be a formal part of this book is an honour I shall always cherish.

Behind every author who finishes such a massive project there is often a surprised and probably relieved spouse! To Flavia, my wonderful, resourceful wife, my partner in life, and my greatest critic, I say, thank you. Flavia is an old Girtonian with uncompromising standards: I know if she's pleased with my work, then I will at least have a chance to win the knowledgeable skeptic vote.

The making of *Whom Fortune Favours* has been many things. It has been a remarkable privilege to interpret for this generation a founding Canadian institution. It has been a joyous experience, even in the most solitary moments, because of the belief and support of friends and supporters. And it has been a humbling experience to realize that one cannot achieve great things alone.

In this era of short-term thinking, when the value of long-term experience and analysis is under pressure but the need for it has never been greater, this book is a sign of contradiction that urges us on to remembrance, reflection, and response as we contemplate the past, present, and future of the single, singular North American institution that is the Bank of Montreal.

Dr Laurence B. Mussio
Toronto, Canada
September 2019

TABLES AND FIGURES

Tables

1.1 Structure, organization, ownership
1.2 Policy and approach
2.1 Reserve funds, 1819–40
6.1 Bank of Montreal senior management
6.2 Capital-stock increases, 1872–1918
6.3 Dividend payments, 1870–1918
6.4 "Character Book" codes for estimated net worth and creditworthiness of customers
6.5 "Character Book" general characteristics of customers
6.6 Bank of Montreal domestic branches
8.1 Bank of Montreal mergers, 1903–25
9.1 Bank of Montreal dividend payments, 1913–27
9.2 State of Canadian banking, 1929
9.3 Branch presence of Canadian banks, 1933
9.4 Bank of Montreal in Mexico, 1918–23
10.1 Large loans requiring special attention of executive committee, 31 October 1931

Figures

3.1 Notes in circulation, Bank of Montreal 1847–59
3.2 Deposits, Bank of Montreal, 1847–59
3.3 Assets, Bank of Montreal, 1847–59
6.1 Assets, Bank of Montreal, 1871–1918
6.2 Notes in circulation, Bank of Montreal, 1871–1918

6.3 Profits, Bank of Montreal, 1871–1918

6.4 Share price, Bank of Montreal, 1881–1902

6.5 Total dividend payments, Bank of Montreal, 1870–1918

10.1 Assets, Bank of Montreal, 1928–39

10.2 Profits, Bank of Montreal, 1928–39

10.3 Total dividend payments, Bank of Montreal, 1928–39

10.4 Rest fund, Bank of Montreal, 1928–39

12.1 Notes in circulation, Bank of Montreal, 1927–36

12.2 Gold and subsidiary coin, Bank of Montreal, 1927–35

12.3 Profits, Bank of Montreal, 1927–37

12.4 Assets, Bank of Montreal, 1927–36

GENERAL INTRODUCTION

Historical experience can be a frustratingly evasive and demanding thing to capture. A faithful synthesis of any experience demands both recall and reflection, evidence and analysis. Time and distance confer perspective. Patterns begin to emerge. New evidence comes to light. Yet time and distance can also dim the realities of the past. Evidence is lost; pieces fall away; the demands of the moment impose their imprint on new interpretations.

People exist in time; so do institutions. Everybody runs out of time someday; so do most institutions. From the historian's perspective, time-defined lives make the job of crystallizing experience easier. Time also gives a distinct shape to the narrative. Things have a beginning, a middle, and an end. By contrast, institutions that manage to survive pose the greatest historical challenge – and the greatest opportunity for understanding how successful organizations not only persist but adapt, grow, and prosper.

In the North Atlantic world, the small number of private and corporate institutions that have persisted for two centuries form an elite club. Rarer still are those companies that have retained their prominence through continuous transformation, innovation, and adaptation. In Canada, very few companies can claim such a long pedigree: the Hudson's Bay Company (founded in 1670) and Molson (1786) come to mind. Yet even these are now managed, or owned partially or wholly, from the United States. In this sense, fortune has favoured one singular Canadian institution: the Bank of Montreal (BMO).[1] Established in 1817, the Bank of Montreal was Canada's first bank and is *the subject of these two volumes.* Over two hundred years of continuous operation represent a remarkable Canadian achievement. Today, BMO is the eight-largest financial institution, by assets, in North America.[2]

The Bank through Time

Capturing the experience of any institution as deeply rooted in the history of Canada as the Bank of Montreal is a challenging task. The Bank's roots are two centuries deep and a continent wide. They reach back half a century before Canada became a nation, or for that matter, before many of the principal nation-states of Europe were born. For financial institutions in particular, persistence in time and over centuries can be the reward for adaptability, evolving strategy, and capability for renewal. Prospering over time also represents a premium for responding successfully to the dynamics of complexity, risk, and uncertainty.

Engaging the cycle of response, regeneration, and renewal, generation after generation, from shortly after the end of the Napoleonic era early in the nineteenth century to the contemporary technology-dominated era of the twenty-first century, is an achievement worthy of celebration and admiration. Even on fast-forward, the last two hundred years are a jerky newsreel of astonishing proportions – encompassing the rise and fall of empires, the emergence of nation-states, panics, depressions, world wars, the growth of the middle class, the broader participation and emancipation of peoples, globalization and new borders, new technologies and information flows, new social and political forces, changing economic hegemonies, revolutions in science, education, culture, style, fashion, and thought. In the same time, banking underwent similar transformations in its products, personnel, services, markets, technologies, and approaches.

If it is worth pausing and reflecting on the magnitude of the transformations of our world, it is also necessary to insist on the continuities. Early-nineteenth-century bankers transported to the trading floors or executive suites of 2019 would undoubtedly live up to the time-travelling stereotypes we would expect. They might marvel in dumbfounded amazement at the extent of the products and services, the millions of transactions and trades pushed through in a day, the ease and extent of bank operations, the ability to transmit data in microseconds, the informality of the relationships, perhaps also the presence of women. Yet, once the novelty wore off a bit, they would likely recognize that, at its core, the functions of banking – deposit-taking, lending, investing, serving clients and customers – have not fundamentally changed. Our time-travelling bankers would also grasp instinctively the close nature of the bank's relations with its customers, its competitors, and the state. In other words, if Peter McGill or Lord Mount Stephen, two prominent nineteenth-century presidents of the Bank of Montreal, were to job-shadow twenty-first-century chief executive Darryl White for a day, they would likely understand the nature of the challenges facing the contemporary leadership and the demanding relationships imposed by a competitive and fluid global financial market, though they might be flabbergasted by the sheer volume of information available to their contemporary successor. They might even be surprised at the intensity and relentlessness of the pace. Some things change, some things stay the same.

But mere longevity must only be the beginning. It is a point of reference: an orientation that leads us toward the more substantial, multi-faceted, and mostly astonishing story of the last two centuries – the triumphs, the challenges, the panics and depressions, the rebellions and uprisings, the world wars and the new technologies. This book represents a unique generational opportunity for several reasons. The Bank of Montreal's two centuries of experience give us a chance to explore a vital aspect of the history of the country through the lens of banking, finance, and investment. In this sense, the Bank constitutes a vital source of knowledge about the evolution of Canadian capitalism. The curtain is pulled back on how Canadians generated wealth and what they did with it. The Bank's history provides us an opportunity to see how bankers created, maintained, and managed relationships with customers, cities, provinces, states, and nations. Capital flows through both private and public channels: how it is used and deployed is therefore both a private and a public matter. Not least, the Bank's history is also an opportunity to examine leadership, strategy, performance, corporate organization, regulation, policy, and technological change in a key Canadian institution.

The Bank of Montreal's history offers us an additional perspective not just because of its roots but also because of its role. This is Canada's first bank, its most influential bank, for a century or more the coordinator-in-chief of the Canadian chartered banks before the establishment of the Bank of Canada. The Bank of Montreal was the government's banker, the financier of vital public infrastructure from the telegraph to the railroad to innumerable public-work projects. Its size, strength, and stability made it a natural standard bearer for Canadian finance in the major capitals of the world. In concert with a small group of Canadian chartered banks and the federal state, the Bank helped to shape the character of Canadian banking operations, regulations, and policies. The prominence of its leaders in the nineteenth and twentieth centuries – from the mercantile elites of early-nineteenth-century Montreal stretching to the executives of the post-war era – illuminates the interconnected nature of Canadian capitalism. The Bank's capital was not just currency-based, gold-based, or backed up by reserves – both its success and persistence over time depended upon large reserves of reputational capital as well. Class, social, and cultural forces have never been far from the surface in the history of Canadian banking.

From a broad perspective, the Bank's history also provides a chance for this generation to understand the genesis and evolution of our financial system

and the important role of banks and banking in national economic development. The Bank of Montreal played either a central or supporting role in the
capital formation of British North America, the transcontinental expansion
of Canada from the Atlantic to the Pacific, government finance and the birth
of the Dominion of Canada, the industrialization of the country, and the
financing of countless projects and initiatives across sectors, regions, and
economies. Its influence expanded to embrace the American Midwest and
outward internationally as circumstances permitted. The Bank's experience
also gives us a chance to observe how dramatically our relationship to money
and wealth has changed – how we earn it, how we keep it, how we invest it,
lend it, and borrow it. Most recently, it allows us to look at the financializa-
tion of the economy, its integration into the mainstream, and the nature of
organizational change. Leadership and change are two powerful, overarching
themes that emerge throughout.

At the Bank level, the organization offers students of business an opportunity to see how strategy and structure evolve and adapt to competition,
opportunities, and threats, and how they emerge empowered or weakened
from the encounter. We also bear witness to multiple transformations of
bankers, clients, and customers.

The Flow

It may be useful to think of the Bank's history over two centuries as a type
of complex watershed. In each era, in each of its twenty decades, the Bank
of Montreal's experience revolved around its ability both to shape and to be
shaped by changes in the ecosystems of finance and banking. It is appropriate
that the Bank's first major loan facilitated the completion of the Lachine Canal
in 1821 to liberate navigation to the west. The Bank's first generation knew all
about flows and circulation in both their literal and metaphorical senses. On
the literal ones they travelled, sent and received goods, explored and settled.
On the metaphorical ones, they imagined a more connected country and continent with Montreal at its centre. Like the great lakes and watercourses that
define lands or have their courses altered by human will and natural events,
there are flows and circulations that shape and characterize the Bank's own history. In fact, flows and circulation played a key part in the history of the Bank
from its earliest beginnings. Circulation of bills, loans, currency, paper, and
specie was not only key to the business: it *was* the business. The historical and
contemporary flows that shape it are capital flows and information flows, flows
of knowledge and expertise, flows between competing metropolises, and trade
flows that move across regional, national, and international borders. That history is also shaped by the flows of human capital, inside the Bank and outside of

it. Historical time flows between public institutions and private ones, between government and enterprise, inside and outside established networks. Freeing all those flows to generate wealth, opportunity, and growth was the number one challenge for the Bank's leadership.

These multiple flows, the interaction between them, the attempts to channel and control them, create new ones, to ride the rapids and avoid the floods, together form the great circulatory system – the life-giving experience – of the Bank of Montreal. Those flows combined to create an interdependent web of relationships connecting people to capital, and capital to markets, and to new opportunities in a complex and fast-evolving way. Across the last two centuries, these flows and networks were able to bring together wealth, resources, capital, and technology with ideas, visions, and projects. The Bank's leaders contrived plans to generate wealth, establish infrastructure, broaden their presence in the industry, and respond to competitive disruption and changing environments. Naturally, results varied. The response of complex systems to emergent circumstances depended on time and context.

There are other, subtler yet still-pervasive subterranean flows that are harder to see and still harder to control. Yet they influence the ecosystem all the same. In London, England, for example, on the north bank of the Thames, over a dozen rivers run underneath the megalopolis, rivers that have become transformed into mere place names – from Hackney Brook and Stamford Brook to the River Fleet and the Moselle. The same is true for Montreal, Toronto, Chicago, and New York City: underground rivers criss-cross the topography of these urban centres. Some of the rivers were built over, some were forced down by development, and others were diverted. But they are there still, seen or unseen, and they still have stories to tell. Similarly, in the Bank of Montreal context, think of those subterranean flows as a territory that is harder to define and quantify – the development of a way of doing things (strategy, approaches), a corporate culture (risk averse, organizationally complex), and a set of assumptions (about the bank's proper role in the lives of individuals and economies) that one sees only when deliberately searching for it beneath the foundations of the institution. There are other rivers that run through the history of banking in Canada and elsewhere that are not immediately evident unless you are actively seeking them – the shift in our relationship to money, to credit, to status and ownership, to wealth and prosperity, and to the changing role of private and public institutions. Ecosystems shape the landscape and set the boundaries of possibility for how people can make it prosperous and productive. The Bank of Montreal's ecosystem was shaped by the will of its leaders as much as by its overall experience in space and time. When it comes to banks, resilience and adaptation are absolutely vital, as are strength, size, and stability.

A New History for a New Era

Some of the Bank of Montreal's history is known. Over half a century has elapsed since the journalist and popular historian Merrill Denison produced *Canada's First Bank*. Denison's work was an impressive undertaking for the time, beginning in 1955 and ending in 1967 with the production of the second of two volumes. The making of that work might deserve examination in its own right, since it was an early attempt at writing corporate history that, among other things, involved the transfer in summertime of station-wagon loads of archival documents from the National Archives of Canada to Denison's cottage, courtesy of the Dominion archivist, W. Kaye Lamb. Denison took his writing duties seriously. Of course, times have changed: access is a little different these days, as anyone at Library and Archives Canada (LAC) reading this might nervously acknowledge. Scholarly styles and approaches have also changed. Denison's corporate chronicle shed light on a lot of interesting material but never claimed to be scholarly or independent. *Whom Fortune Favours*, by contrast, is designed to be both. In fact, it sets out to accomplish four well-defined objectives.

First, it not only seeks to bring the Bank's history up to the present but also recasts that history by grounding it firmly in the most extensive archival evidence possible. At the same time, it endeavours to put the experience of the Bank into its proper historical context by connecting it to the very best and most recent scholarship and analysis in the field. By the same token, it tries to some extent to *unfamiliarize* the reader with the standard or familiar historical inquiry by introducing new perspectives and evidence available to the author – to shed new light on and offer new interpretations of well-known events.

Second, this history represents a generational opportunity to provide a fresh understanding of the Bank's experience through the passage of time and contingent circumstances – by mapping its networks, decisions, and interactions as a prominent financial organization – as its operations evolved from city to province to nation to the North Atlantic world and beyond. It gives us a chance to analyze and understand how successful firms dealt with the transformations either generated by will or imposed by circumstance.

Third, this history of Canada's first bank also offers a view of both Canada and the Bank of Montreal's major markets as seen through the lens of banking and finance. Equally, however, the Bank's own internal experience – through global events and in personnel, organization, technology, leadership, and competition – illuminates the evolution of the corporate form. The long-run experience of the Bank of Montreal is a stage upon which some of the best exemplars of Canadian economic and financial leadership developed and implemented their strategies in every era from early colonial times to the present.

Lastly, in the distant past, the Bank of Montreal's status as Canada's first bank and its vital role in the development of the country are in some ways understood. In the more recent past, mergers, acquisitions, and international expansion may more easily come to mind. The approach of this history is not to produce a simple chronology of events. Rather, its thrust will be to analyze and examine how the Bank of Montreal performed as an organization in time – how it channelled or was carried by those flows discussed earlier. In addition to the overall narrative flow, this book focuses on some specific themes in the experience of the Bank – themes that underline the possibilities and the perils of constantly being at the forefront of Canadian banking. Some of the subjects include political economy, economic development, the role of reputation, and, at various times, disruptive technology.

The effectiveness of the Canadian banking system and of Canada's regulatory architecture over the years has been a point of pride for Canadians, especially considering the failures of banking and government regulation elsewhere in the North Atlantic world. This history offers an opportunity to test these assumptions, to trace how the Canadian system came to be so undeniably strong, secure, and resilient. It is also a chance to examine the interdependence of public and private in the building of the Canadian banking system. The Bank's experience in key locations – London, New York City, Chicago – allows us to see Canadian capitalists in action in larger markets, and on a larger stage.

Canadian banks and banking as historical subjects are generally considered to be an under-served area of scholarship, unlike their counterparts in the rest of the world. There are a number of reasons for this. Business history in Canada is practised by only a handful of professional or academic historians; banking historians are even rarer, though sometimes the field attracts its share of well-meaning amateurs. While writing on Canadian banking appears in various places in the international literature, almost all of it depends on useful but ancient sources from the nineteenth century, and almost none of it is the product of fresh archival investigation. Historians Adam Shortt and R.M. Breckenridge each chronicled the rise of the Canadian banking system from their perspective of the late nineteenth century. There are, of course, notable contemporary exceptions to this rule, including Duncan McDowall's history of the Royal Bank of Canada and the work of James Darroch on Canadian banking in an international context.[3] Andrew Smith has much more recently examined aspects of Canadian banking in the 1860s and 1870s through the lens of the regulatory foundations of the Bank Act. Another class of writing either brings a more polemic and combative tone to banking history or, alternatively, uncritically sings its praises based on recent successes, especially after the Great Recession of 2008. The Bank of Montreal and the Canadian banking system share histories that are far more complex, and more interesting, than either approach would have us believe. That history therefore deserves to be grounded in archival evidence and reinforced by analysis – an approach that is at the heart of this book.

Fortunes

A word of explanation about the title, *Whom Fortune Favours*. I intended this title to play on the transliterated Latin saying "fortune favours the bold." The connection between "fortune" and "bank" is straightforward enough, since a financial institution deals in wealth – creates it, accumulates it, amasses it, allocates it, and invests it. But the title also points to a stronger, classical reference. Fortuna is a goddess of the Roman pantheon, patroness of chance, luck, wealth, and prosperity. It is interesting to note that one commonly mentioned cognomen of Fortuna is *primogenia*, first-born of the gods – a name that is thought to attest to her great antiquity. Since the Bank of Montreal is the first-born of the Canadian banks, the title therefore seems apt. The formulation "whom fortune favours" is also equivocal. Fortunes are made and safeguarded, invested and extended, deployed and dispersed. They can also be lost, robbed, competed for, and so forth. The fortune involved not only refers to wealth but also implies chance and destiny. Both the ambiguities of chance and the clarion call of destiny are well familiar to the Bank's leaders through time.

Fortune has often favoured the Bank of Montreal – its leaders, employees, and clients – and has also embraced and supported local, regional, and national destinies. Of course, fortune has not favoured the Bank in every case. Fortunes shift, as do the times. Destinies are also interconnected – intertwined with those of industries, markets, and nations. Matching capabilities to aspirations, the right strategy to an evolving competitive environment, year after year for two hundred years, is bound to result in challenges and reversals. The story then turns to the comeback, the rally, and how the leaders and people of the Bank of Montreal responded.

If You Are Reading This

Prospective readers of *Whom Fortune Favours* will be drawn from a wide audience. They will also have diverging expectations of what this book ought to deliver. Here is what I hope it offers. At a fundamental level, it is the story of Canada's first bank and one of the country's founding institutions. For students of history and specifically of banking and financial history, this book provides a comprehensive and sustained examination of the evolution of one of North America's oldest and most prominent institutions. In doing so, it supplies new perspectives and new evidence from the perspective of the Bank. The Bank of Montreal's history intersects with important currents and cross-currents in Canada's development and that of the North Atlantic world. Analyzing that history provides an opportunity to examine how complex organizations survive and prosper, compete and persist, over time.

Posterity often preserves historical actors in the embalming fluid of permanent acclaim or disrepute. That process makes it difficult to *unfamiliarize* ourselves with what we think we know in historical inquiry. The actors become locked in an historical hologram, moving in predictable and almost predetermined ways according to their interests and linked irrevocably to the outcomes with which we are familiar. If history is presented that way, no wonder people will smile politely and run for the exits. What I hope to show with this book is that, at key points, the Bank's leaders and everyday staff had hard choices to make, risks to take, strategies to pursue, and competitors to contend with. At its most heroic, the story is about people who not only created a bank but who helped to build a city (Montreal) and a nation. It is also about an organization that was central to the development of a Canadian and North American capital market, as well as a distinctive style of Canadian banking. In other words, the Bank of Montreal was a cardinal point of reference for the development of Canadian capitalism at various stages. It played this role in various ways – sometimes as a key player, sometimes as a dominant one, at other times as part of a larger group of actors – in the midst of often fast-flowing and quickly evolving circumstances.

As with any organization, the heroic or transformational moments are necessarily rare. But they do punctuate the history. Those moments also allow us to focus our attention on a major event that reveals the strategic capabilities of the firm, its mobilization, agility, and follow-through. At its most prosaic, the history involves long periods of routine, the ordinary daily transactions that are the foundations of the Bank's business, from deposit-taking to loans to exchange to investments. The millions of individual actions cannot interest the reader, but what should do so are the unique patterns and organizational rhythms over time, how they persist and how they are changed, as well as the organizational and corporate culture created by the Bank. Understanding its history involves exploring not only the why but also the how: a task that requires us to disengage from the present and to look retroactively at the depth of the Bank's experience.

The history of the Bank of Montreal obviously provides a way to appreciate better the achievements and failures of the organization over time. But it can also have a contemporary relevance. Understanding how previous generations of Bank of Montreal leaders handled competition, volatile markets, regulatory constraints, the challenge of regional and international expansion, and organizational rigidities can provide useful, specific context. In some ways, this history captures the things that people and institutions forget to remember. A deeper grasp of the capabilities of the organization can emerge – how the culture evolved, how its assumptions have been defined, how the organization has responded to emerging events, and so on. Understanding patterns of behaviour and organization can be instructive not just from an historical perspective but also from a contemporary one.

Historians with an understanding of the way business works also recognize that drawing a simplistic line between the history they write and potential managerial "lessons" of history is a dubious proposition. Yet a deeper knowledge of how the organization shaped and was shaped by its environment in specific situations and at key turning points offers the contemporary executive a point of reference. Access to institutional memory can be good for institutions, but only when combined with the analytical acuity required to assess past and present operational situations. The proverbial generals waging today's war by applying strategies and tactics from yesterday's war is a good example of taking the wrong lessons from history. Understanding what worked and why, how organizations responded and why, and how results were achieved or missed, as the case may be, is both germane and salient, relevant to the point being made here.

All of these audiences would be ill-served by simply an updated chronicle of events. Rather, *Whom Fortune Favours*'s animating spirit has been the desire to understand the major events and developments of the past – the cultures, continuities, and transformations in the life of the Bank of Montreal. Indeed, the book was conceived as an attempt to explain how the Bank's history intersects with some of the main historical changes in the North Atlantic world in the last two centuries. This goal offers a sharper angle of vision into the Bank's experience. It provides both a useful and a practical way to proceed, allowing us to focus on what mattered to different generations of Bank leaders. Understanding the history of any institution over two centuries is a daunting task if it is to be actually useful to the current generation. To that end, there are a few observations that apply not only to the Bank of Montreal but also to how business historians approach the life of organizations in time.

As my colleagues Philip Scranton and Patrick Friedensen have observed, contemporary actors have a temptation to present the course of business through accounts that make rational sense of often diverse happenings. Those "professionally rigorous summaries and analysis of orderly dynamics" of the past can be misleading because we tend to rationalize retrospectively business performances that were often "experimental, chaotic, indeterminate and conflictual."[4] The history of the Bank of Montreal, particularly but not only in its first several generations, often fits that description. If you ask a successful and professionally well-formed contemporary executive today what his or her greatest challenge (and perhaps stimulation) is, it would most likely be dealing with the opportunities and challenges of managing risk and uncertainty for advantage. Yet organizations must achieve this through imperfect structures, problematic technology, and fluid participation rather than through "rational planning, reliable technology and effective hierarchies."[5]

We must also recognize that, in the Bank of Montreal case as with other institutions of such long pedigree, different eras called forth different leaders responding to different conditions and serving different constituencies. The founding generations of leadership confronted the problems of establishment and expansion. Recent generations are confronted with organizational complexity, rededication to purpose, and the challenge of avoiding comfortable complacency.[6] Here, the long-run experience of an institution can provide valuable insight, shedding light on historical change over time as a category of managerial analysis and decision-making. The bank's "decision engine" works best when it is fuelled by the highest-grade analysis possible, and that must include the long run.

The approach I have taken here is to focus on the Bank's approach to the risk and uncertainty that is a prominent feature of the financial history of the North Atlantic world and its markets. Bank of Montreal bankers throughout their history had to deal with varying access to reliable knowledge, and no reliable knowledge at all about the future. Risk and uncertainty end up becoming not infrequent historical actors in the unfolding of the Bank's history. As Scranton notes, the difference between the two concepts – risk and uncertainty – is important. Risk is complicated, subject to rationality, and involves knowable options, steps, and opportunities. Uncertainty, by contrast, is complex and extra-rational.

Bank of Montreal leaders at times faced considerable uncertainty generated by both ancient and contemporary sources of uncertainty – politics and authority, finance and technology. Periodically, a single element was in the ascendant.[7] Politics, for example, seemed to mark the history in specific periods, and sometimes quite sharply: in the first generation of the Bank's existence, then in the 1860s and 1880s, and again in the 1930s, 1960s, and 1990s. When the rules of the game change in finance, regulation, and the industrial organization of the sector, winners and losers emerge among bankers. Financial uncertainty came to the fore at various times through panics, recessions, and depressions (1837, 1857, 1873, 1893, 1907, 1929, and so on). In fact, that uncertainty is a typical feature of the system, but in the years listed it was of a different order entirely. Technology was a relatively stable element for long periods of the Bank's history, only to occupy centre stage in the information and control-processing revolution of the late nineteenth century and again in the late 1960s, in the 1980s, and with the dawn of the Internet in the 1990s. Financial uncertainties have involved the credit and creditworthiness of not only individuals but also companies and countries. These uncertainties ran largely in the background as a permanent feature of the business but occasionally burst onto the scene in spectacular fashion. The severe economic contraction of 2008 is probably the event that is most seared into the memories of the current generation of Bank of Montreal bankers.

The research and writing that has gone into *Whom Fortune Favours* has been, among other things, an exercise in the preservation and interpretation of the historical memory of the Bank of Montreal. The Bank of Montreal Archives – both in Montreal and Chicago – was naturally the major source of the evidence for this book. But the corporate archives were only the beginning. I consulted a vast array of regional, national, and international archives in Canada, the United States, and the United Kingdom. The story of the Bank has unfolded in multi-faceted ways in an astonishing variety of fonds, collections, correspondence, private papers, state, and regulatory repositories from the Colonial Office of the nineteenth century to the cabinet office of our own day, secret cabinet papers, circulars, memos, and more. The documentary evidence in these many repositories and archives has been amassed, collected, sifted, sorted, catalogued, and analyzed with the sole intention of offering as complete and definitive a history as possible. Thanks to the far-sighted decisions the Bank made about preserving its past, we can also draw on a series of well over a hundred recent oral interviews with many of its major figures. Those confidential interviews represent by far the most important recent contribution to the preservation of the historical legacy of the Bank of Montreal. In addition, the book also depends on a range of supplementary interviews to fill in the gaps where the record is silent, unavailable, or non-existent. Here, the book is careful to distinguish between the four dimensions of memory – the private, the public, the organizational, and the historical or professional. While each of these collectively contribute to the book, the last one is the most important since it seeks to link personal recollection with the broader forces shaping the Bank.

The Roadmap

Whom Fortune Favours is divided into two volumes, seven sections, and an Epilogue. Volume I, *A Dominion of Capital, 1817–1945*, examines the period from the establishment of the Bank in 1817 to the end of the Second World War in 1945. It also contains the first four parts. Part One, In the Beginning,

1760–1817, examines the challenges of establishing the Bank of Montreal in a difficult colonial/imperial/continental environment. Part Two, Forging Canadian Finance, 1817–1870, studies in greater depth the foundations of Canadian banking through the lens of the Bank of Montreal. Its chapters deal with the struggle for stability in early colonial Canada, the importance of reputation, and the paramount relationship between Montreal bankers, colonial governments, and the imperial authorities in London. This period also covers the tumultuous 1860s, a dangerous yet transformational decade in the life of the North Atlantic world.

The three chapters in Part Three, Fortune's Faithful Disciples, 1870–1918, analyze the further development of Canadian banking, the efforts of Montreal bankers and Canadian capitalists to forge a transcontinental nation, and the growing importance of Canadian financial institutions, which, by the turn of the nineteenth century, had reached in some ways the zenith of their power and influence. These are also the years when the Bank of Montreal came into its own as Canada's premier bank. At the same time, the broader Canadian financial system matured, produced new competitors and new forms of financial instruments, and eventually lay down the four foundations of the Canadian financial system (banks, insurance, trust companies, investment firms). This is also the period when public policy began to shape the system.

The five chapters of Part Four, A Changeful Fortune, 1918–1945, focus on banking and political economy in a complex era of shifting power relations between the state and corporate interests. The tumults provoked by boom, bust, and depression caused a veritable earthquake in the Canadian banking system, and the Bank of Montreal was at the centre of the action. There is also a special thematic chapter on the fascinating role of Montreal and Canadian bankers in the dire financial situation of the Dominion of Newfoundland in the early 1930s, when a threatened default absorbed the attention of Canadian and imperial governments and bankers and led to the suspension of responsible government for a decade and a half. This part concludes with an examination of the Bank of Montreal's role in Canadian wartime finance during the Second World War.

Volume II, *Territories of Transformation, 1946–2017*, opens with Part Five, The Magnificent Facade, 1946–1974, which traces the post-war development of the Bank, its extended decline in the 1950s and 1960s, and the efforts of Montreal bankers to modernize technology and organization. Part Six, The Road of Return, 1974–1989, places particular emphasis on the leadership of William D. Mulholland in successfully pulling the Bank back from the brink and putting it on a solid foundation. Thematic chapters also focus on an epoch-making expansion into the United States and the extension of bank operations to the international field.

The end of Part Six represents the frontier of the scholarly history of the bank; beyond 1990, the Bank of Montreal Archives are closed, as the introduction to Part Seven, A Time to Every Purpose, 1990–1917, discusses. Part Seven consists of two chapters that cover the fascinating events of the 1990s, the first decade of the twenty-first century, and the 2010s up to the end of 2017. They are separate from the rest of the work, as I have had to rely on only partial access to the overall historical record. At the same time, the account is enriched by interviews and observations that will surely provide grist for the mill when the full, scholarly history of this period is written. Finally, there is a short Epilogue in which I step outside the history to provide a few concluding remarks about how the Bank's remarkable story connects to the present generation of BMO's leadership and workforce.

In case the reader hasn't noticed, *Whom Fortune Favours* is a substantive work by weight and volume; my hope is that it will also be of a similar weight in contribution and insight. When I started this remarkable project, I had only a vague idea of just how big a history of the Bank of Montreal would be. Eventually, I understood that, to do justice to the entirety of the bank's story, the coverage would have to be extensive, in terms of time and themes. The committed reader who explores the book from cover to cover will be rewarded, I hope, with a wide-ranging grasp of the full history of the Bank of Montreal. But even those who focus on their special interests – the nineteenth century, the early twentieth century, political economy, and so forth – will be repaid for their attention. Those with a more contemporary focus or those anxious to answer more directly the question "How did the Bank get to where it is today, in my lifetime?" might concentrate on Volume II. *Whom Fortune Favours* is written to satisfy a wide audience. The narrative that unfolds here is a powerful antidote to the conceit that only the present really matters. As a great Canadian businessman once told me, the higher the corporate ladder you go, the more context matters.

That insight about the importance of context is not exclusive to corporate leaders: it is also shared by those who intimately understand the human spirit. The one-time bank clerk, poet, and Nobel Laureate T.S. Eliot spoke eloquently about the importance of tradition and the historical imagination as a living organism "comprising past and present in a mutual interaction."[8] In *Little Gidding*, Eliot writes: "We shall not cease from exploration / And the end of all our exploring / Will be to arrive where we started /And know the place for the first time."[9] Eliot here points us in the direction of an historical sensibility: an engagement with history with the objective of more deeply understanding places we have taken for granted and the experiences that have made us. Only when we arrive where we started from – at the end of our journey – will we be able to "know the place" – to really know the place – for the first time.

For this book, that "place" is the Bank of Montreal – an institution that holds an essential place in the story of Canada. Let us therefore begin our exploring in the struggling, ethnically riven British colonial city on the St Lawrence River – in Montreal, in the hard years following the War of 1812, where the struggle for Canadian finance began.

PART ONE

In the Beginning, 1760–1817

CHAPTER ONE

An Unchartered Territory

The establishment of the Bank of Montreal in November 1817 was the culmination of a powerful set of currents coursing through the North Atlantic world of the early nineteenth century. With a population hovering between 15,000 and 20,000, Montreal was positioned in the centre of a growing network of flows. Trade flows from the fur trade and the staples trade, as well as agricultural products of every sort, reached deep from the interior of the west country (Ontario and west) and were channelled back into Montreal. There, the trade flows split into three streams – one travelling down into the American republic, one to the West Indies, and the third across the Atlantic to Britain – and back again with manufactured goods, tools, textiles, rum, and molasses. Two-way capital flows from Montreal to the growing financial centres of New York and London intensified steadily as well. These capital flows were comparatively small. But they were nonetheless sufficient to push Montreal merchants to establish institutions that would facilitate the movement of capital. They were also looking for a vehicle – a channel – to carry forward their vision of Montreal as a serious metropolitan competitor in the North Atlantic world.

The late-eighteenth and early-nineteenth-century prologue to the establishment of the Bank of Montreal was an era of transformation, confrontation, and struggle. This chapter will provide a brief tour of the highlights of that history, focusing on the changes to the financial system before the establishment of the Bank in 1817.

A Pre-Bank Canadian Economy

In economic terms, British North America in the late eighteenth and early nineteenth centuries was a struggling pre-industrial backwater. New systems of trade increasingly rested upon a chronically sclerotic system of exchange held back by eternally insufficient quantities of specie and a proliferation of monetary instruments (from Sterling to Mexican or Spanish silver dollars to an astonishing variety of foreign currency, including the Portuguese Johannes, the German Carolin, and the French pistareen) that were of unreliable value.[1] The money supply in the Canadas mainly consisted, therefore, of foreign gold, silver, and copper coins for everyday transactions and some merchant scrip (*bon pour*).[2] The British North American colonies were astonishingly dependent on American supplies of specie currency, especially during the Napoleonic Wars (1806–15), when British treasure flowed to finance the European conflict.

In the decade before the establishment of the Bank of Montreal, three major events added both urgency and complexity to the financial situation facing Montreal merchants. The French blockade of the Baltic Sea during the Napoleonic Wars, the US embargo of British goods in 1808 (the Jefferson Embargo), and the War of 1812–15 between Britain and the United States each in its own way exerted major pressures on the Canadian financial system.

In some ways, blockades, embargoes, and military conflict were good for Canadian business. The British turned to North America for timber and a host of other goods once provided by the Baltic states. The Embargo Act of 1808 led New England traders to shift from selling to Britain to trading with British North American colonies, in spite of the act's direct prohibition of inland trade with the British colonies in Canada.[3] Residents of the Champlain valley were tied to Montreal and Quebec City for both the export and import trade. The trade in livestock and lumber for staples such as salt, coffee, and cloth continued virtually unabated. In fact, the embargo was honoured more in the breach than in the observance – overland via Vermont and New York, via coastal or maritime routes (thence to Canada or Spanish Florida), and through direct clandestine sailing from US harbours to foreign ports without clearance.[4] American goods in Canada could command up to eight times their American value, moreover. The cross-border price differential made running the embargo a calculated risk. For their part, the British actively encouraged breaking the embargo to keep trade flowing between the two countries.

The outbreak of hostilities between the United States and Great Britain in 1812 posed a direct threat to colonial capital flows. Exports, import duties, immigrant funds, and government spending all came under severe pressure

– at least at first.[5] The War of 1812 caused a flood of imperial bills to flow into Canada to support the military and civilian infrastructure. The spike in the triangular trade between Canada, the United States, and Great Britain created an expanding exchange in currency and exchange between London, Montreal, and New York. The Canadian specialization in foreign-exchange transactions therefore runs very deep indeed.

Collapse of the Old System

The information infrastructure of colonial financial intermediation was simply unable to handle the kind of demands increasingly made upon it for notes in exchange for deposits, discount bills, and issues of long-term credit. Paper currency had been used in New France before the Conquest of 1759, but its disastrous depreciation had sealed the reputation of the paper currency for two generations or more with the country's French Canadian inhabitants.

Two attempts were made to begin a banking business in the years before the conclusion of the Napoleonic Wars. In 1792 London merchants attempted to establish a banking concern in the colony, to no avail. Fifteen years later, in 1807, a second attempt was made under very different economic and political conditions. The Bank of Canada (or the Bank of Lower Canada) initiative was very much a product of the changing commercial and political conditions for colonial capital. The capitalists created through these ventures, as much as the nature of the initiatives themselves, flowed from the trade, capital, and political currents in the North Atlantic world of the early nineteenth century.

The champions of the banking company were drawn from the English commercial party of Montreal, a small group of merchants. They comprised some of the luminaries of the North West Company who had made their fortunes in the North American continental fur trade and in mercantile endeavours. One man, John Richardson, spearheaded the initiative, just as he had the 1792 attempt at establishing a bank. He attracted support from a large swathe of the English merchants in Montreal. The ties to Montreal's New England partners were also very much in evidence, with Horatio Gates, George Platt, and other merchants engaged in the Vermont trade supporting the idea.

John Richardson's petition requesting an act to incorporate the Bank of Canada made it to the floor of the Lower Canadian House of Assembly in February 1808. The committee struck to study the matter neatly outlined the increasingly difficult challenges facing Lower Canadian commerce as a result of the lack of financial intermediation. The establishment of a bank, the issue of notes, the extension of credit, the discounting of bills, and the ability to take deposits and cash receipts were necessary conditions to ensure the continued growth and prosperity of the colony. The momentum for the Bank of

Canada continued to grow in the spring of 1808. The bill providing for the bank's incorporation carefully set out conditions of organization, share capital, £250,000 liability, and bank-note circulation. Counterfeiting – a widespread art at the time – was raised to status of a capital crime, punishable by death. Provisions on stockholder voting, director liability, and total indebtedness (no more than three times the paid-up capital) were also spelled out. The bank could not hold real estate as a major asset but could hold mortgages on real property.[6]

Other, more subtle flows also contributed to the increasing momentum to establish a financial institution along the lines of the proposed Bank of Canada. There were currents of ideas, models, and examples that inspired the merchants of Montreal. The new bank had to conform to the particular requirements of the Canadian situation. Its organization and capital structure would have to be familiar to Montreal metropolitan capitalists. It would also need to have a proven track record of successful banking based on specie capital and mercantile credit. The first Canadian bankers sought familiarity, good reputation, and trust in their relationships and networks, as well as in the models they sought to emulate.

For Richardson and the other founders of the Canadian banking system, models were found in the American republic, namely the Bank of North America (1781), the Bank of New York (1784), the Massachusetts Bank (1784), and especially the First Bank of the United States (FBUS) (1791). Each of these banks had a common root in the mind of Alexander Hamilton, the first secretary of the Treasury under President George Washington and the father of the American banking system. The model that most suited Canadian needs and Canadian aspirations was Hamilton's creation, the First Bank of the United States. Hamilton envisaged the banking system at the centre of a financial infrastructure. The main bank would act as the government's financial agent, but it would do so as a private corporation with private shareholders. Private ownership and management were intended to ensure the expansion of commerce, while government participation acted as a guarantee of stability. The FBUS was incorporated by an act of Congress. The essential provisions of its charter – from the strictures on real estate holding and mercantile speculation to note issue and the emphasis on convertibility – were broadly those that found their way into the founding principles of the Canadian banking system. As Merrill Denison notes, "the Canadian charter was a direct replica of that of the First Bank of the United States" save for one or two minor adjustments.[7]

Here, the Canadian merchant experience and affinity with New York and New England forged a common interest and outlook. The networks spreading through trade across the St Lawrence, New York, and New England forged strong ties. Richardson himself worked in the New York office of Phyn, Ellice and and Inglis, and since that firm had close connections to the emerging banking establishment in the United States, he did not have to look beyond the FBUS for a banking model to emulate.

The American declaration of War on Great Britain in June 1812 was to have far-reaching consequences for the economy of British North America. A sustained burst of military spending in the colony resulted in some career-making profits for some well-placed merchants, and especially those in Kingston and York.[8] (Smaller merchants, particularly in the western sections of Upper Canada – modern-day Ontario – were not so fortunate.) That's not saying much, however, because the colonial economy was massively under-developed and barely able to surpass subsistence level.[9] From a banking and currency perspective, it was the way the military financed the war that produced a decisive break with the past. Army bills created a de facto paper currency in the British North American colonies. The bills in circulation reached $6 million Spanish dollars of varying denominations.

Here, the Commissariat Department deserves special mention. This civil administration under the command of a commissary-general reported not to the military but rather to the Treasury. It was responsible for payment and provision of supplies and retained accountability for military spending.[10] The sprawling infrastructure of procurement and provisioning of supplies for the 48,000 men fighting under the Union flag during the war rendered the Commissariat of critical importance in a time of great scarcity and personal privation.

During the War of 1812, the commissary-general for British North America, William Henry Robinson, had only sixteen officers to maintain posts and provision depots along a 1,700-mile supply line. He was assisted by a deputy commissary-general in Upper Canada who controlled a number of officers, storekeepers, and clerks at various posts throughout the province.[11] Chronic problems with payments, delays, lack of supplies, and other issues made for a volatile situation for the Commissariat, which played a vital role in keeping the primitive Canadian economy afloat and protected against excessive profiteering and inflationary pressures. At war's end, military expenditures amounted to £5.92 million, £3.44 million of which had been issued in army bills. The financing of the war need not concern us here. The structure of financing and circulation, however, was crucial for the further development of the system in Canada.

This imperial currency was a qualified success – as a circulating medium (for exchange) as well as for investment purposes (the larger bills bore 6 per cent interest). The guarantee of the imperial government in London also ensured that the bills could be bought and sold at a premium. They were much in demand in the United States, too, demonstrating that a sound currency redeemable for specie could cross even the most contested of barriers in the most contested of circumstances – war. In spite of the multiple inconveniences – chronic shortages of funds, hoarding, and counterfeiting and forgeries especially of the lower value denominations – the bills succeeded in providing a measure of circulation to the British North American colonies.[12] Private scrip, issued by private associations or businesses of varying denominations, further assisted in the circulation of an exchange medium, though this was more prominent in Upper Canada than in Lower Canada (modern-day Quebec).

Winners, Losers, and Bankers

If Canada had won the war, it lost the peace. Canada's post-war economy struggled in the wake of substantial war losses. The adoption of protectionist measures on trade and immigration by the Upper and Lower Canadian legislatures, as well as the paring down of public-work projects, drained the vitality from the colonial economy. The retirement and redemption of army bills further restricted currency circulation.[13] Canada's economy was subject to a series of post-war pressures: dramatic falls in public spending, serious falls in consumer demand, disastrous falls in prices, and devastating falls in available and circulating capital. The army bills did offer a glimpse of the possibilities that a paper currency could bring, while local conditions offered a powerful incentive to establish policies and institutions that would at least offer the colonies an opportunity to craft a sustainable economic program.

The Bank Project

After the war, fresh banking proposals were proposed in the Lower Canadian legislature in 1815 and again in 1816, commanding significant support from the merchant communities of the two largest cities in the colony, Montreal and Quebec. Each time, the bills fell victim to the broader and much more intensive political battles being waged between the French Canadian majority and the English governors over judicial appointments.[14] For John Richardson and his group of bank promoters, continued political deadlock between governor and legislature demanded bold action: the establishment of a bank without legislative charter. In May 1817, twenty-five Articles of Association were drawn up, posted, adopted, and published in *Le Spectateur Canadien* (26 May). The strong sentiment in favour of the venture in both the French Canadian and English commercial press must have been encouraging to the original group that formed the Bank of Montreal and in particular its driving force, John Richardson.

More broadly speaking, the Montreal Bank was the project of the city's entrepreneurial merchant class. Its establishment perfectly reflected the character, experience, needs, and aspirations of Montreal capitalists. The bank project represented the merchants' best and most effective response to a demonstrated need for stable financial intermediation. The new Bank also carried with it the aspirations to establish and consolidate Montreal's metropolitan position and financial predominance. The Montreal Bank would ensure that the city's trading and commercial networks could be potentially reinforced and extended so as to attract and deploy the circulation of capital. The venture was, moreover, deeply rooted in in the bold vision of some of its most enthusiastic promoters who had proposed similar but abandoned banking initiatives in 1792 and 1808. The original nine signatories of the Bank of Montreal's founding articles were motivated by necessity, conviction, and, increasingly, ambition.

As a group, the "Montreal Nine" joining together to form the Bank of Montreal were some of the most skilled, experienced, and shrewd businessmen in British North America. Through their activities, interests, and enterprises, they collectively represented a cross-section of the colonial business elite. Further, their association with the Bank conferred the three kinds of capital a bank needed to succeed. First came the real kind, that is, the actual money required to move forward with such a venture. The second kind of capital was the political capital required to establish and preserve such a potentially vital institution as the country's first bank. A project of that scale demands protection in the midst of controversy and that protection must be embedded in law and statute. The third kind of capital is the reputational kind. If reputational capital is important in any business involving exchange, confidence, and trust, it is absolutely critical to banking. For the Montreal Bank to have a hope of surviving and prospering, the founders had to possess all three kinds of capital in abundance. They did. Real capital flowed from Montreal and Lower Canadian merchants and businessmen, naturally. But it also flowed across borders, and in quantity, from New England and New York through numerous shareholders and, to a smaller extent, from capitalists in London. Most of the founders were of the businessman-politician class so common among the prominent of Montreal society.

The reputational capital of the Montreal Nine was generated from the range, extent, and scale of their activities and their contributions to British North American economic and political life. Four representative examples will illustrate the point: Austin Cuvillier, Horatio Gates, George Garden, and John Richardson.

The Rainmaker: Austin Cuvillier

Augustin (Austin) Cuvillier was the sole French Canadian founder of the Montreal bank. Cuvillier was a member of the first post-Conquest generation, born in 1779 at Quebec. His calling, as it were, was as an auctioneer in Montreal, chiefly of wholesale dry goods, where he developed a large network of contacts, understanding of markets, and a growing acuity in banking and finance. Combative, ambitious, and entrepreneurial, Cuvillier achieved sufficient success in the British colonial commercial circles that he changed his name to the more Anglo-friendly "Austin" by 1800.[15] The vicissitudes of commercial life in the auction business meant that success was coupled with setback throughout his career. As his biographers note, however, "Cuvillier's financial difficulties ... did not undermine his prestige."[16] During the War of 1812, Cuvillier served as a lieutenant and adjutant in the 5th Select Embodied Militia Battalion, known as the "Devil's Own," ended his military career as a captain in the Chasseurs Canadiens, and was awarded a medal and land for his efforts.[17]

Cuvillier also distinguished himself in the political realm, winning election in 1814 as a nationalist in the Parti Canadien, the legislature's dominant party. His knowledge of economic affairs made him an important figure in French Canadian politics. But he was equally appreciated in the business community. As a familiar and trusted presence in the English-dominated mercantile circles of the city, he used his influence to soften the outright hostility of French Canadian nationalists to English commercial interests. Louis-Joseph Papineau and John Neilsen, the two leaders of the Parti Canadien, relied on Cuvillier in their attempts to gain legislative control over colonial finances.[18]

Cuvillier's unique place between factions perfectly positioned him to become the driving legislative force for the creation of a Montreal bank in 1815. As we have noted, broader political considerations scuttled the first venture. Yet that failure masks the more subtle success achieved, as a result of Cuvillier's efforts, in gaining acceptance or at least acquiescence for such a project from the French-dominated legislature. This was a hugely important achievement, considering the power of the Parti Canadien throughout the period. After the Bank of Montreal was established, Cuvillier twice piloted a bank charter through the legislature, succeeding in 1821. In 1822 the charter finally achieved royal assent. Cuvillier's later vaulted to prominence in the 1820s in the colony's most controversial and consequential debates – over government spending, arbitrary exercise of power, and the financial reorganization of the local government.

Cuvillier's extraordinary ability to bridge the gap between the British merchant community and French Canadian nationalists was of signal influence in easing the way for the establishment of the Bank of Montreal. As his biographers say, it was in this period that "Cuvillier was able to reconcile the antagonistic interest of the two groups."[19] At least until the 1830s.

An American in Montreal: Horatio Gates

Horatio Gates is another founder whose career, relationships, and connections exemplify the kind of reputational capital so crucial for the success of the Bank of Montreal project. Gates was an American by birth (born in Barre, Massachusetts in 1777) who, by his early twenties, had become involved in the marketing of agricultural products from Vermont and New York to Montreal and the St Lawrence valley.[20] In 1807 he moved to Montreal and established a store with Abel Bellows, a fellow American, on St Paul Street. The War of 1812 provided Gates with an opportunity to connect the sudden spike in British military demand for provisions in the Canadas with American supply in meat and produce. His American connections and Canadian clients in a time of war required nimble diplomacy and reliable intelligence on both sides of the border. Gates was ready to sell his holdings and leave Lower Canada should the circumstances warrant it. He reluctantly took the oath of allegiance but obtained an exemption from taking up arms against his home country.[21]

Gates's business interests flourished in the aftermath of the war, as he became a major supplier of provisions to Lower Canadian garrisons below Quebec. He engaged in multiple business partnerships, from provisioning to the importation of British and American finished goods, to the exportation of potash, wheat, flour, pork, and staves. In this extensive range of business activity, Gates developed an impressive network of contacts through which passed hundreds of transactions involving bank notes, cash, and bills of exchange. As the Lower Canadian economy moved away from the fur trade and toward participation in a more diversified, continental, and transatlantic economy, payments, transactions, and matters of credit became increasingly urgent matters. Gates's sophisticated grasp of the need for financial intermediation was only part of the story, however. He also understood the relationship between credit and information flows about commercial, trade, and general conditions affecting business. His biographer notes that he published correspondence and circulars on the subject of Canadian trade in the United States, especially on prices, crops, and inventories, as well as vital credit information.[22]

The contribution of Horatio Gates to the establishment of the Bank of Montreal was indispensable. As a prominent Montreal merchant with continental networks, as an agent for the New York bank of Prime, Ward and

Sands, and as the founder most able to access American capital and share-holders for the venture, he played a key strategic role. His deep involvement in the first decade of the bank's activities underscores his conviction that properly functioning, effective banking institutions would be vital for the future prosperity of the colony. Indeed, he was so convinced that he also participated in the foundation of the Bank of Canada, a bank established to specialize with the United States trade in 1822 and which was merged with the Bank of Montreal in 1831.[23]

Gates's social standing in Montreal, his cultural and philanthropic commitments, and his active participation in church affairs placed him among the leading citizens in the city. At the same time, his conciliatory disposition allowed him to serve as a bridge between his fellow Montreal merchants and the Parti Canadien. As Jean-Claude Robert notes, Gates's career closely parallels and intersects with Montreal's rise as a metropolis in the first three decades of the nineteenth century. Starting from a position of economic weakness, the city was able to become, thanks to the efforts of its middle class, the pre-eminent economic power in Lower Canada.[24]

Presbyterian Powerhouse: George Garden

Another founder, George Garden, was a Scottish-born businessman, entrepreneur, and politician who participated in a number of partnerships in wholesaling with Alexander and George Auldjo. His interests also included the often-tricky business of fire insurance in Lower Canada, and he associated himself closely as well with improved transportation and communications between the Canadas, including the Lachine Canal's construction. He joined with other Montreal merchants to advocate for more open markets in Britain and the West Indies for Canadian agriculture and commerce.[25] Garden's reputation and economic standing in the late 1810s was reflected in his social standing – as a leading Scotch Presbyterian, governor of the Montreal General Hospital, member of the legislature for Montreal West, and justice of the peace.[26] His contribution to the Bank of Montreal crossed all categories – from resources to experience to reputational capital.

The Key Man: John Richardson

No founder, however, better captures the spirit behind the establishment of the Montreal Bank than John Richardson. Richardson was born in 1754 in Portsoy, Scotland, and studied arts at King's College, Aberdeen. In 1774, drawing on family connections, he entered into an apprenticeship with Phyn, Ellice and Company at Schenectady, New York. Richardson's business experience included working with the main supplier of British troops in New York during the American Revolutionary War as well as captaining the marines on the privateer ship *Vengeance*. His exhilarating experience with the *Vengeance* included being attacked and sunk by a British Navy vessel in May 1779.

Richardson's American business experience was extensive. In 1780 he established a shop trading in export consumer goods in Charleston, South Carolina After 1783, he represented the interests of his old firm, Phyn, Ellice, in New York State. By 1787, Richardson had moved to Montreal to help in the reorganization of Robert Ellice and Company and to rationalize that firm's over-extended operations in the Michigan territory. His position at the metropolitan centre of the fur trade, Montreal, and his role in such a prominent company, put Richardson at the centre of the action, allowing him to observe fur-trade flows, the market in bills of exchange, the relationship of Montreal merchants with local and imperial governments, and especially the provisioning of Loyalist and military settlements. In 1790 Forsyth, Richardson and Company had emerged as a successor firm to the Ellice company. Exploiting its knowledge of the forwarding trade to the west (Kingston and Toronto), it expanded the shipping business on the Great Lakes and fought vigorously for the retention of British military posts on American territory to protect the fur-trading concerns of Montreal merchants.

Richardson's political career began virtually moments after he took up residency in Montreal in 1787. He championed the merchants' demands for an elected assembly and the introduction of English commercial law as opposed to French civil law, and he fought a colonial administration decidedly anti-commerce in its outlook. His election to the Lower Canadian legislature in 1792 initiated a long career in shaping public policy and legislation, particularly in relation to finance, trade, and economic affairs in general, as well as in expanding legislative authority over money bills. In the 1790s, Richardson led the charge in securing the colony from the "contagion" of ideas and influences of revolutionary France. He played a central role in tilting the Militia and Alien Acts to a more aggressive posture. His reputation as an uncompromisingly loyal subject was rewarded with an appointment as justice of the peace during a time of civil unrest. In 1796 and 1797 he led Lower Canadian counter-intelligence efforts against French revolutionary penetration from the United States, and he took a leadership position in the defence of Montreal from foreign and domestic enemies.[27] His work in the Lower Canadian counter-intelligence service was particularly important during the war against Napoleonic France. Richardson's operations on behalf of the imperial government involved a network of informers, double agents, and the gathering of intelligence about French military plans for a possible attack on the colony. His efforts in this vein also extended to rooting out those suspected of treason.

In the early 1800s, Richardson's broader political involvement would be felt across the spectrum of public policy and in numerous statutes dealing with everything from taxation to jails, to transportation and navigable waters, and the like. But his most remarkable achievement lay in his championing of Canadian commercial interests. Richardson's passionate advocacy for the establishment of a bank – prematurely, perhaps, in 1792 and especially in 1808 – put banking squarely on the public-policy agenda. The April 1808 bill to incorporate a "Bank of Lower-Canada" was an opportunity to set out the principles of banking, parry objections to it, gather a base of support, and generally make the case for the benefits of the establishment of a banking system and paper currency.[28]

Richardson's passion after politics was to improve the business environment for Lower Canadian merchants by strong lobbying of imperial authorities over a range of issues, including better terms of trade, protection from American competition in imported goods, and the reduction in excise on a range of imported goods. Montreal's deep and abiding interest in the fur trade – in which Richardson and McGillivray prominently participated – was of particular concern. John Richardson presided over a vast range of business activities during his career. Those activities had their epicentre at Montreal but extended into economic, commercial, and political networks that projected the interests of English Montreal merchants to the southwest country (Ontario and Michigan), down to New York and New England, and across the ocean to the seat of the Empire. Richardson pursued his interests in both dangerous and often desperate times, and he often could be found at the centre of multiple contests. In the commercial realm, the struggle involved the fur trade, the establishment of a grain and timber trade, the promotion of imports and exports, and the levying of duties and taxes. In war and the affairs of nations, Richardson was an active and shrewd protagonist who exercised considerable influence, especially in the west country in the War of 1812. In domestic politics, he was focused on trade promotion and the defence of the mercantile interests of the English commercial party against an often-hostile French Canadian majority, as well as the establishment of a legal and regulatory framework to facilitate business development. By the 1810s, Richardson was uniquely prominent among his peers in the colonial business community, supremely active in the support of that community's commercial, political, and philanthropic interests, fearlessly loyalist and conservative in his politics, and passionately committed to the defence and promotion of British institutions, laws, and customs. His biographer says of Richardson that he "had the instincts of an outstanding team-player, although prone at times to define personally the true interests of the team. These instincts gave him superabundant energy and generated fierce and often selfless loyalties."[29]

Of all the intersecting interests and passions of John Richardson, his most enduring one was finance. His attempts at establishing a bank in 1792 and especially in 1808 were prologues to his success in 1817 with the Bank of Montreal. Richardson's strong advocacy of banking and paper currency in 1808 found much approval and favour in the Montreal merchant community of 1817. Both the arguments and the articles defining the operations and character of the Montreal bank were essentially Richardson's, though paradoxically he never held a formal position in the Bank beyond his chairmanship of the founding committee. His seminal influence in the early years extended to his personal negotiation at the Colonial Office for royal assent to the Bank's incorporation in 1822 and some key interventions in the Bank's affairs in the mid-1820s when a crisis threatened to blow up the venture.

John Richardson's extraordinary career and life in many ways epitomized the networks, relationships, experiences, and influences that lay the foundations of the Bank of Montreal. His financial ideas flowed from a deep knowledge and understanding of colonial, continental, and transatlantic economies in which he participated and through which he flourished. The kind of long-term intellectual research and development required to establish Canada's first bank was built upon an understanding of trade, exchange, and finance developed in the 1780s. Richardson's American apprenticeship provided not only commercial experience but also models of banking and finance – the First Bank of the United States and the Bank of New York – that found their way directly into the draft articles of the Bank of Montreal. The Bank of Montreal has, therefore, at its deepest layer of origin, an American design or at least inspiration. The Bank was also, from the beginning, continental in scope, paralleling the interests, connections, and trading relationships of its founders from Montreal to New York to New England.

If the blueprints for the Bank of Montreal were inspired by American models, and if its character was continental by virtue of its relationships, two major factors would mark it as Canadian or British North American. First, the Bank's establishment responded to the growing need of Canadian, mainly Montreal, merchants for stable financial intermediation and above all increased capital flows to stimulate the rudimentary economy of the colony. In essence, then, the Bank's establishment was very much the project of the Montreal commercial class. As Jean-Claude Robert writes, Montreal merchants surely amassed private fortunes in the process, but their commitment to the city's economic power was equally in evidence.[30] The mercantile community of Montreal well understood the importance of establishing institutions and instruments that not only enabled business to function but allowed Montreal to evolve into a Canadian metropolitan capital.

Another point worthy of note concerns the Bank's close association with the state, both local and imperial. The state helped to fundamentally shape the Canadian banking system from its earliest beginnings. Colonial legislatures and governors set conditions and demands that reflected local concerns and compromises. Simultaneously, through its representatives in Canada, the imperial government set parameters, regulations, and requirements while also providing detailed advice and direction on the shape and character of Canada's emerging financial system. The imperial influence would be most dramatically exercised in the first generation of the Bank's existence – a subject that will be discussed in later chapters.

Relationships with the state could become complicated. As we have seen, attempts at establishing a bank in the colony through the colonial legislature failed twice – first in 1792 and then in 1808, though only on the latter occasion were the arguments for the venture well articulated. Again in 1816 and 1817, the deadlock between legislature and governor on unrelated issues produced a similar result on similar proposals. The demands of the Montreal merchant class proved secondary to the larger battle between the French Canadian majority and successive governors of the colony on explicitly political matters. The establishment of a bank and a financial system in this context was not a priority. Later, the difficulty with which the Bank did finally obtain a charter – after intensive lobbying and advocacy by John Richardson in particular – underlines the point.

Subsequent petitions of the stockholders of the Bank of Montreal to the Lower Canadian House of Assembly capture some of the hopes and aspirations surrounding the Bank from its inception. The petitioners argued that "all persons desirous of promoting improvement look to the continuance" of the Bank of Montreal as necessary to give "scope and encouragement to agricultural and commercial enterprise."[31] In the eyes of its promoters, the Bank was "essentially conducive to the prosperity of the country, and a powerful means of developing its resources."[32] Yet not everyone agreed. Political deadlock compelled the promoters of the Montreal Bank to proceed without a legislative charter. A charter was the preferable route, but it was blocked by circumstance.

Some other way had to be found. Ultimately, the soundness of the twenty-five Articles of Association and the public's familiarity with the outlines of the venture and the acceptance of the need for a banking institution facilitated the Montreal Bank's emergence. The considerable reputational capital of the original nine signatories among the Montreal commercial class provided assurance that the Bank would enjoy the support and confidence of the wider community. In addition to John Richardson, the pre-eminent business leader in Montreal of his day, the other founders were either prominent or becoming so in their own right. George Garden and George Moffatt were partners in two of the leading firms of the city. Moffatt would go on to an illustrious career within the Bank and in politics. James Leslie and Robert Armour were similarly prominent businessmen. Austin Cuvillier prospered as an importer and served as a vital link to the French Canadian community in Montreal. Americans Horatio Gates, Thomas Turner, and J.C. Bush provided the continental American links to New York and New England.

The decision not to go "through" but "around" the legislature was a strategy that could have been pursued successfully only by people of such prominence, for banking is a business where reputation, trust, and confidence can mean everything. There was an implicit understanding that the character of the signatories and the soundness nature of the Articles of Association were sufficient guarantee of the probity of the venture.

The Constitution of Canadian Banking

The Articles of Association of the Montreal Bank, as posted at the Montreal Court House on 19 May 1817, represent the original constitution of the Canadian banking system. The provisions are in reality the foundations of a bank system that can be said to be American in design, continental in scope, and British in character. They were also a distillation of the experience, observation, and prudential judgment of Montreal's best minds on the subject. It would be tedious to review each article in the association agreement. Instead, we shall focus on the most pertinent ones that directly gave shape to Canadian banking. The articles set out the following key provisions, in addition to a range of administrative directives as presented in tables 1.1 and 1.2 below.

By the early 1820s, the Bank of Montreal had successfully emerged as an institution fresh from the struggles of the previous decade. As the chief financial project of Montreal merchants, it had overcome formidable obstacles in its establishment – from political turmoil, to imperial-colonial complications, to economic headwinds. The project was at least a quarter-century in the making and, to become a reality, required the full and energetic commitment of Montreal's commercial elites, their capital, their connections and their reputation. The success or failure of the project in the decades to come would demand a sustained and evolving commitment to confronting the massive challenges that awaited the new Bank of Montreal as the Canadian banking system was built – in the political arena, in the market, and as an organization. It is to these three major challenges that we now turn.

Table 1.1 | Structure, organization, ownership

Capitalization set at £250,000 with 5,000 shares at £50 each
13 directors on board; provisions for director turnover to ensure new perspectives enshrined; no salaries or "emoluments" to be provided
No citizenship requirements to hold directorship; certain provisions for residency in Montreal or colony for a period of time
Limited liability of shareholders
Graduated shareholder voting system capping one shareholder at 20 votes for 100 shares

Table 1.2 | Policy and approach

Note issue to be completely convertible, and backed by gold/silver reserves only – no real estate
No government participation/ownership as shareholder
No mortgages to be issued and no ownership of "lands and tenements" (real estate) permitted (except for banking business)
Focus on commercial enterprise
Debts cannot equal three times the paid–in capital stock
Provisions made for meetings, publication of reports
Books open to directors, but not individual accounts
Half–yearly dividends to be paid

PART TWO

Forging Canadian Finance,
1817–1870

The Bank's experience in its first half-century reflected the broader fortunes of the Canadian colonial economy. In an important sense, the Bank's "Generation Alpha" – its first generation of leadership – was challenged to navigate a treacherous set of circumstances while exploiting often-fleeting opportunities. These bankers had one task that ranked above all others: to create an institution of finance that would carry the ambitions and vision of the city, the colony, and the nation, and to project that institution into the financial markets of the North Atlantic world. How they performed this task was principally tied to the economic context of the Canadian colonies. That context – a sparse population and a staples-led, agriculturally dominated economy – provided the restraints, challenges, and opportunities for the evolution of Canadian finance.

Part One covered the context surrounding the establishment of the Bank. The period this section considers – 1817 to the 1870s – generally coincides with the first couple of generations of the Bank's existence. The chapters in Part Two examine the factors that gave the Bank of Montreal its particular character: the circumstances it faced, the decisions it took, the forces, ideas, and institutions that shaped it, and the strategies it deployed. The first generation's mission can be crystallized as one dedicated to building a solid foundation for bank performance and strategy based on three elements: reputations, relationships, and networks.

The Role of Montreal Bankers in British North America

From the retrospective gaze of posterity, becoming Canada's first bank is rightly considered a unique honour. Yet, to the founding generation of Montreal men in Canada's first banking institution, honours were the last thing on their minds: creating a viable, profitable bank was all that mattered. To them fell the responsibility to establish, define, promote, and expand Canada's first bank. That meant building a bank in an economy that, while growing, was prone to cyclical extremes and proliferating competition.

The first generation of Bank of Montreal bankers shaped its approach to banking within a deeply flawed and ethnically riven colonial political system with at least half a dozen potential flashpoints present at any given time. Generation Alpha also had to constantly negotiate arrangements within the political and administrative machinery of the Empire. What is more, it was laying the cornerstone for a Canadian financial system in a fundamentally continental – that is, North American – context. That context was known for periodic instability and with a proven capacity to erupt into military conflict, trade wars, or cyclical swings. Complicating the founding generation's work still further was the fact they were building a financial institution with a only few imported models as inspiration and a slender capital base to realize their goals.

Three Interpretive Keys

It would be tedious even if it were possible to document each decision, each step, each loan, each deposit, each board decision, each circular, and each change of rate of interest that together mark the first four decades of the Bank's history. Such an exercise would bring us no closer to understanding the importance of this vital Canadian financial institution. For the contemporary observer, the density of the history of the colonial period is hard to penetrate. So many forces seem to be working to shape the emerging institutions of state and civil society, the market, and financial intermediaries.

Part Two suggests a streamlined yet hybrid approach to this period. It begins with an examination of the historical record from the perspective of three interpretive keys. Those keys are reputation, relationships, and networks, at least as seen through the prism of the evolution of bank strategy. It then proceeds to a special focus on a fundamental, defining relationship that really did define the shape and contours of Canadian finance: that of the state and the Bank of Montreal. Next, Part Two turns to the 1860s – a decade whose challenges and opportunities were enough to break, or make, the Bank.

When the actors, the strategies, and the thousands of actions and decisions, along with the competing contexts and connections, are brought together, these three vital themes – reputation, relationships, and networks – emerge as central to the history of the Bank. Each of these themes courses through the first four decades of the history like a subterranean river – shaping decisions and strategies, influencing outcomes, and defining responses to challenges and opportunities alike.

A word of explanation about those three keys, and how they are used there to understand the experience of the Bank's Generation Alpha, is now in order.

Reputation

Bank of Montreal bankers were in some ways Canada's foremost nineteenth-century reputational capitalists. An analysis of the way in which the first generation of Bank of Montreal bankers exploited personal, business, and political reputations to establish the Bank, and then consciously and carefully built the Bank's reputation, is vital to understanding why the Bank leadership pursued certain lines of development while avoiding others. In banking in general, reputation can mean everything. In mid-nineteenth century Canada, it often did. Montreal bankers grasped this point as well as anyone.

Relationships

Montreal bankers spun a web of financial, social, and reciprocal relationships within the colonial economy and in the wider North Atlantic sphere – relationships involving clients, investors, debtors, officials, politicians, and regulators. Those relationships deepened and multiplied over time and as a result powerfully defined the Bank's character and reach. They can be thought of as overlapping concentric circles extending ultimately outward within the expanding metropolis of Montreal and Lower Canada, to the competing colonies to the west, and to the major metropolitan centres in the North Atlantic world – London, New York, and Chicago. These relationships also involve the business and mercantile interests that formed the Bank's clientele, as well as, crucially, administrators in local and imperial colonial administration – especially those who set the rules of the game: the Colonial Office and the Lords of the Treasury at Whitehall, London, for example.

Networks

In this context, networks encompass vehicles of information, control, and authority inside an expanding banking system. They also refer more conceptually to ideas and models in financial institutions and banking that influenced the direction and thrust of Canadian banking.

Summary

Reputation, relationships, networks: as broad categories of analysis, these three categories take us away from the traditional approaches to financial and banking history (chronologies, for example) to emphasize the deeper character of how success is made and sustained. Reputation can cut both ways. Relationships can be sometimes an encounter of equals. At other times, they are asymmetrical. They are almost always subject to change over time. Networks can form, dissolve, or reform in the face of events, or they can expand, grow stronger, and extend wider. As categories, they embrace far more than the financial element to include the social, political, and regulatory connections – threads that constituted the fabric of nineteenth-century Canadian economic and political life.

Of course, these categories are never watertight compartments. As events unfold in our story, reputations, relationships, and networks prove to be remarkably interdependent categories throughout the first four decades. The main point to remember is how the Bank had to dominate each category. At play was both the Bank's long-term success and the broader development of Canadian banking.

Context: Competing Worlds and the Canadas

The Canadas existed between competing worlds. The middle decades of the nineteenth century – from the mid-1810s to the eve of the US Civil War – were formative ones for the political, economic, and social life of British North America: nations were formed, economies grew, institutions established roots. The colonial settlements of Lower and Upper Canada found themselves struggling to establish their economic and political relevance in the North Atlantic world. These British North American colonies also very much existed *within* worlds – class, commercial, political, social, religious, and ethnic – and *between* often competing forces: continental vs. imperial, centre vs. periphery, rural vs. urban, French vs. English, Catholic vs. Protestant, First Nations vs. European, nationalist vs. imperialist, loyalist vs. annexationist. At this time, the term "competing forces" should often be taken quite literally: standing armies fighting for territorial expansion, trade, and competitive advantage. Wars, uprisings, and rebellions punctuated the history of the hemisphere in spite of the overall peace that reigned between the Great Powers after 1815.

In colonial Canada, these multiple contests were mainly fought in the realm of politics, ideas, and competing economic models – conservative vs. reform, free trade vs. protectionist, republic vs. constitutional monarchy, workers vs. capitalist, industrialization vs. agriculture. The competing forces at play fundamentally shaped the environment in which mid-nineteenth-century Canadians lived, worked, and made decisions. The fault lines that ran through the colonies often made for a contentious and challenging operating environment for financial institutions. The sharp expansions and contractions of the colonial, continental, and imperial economic system could often add drama and urgency to the conduct of business in British North America. This period of the nineteenth century can fairly be characterized as fluid, fermenting, and unpredictable.

Colonial Canadians, in other words, lived in a tough and unpredictable neighbourhood, compelled constantly to negotiate both inside and out to maintain the kind of rough equilibrium that forms the basis for economic development and growth. In this period, a small but growing capitalist and political elite began turning their attention to establishing the conditions, the mechanisms, the practices, the rules of the game, and the financial institutions that could position Canadians to take the greatest possible advantage of the country's potential and allow its businessmen both to connect, collaborate, and compete within British North America and to unlock the opportunities awaiting them in the broader North Atlantic world.

Canada's Economy in the Nineteenth Century

The pre-Confederation Canadian colonial economy can be described as a primarily agricultural and staples-based one perched on the periphery of the North Atlantic world. It was especially exposed to international terms of trade, notably between the United States and Great Britain. The Canadian colonies, moreover, were also susceptible to the cyclical economic upswings and downturns produced by staples-based trade (fur, lumber, wheat) and the vagaries of North American and European financial markets, particularly those in London and New York. Metropolitan competition between Montreal and the commercial "empire" of the St Lawrence, on the one side, and New York, on the other, was resolved in favour of the latter by the 1840s.

Advances in transportation and communications in the mid-nineteenth century focused on the construction of large public-work projects such as canals and railways. The capital required to fund these large projects, however, came primarily from public funds drawn from the imperial centre or from the United States. On their own, the Canadian colonies were then too small to be major underwriters of continental economic development. Small, pre-industrial, staples-based, vulnerable to cyclical economic swings in the wider environment: that description essentially captures in broad strokes the pre-Confederation central Canadian economy. The population of the Canadas in this period grew steadily from 452,065 in 1822 to 792,226 in 1831. By 1848, the population had grown to 2.4 million, and by 1870 it had reached 3.17 million.

This, in brief, is the political-economic context in which the Bank of Montreal had to operate: a society vulnerable to economic swings, vulnerable to terms of trade, vulnerable to events, vulnerable to politics, and vulnerable to decisions of foreign capital and policymakers in foreign capitals. In the roughly four decades that Part Two covers, the Bank had to navigate cycles of boom and bust, at least four panics, a rebellion, several European military conflicts, and bursts of public works, railway and canal expansion, road building, and the like.

Generation Alpha: The Key Players

The leadership team that would generate the reputation, build the relationships, and expand the networks of the Bank in the first generation were drawn from Montreal's commercial and mercantile elite. The team was remarkably stable. Samuel Gerrard's tenure as president (1820–26) was followed by that of John Molson Sr (1826–30), John Fleming (1830–32), and Horatio Gates (1832–34). The Bank's vice-presidents in these years were Thomas Thain (1822–25), John Forsyth (1825–26), John Fleming (1826–30), and Peter McGill (1830–34), the last of whom would then serve as president from 1834 to 1860. Alongside McGill were two vice-presidents: Joseph Masson (1834–47) and T.B. Anderson (1847–60). Two general managers guided the everyday operations of the bank – Benjamin Holmes (1827–46) and Alexander Simpson (1846–55). David Davidson was the last cashier to hold the title, from 1855 to 1862. Thereafter the post was renamed general manager.[1]

The directorship of the Bank was also relatively stable, with most directors serving long terms. Like the presidents, vice-presidents, and general managers, they were drawn from the merchant elite of Montreal. A few of the directors – John Molson, Joseph Masson, and John Redpath, for example – were also the largest shareholders, though they rarely individually held more than around three hundred shares.[2]

The day-to-day operation of the Bank was the business over time of a relatively small number of key employees in branches. The Bank's first cashier, Robert Griffin, in the 1820s could rely on a small but tightly knit team that included a notary (Henry Griffin), a first teller (Henry B. Stone), and a second teller (James Jackson) as well as an accountant (Henry Dupuy), a second bookkeeper, and a porter.

The Bank of Montreal's first years were marked internally by a focus on the establishment of the fundamentals of a banking business. In November 1817, the Montreal bank was officially in operation, and by the following year it had opened offices in Kingston and York, appointed agents in New York and London, and begun transacting foreign-exchange business in Boston. The Bank, of course, also began to issue the first paper-note currency in the colony. The fact that the first Bank of Montreal currency was printed in Hartford, Connecticut, was a practical decision but neatly symbolic of the ties that bound the colony to the republic to the south.[3]

Many of the Bank's customers were mercantile houses in Lower Canada closely allied to the Bank itself, and whose main merchants were directors. Forsyth, Richardson and Company, Horatio Gates and Company, Gillespie Moffat and Company, Peter McGill and Company, and John Torrance and Company are all typical examples.[4] Banking in British North America was a closely knit affair tied to merchant activity. Not surprisingly, it was to be found where the money was. And, in mid-nineteenth-century Canada, that money was very much to be found streaming out of the public treasury and into the hands of civil authorities, who then channelled it into public infrastructure and the military. As was suggested in the last chapter, the commissary-general occupied a prominent place in the early days of Canadian finance.

The Bank of Montreal was not the only bank in the colony: the Bank of Quebec and the Bank of Canada were both established in 1818. In Upper Canada, the Bank of Upper Canada (BUC) was established in 1819 and re-chartered in 1822. The BUC would prove to be a serious rival of the Bank of Montreal in the first generation. In the 1830s, a new crop of banks emerged: the Agricultural Bank of the City of Toronto (1834), La Banque du Peuple (1835), the Gore Bank (1836), the Farmer's Bank of York, Upper Canada (1835; renamed the Bank of the People in 1836), and the Bank of British North America (BBNA) (1835). In the United States, by contrast, a different approach to banking – one that discouraged branches – led to a proliferation of institutions. By 1834, for example, the United States had 505 banks; by 1839, 840.

The Bank's strategy, structure, and performance rested on several foundations: reputation, strategy, relationship with the state, and evolving systems of credit. Each of these is examined in the chapters that comprise Part Two. First, in the next chapter, we examine the importance of reputation to the first generation of the Bank and specifically how three key reputational "battlegrounds" emerged to shape the Bank's experience, approach, and identity.

CHAPTER TWO

Canada's Reputational Capitalists

Once colonial bankers were in possession of a sufficient amount of the "real kind" of capital, other kinds became important. First, success in Canadian colonial banking as elsewhere depended upon its organization, its management, and its political and market relationships. In other words, bankers needed to harness the intellectual and knowledge capital created by virtue of learning and experience. In addition, political capital in the form of influence, persuasion, and action was also vital in the legislative and imperial contexts. But, crucially, long-term success depended on "reputational capital" – the kind of relative assessment of the economic, financial, political, and social standing that formed the basis of financial transactions in an uncertain and information-challenged environment.

Reputation can mean everything in banking. Banks work hard to earn and keep good reputations. They know that reputations represent a tremendous intangible asset, a comparative judgment, and an assessment of performance.[1] The value placed on reputation in the nineteenth century was in some ways more consequential than it is today. Nineteenth-century bankers and financiers had to establish networks of trust over long-distance relationships. They also had to do so in what would comparatively be considered a "low-information environment." Evaluations of reputation took different forms, but people and institutions understood the value of it. Reputation mattered. Reputational capital, in other words, has been an important element in the long-term success of banking firms. It certainly was key to the success of the Bank of Montreal in the early decades of the nineteenth century.

Canada's First Bank and the Reputational Battlegrounds
of British North America

A contemporary definition of reputation characterizes it as a "collective representation of a firm's past actions and results that describe a firm's ability to deliver valued outcomes to multiple stakeholders."[2] Five key attributes form an essential part of the definition: reputation is based on perceptions; it represents a collective judgment of all stakeholders; it is comparative; it can be positive or negative; and it is stable and enduring.[3]

Three "reputational battlegrounds" shaped the destiny of the Bank in this period: 1) the nature and character of its banking enterprise; 2) the political environment of politics in a tumultuous period; and 3) economic performance in the context of chronic economic instability. Those three key factors later established the foundation for how the Bank put a premium on the strict maintenance of its reputation in its operations and relationships.

It was in this formative period – between 1817 and roughly the end of the 1830s – that provided the basis of the Bank of Montreal's long-term reputation as the most important and consequential financial institution in nineteenth-century Canada. Not only did the Bank of Montreal in these years become Canada's premier bank; its leaders also became Canada's reputational capitalists. The term "reputational capitalists" is used to capture the idea that those leaders came to an understanding of the importance of reputation to their business. They sought to create, preserve, and extend the Bank's reputation through their social, professional, and trade and business networks, through shaping the Bank's character and values, and through the Bank's performance.

Reputation as a force can facilitate or constrain market exchanges, deter malfeasance (given the threat of a bad reputation), and "legitimiz[e] firms and the institutional web surrounding them." In other words, corporate reputation as a concept can be applied both to individual firms and to broader corporate networks.[4] The experience of the Bank of Montreal in its first generation would certainly suggest that matters touching upon the genesis, development, and extension of its reputation did all of that.

Recent work on the subject has agreed that firms transacting long-distance exchanges have "almost invariably" relied on reputation, especially in markets that were undeveloped or poorly regulated. In situations where there were obstacles to gathering information or contract enforcement was difficult, reputation acted as an important historical force.[5] This has been especially true in the banking sector. The most famous international examples that come to mind are the Rothschilds and their preponderant influence in early-nineteenth-century finance, the House of Brown, and the case of the

Morgans and investment banking.[6] Reputation also cut both ways – the credit-reporting agencies in the mid-nineteenth century answered a massive need for information on the creditworthiness of the widest possible range of potential lenders. Bankers and their clients, therefore, had an acute awareness of reputation and a strong recognition of its power to persuade.

One private banker in the late nineteenth century remarked that "if that [reputation] is gone, our business is gone, however attractive our show window might be."[7] Social networks played a key role in the creation of reputation in financial firms: so did culture.[8] Such mechanisms functioned to discourage bad actors as well as to share exclusive or privileged information. One historian sums up the importance of reputation in nineteenth century banking: "To the extent that accurate economic information remained opaque or unclear and as long as personal relations mattered, social networks had an important role to play in the development and maintenance of a bank's reputation. This was true even when the social networks were fragmented and conflicted."[9] As the Bank of Montreal moved into the modern era in Generation Alpha, it developed a more differentiated organization, a workforce, a set of protocols, and an increasingly elaborate system of rules and regulations, all of which facilitated more impersonal interactions and the expansion of trade. Yet even what we consider "modern" interactions remain embedded in social relations. "Social capital" is therefore a relevant force, and "reputational capital" can determine whether social relations are effective and successful in an economic context.[10]

Historians have illustrated the many ways in which reputational capital in this context can supercharge social relations by operationalizing business and corporate networks and influencing decisions on jobs, capital, information, and security.[11] Membership in a particular elite social group can benefit from the reputation of the groups themselves and facilitate access to resources.[12] This was very much the case with the Bank of Montreal.

Bank of Montreal leaders, like their colleagues in banking in the North Atlantic world, well understood that "their reputations were non-replicable assets that were worth protecting."[13] As the Bank of Montreal grew, moreover, Canadian colonial elites were more inclined to trust it, regarding the Bank as a large and established player that was assumed to be in the market for the long term and consequently had much more incentive to avoid reputational damage than smaller players. It also helped that the Bank's leaders were increasingly connected to colonial, American, and imperial financial institutions, government finance, and key business enterprises in Montreal.

We have seen how fluid and contested the economic and political landscape of British North America could be. Reputations had to be fought for and won, earned and maintained, in constantly shifting territory. Ideas about what was appropriate and acceptable in banking were very much a matter for debate in the North Atlantic world of the mid-nineteenth century. Currency and exchange were far from settled entities and concepts. Paper currency was new, untested, and prone to counterfeit. An economy based on a succession of staples products such as fur and timber rendered the colony especially vulnerable to the vagaries of international markets and the terms of trade. A restive politics pitted factions favouring greater local control and responsible government against those who wished to maintain the imperial/colonial status quo. Regional rivalry between Lower Canada and Upper Canada manifested itself in many ways, including the blocking of commercial initiatives from the competing province. Armed insurrections in both provinces in 1837–38 caused further upheaval and uncertainty in the colonies. Finally, a mercurial Colonial Office and Treasury in London often generated challenges of its own, as we shall see in the next chapter.

These conditions meant that Canadian bankers had to be constantly mindful of their reputational capital as well as of the real kind of capital. Bank of Montreal bankers had to generate, create, use, and defend their reputational capital in the nineteenth-century Canadian context in order to survive and prosper. In fact, maintaining and expanding that capital became a critical foundation of the Bank's strategy.

Generating Reputational Capital: The Bank of Montreal's First Generation of Leadership

The new Bank's founding generation was drawn from the highest social and commercial ranks of the colonial elite. A few examples will suffice.

John Gray, the Bank's first president, was a prosperous merchant and trader in the North West Company. Thomas A. Turner was a member of a prominent merchant firm in the city. John Forsyth was a partner in Forsyth, Richardson and Company, the most prominent commercial house in Montreal at the time, and later a member of the Legislative Council. George Garden, also a leading merchant, became vice-president of the Bank in 1820. Horatio Gates, a New England merchant whose connections in Boston and New York made it possible to gather the necessary capital for the establishment of the Bank itself, became its president in 1826. Samuel Gerrard (president, 1820–26) was also a prominent businessman, as was John Fleming (president, 1830–32) and John Molson, a pioneer in steamboat navigation, the eponymous founder of the brewery, and a member of the legislative and executive councils who became a director of the Bank in 1824 and its president from 1826 to 1834.

Businessman, trader, and merchant Peter McGill joined the Bank in 1819 as a director, much later assuming the vice-presidency in 1830 and the presidency from 1834 to 1860. Once called by a contemporary "perhaps the most popular Scotchman that has ever lived in Montreal," he was considered to be the ex-officio head of the Montreal business community,[14] with interests including railways, transport, and finance. His political involvement as a member of the Legislative Council of Lower Canada and subsequently of the United Canadas after 1841 underlined those interests.[15] McGill's extensive import business, encompassing British goods and West Indian produce, generated a wide network of contracts. His mercantile partnerships and financial connections, as well as his political and administrative posts, made him one of British North America's most prominent men. Social and family ties, as well as his deep involvement in the Church of Scotland and Masonic Lodge, helped him to exert a measure of influence and reputation in both colonial and imperial circles.

These men, especially Molson, Fleming, Gates, and McGill, brought with them a network of connections that spanned the North Atlantic world, notably London and New York. They were experienced businessmen who now started gaining experience in banking as well. They were also familiar with foreign exchange through their other businesses in shipping and importing.[16]

The social, political, and business networks of the Bank's first generation of leaders conferred a strong guarantee of the Bank's probable success in establishing its own independent reputation. The members of the Montreal commercial elite who established the Bank of Montreal knew that they were setting foot in a vastly underdeveloped field. Canadian financial intermediaries began to appear in the first decade of the nineteenth century in the form of fire- and casualty-insurance companies (1809).[17] The chartered banks acted as the main suppliers of the medium of exchange and short-term credit. Alongside the new banks were trustee savings banks, Quebec-based savings banks, fire-insurance companies, and eventually the first Canadian life-insurance company, Canada Life. In the first half of the nineteenth century, building societies and joint-stock loan companies operating under royal charter rounded out the Canadian financial scene.[18]

The Canadian colonies were then struggling to find a reliable medium of exchange and a reliable currency. Restrictive bank charters were issued in the 1820s – to the Bank of Montreal, the Quebec Bank, the Bank of Canada, and the Bank of Upper Canada. The Bank of Montreal, for example, was limited to a ten-year charter, could not own real estate except for office premises, could not lend on mortgages or any property, was required to produce an annual report, and could not charge an interest rate on any loan higher than 6 per cent per year. Some of those provisions, such as the mortgage prohibition, lasted for a century and a half. As E.P. Neufeld writes of this early period in Canadian financial history, "government control was to take the form, not of detailed investment prescriptions, but of general and increasing supervision based on a progressively more detailed system of reporting and inspection."[19]

From a reputational standpoint, the early years were ones in which the Bank of Montreal's leadership sought to firmly anchor the Bank itself in the city and region. The directors soon contracted to build a "large and elegant building of cut stone," "ornamented in four compartments with emblematical devices of Agriculture, Manufactures, Arts and Commerce."[20] The new bank opened on Place d'Armes in 1818, and a generation later, in 1847, it built an entirely new edifice on the same site.[21] Outside the city, only two weeks after the Bank had opened in 1817, the directors appointed an agent at Quebec. In 1818 agents were then appointed at Kingston and York in Upper Canada. The Bank also later managed to become the custodian of the government account, which conferred upon it competitive advantages as well as envy from competing institutions.

Reputation and the First Corporate Governance Crisis at the Bank

The first and defining reputational battleground of the founding generation was the struggle to transform the Bank from a mercantile partnership marked by a personalist and insider-lending approach to a financial institution run along professional lines. In the early 1820s, Bank President Samuel Gerrard made loans and generally treated the Bank as if it were an extension of his own business. As Naomi Lamoreaux has shown for New England in this period, this type of insider lending within banks and between associates was very much par for the course in early American banking. In the case of Canadian banking, however, the situation was somewhat different, with rather less tolerance for the "investment club" type of banking prevalent south of the border in New England.[22] At the time of the 1825 crash, the Bank of Montreal had loans equalling a quarter of its paid-up capital – loans that were lent by Samuel Gerrard, who made no mention that he was doing so in his capacity as president.[23] The recovery of those outstanding debts was very much a matter of contention in the wake of the crash.

Outraged at the president's actions, three directors led a revolt. George Moffatt, a "dominant figure in the city's commercial life,"[24] James Leslie, a brilliantly successful wholesaler and American-born Montreal merchant, and Bank of Montreal founder Horatio Gates attempted to force Gerrard's resignation, succeeding, after several attempts, in the summer of 1826.[25] Gerrard was declared in default to the Bank and charged by the directors with irregular conduct. Specifically, he was found guilty of having granted discounts on behalf of the Bank without his colleagues' knowledge. Having granted those discounts, he then also augmented the debt of a borrower beyond the permissible limit of £10,000.[26] The board's decision, however, was a near-run thing; Moffatt's position on the matter was upheld by the slimmest possible margin: five for, four against.

The crash of 1825 seriously affected the Canadian colonial economy. A number of prominent Montreal firms suffered severe difficulties, and many fell into bankruptcy. England's economic position was not much better, either. There, the Bank's London agents, Thomas Wilson and Company, were also in straitened circumstances owing to over-extended South American investments. The situation for the Bank of Montreal was so dire that the directors departed from the normally spare, matter-of-fact reporting of their proceedings in the Bank's "Resolve Book" to record the following for the July 1826 meeting: "The Board, having had under its consideration the evil tendency of disagreement among the officers of the Bank, deem it necessary to declare it is their bounden duty individually and collectively to uphold the character and respectability of the Institution by the performance of their daily avocations with temper and forbearance – thereby conciliating the confidence of the public and the respect and esteem of each other – And the Directors are fully determined to mark any instance of neglect of such duty or breach of decorum in the Bank with the severest displeasure of the Board."[27]

The central worry here was the Bank's reputation, and its preservation in spite of economic downturn, directorial disagreement, and angry feelings on the part of some of its members. The unease of the directors was made worse by rampant talk of the Bank's mounting losses. The Bank's high charges for offering English exchange in Montreal – rates dictated by the market, not the Bank – further irritated a public that blamed the Bank for the added misery of costlier exchange. In addition, the Bank's insistence on enforcing an absolute news blackout on its losses seemed to do nothing but incite rumour mongering. The bankruptcy of the prominent merchant Simon McGillivray, who had close links to the Bank and, more importantly, sizeable loans drawn on it, became grist for the gossip mill in the city.

The resolution of the crisis did not come without a struggle. Long-standing and serious tensions among the directors of the Bank boiled over. The old guard of merchants on the Bank board supported the man at the centre of the controversy, Samuel Gerrard, and did not by any means go quietly. That faction of greybeards included the young Peter McGill, Gerrard's protégé, who helped to drag the issue out over a lengthy period and who assisted in softening the final blows when the final decision became inevitable.[28]

George Moffatt's campaign to put the Bank's operations on a professional footing – and especially to end insider dealing and favoritism in banking – came to a head in the summer of 1826. A special meeting of the Bank's stockholders was held to consider and eventually pass a sweeping revision to the by-laws of the Bank and the establishment of new rules and regulations to prescribe and control the conduct of the president and the cashier, as well as subordinate officers.[29] The key provisions of the revised code restricted the discretionary powers of the senior officers of the institution and set down strict rules for bills-of-exchange discounts.

Industrialist John Molson Sr acceded to the presidency in 1826, followed by John Fleming and Horatio Gates. In 1834, after the deaths of Fleming and Gates, Peter McGill assumed the presidency as the senior member of the board. As McGill's biographer writes, he benefitted from the sweeping changes that Moffatt and Leslie had pushed through the board, though he had previously strenuously opposed the changes in his defence of his partner and patron Samuel Gerrard.[30]

The issue of bank policy and practice was the key reputational battleground for the Bank of Montreal in its first generation. The victory of the Moffatt group was decisive. They wanted to push and pull the Bank into a more professional understanding of its mission and charter. The old guard, for valid reasons of their own, had every incentive to continue to use the Bank's resources for their personal and business projects. The small size of Montreal's business community made some sort of insider trading all but inevitable. The changes championed by Moffatt, Leslie, Gates, and Fleming, however, laid an essential foundation for the Bank's self-image and its signal to the wider world about its operations.

Reputational Battleground: Politics and Economics

The second reputational battleground for the Bank was in the political arena and was closely tied to the larger economy. Lower Canada was a deeply divided polity which separated the majority, Roman Catholic French Canadians, from the minority, Anglo-Protestants. The colony had a legislature and an executive, but the latter was not responsible to the former. Responsible government was many years away. An Anglo-Protestant commercial elite dominated the economic life of the colony – many connected to the Bank of Montreal itself. ""The checks imposed by an absorbing political strife,"[31] both within the colony and between Lower Canada and Upper Canada, absorbed the energy and attention of the political class. Cyclical economic downturns, dependence on a staples-based economy, and a host of other challenges provided more than enough fuel for tensions to spill over when life was not so sweet and people grew desperate enough. In addition to ethnic, regional, religious, political, economic, and social differences, there were competing ideas circulating about the nature of money, banking, and finance. Add to that the use of politics for private, local, or sectional gain, and one has a good picture of the political life of the British North American colonies in the mid-nineteenth century.

Politics in the colonies was, therefore, was anything but dull. In fact, it was rather too exciting for bankers in general. Predictably, success in troubled times attracted both friends and enemies. In the 1820s and 1830s the Bank could be seen either as a model to emulate or an overweening institution to bring down, depending on where the observer stood. In the legislature, it was the subject of harsh criticism for its practice of not discounting foreign bills when it purchased bills of exchange from the commissary-general. There were accusations that the Bank had not acted in the public interest, that it had injured Quebec interests by establishing a branch in that city, and that it had committed a host of other more banal sins.

An 1829 committee of the Legislative Assembly investigating these charges concluded several things: that the Bank had acquitted itself properly in the trading of notes; that the Quebec branch had been a great benefit for commercial and agricultural interests of the city and district of Quebec; and that the affairs of the Bank had been conducted on fair and equitable principles.[32] The committee also found that the Bank's practices of redeeming issues and discounting notes, as well as combating counterfeit circulation, had been up to the standard of the best and most reputable banks in the North Atlantic world: the Bank of England, the Bank of Scotland, and the Bank of the United States.[33]

The conclusions of the Legislative Committee followed lengthy testimony on the part of Benjamin Holmes, the Bank's cashier. The Bank had sent Holmes rather than more senior figures in the Bank to avoid further controversy and conflict. What is more, Holmes's job as director of operations for the Bank allowed him to speak authoritatively and clearly on best practices in banking. His reputation as a stickler for procedure likely impressed the committee members.[34] His biographer also suggests that his non-political demeanour was a great asset for the Bank in this dangerous passage through the often-hostile proceedings of the committee.[35] Holmes testified about the methods of the Bank in dealing and redeeming its own paper. He also pointed out that the gold and silver channelled through the Bank of Montreal that was used to pay taxes or for buying English or American exchange had been provided mainly by the Bank itself.[36]

The committee's findings did not, however, end the peril faced by the Bank. Political attacks on the banks and on banking were increasingly common in this period in the United States, and those flames spread across the border in the early 1830s. In fact, while the committee's report had exonerated the Bank of wrongdoing, it had a much less positive effect in the court of public opinion. The committee's conclusions left many with the impression that the Bank's political powers of persuasion must have been considerable to obtain such a favourable result (irrespective of the merits of the case). The involvement of many of the Bank's leading lights in the political issues of the day – prospective union of the Canadas, questions over land tenure, the nature and powers of the judiciary – was controversial as well. The renewal of the Bank's charter in 1831 elicited intense opposition from radical/reform elements of the legislature, especially from their leaders, John Neilson and Louis-Joseph Papineau (the speaker of the house). Papineau argued forcefully that banks were not private but rather public and political institutions answerable for their conduct to the authority that created them. He charged that the Bank had failed to live up to the demands of the public and therefore should be denied its charter. "Private interests invariably more or less sway men in their public capacities," Papineau concluded, "and it is necessary that establishments of this kind be jealously looked at."[37]

The early 1830s also produced opposition to the Bank's conduct in other areas. In an extraordinary set of letters, a writer ominously named "ANTI-BANQUE" claimed that small bank-note issues had driven metallic currency out of the country. The Bank of Montreal's monopoly of government exchange therefore drew particular fire. Paper money, moreover, had a very low reputation among French Canadians, who had a bitter experience with that medium of exchange. In the end, the charter eventually passed but was extended for six years only, to 1 June 1837.

The political tumults of the 1830s put the Bank squarely in the sights of the fight between English and French in Lower Canada. The following anonymous warning was posted in the heat of the parliamentary elections of 1834. Translated, it reads:

NOTICE TO CANADIANS
From the public press you will have learned that the confidence of the public of Quebec in the Bank, and above all those of Montreal, has ceased, that within a few days £12,000 has been withdrawn from them, and that the principal Bank at Montreal has been forced on two occasions to send hard coin to its branch in Quebec. Those of you who have bills of this bank in your possession, and who do not wish to be exposed to the risk of losing their value, wholly or in part, would do well to exchange them as soon as possible, for hard coin at the Bank of Montreal, St. James Street. Let the example of the United States be a warning to Canadians. Several hundred banks there have failed, and all those who had confidence in these institutions, which are enemies of the liberty of the people, have sustained considerable losses on their rags of paper, which they pretend to be equivalent to hard coin. Be on

your guard, Canadians! Take no more bills, and rid yourself as soon as possible of those that you now have!
8 November 1834

As we have seen, the commercial activities of the Bank's directors touched virtually every aspect of Montreal economic life. Leading Bank executives such as George Moffatt and Peter McGill were also involved in immigration and land settlement initiatives in the Eastern Townships through the British American Land Company. The company sought to buy land for the settlement of British emigrants, but it ran into trouble once it was realized that the majority of the emigrants could not pay for their passage. The political environment of the 1830s also proved to be a serious problem for the company, whose directors had somehow not anticipated the virulent opposition of the French Canadian majority to plans for the British colonization of the Eastern Townships.[38] The tensions of the mid-1830s between the French Canadian majority represented in the Assembly and the governor and Colonial Office were reaching the breaking point on this and other issues. The battles fought over constitutional arrangements – specifically the power of the Assembly – were made all the more complicated and intense by the deep ethnic divisions in the colony. As Governor Gosford wrote to Lord Glenelg in March 1836, "the English portion of the community and especially the Commercial Classes will never, without a struggle, consent to the Establishment of what they consider little short of a French Republic in Canada."[39] Such was the atmosphere in the Canadas in mid-1830s. It was about to get a lot worse.

The Unravelling Colony

By the mid-1830s, Lower Canada's political life was in a state of crisis. At the heart of the crisis was a contest for greater self-government, advocated especially, but not exclusively, by the French majority. Matters deteriorated to the point of agitation, boycott, breakdown of trial by jury, and ultimately rebellion in 1837–38. Bad harvests in 1836 presaged an economic contraction. Some banks made matters worse. The proliferation of banks in Upper Canada making unsecured loans led the financial agents of that province to suspend payments in London in 1837. That May, American banks followed with an even greater blow, suspending the payment of specie, which forced the Lower Canadian banks to do likewise. As if this were not enough, exploiting the laxity in existing regulations, sixteen banking institutions – without charters, mainly consisting of groups of individuals operating from Buffalo, New York – began circulating notes throughout the United States and British

North America. When those notes were offered for redemption, the banks promptly disappeared.[40]

The political, financial, and economic crisis faced by the Canadas stretched their financial institutions to the breaking point. The Bank of Montreal, with a reputation for resilience and prudent management, was able to remain afloat. Even so, dividends between 1837 and 1840 were cut in half.

Chartered banks dominated colonial commercial banking and the Canadian capital market in general in the nineteenth century. That does not mean, however, that those chartered banks were assured their position for decades to come. Between the 1820s and 1837, numerous attempts were made at establishing private note-issuing banks "under deed of settlement." Banks such as the Farmer's Bank, the Bank of the People, the Niagara Suspension Bank, and the Agricultural Bank of Toronto all failed. Besides the Bank of Montreal, one of the survivors was the Bank of British North America (established in 1836) – a British bank but with the authority to sue and be sued in the name of the resident officer and with the protection and prestige of a royal charter (1840).

The Bank of Montreal's assistance with large public-work projects such as the Lachine Canal (completed in 1821, at a total cost $440,000) and private infrastructure initiatives (Champlain and St Lawrence Railroad, built in 1832), along with its sound banking practices in exchange dealing, began to earn it a solid reputation. Consider one example: the Bank became the largest dealer in exchange in both Upper and Lower Canada, employing Prime, Ward and Sands as its agents in the New York market to obtain a more favourable sterling exchange than was available in Lower Canada. The channelling of funds through New York provided a favourable market for sterling bills, a source of supply of specie. The strategy of keeping large secondary reserves both in London and in New York was becoming typical of the Bank's conservative strategy.[41] Coupled with an upswing in colonial economic fortunes, the Bank's business became more voluminous and profitable, with its shareholders deriving between 12 and 14 per cent dividends on their stock between 1832 and 1836.

The Bank of Montreal's growing reputational capital in the 1830s consolidated its position in the Canadas. For one thing, it did not fail, nor did it come close (though the "Rest" or reserves were drawn upon a few times to a significant extent). In fact, the "Rest" maintained an impressive health even during the troubles, as table 2.1 shows.

The Bank's established record as a stable and cautious institution marked by a stringent set of rules and vigilant directors set it apart from others. The adroit management of its affairs resulted in its admission to conduct business in Upper Canada, where it had been barred from doing so (for political reasons) except through a subsidiary bank (the Bank of the People). When Upper

Table 2.1 | Reserve funds, 1819–40

Year	Reserve
1819	£1,042
1825	£7,570
1830	£7,840
1835	£20,165
1840	£22,370

and Lower Canada joined to form the United Province of Canada in 1841, the Bank was given a new, twenty-one-year charter and authorized to increase its capital from £250,000 to £750,000.[42] The Bank leadership took full advantage of the prevailing tailwinds of the 1840s and established a number of agencies across the emerging towns and cities of what is now southern Ontario. The Bank's ability to weather subsequent reversals of every sort – the suspension of specie payments by the Bank of the United States, Anglo-American tensions over the Oregon territory in 1845, the arrival of 100,000 destitute Irish in 1847, a banking crisis in England in 1848, frenzied railway speculation, and sudden and sharp declines in agricultural and timber prices and in the construction of colonial ships – all tested the mettle of the Bank, which incurred considerable losses but remained stable. The response typically would be to gauge the risk and adjust loans and outlays to conform to the strict maintenance of the Bank's reputation for probity and sobriety in financial transactions.

In the 1840s, the Bank's reputation was well established and also well defended. Bank leaders in the McGill administration ensured that any threats to that hard-earned reputation would be dealt with. Two events in the 1840s illustrate the point. The first one was political. Cashier Benjamin Holmes had entered the combative world of colonial Canadian politics, with the result that, in the course of his political career, he had to endure an onslaught of political hostility and rough treatment at the hands of the opposition. One particularly sharp skirmish with the Executive Council over canal expenditures in 1845 got passions so aroused that the Council withdrew all government accounts from the Bank in a fit of fury. Some months later, in 1846, Holmes resigned his position as chief cashier with the Bank in favour of Alexander Simpson. Thereafter, the Bank's officers studiously shied away from any overt political involvement as too risky and potentially damaging – not only in a reputational sense but also in a financial one. The government accounts soon returned to their normal status with the colonial authorities and business proceeded apace.[43]

The second event in the 1840s focuses on a curious contretemps concerning the shareholding ownership of the Bank. Its leaders were under increasing pressure to release who, exactly, the shareholders were and where they came from. In response to growing concern about possible American influence, the Bank in 1845 released some statistics showing that, in fact, only 73 of the 15,000 shares were held by US interests. The majority (9,739) were held in Canada East (southern Quebec), followed by Great Britain (2,660) and Canada West (1,186); army and navy officers held 873. The Annual Report of 1845 also suggested that the shares were relatively widely held in the colony, with "parties directly engaged in trade" holding 4,401; lawyers and doctors, 815; and "other professionals and private individuals," 10,144.[44]

Both incidents – one focused on political perception and the other on public perception – underscore the importance that Generation Alpha continued to place on reputation. The Bank of Montreal's experience in the three key reputational battlegrounds suggests that its leadership had come to an intuitive understanding of the role and impact of reputation in nineteenth-century British North America. Bank of Montreal bankers acted to create, generate, and preserve reputation. Internal crises over banking practices in the 1820s and the conflicts of the 1830s speak directly to the shifts in the "micro-culture"[45] of the Bank. That micro-culture comprises values and beliefs that determine or shape reputation from inside the firm (in other words, its own internal image). The battles over the Bank's proper command structure, its loan policies, its voting procedures, and administration and by-laws provided an opportunity to come to a new understanding about how the Bank could connect its expanding banking capabilities to an emerging set of values and beliefs that emphasized a more professional approach to the Bank's operations. The reputation that was being shaped inside the firm in 1825 and 1826 was deteriorating so rapidly that only an urgent set of actions could have saved the Bank from a cruel fate. The success of the reforms and the elimination of certain key figures helped the Bank to reverse course and begin to exploit is growing capabilities in the sector.

The Legislative Assembly's scrutiny of the Bank's operations in 1829, as well as its discussions over the renewal of its charter in 1830–31, made for a potentially contentious and perilous operational environment for the Bank. Yet, in the end, the Bank survived. In this outcome, the support of the British commercial elite, or at least enough of it, was vital. The views, moreover, of the Colonial Office and Treasury in London could and did have an impact as these bodies passed judgment through their intermediaries about the status of the Bank and its operations.

The relative success of the Bank of Montreal in weathering the difficult times of the mid- to late 1830s suggests strongly that its reputational capital, built on careful management of its affairs, was considerable. But that would only be part of the story. Many of the principals of the Bank, McGill, Moffat, and Holmes, for example, were passionate supporters of the United Canadas and of loyalty to the crown. At the time of the Rebellion, some of them earned the praise of the community through their participation in the military campaign against the *Patriotes*. In insisting on harsh punishment (including hanging) for the rebels, a number of Montreal merchants made it clear that they were not especially concerned about how the French Canadian population perceived them, at least while passions ran so hot. Bank of Montreal leaders were more concerned with their reputation in their own community and with the imperial government. This attitude persisted over some time and was expressed again in connection with the issue of indemnification for rebel losses incurred during the unrest. Yet slowly, even as early as the 1840s, relations between the two communities began to improve as the British North American colonies evolved into a more politically mature entity. The Bank's leadership also moved steadily away from out-and-out political involvement, preferring to exercise its influence behind the scenes and away from the glare of the public spotlight.

The Bank of Montreal in the 1820s was essentially a mercantile partnership that showed signs of becoming a more complex institution. In time, the champions of more stringent governance within the Bank could declare victory on various reputational battlegrounds. The Bank's leadership increasingly boasted of a strong reputation – for careful management, for its network of connections, and for its financial performance (which had the virtue in tough times of not leading it to failure, as was the case with so many other banks). As the subsequent history of the Bank shows, those reputational assets facilitated an increasing number of profitable exchanges and interactions – through expanding branches, greater investment opportunities, and a growing network of agencies in the United States and London. This period, in other words, marked the beginning of the Bank of Montreal's reputation as the premier Canadian bank – a reputation tried, tested, and earned.

As we have seen, three "reputational battlegrounds" shaped the destiny and future of the Bank in this period, defining the Bank's essential nature, character, and values. The Bank's struggles with both internal and external pressures created an institution with a solid reputation and one in which the importance of reputation was keenly recognized. In the process, the Bank of Montreal became not only Canada's first bank but also its premier bank for the greater part of the nineteenth century, while its leaders became Canada's foremost capitalists.

CHAPTER THREE

Style, Strategy, Stability

Reputation was one thing: strategy was another. Both intersected, of course. But successful strategy was multi-faceted, combining reputations, relationships, and networks. The Bank was called upon to develop the strategy and organizational capacity to be able to perform a number of vital functions for the colony.

The Bank in this period adhered to what can be called the Stability Strategy, which embraced a conservative, careful approach to loans, a preference for a large build-up of reserves for contingency, and an overall outlook that emphasized deliberate growth, even if it were at the expense of quick profits. The Stability Strategy fit well with the stature of the Bank, the tendencies of its principals, its fiduciary role as the largest Bank, and its role as government banker. All those signposts pointed to the need for stability in banking, an imperative for survival in the colonial era. Success for the leaders of the Bank of Montreal was possible in this climate only if they could successfully manage the tension between two contradictory forces: growth and risk. Of course, all banks must manage that tension in order to survive and prosper. But in colonial Canada, both forces were typically unpredictable and often suddenly subject to sharp reversals.

First, the Bank was called upon to leverage the existing strengths of a weak and capital-deprived Canadian colonial economy to facilitate the interests of broader economic development. Its greatest challenge was to help build a capitalist system that would promote local development and provide crucial banking facilities in circulation, foreign-exchange services, and capital flow and transfer, as well as deposit and loan for public and private demand. It would have to do so at the pulse and rhythm of the colonial economy, moreover. The rise of the Bank of Montreal system demanded the growth of a network of financial intelligence and contacts that had to be developed in the markets that mattered: locally, of course, but also in cities where Canadian financial and mercantile interests needed to be represented: New York, London, and Chicago.

The Bank's developing policies and institutional arrangements also had to be able to withstand periodic but sometimes sharp contractions or economic shocks to the colonial economic system. The need to manage market risk often collided with popular pressures upon the bank to liberalize loan facilities, open branches in developing areas of the colony, or provide capital for large public projects. Occasionally, those pressures were intense.

Balancing these two centripetal forces through four decades demanded an agreed-upon strategic vision and a disciplined leadership with the shrewdness to judge how to build, when to strike, when to risk, when to pull back. If the Bank had merely followed a tight-money policy and refused to support any but the most secure ventures, Canadian economic development would suffer – affecting, not least, Montreal merchants who were at the centre of trade. By contrast, if the Bank's leadership succumbed to the temptation of engaging in more speculative ventures, it stood to jeopardize not only its own standing but perhaps its very existence. The prospective failure of the Bank would have had incalculable consequences for Canadian economic fortunes both at home and abroad. Its dual roles as the financial establishment of Canada's metropolitan capital and as an anchor of Canadian financial stability surely must have been obvious to both management and board of the Bank. Its close relationship with successive colonial governments would only underline this sense of the public importance of the Montreal bank establishment.

The Bank, therefore, pursued an adaptable, long-term strategic vision that embraced and sought to balance these two contradictory forces. Between the 1830s and the late 1850s, the Bank's leadership approached questions of expansion, development, competition, market penetration, organizational development, and policy evolution through this lens. It did so on the intuitive understanding that it was responsible not only to its shareholders but also, in a much larger sense, to society at large. Canada's prospects as a colony and as an emerging player in the North Atlantic world depended on its performance.

As we shall see in the next chapter, the regulation of banking had a profound effect on the way that banking in Canada in general, and the Bank of Montreal in particular, evolved. Canadian banks and their restrictive charters were substantially the product of a political economy of banking in Canada.

The strategies pursued and the decisions made, however, flowed from the Bank of Montreal's Stability Strategy.

The Stability Strategy – in some ways unique to the Bank of Montreal – featured a careful approach to lending and discounting, a policy that is not altogether surprising in a capital-scarce and information-challenged environment. It also at least partially accounts for the selective and discriminating nature of the Bank's loans and investments, particularly in railways, a class of investment that the Bank typically sought to avoid, except in special circumstances. The policy accounts as well for the timing and opening of new agencies and branches after considerable deliberation and not infrequently after much petitioning from local communities; and it propelled the Bank to focus, sometimes to a fault, on the pursuit and maintenance of consistently high reserves – beyond that which was required by legislation. Finally, the Strategy puts into context the Bank's operational focus on building organizational capacities and financial capabilities in New York, Chicago, and London. The necessity to move carefully, and with caution, was reinforced by the Bank's role as government banker in crucial periods through the first generation of its Bank's existence.

Developing financial institutions depended on an ability to respond to an impressive and often fearsome array of organizational, business, and strategic challenges facing nineteenth-century finance. Some of those challenges were common to all banks: organization, strategy, structure, policy, rates, and regulation. A few were specific to the Canadian context: an awesome geography, a peripheral and cyclical economy, the limited autonomy of colonial government, the ethnic divisions of colonial society, and a continental and metropolitan rivalry with the United States and its emerging financial capital, New York City. As the market slowly developed, new banking establishments added to the challenges of competitive pressures.

The Bank of Montreal's first generation of leadership was therefore summoned to tackle a powerful, unpredictable, and often dangerous set of economic and political circumstances over time. Montreal merchants were developing greater economic capacities in manufacturing and wholesaling, but progress was slow. The Canadian capital market was barely beginning to form. The colonial economy was deeply tied to the terms of imperial and continental trade, moreover, and therefore susceptible to the rising and falling tides of international economic fortunes. Bad harvests, the fluctuations of trade in staples, and periodic financial panics formed an important part of the economic landscape. The advent of large public-infrastructure projects – canals, railways, telegraph networks, for example – all provided both opportunities and risks for investors. Settlement and expansion in southern Ontario especially also provided new potential for investment and development. Banking itself was a young and unproven new financial instrument, its methods and approaches yet to be fully tested or completely accepted.

Success or even survival for young financial institutions is never assured in any environment – and particularly not in a volatile one such as that of colonial Canada. The stakes were high, and not just for the Bank of Montreal's leadership and its promoters. Canadian fortunes, Canadian enterprise, and Canada's presence and participation in emerging North Atlantic financial networks were all deeply implicated in the potential success or failure of the Montreal Bank. In many ways, the Bank of Montreal over the course of that generation had become the principal standard bearer for Canadian finance – its embodiment and exemplar. This was in spite of the fact that the Bank had plenty of competitors, plenty of detractors and critics, and more than a few enemies.

A vital element of the Bank's success in the first generation was its creation of an administrative, organizational, and information architecture. That architecture would have to be strong enough, in the face of adverse economic conditions, to guarantee the proper flow of information on credit, conditions of trade, and the like. By the 1850s, the structures, strategies, and networks that came to define the Bank's character and style in its first generation were firmly in place.

Stability as a Style

The reputation of Canadian banking for stability has been attributed to Canada's "institutional foundations" – in other words, the regulatory and political context and the branch system – as well as the slow evolution of Canadian securities markets. The Canadian system therefore limited sources of systemic risks by its very nature.[1] That Canadian style of banking in this period had its roots in the early to mid-nineteenth century and was shaped both by political struggle at home and by imperial oversight. But to leave it there is only to understand half the picture. As the principal player in the banking system, the Bank of Montreal had to operate within the rules of a conservative approach to banking. The evolution of its policy and the implementation of its banking strategy performed an important role in defining the trademark approach of Canadian banking.[2]

A Developing Capability

"The Montreal Bank is said to have commenced with quite an unexpected confidence from every class of the community," the *Daily National Intelligencer* of Washington, D.C., reported in December 1817. "So much so," it continued, "that the merchants are realizing more convenience than they ever anticipated." Deposits were reported to be "immense" since it began business in November of that year.[3] This account of the Bank's auspicious beginning is interesting for two reasons. First, it captured a sense of the demand for banking services among merchants in Montreal. Second, the fact that Americans were taking an interest points to the natural continental ties that were such a prominent feature of the Bank's activities and the profile of its promoters.

Exchange

The Bank's early efforts were directed toward the establishment of the essentials of the banking business. One of its earliest strengths was in exchange, exploiting its connections with London in the British market and New York in the American market. In the latter, the Bank of Montreal developed a profitable business in sterling exchange, serving the New York trade. It also remitted bills to London for indebtedness arising from the importation of goods and especially specie. Of the two capitals, however, New York held the most appeal as a market for sterling bills and specie and even for the deployment of reserve funds. The circulation of coin, currency, and specie was a major preoccupation for the bank, since it involved a high degree of risk. The hazards of physically moving gold, specie, and valuables across the forbidding terrain of the Canadian colonies were considerable.

The Bank's burgeoning traffic in exchange in the late 1820s is revealed in the numbers. Between 1827 and 1829, bills bought of the government increased 208 per cent from £47,000 to £145,000, in private bills from £18,729 to £60,610. By 1831, the debts due to the Bank were just shy of half a million sterling; deposits stood at £129,285; and notes in circulation amounted £223,558. Of the debts, the directors were responsible for a sizeable proportion of the loans – over 35 per cent. The reason is relatively straightforward: the directors were the main merchants in the city. In later years, the percentage of debt held by directors would decline as the business grew and was eventually capped by statute at 10 per cent of all loans in the 1840s.

The Bank's early specialization in exchange and mercantile credit helped to establish its foothold not only in Montreal but also in the larger markets of London and New York. As we have seen, its success was not always well received: a petition to the House of Assembly in 1829 delivered a coruscating attack on the Bank's policy of apparently restricting its loans to those engaged in trade, thus "depriving the public of those advantages which in countries where the banking system is better understood, are considered as important to the agricultural, professional and general interest as to that of the mercantile part of the community." The petition continued that the Bank had displayed the "narrow, mistaken and selfish views of those who cannot drop the trade when they assume to be bank directors."[4] The outburst seemed directed at broadening the banking facilities in the colony, something that the directors believed ultimately desirable but premature.

Early Banking and Lending

The Bank of Montreal represented Canada's arrival in the capital markets of the North Atlantic world. The challenge was that Canadian capital in the mid-nineteenth century rested on primitive economic foundations.

The continental struggle for advantage between the United States and Canada unleashed a wave of infrastructure projects that began with canals in the 1820s. The landmark American construction of the 363-mile Erie Canal linking the city of New York to the Great Lakes (1825) prompted Canadian interests to build competing networks north of the border. The Lachine Canal was Montreal's entry into the "canal-mania" of the day, as one historian has put it. The nine-mile canal would connect the port of Montreal to Lachine and allow shipping to pass into the Great Lakes system without the enervating business of unloading and loading cargo arriving in Montreal and bound for the west. Its completion in 1824 allowed Montreal and the Canadian colonies to compete with the American states. Its construction engineer was John Richardson, a key figure in the organization of the Bank of Montreal. Generally, however, the Canadian capital market was simply not ready to take on the capital-intensive public-infrastructure projects demanded in the Canadas. Canadian capital in this period was just beginning to show signs of life in the 1820s and 1830s. The mid-century boom in railways and telegraphy was largely financed by government debt and foreign capital.

The Bank of Montreal and other Canadian banks also provided Canadian investors with a nascent securities market. In fact, bank shares were virtually the only game in town, with the Bank of Montreal's shares the most heavily traded security for a good part of the nineteenth century, beginning virtually at the Bank's inception in 1817.[5] As David McKeagan notes, bank shares were traded directly between shareholders, with bank directors or employees as intermediaries.[6] In the 1840s, commercial activity, agricultural expansion, and improvements in communications led to a more formal organization of commodity trading. The emergence of brokerages and commodities exchanges in Montreal put Canadian finance slowly but surely on the road to a more professionalized system of securities trading. The Board of Brokers (1848) eventually became the Montreal Stock Exchange in 1870, with its legal incorporation in 1874. But Montreal would remain a regional market for securities whose transactions mainly focused on financial institutions such as banks and insurance companies and utilities-based firms (gas/light), railways, and shipping lines.[7]

The Bank's involvement in the developing securities market of the 1840s and 1850s is evidenced by the multiplying activity recorded in the Bank's stock ledgers.[8] The Montreal securities market began to attract a more specialized class of brokers and traders buying and selling a modest but increasing number of securities. As the brokerage profession began to take shape, Bank of Montreal officials were less and less involved in the direct selling of the Bank's shares or "over the counter" – a function gradually taken over by professional traders.[9]

The Bank Abroad

The Bank of Montreal's links to the major capital and securities markets of the North Atlantic world, especially in New York and London, represented a crucial Canadian contribution to the development of the financial system. These links provided essential opportunities and intelligence networks flowing across the Atlantic and continentally. The networks were small but growing in the 1820s and 1830s. By the 1840s and 1850s, railway construction and the arrival of the telegraph had given securities markets a major impetus.[10]

The Bank's networks in London were primarily linked through agents established in the city. Routinely, the Bank placed advertisements in the *Times* to attract depositors who were considering emigration, or "who may be desirous of remitting money to Canada." In the 1830s, the chief agents were Thomas Wilson and Company, with offices in London and Liverpool. The Bank offered the facility of deposits in Britain and withdrawals at Montreal, "or at any of the agencies of the institution in Upper or Lower Canada, free of charge, with the current rate of exchange."[11]

The Challenges and Opportunities of Investing

The truth of the matter is that the Canadian economy before 1850 was a predominantly agricultural one with a focus on the primary producing sector. Canadian economic development was halting and limited; Canadian capital was scarce. Yet Canadian economic potential as perceived by both British and American investors was considerable. In the nineteenth century, the great vehicle for exploiting that potential was the railway company. Two great sources of securities and investment therefore defined the Canadian market: governments and railways.

The Bank of Montreal was the principal investor in the Champlain and St Lawrence Railroad (constructed in 1832), a small railway by the standards of the later ones. Yet Canadians alone could not possibly hope to deploy the massive amounts of capital required to develop the potential of railways. The Great Western Railway of Canada (1845) and the Grand Trunk Railway (1852) were almost completely British-financed.[12] The Bank of Montreal did, however, provide significant amounts of capital to fund the secondary market – the contractors, engineers, and construction firms – that was a vital part of the construction of the Grand Trunk. Later railways connecting Canada to the United States were almost completely underwritten by American or British investors, with the shining exception of the Canadian Pacific Railway in the 1880s.

Nineteenth-century Canadian economic development was therefore a collaborative effort drawing in capital and investment from public and private sources in the North Atlantic world. As a colonial junior partner, Canada in the pre-Confederation era very much relied on the terms of trade and on foreign capital to underwrite economic development. The one exception to this rule was Canadian banking itself. Canadian banks had the distinction of being predominantly Canadian-owned and controlled. The Bank of Montreal, for example, had initially a large American shareholding, but by 1830 the shares had mostly reverted into Canadian hands. The Bank of British North America was a British-backed bank which two generations later was absorbed by Bank of Montreal. Bank securities were virtually the only game in town in terms of generating securities in the early Canadian market.

Relationships and Networks in the 1840s and 1850s

The Bank's challenges in the 1830s intersected with politics, the market, and the larger colonial and imperial context. Building a reputation as a bank in these circumstances was a tough challenge but one that the Bank overcame. In the 1840s and 1850s, the battlegrounds were only slightly less dramatic. The Bank's attention in those decades turned to developing the strategy and performance required to remain competitive in a rapidly changing environment.

The competition between banks in the 1840s and 1850s can be described as relentless and sharp. For example, in September 1841, the Commercial Bank of the Midland District redeemed in one single day £40,000 in sterling in Bank of Montreal notes it had been hoarding – equivalent to about a third of the coin and bullion in the vaults – in order to attempt to destabilize its Montreal rival. The gambit did not succeed, of course, but the tactic was typical of the competition in colonial Canada.[13]

Generally speaking, Bank decisions in the 1840s fit completely in line with the Stability Strategy. The Bank's leaders kept a close eye on conditions of credit, and when changes were in the air, they restricted commercial loans. The Bank also instituted a series of sixty- and ninety-day payment regulations. Of course, the main instrument available to give effect to the Stability Strategy was the enhancement of reserves or "rest," which almost became a management obsession.

The Bank also consolidated its position in Canada West in the 1840s, expanding its branch network to Toronto and Ottawa in 1842 and to Kingston, Hamilton, Cobourg, Brockville, London, St Catharines, and St Thomas at various points in the 1840s. Other towns in the Bank's territory flooded the Montreal headquarters with petitions for branches. The reason was straightforward: the appearance of a Bank of Montreal branch signified a powerful economic stimulus for local areas and brought with it the power and prestige of the Bank's organization. Loan and discount facilities were as vital to the growth of the undeveloped parts of the colony as to that of the more developed ones. In keeping with its strategic preference for stability, the Bank extended its branch network and its loan facilities with a view to minimizing downside risk. That meant in practice that the board would say "no" to branch-establishment requests much more frequently than "yes."

Branch expansion throughout the 1840s and especially in Canada West (southern Ontario) was accompanied by a corresponding expansion in the ranks of the Bank's representatives. Tory politicians William Wilson and William Henry Draper, for example, both became important representatives of the Montreal Bank in Canada West. The network of managers and representatives of notable rank in the colony gave impetus to the expansion plans of the Bank.

The focus in the 1840s was the financing of public works and infrastructure projects. Here again, the Bank's experience motivated it to tread carefully and deliberately, where other banks often rushed in. Public-work projects dominated the 1840s as Canada began to build a network of harbours, waterways, lighthouses for navigation, timber slides, custom houses, courthouses, jails, post offices, legislative buildings, quarantine stations, and marine hospitals. Those public works were financed by government with loans arranged by the banks. In the case of the Bank of Montreal specifically, it financed public works through contractors via the security of their engineers' vouchers channelled through individual branches. By 1845, the total discounts reached $1.48 million, of which $330,000 were provided in Canada West.[14] The Bank's loan and investment activities also extended to the funding of the Magnetic Telegraph Company – which built the first telegraph line between Montreal and Toronto in 1847. The company obtained a £2,000 loan secured on the credit of the individual directors of the Bank.[15]

The Bank's reputation for a tight money policy was often a source of public criticism rather than praise in this period. The voices of criticism, however, tended to be silenced when the economic cycle would produce a panic or depression. In 1848, for instance – a year that President McGill called "one of the most calamitous in the commercial annals of Great Britain" – a financial panic occasioned "disastrous failures" right across the colonial landscape.[16] The Bank itself managed to hold its losses to £90,514.[17] It was able to survive such cyclical economic misfortunes by sticking to its tight-money policy and avoiding plunging headlong into any "mania" of the day. The Bank's first-generation leaders were not only careful, they were wary of any project that would entail what the management considered to be excessive risk.

The Bank's Stability Strategy was most notable in railway financing. In the nineteenth century, railway construction represented the most attractive – perhaps one can say the most seductive – investment possible for banks and investors. Bankers were often swept up in the excitement. By the end of the 1850s, two thousand miles of track were in place in Canada, financed mainly by British capital. The Bank's policy in this context was to assist the development of railway projects such as the Grand Trunk and the St Lawrence and Atlantic by extending loans secured on the security of the principals involved, giving assistance to the placing of public debt on the London market, or securing backing provided by the government itself. The Bank also advanced loans and discount facilities not to the railways themselves but rather to the contractors who were building the lines. Debts were safer and more recoverable that way. In addition, the bank financed the purchase of rolling stock.

Performance

By the late 1830s, the Bank had consolidated its place of prominence over its provincial rivals, as much for its business as for its developing expertise in banking. In 1839, for example, the news that the Bank of Montreal was proposing to extend its operations to the Upper Province, Canada West, was welcomed because of the expertise it would bring into that province's underdeveloped banking system: the Bank, it was said, would "instruct our directors in the system of commercial banking, which very few of them understood."[18]

The Montreal Bank's role in the growing Canadian system of monetary circulation involved an increasing traffic of coins, bills, and specie that demanded a relatively high level of organization and security not only between the central office and the branches but also across borders. The specie flow in Canada typically followed a circular pattern from the United States and Upper Canada to Montreal, and then from Montreal to Quebec. At the two latter points, the specie would pass into the hands of the provincial and imperial governments for duties and to redeem bills on Britain. Finally, government expenditure for civilian and military purposes would close the circle and return the specie to trade.[19]

The Bank's growing expertise was put to the test during the economic and political troubles of the late 1830s. Between 1837 and 1840, the suspension of specie payments arising out of the economic crisis forced banks to redeem their liabilities in foreign exchange. By so doing, the banks were able to add premiums to the exchange transactions that allowed them to recoup some of the losses incurred.[20] One of the more interesting features of this difficult period for Canadian banking was the fact that notes were being redeemed that were "irredeemable" between the banks themselves. Debtor banks were forced to hand over in settlement some of their most prized discounted paper. As the Canadian Bankers Association (CBA) later noted, "these notes were redeemed in due time, by the makers, leading export merchants, by sterling bills drawn against shipments of grain, potash, ginseng and timber."[21]

The three-year period of economic crisis between 1837 and 1840 was a testing period for the Bank of Montreal, no less than its competitors. The banks in tandem, however, managed to weather the crisis and emerge with a stability and strength that served the colony well. They were therefore better positioned in the ensuing upswing in the early 1840s as prices rose and conditions of trade became moderately favourable.

A depression in 1848 – occasioned by a number of factors, including a railway-investment crash in England and the colony's loss of its imperial preferences in timber and other natural products – gave rise to a new set of challenges for the Canadian banking system. But, once again, the Bank of Montreal was able to execute its stability strategy. Its leadership's main preoccupation was with the establishment and build-up of a reserve. In prosperous years, the reserve would deepen while in the challenging years, such as 1848, the Bank could draw upon its reserve while maintaining a healthy sense of solvency and maintaining specie payments. Any losses would be borne by the shareholders alone.

Performance: A Closer Look

An analysis of the Bank's performance in the 1840s and 1850s shows that the Stability Strategy functioned as it ought to have. It did, however, harbour both advantages and disadvantages. Three charts will illustrate the point with respect to circulation, deposits, and assets for the period 1847–59 (see figures 3.1, 3.2, 3.3).

In figure 3.3 in particular, we see the results of the Bank of Montreal's focus on careful extension of its operations. The assets tend slightly upward, even after the economic and political crisis of 1848 in the North Atlantic world. By 1850 (in the wake of a colony-sparing imperial loan), they resume their significant upward trajectory; by 1853 and the return of prosperity and rising

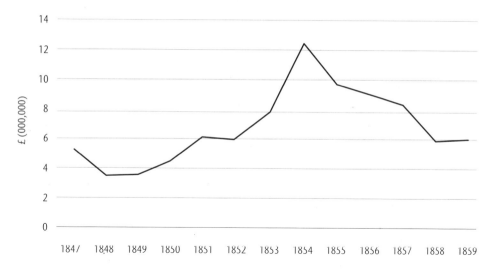

Figure 3.1 | Notes in circulation, Bank of Montreal, 1847–59
Source: Bank of Montreal Annual Reports, 1847–59.

fortunes, the curve climbs significantly to over £3 million. Even after the crisis of the 1850s, Bank assets remained at £1.8 million before returning to over £3 million in 1860.

Taken together, the charts allow us to draw a couple of general observations. First, the Stability Strategy produced positive but often mixed financial results. Assets show a strong trend line upward, but that is not the main story. The main story is the ability of the Bank to register this trend in spite of the strong cyclical spins that so characterized the Canadian economy in this period. The Bank certainly did not and could not escape some collateral damage. Second, as the Bank's capitalization grew during the 1840s and 1850s, loans and discounts generally kept pace, suggesting that the conservatism in loan policy was not as stringent as previously supposed. It never seemed to push the limits of safety but did go as high as £2.6 million in 1857.

By the late 1850s, the Bank's Stability Strategy had positioned it as a smart, careful competitor atop the Canadian banking system. In 1856, the Bank operated 21 branches and 3 subagencies and employed 112 people. The circulation of Bank of Montreal notes was approximately £900,000 that year, a growth of 100 per cent from the beginning of the decade.[22] The Bank expanded to accommodate the wider range of economic activities in the United Province during the boom years of the 1850s. "Accommodation" was the order of the day but, of course, always within the limits of the Stability Strategy.

Figure 3.2 | Deposits, Bank of Montreal, 1847–59

Source: Bank of Montreal Annual Reports, 1847–59.

Figure 3.3 | Assets, Bank of Montreal, 1847–59

Source: Bank of Montreal Annual Reports, 1847–59.

A Sure Foundation

By the end of the 1850s, the Bank's Stability Strategy, its growing organizational capabilities, and its extensive relationships locally and in the North Atlantic world had worked to make Montreal bankers a force to be reckoned with in the banking system in Canada and a respectable brand in the markets of New York and London. The Bank's restriction of discounts and circulation was not always popular, and often frustrating. But it ensured that the Bank was there through thick and thin. The Bank's expansion of its networks – of branches as well as of intelligence and credit information – proceeded steadily.

The Bank's architectural plans throughout the period offer a concrete testimony to its rising reputation, developing relationships, and expanding networks. In 1845, plans for the new head office in Montreal were drawn up. When the new building opened in 1848, it was an impressively faithful tribute to its inspiration – the domed neo-classical head office of the Commercial Bank of Scotland in Edinburgh. The Commercial Bank was likely an inspiration in other ways – in its methods of banking, its joint-stock ownership structure, and its success in the Scottish banking market. A decade later, John Redpath, the head of the Bank of Montreal's building committee, moved to build a series of new branch buildings in Toronto, Hamilton, and elsewhere.

The Bank's competitors, however, were gaining fast, especially the Bank of Upper Canada, which had experienced spectacular growth in the prosperity of the 1850s. In 1855 five new banks emerged: the Molsons Bank, the Bank of PEI, the Bank of Toronto, the Niagara District Bank, and the Bank of Canada (later the Bank of Commerce in 1867). Competition was intensifying in the context of a small colonial base. The Bank of Montreal was by no means immune to these competitive pressures. By the end of the 1850s, however, its reputation was established, its relationships were solid and productive, and its networks made it a clear leader in Canadian banking. Whether or not the Bank's incoming leaders would be able to sustain that, or whether they would be eclipsed by bolder, more aggressive banks, was the most serious question on the horizon as the first generation of the Bank's leaders faded from the scene.

CHAPTER FOUR

Legislator, Lord, Banker

In the last chapter, we saw how success in banking in mid-nineteenth-century Canada depended on a network of intersecting personal, business, and institutional relationships in the North Atlantic world. Those relationships shaped Canadian finance. One set of relationships, however, most defined the style, character, and rules that governed the Canadian banking system: the relationship between legislator, lord, and banker. In other words, the dynamic between colonial politician-legislators, the lords of the Treasury in London, and Montreal bankers was a central one in shaping the Bank of Montreal's sphere of action and the overall contours of the Canadian financial system. That is the reason this particular relationship demands its own examination.

More than at any other period during its two centuries of existence, the Bank of Montreal's relationship with the state in this first generation was at its most intense and its most consequential. It was intense because the Bank's activities were closely monitored, regulated, and scrutinized by both colonial politicians and imperial administrators. That intensity was magnified because of the Bank's central role in the financial security of the British North American colonies. If the Bank was not yet "too big to fail," by the 1830s it had become too "important" to leave to mere fate. Its specific role in the military-payments structure elevated the Bank's activities to matters deserving of imperial military security.

The triangular relationship involving legislators, lords, and bankers ensured that Canadian colonial banking was responsive to local demands while also adhering to imperial standards of safety and sufficient capitalization. But it also involved a great deal more: collaboration and coordination on questions of the military-payment structure and the stability of the colonial system. The parties acted sometimes in concert, but often, too, they were at odds over specific questions of finance. This was an era in which the struggle to establish the rules of the game and the boundaries of the field of action was most intense. The Bank of Montreal was a central participant in this struggle. The defining features of Canadian banking were then being negotiated – everything from proper capitalization of banks to questions about which currency Canada should use. The Bank of Montreal's decisions and actions reinforced its importance as a key player in the unfolding of the Canadian economic and financial system – a role that in turn gave added support to the Bank's prudential strategy in the market.

To be clear, the Bank's role as the leader of Canadian banking was one that would unfold over time. The mid-nineteenth century was an experimental period of market organization in banking in Canada. The state in this situation acted as referee, rule-maker, and client. The imperial government's ability and willingness to dispense rents to economic agents in the colonies was intended to serve two purposes: facilitate its own credit and payment systems in British North America, and give aid to the development of a financial infrastructure. In vital ways, then, the state-bank relationship put the Bank of Montreal on a specific evolutionary path in Canadian finance – as leader, guarantor, and Canadian banking point of reference – characteristics that would inform its approach to banking, underline its preference for stability, and reinforce its prudential approach to fundamental banking questions. In key respects, the political economy of British North America played a central part in the destiny of the Bank of Montreal. The public power to grant banking charters and set specific conditions for banks meant that politics and administration had a defining role to play in the making of the Bank of Montreal.

Primum Inter Pares

Between the 1820s and the 1850s, the Bank's relationship with the state was in many respects the same as that of all other banks in the colonies. Every Canadian bank was compelled to pass through legislative and regulatory scrutiny. Every bank also had some level of relationship both with legislatures and imperial authorities just by nature of its business. There are, however, a few elements that set the Montreal Bank apart from the rest. The Bank's importance to the emerging Canadian financial system was absolutely central. Its primacy among Canadian banks by virtue of its size and reach, extensive networks and relationships, and solid reputation conferred a special status on its activities. The Bank's ability to weather the periodic financial and economic instability of the colonial and North Atlantic economic systems gave it a privileged position in British North America. As the colonies grew, as the Canadian financial system began to take shape, the Bank of Montreal was at the heart of the action.

As the title of this chapter suggests, the Bank's relationships with public power took place on several fronts, each requiring a different set of diplomatic and political skills. Closest to home was the colonial legislature, which passed banking laws, approved terms, imposed conditions, and established regulation and supervision mechanisms. In the Assembly and its committees, the Bank underwent often very close and critical scrutiny that could at times turn hostile or contentious. The legislative arena in colonial British North America was an especially contested environment where economic initiatives were often subordinated to other more urgent concerns encompassing politics, ethnic divisions, military expenditures, trade, tariffs, and commerce.

The Bank also had direct links with the imperial government, specifically the Colonial Office and the lords of the Treasury in Whitehall, London. Together, these branches of the imperial government formed a well-coordinated information and intelligence network on banking and financial matters. Advice flowed from colonial officials and military officers in the Canadas to London, which was thereby kept informed of local issues and circumstances.

To the Commissariat Department, responsible for the payment and provisioning of troops, the relationship between the crown and the Bank of Montreal was a matter of *military* security. To the lords of the Treasury, who oversaw the vast finance, trade, and commercial interests of the British Empire, it was a matter of *economic* security. The Whitehall-based offices of the Treasury were the hub of an information network that received commercial intelligence relayed from men on the spot in the colonies. For their part, the lords of the Treasury were responsible for ensuring the orderly, careful development of colonial financial institutions. The lords provided advice on the royal assent of bills (which bills should be proclaimed law), on disallowance, on possible amendments, and on the structure and regulation of banking. Always keeping a close watch on Canadian developments from an imperial perspective, they were at times at loggerheads with the colonial legislature. They were far from being impartial observers or participants in colonial financial affairs. There is no question, however, that Canadian banking bore imperial markings of either approval, disapproval, or acquiescence.

Between the 1820s and the 1850s, the imperial government exerted considerable influence on the emergent Canadian banking system. A conjunction of factors made it so: colonial banking was young and impressionable – in its foundation phase. Periodic crises such as the Panic of 1837 in the

United States, when a number of banks failed, sharpened imperial interest in colonial affairs. The limited autonomy of Canada's parliamentary institutions was also a factor. With the advent of responsible government in 1851, the Treasury's direct authority over, and interest in, Canadian banking gradually receded as local institutions and priorities asserted themselves in the development of colonial finance. But until then, London was a key player in the forging of Canada's system.

Legislators and Bankers

The first defining relationship was between the Bank and the colonial legislatures (first that of Lower Canada [1817–41] and thereafter with that of the United Province of Canada [1841–67]). The colonial legislature was the political arena into which the Bank of Montreal and its promoters would descend to have charters approved and rules set, to explain their vision of the enterprise, and to see off any challenges. Passage of the Bank's successive charters through the legislative process established rules of operation and conferred legitimacy, but as we shall see, the process could be hotly contested. As a central economic activity, banking and financial matters could act as lightning rods for other forms of discontent. Banking in the nineteenth century did not operate in a separate sphere but rather was intimately connected with the political, economic, and social concerns of the colony.

In the previous chapter, we noted the challenges the first promoters of the Montreal bank faced in getting a charter through the Lower Canadian legislature and the torturous path to royal assent. But even then, the newly minted Canadian bank had to wait a year as the governor did not enshrine the charter into law until 1822. For the "President and Directors of the Bank of Montreal," its second, legislative birthdate would be 22 July 1822 when its existence was officially proclaimed. The Bank's charter would run until 1 June 1831.

The Bank's original charter was impressively prescriptive. The 144 shareholders elected 13 directors, all of whom had to be British subjects meeting residency requirements for the city and the province. The charter set out in considerable detail the rules surrounding conflict of interest (no director could act as a private banker), liability (which was limited to directors' shares), appointment of offices, charging of interest (with a 6 per cent maximum on any transaction), bookkeeping, transfers of stock, annual meetings, debts, circulation of notes, receipt of deposits, and dividends. There was even a provision for the dissolution of the Bank in the event that the legislature established a provincial bank seven years after the original Bank of Montreal charter. The Bank's charter thenceforth acted as a template for the other banks that followed in the province.

The Bank's directors and promoters were frequent guests before the Lower Canadian House of Assembly. There, as we have seen in previous chapters, the Bank was often the subject of criticism or cross-examination by politicians representing the interests of its competitors. The political and legislative arena was an often-unpredictable one for the Bank and its promoters. Looking back in hindsight, however, a Legislative Committee commended the "good effect of [the banks'] careful policy and the restraints imposed by law, by circumstances and by their mutual competition" that led the Canadian system to retain its strength and stability until the commerce and agriculture finally revived in the early 1830s.[1]

The 1840s and 1850s

The 1840s and 1850s provided a quieter context than the 1830s. After the creation of the United Province of Canada, which comprised the former colonies of Lower and Upper Canada, the politics of banking continued under the statutory styles and systems set up by previous legislatures. Lawmakers introduced, debated, and approved changes to charters, focusing on capital, security, or other organizational elements of bank operations.[2]

Some of the Bank of Montreal's key protagonists in the early 1840s decided to run for the Legislative Assembly of the new United Province. Benjamin Holmes and George Moffatt were not only central to the Bank's early success; they were also valued as articulate representatives of the Montreal merchant community who had played an active part in shaping the constitutional future of the colony. George Moffatt, for example, was an important member of the delegation of the Constitutional Association of Montreal which had gone to London to urge the necessity of union on the government there.[3] "It is sufficient to say," wrote an editorialist in the *Montreal Gazette* in March 1841, that "they are in every respect worthy of representing such a metropolis in any situation whatsoever," that their re-election will "reflect everlasting honour on our fellow citizens," and that "while their [Montreal merchants'] interests and civil liberties can continue to be entrusted to the guardianship of such delegates as Holmes and Moffatt ... they will never be compromised and betrayed."[4]

George Moffatt in particular was an outspoken advocate of the promotion of British culture and interests. He was a tireless opponent of the French Canadian Parti Patriote – successor of the Parti Canadien – and looked forward to the peaceful anglicization of Lower Canada. The republican elements in the Parti Patriote, he argued, aimed at "the establishment of a French Republic on the banks of the St. Lawrence." In the wake of the Rebellion of the 1830s, such perspectives and sharp divisions were entirely to be expected. The tensions between English and French, Protestant and Catholic, were never far from the surface as legislators got to the difficult but necessary business of governing a regionally and culturally divided polity. What is extraordinary, however, is that the early forays of bankers into frontline politics did not continue much beyond the 1840s and 1850s. Leaders of the Bank of Montreal increasingly preferred to stick to banking and remain either behind the scenes or on the sidelines.

The pressure points on the subject of banking in Canadian politics in the 1840s were primarily about economic growth, monetary circulation, and capital flows. The creation of the United Province offered a fresh legislative opportunity to tackle some key questions about the emerging Canadian financial structure. In this process, the Bank's leaders were protagonists and key participants, focusing on such matters as bankruptcy and real estate laws, usury, and – of special importance – the idea of a government central bank as the sole issuer of currency. In all of this, the shaping of Canadian finance in the mid-nineteenth century was indeed the outcome of a triangular contest between legislators, lords, and bankers. But in other ways, the divisions on banking matters pitted colonial Canadians and their judgment and experience against the judgment and experience of the decision-makers of the imperial government.

Conflicts over Currency

One of the key conflicts in the developing relationship between the state and banking was whether or not Canada should adopt the pound sterling. To most Canadians, the answer was no. Conversion to sterling would not only affect the prices of commodities but also create confusion across the commercial dealings of the province, especially with the French population. Bank of Montreal cashier Benjamin Holmes testified that, if there was to be any change in the money of account, it would be much more desirable to follow the American lead and introduce the decimal currency, with the dollar as the medium, not the pound.

British observers had strong opinions about plans for the Canadian currency, especially Canadian resistance to the adoption of the pound sterling.[5] "The history of the Currency of the British Colonies affords ample evidence," one Treasury memorandum suggested, "of the necessity for the exercise of the controlling power of the state. All the anomalies which have arisen in past times and the difficulties which in some cases still remain to be adjusted may be traced to the ill-considered and partial proceedings adopted in the Colonies, in the absence of a systematic and judicious superintendence on the part of the Home Government."[6] And again: "The character of the Legislation recently proposed in more than one colony leads this Board to apprehend that the past experience would be of little avail if the Colonial Assemblies were left to legislate on these subjects without control, and that those bodies would still be governed by partial and restricted views instead of broad and general principles."[7]

The lords of the Treasury in Whitehall were strongly in favour of unifying the currency of the entire Empire on the British model. They also had an outspoken advocate in Commissary-General Randolph Isham Routh, the most influential imperial public servant in the shaping Canadian banking. Born in Poole, Dorset, in 1782, Routh was educated at Eton College from 1796 to 1803. He entered the Commissariat in 1805 and served in a number of progressively senior roles, including at Waterloo (1815), Malta (1816–22), and the West Indies (1822–26). In August 1826 Routh was promoted to the highest office in the Commissariat and sent to the Canadas as commissary-general.[8] He was to have a seventeen-year run in the posting, at a period when Canadian finance was beginning to acquire its fundamental characteristics.

Routh was an outspoken advocate of the pound sterling for Canada. From the imperial perspective, the emergent Canadian banking system was too dependent on American money markets, particularly for specie. Routh also viewed the exchange business of colonial banks and their issue of small notes as costly and inefficient. More to the point, the success of the Canadian bank notes was hampering the introduction and circulation of British silver coins. Routh's particular passion was the introduction of a sound currency law, dealing with legal tender and preventing the banks from charging any premiums on exportable metallic money so long as bank notes were freely redeemed in specie.

Routh argued that the adoption of the British sterling as the official medium of exchange in Lower Canada would end the confusion surrounding the variety of foreign currencies in use in the colony. From the vantage point of London, this would have made eminent sense. Yet it made significantly less sense to the colony, whose trade links with the United States were important and growing. And it made almost no sense at all to the Bank of Montreal, whose increasing specialization in foreign-exchange currency trading was a profitable business. Routh's proposals were unsuccessful, with the Bank of Montreal's leaders ensuring they would remain so.

There was another point of controversy, too. In the early 1840s, the governor-general of the United Province, Lord Sydenham, pushed hard for the adoption of a sound paper currency by means of a state bank of issue (to be called the Bank of British North America and headquartered in London). The plan met with considerable resistance from the chartered banks themselves, which argued that the chartered banks had come out of the recent crisis well enough and none had defaulted on their notes. The loss of the privilege of issuing their own notes would not only result in diminished profits but also reduce the number of branches and diminish the loanable credit at their command.[9] Local banking interests also made the case that discount accommodation would be curtailed in the province and that surrendering the power of note issue would put even greater powers at the disposal of the unaccountable provincial executive.

The initiative to create a Canadian state bank of issue, like the proposal to adopt the pound sterling, ultimately failed in the face of the opposition from chartered banks. Opposition to the initiative had also come from many French Canadians, who saw in the idea of a state bank an attempt by the executive to augment its power at the expense of the legislature, as well as an imperial intrusion into colonial affairs.[10] "We had ventured to hope," the Legislative Committee considering the matter wrote in September 1841, "[based on] the tenor of the recent Despatches of Your Majesty's Secretary of State for the Colonies to Your Majesty's Representative in His Province, that non-interference in those affairs would be the principle on which Your Majesty's Councils would thenceforth [operate] ... in reference to the affairs of this colony."[11]

Despite these disagreements, regulations passed in the 1840s set the stage for the further development of Canadian banking and finance. The Select Committee on Banking and Currency made a number of recommendations and established a series of restrictions that were eventually passed into law. Regulations were adopted governing capitalization, what banks could safely loan, and the need to pay on demand and in specie. The regulations of the 1840s also directed chartered banks to stay out of the mortgage market and confine themselves to discounting commercial paper, offering negotiable securities, and "other legitimate banking business." The banks were required as well to publish detailed financial statements and to furnish to the Treasury whatever information it sought in connection with banking.

In the late 1840s a series of severe economic contractions – particularly in the wake of the English railway crash of 1847 and the extreme depression of 1848 – led to a fresh appraisal of the need for additional banking facilities. The stability of the banking system in the face of these reversals held firm, not least because of the caution and prudence of most bankers. The Bank of Montreal was forced to reduce its reserve at the height of the trouble by £60,000, while other banks – especially the Bank of Upper Canada, its main rival – was awash in a sea of losses. Yet no chartered bank failed, payments were maintained, and losses were borne by shareholders and them alone. The main charge against Canadian banking, especially the Bank of Montreal, in the late 1840s was paradoxically the source of its reputation for stability: its great caution in financial affairs and its conservative lending policies. As parts of the country were settled and integrated into the larger economic system, the demand for capital soared. More capital, more branches, more banking facilities: the chartered banks could not keep up with the demand.

Most banking start-ups in the 1840s had not succeeded in securing the required minimum capital and therefore forfeited their charters. Meanwhile, the chartered banks were not able to meet the demand for capital in the more rapidly developing parts of the province. In the public imagination, at least, the issue was not enough banks, not enough facilities, and not enough capital. The problem was that Canada was simply not attracting the kind of banking investment and capital to justify a large territorial expansion. By the late 1850s, banks were granted additional facilities in commercial transactions and were permitted to acquire title to goods, wares, or merchandise in lieu of credit. Twelve new chartered banks joined the Canadian banking system, with £6.3 million of currency added to the authorized banking capital of the province. This was more than double the total paid-up capital of the banks in 1851.

By the 1850s, the legislator-banker relationship had settled into a more routine posture. There was no absence of contention on specific matters such as currency, capitalization, structure, and credit. Government financing could be a particularly thorny subject, especially as regional and metropolitan rivalries came to the fore. But, as far as the actual operations of the Bank were concerned, the legislative arena was seen as a more contained environment where bankers could expect fewer unpleasant surprises.

Lords and Bankers

The Bank of Montreal's other fundamental relationship – with the imperial government – grew to be close, comprehensive, and complex in this period. It was also sometimes contentious. That was what made it such a defining one for Canadian banking. The Bank played an integral role in financing imperial military obligations in the colony. At the same time, the imperial government was keenly interested in banking charters, and especially in the political and economic implications of finance in the colony. It was, therefore, a client, a regulator, and a closely involved observer of the contested political, economic, and social environment in the Canadas.

The Bank of Montreal was by no means the only Canadian bank in British North America to receive such attention, but, constituting as it did the key pillar of the emerging Canadian financial system, it was the most important. Payments, capital flows, exchange, specie, and currency questions were not just financial matters: they were also political ones to be seen and understood in an imperial context. Through the Treasury and the Colonial Office, London exerted both power and influence on the Canadian banking system that set the boundaries of the possible in the British North American context. Legislatures in Canada gained increasing authority, especially with the advent of responsible government in 1851 and the achievement of Confederation in 1867. Historical writing, however, has undervalued the role of the British government in the making of the Canadian banking system.

Oversight

Imperial oversight of colonial banking took several forms. The disallowance of colonial bills related to finance was the favoured and most direct instrument, but it was not the only one. Throughout this period, the Committee of the Privy Council for Trade and the lords of the Treasury in London issued a series of opinions, regulations, and orders that shaped Canadian banking. In the 1830s, the regulations – mainly concerned with the proper capitalization of banks and the potential creation of new banks, especially in Upper Canada – were designed in large part to avoid the excesses and perils to the public interest that characterized the US banking system. The Upper Canadian legislature of the 1830s came into periodic conflict with the imperial authorities over the Assembly's more liberal approach to banking matters. As Roeliff M. Breckenridge notes in his early history of Canadian banking, the relationship was a fraught one, involving both protests and petitions to the crown as a result of unpopular regulations as well as the threat to exercise the royal prerogative to disallow any bills that were not properly amended.[12]

Government as Client

The Bank of Montreal's central involvement in colonial capital flows – specifically in the flow of specie – brought it into close contact with the imperial authorities. Specie would flow from the south and the west – from the United States and Upper Canada – to Montreal. Provincial and imperial governments were the largest receivers of specie for custom duties and bills of exchange drawn on Britain. In turn, the government incurred expenditures in meeting its civil and military responsibilities in the colonies. The Bank's increasing specialization in currency and exchange in specie and government bills, as well as its bustling trade in private bills, attracted notice. The Montreal bankers were so proficient at it that by the late 1820s competitors accused the bank of "monopolising the exchanges of the country."

By the early 1830s, the Bank of Montreal had begun to look like a more and more useful and trusted place to put the funds of the imperial government. Writing in May 1831, Lieutenant-Governor Aylmer of Lower Canada noted that the "banks of the Province are of the most respectable kind" and also subject to the supervision of the provincial legislature. His only concern related to the close ties colonial banks had with the United States. In peacetime, there would be no difficulty in deploying the funds in Canadian banks. In the case of any crisis, however, there might be trouble. The issue was the command of specie – an absolute necessity for London in periods of war. Under the existing conditions, it might be difficult to convert the paper into specie. Add to this Lord Aylmer's conviction that all US banks were "little better than gambling speculations" and one has a good idea of the attitude of London and its representatives toward banking in North America. The imperial administration's expanding need for credit and exchange led its agents in the Commissariat Department to establish closer and more formal links with the Bank of Montreal. In January 1833 the *Quebec Gazette* reported that all demands against the Commissariat Department were now to be paid by cheques on the Bank of Montreal, marking the first deployment of Canadian banks in making payments by London.[13]

As the principal financial agent of London in the colonies, the Treasury's representatives in the Commissariat held a uniquely powerful financial position. Its relationship, therefore, with the Bank of Montreal was a both a close and an important one. The Bank increasingly acted as a government banker for substantial sums flowing through the colonies from large financial concerns such as the East India Company (whose agents in Montreal, Forsyth, Richardson and Company, were also among the founders of the Bank of Montreal). As we have seen, Commissary-General Routh oversaw the financial transactions of the British Army in the Canadas. The Military Chest of the Canadas, under the commissary-general's control, commanded resources that equalled or exceeded Lower Canada's entire public-accounts budget. Consequently, Routh's influence on the emerging Canadian banking system was substantial, though his views on finance sometimes put him in direct opposition to local interests in the colony. His positions on two key matters – currency and the proposal to turn all the financial business of the military over to local banks – created the most controversy. They would also put him on a collision course with the Bank of Montreal.

Routh's target in the mid-1820s was the Bank of Montreal and its growing influence – an influence that he believed competed with the authority of the state. His prospective weapon was a new policy that would impose restrictions on the bank in dealing in bills of exchange – one of its most profitable business lines – and in issuing bills for small sums. In the event, the large public-work projects undertaken by the imperial government, such as the Rideau Canal, as well as its sizeable military expenditures, meant that London needed the banks to provide the required capital. The plans surrounding currency were quietly shelved – at least for the time being.

Again in 1832, Routh expressed an uneasiness with the emerging power of the Bank of Montreal, especially in connection to the Treasury. In 1832 the Treasury sanctioned the transfer of the money provided for military expenditures from the Commissary Department to the principal Canadian banks. The Bank of Montreal was particularly favoured because of its reach in both Upper and Lower Canada, along with the York Bank.[14] Its effective network and its successful management of the government accounts for both Upper and Lower Canada aroused some resentment in the upper colony – so much so that Routh feared growing resentment against Montreal capitalists if responsibilities were not distributed more equitably.[15] The Montreal bank's success would, he worried, come at the expense of Upper Canadian interests. "Our fear," Routh wrote to the Treasury in November 1832, "is that either a want of confidence or some misapprehension has caused undue preference to be given to the Bank of Montreal in opposition to another equally solid establishment."[16] The preference for the Bank of Montreal "inadvertently no doubt affords an undue encouragement to a species of rivalry not contemplated in the charter of the former." As a result, Routh suggested that the Bank of Upper Canada should take over the accounts of the government in that colony.

The relationship between the agents of the imperial government and the Bank had multiple points of contact. Correspondence – on account payments, pay lists, and the details of arrangements and balances – was prolific between Routh and his superiors in the Treasury. There was also occasional correspondence regarding the inevitable gaps in troop and public payments across the colony.[17] The relationship between the Bank and imperial government could therefore be a contentious one as interests or perspectives diverged, two examples being the currency question and the choice of financial agent for the army in the 1830s. That the far more significant question of the currency was settled in favour of local, not imperial, interests demonstrates the growing influence of colonial institutions.

Of course, the state-bank relationship in banking was played out on a much larger stage than these two policy questions alone. The imperial authorities were also deeply concerned with protecting, preserving, and shielding the reputation of the Bank of Montreal in turbulent times. This was especially so in the mid-1830s, when the Lower Canadian colony was convulsed by political tension, an economic crisis, and a devastating cholera outbreak. In November 1834 everything came to a boil over the Bank's ability to pay its obligations in specie. In other words, there was what seemed to be the beginnings of a run on "a Branch of the Montreal Bank" in Montreal itself. Routh reported to the Treasury that the "panic was very general throughout this district."[18] There were small mercies: had there been a run on both branches in the city – there were then two – to redeem at once all their outstanding notes, the situation would have "created a present alarm and danger that might have led to the most serious results."[19] As it happened, when the confusion was dispelled, there turned out to be no actual run on the Bank of Montreal's main branch after all – "an event which I must consider to be very fortunate," Routh reported to London.[20]

The issue for Routh was that the East India Company was about to deposit into the Bank of Montreal's government account a sum of $100,000. If the Bank was to suspend payment, then those vital funds would become unavailable. The problem was that bank notes had gradually replaced specie, and so, when the demand for specie suddenly spiked, sometimes the Bank could not, at least temporarily, keep up with the demand.

The underlying reason for the Bank's difficulties, however, was in reality political. "The Bank of Montreal is very prosperous," Routh reported to London, offering 8 per cent on dividends and a bonus of 6 per cent. "This profit cannot be made without risk and speculation – probably by high discounts, by purchasing foreign exchange low and selling their own high."[21] Notwithstanding this, Routh pointed to a "strident Party Spirit" in the country ready to deprecate the Bank and its notes. The Patriotes were "labouring hard to promote an anti-British feeling among the quiet Inhabitants, who without knowing the cause or the object, are beginning to apprehend that something is in preparation against them."[22]

In a case where the troops would have to be deployed in the colony itself, the credit and notes of the bank would be rendered worthless. The ultimate "solidity of the institution" would be beside the point entirely, and doubly so since the Bank's dependability was also connected with that of their agents in the mercantile houses of London and New York. Routh described the situation as a delicate one for both the Bank and the imperial government, despite "my firm conviction of the honour of that Establishment to act with prudence and circumspection."[23] The issue, of course, was public confidence in the Bank. On the other hand, Routh also had an obligation to "protect my own reputation as a Public Official and the Interests entrusted to me by the Government."[24]

The precarious nature of early Canadian banking in tough times mobilized imperial officials to offer reputational protection to the Bank of Montreal. Writing in November 1834, Routh stated that he was "sensible of the description of faction which activates the present attack on the [Bank of Montreal] and will most readily find my assistance to defeat it."[25] To put an end to any negative whispering about the Bank, he had deposited there $30,000 in specie as a vote of confidence. He even stayed away from Montreal personally in case his trip "might be construed into an appearance of diminution of confidence" in the Bank. Any actions connected with the "credit of an institution" were to be made with much prudence and judgement, Routh concluded, and "only when they are indispensable."[26]

Routh's concern about the Montreal Bank in the autumn of 1834 was also strategic. As a commissary-general, he, as well as his deputy in Quebec, J.B. Price, were concerned not whether the bank could ultimately pay or its "ultimate solidity" but whether there should be any present hesitation which might paralyze a military movement, "if it became necessary."[27]

The Bank of Montreal and Imperial Security

The prime source of imperial anxiety was the connection between colonial banking and imperial military preparedness. Reliability of payment flows was a matter of military security. As Routh noted in a communiqué on the subject, "if our finances be disordered, Sedition would not be very distant" – and, in that case, what use would it be if the Bank could eventually pay its obligations? "I think it is a time to consider the subject in relation to the security of Specie in these Provinces," Routh wrote to his superiors in London in November 1834. His solution involved stationing an office to acquire specie on the Spanish coast and then have control over the foreign exchange. "It would not be proper," he noted, "to consign [these] remittances to the Bank for in that case it would be applied to the purposes of the Establishment and not to those of the Community."[28]

Routh's views on the Bank of Montreal were somewhat complicated, not least because the relationship between it and the imperial government was similarly complicated. On the one hand, the Bank was the indispensable financial institution for the imperial government in the colonies. On the other hand, conferring too much power on private institutions might pose a practical policy problem for both the army and the government. Routh admired the Bank of Montreal for its operations, and he begged London to "disclaim all unworthy jealousy or hard feeling towards the Bank or upon the subject. The directors were honourable and upright men in the way of their Business." But he feared the consequences of "binding up the Interest of the Army and the Government in our stake with theirs, and I mean only in these representations to consult the Public Safety and to discharge my duty of responsibility to their Lordships."[29]

For his part, Price reported from Quebec City that the Bank of Montreal's reputation there was solid and that he was not aware of "the least disinclination on the part of the Community at large to receive the notes of this Institution or that there is the smallest distrust of their most perfect solidity."[30] The fact is that everybody – legislators, imperial officials, and bankers themselves – had a stake in ensuring public confidence in the emerging Canadian financial system.

The Panic of 1837

The Bank of Montreal's position as lead Canadian bank as well as its North American connections put it at the centre of questions about the financial security of the colonies. At no time was this truer or more dramatic than in the events surrounding the Panic of 1837. That panic was in reality a great depression, devastating in the breadth of its impact. One historian has called it America's first great depression.[31] In fact, it may have begun as an American event, but it soon had catastrophic consequences that encompassed the entire North Atlantic world. The British demand for American cotton goods in the mid-1830s created a super-boom that eventually collapsed in spectacular fashion when economic conditions changed. Meantime, the Bank of England, fearful of the drain of specie from the United Kingdom, raised interest rates just as the boom was becoming a bust, in a sort of inverse Keynesian nightmare scenario. The credit crunch and serious deflation that resulted led to a mighty reckoning for governments of all levels in the North Atlantic world from the United Kingdom to the United States to the British North American colonies. Many US state legislatures that had dreamed of foreign investment replacing taxation for massive public-improvement projects defaulted in droves; banks failed and suspensions of specie payment presaged a decade of serious economic hardship, political dislocation, and social unrest for the United States. As one historian puts it, the Panic of 1837 was as much a political and social disaster as a financial one.[32] American banks in the 1830s were said to be enmeshed in a banking war stoked by the policies of the Andrew Jackson administration. In England, the financial and popular press were horrified that the US banking system was being turned into a "gambling house for the benefit of legislative favourites" – a fate that, some argued, may well have also befallen Britain with the proliferation of joint-stock banks. British merchants began to experience serious anxiety about whether too much British specie had been traded to the United States in exchange for paper that promised high interest rates but would not retain its value.[33] The networks of information exchange as early as 1836 started to transmit very negative views of the ways of American finance, gradually eroding confidence in the financial system itself.

Matters came to a head on 10 May 1837 when New York banks suspended specie payments. The situation for the colonial government and the entire commerce of the British North American colonies was potentially catastrophic. The Bank of Montreal's financial and intelligence networks in New York proved absolutely crucial in managing the Canadian dimension of the crisis. The Bank's contacts, its reputation, and its "very satisfactory position" respecting its liabilities made a determining difference in the outcome.

The Bank of Montreal and the imperial government – in particular, the Bank's cashier, Benjamin Holmes, and R.I. Routh and the lords of the Treasury in Whitehall – were in close contact during the period. The suspension of specie payments at New York hit Montreal particularly hard, since the source of supply came principally from foreign-exchange transactions in New York. Between November 1836 and May 1837, "upwards of £100,000 in gold and silver" had been imported by the Bank of Montreal alone.[34] Now the supply was cut off.

Benjamin Holmes reported to the imperial authorities that the situation was serious but that the bank was in a healthy position in terms of its liabilities and especially its specie reserves at Montreal. The confidence that the Bank enjoyed not only in the "commercial and agricultural sector of the province" but also among officials of the provincial government was completely justified, even if it had, under absolute necessity, suspended for a time payments and specie transfers. The objective was to overcome the worst of the crisis, then resume business. Holmes assured the authorities that the "deposits of Her Majesty's Government" were safe and secure and that nothing should disturb the relation "thereto subsisting between your department and this institution."[35]

In financial crises, access to accurate, actionable intelligence can make the difference. In the Panic of 1837, the principal Canadian pipeline to New York was through the Bank's partners. In early May 1837 Samuel Gerrard travelled to New York "on a confidential mission" to meet the Bank's agents in London, Thomas Wilson and Company. His report to Bank of Montreal President Peter McGill offers an extraordinary window on a rapidly evolving situation and was made immediately available to the imperial authorities through Holmes.[36]

Gerrard arrived at 5 a.m. on the morning of 5 May and soon thereafter entered into crisis talks with Prime, Ward and Sands, the Bank's agents in New York, and other contacts who were "frank and civil" in their assessments of the situation. The bills of exchange were still being traded with premiums as high as 17 per cent. Gerrard reported to McGill that he would not "disprove of the bills in my possession" until he heard from McGill subsequently. He suggested that the Bank's interests in Wilson and Company were on relatively solid grounds and therefore he had "every reason to assure you that I think the bank will lose nothing by them." Yet Gerrard appeared not to be completely convinced of Wilson and Company's assurances, especially since those assurances appear to have been limited to the payments for April 1837, and "were any untoward circumstances to occur," the situation might force the company to rely on more unorthodox means to procure payment.

Gerrard then delivered some very frank advice: "If the smallest run appears" in the market, "lock up every shilling and do not allow yourselves to be fleeced by inventive shavers and speculators." He explained that the sharper elements of the New York market would attempt to get Bank of Montreal specie by buying up and exchanging other notes for theirs for the sake of the premium, with the result that the depositors and stockholders would be the sufferers. Gerrard advised that, though there might be opportunities in the roiling market, the risks to the Bank's reputation and its standing were too great. The "credit of being well-intentioned" with the Bank's supporters and clients would far outweigh the fleeting and dubious advantages of speculation. The Bank would therefore be "able to come forward nobly and without injury" in the trying circumstances. Gerrard wrote that the Bank should not issue a single note unless "you can redeem it with cash."[37]

The supply of specie was, of course, vital to the activities of the British Army, especially since military payments must be made in specie or any notes redeemable for specie at the option of the holder.[38] The Montreal Bank's holdings and strategy were thus closely intertwined with the imperial payments system. Commissary-General Routh was compelled to write to his colleagues in Mexico to ensure adequate supplies of specie as a result of the agitation in the money market and the suspension of payments by the New York banks. The Bank was able to provide a more than adequate supply of specie for the trade of Canada, but the surge in Americans flocking to Montreal to obtain specie was a serious concern from both a financial and military perspective (namely, to prevent sedition).

The request to move specie from Mexico through Bermuda and Halifax and over to Montreal had a practical and obvious objective: to continue the flow of specie payments. But it also had another, more important, objective: to underwrite the confidence and reputation of the financial system in general and the Bank of Montreal's in particular. Routh insisted on receiving the specie "into my own hands" in Montreal – in other words, "in a manner so public as to affect the interest of banks and with that institution those of the community connected with it." He lamented the "elasticity of character" that distinguished Americans from Canadians and that led to an overtrading on credit and a passion for speculation. The result was that the crisis came upon the continent "so suddenly and so unexpectedly" as to put the government in serious difficulty.[39]

Canadian Banking, Imperial System

The imperial authorities, meanwhile, kept a close watch on successive bank acts in the 1830s, anxious in particular to prevent the proliferation of bank establishments with inadequate capitalization. Breckenridge notes that it was "only the firm restraint and cool judgement of these officials" that saved the banking system from a worse fate in the crisis of 1837.[40] The Bank and the imperial government, therefore, worked closely together to safeguard the common interests of the British North American community in its private and public manifestations. This is undoubtedly the reason why the documentary record of the lords of the Treasury is prolific on the subject of the Panic of 1837. The lords kept a close eye on developments in the Canadian financial system. This included oversight over the activities of the legislature, the passage of ordinances, general statements of affairs of the bank, annual reports, and lists of partnerships or companies that related to the Bank.[41] The Bank of Montreal invited closer scrutiny because of its importance to the emerging Canadian financial system. Its original charter, with its rules and conditions, created a model that the lords "thought it necessary that other Banking companies should conform to" as fresh establishments were created in the colony.[42]

The discussion in the council chambers in Whitehall frequently revolved around the right conditions for banking institutions to flourish in the colonies. The minutes of one meeting in July 1830 relating to a possible bank on the eastern African island of Mauritius – about as far away from Montreal as one could get – captures the essence of the British government's approach: "The Establishment of Banking Companies upon the secure Foundation" of ample capital, well regulated and appropriately governed by "certain regulations and restrictions as to the conduct of their business," would "tend to promote the Commerce and general prosperity of the Mauritius or of any other of His Majesty's Colonies in which individual Capitalists might be willing to undertake such Establishments."[43]

The imperial regulations of 1830 for Canadian banking perfectly reflected the British government's approach outlined in the Mauritius memorandum. The Committee of the Privy Council for Trade set down a series of "precautionary principles" that found their way into the acts of the colonial legislatures. One of the major motivations of the imperial authorities was not only the "protection of the public interest" in banking establishments, but also the experience of the "neighbouring states" in the United States regarding the banking system.[44] Later, in 1833, the Privy Council considered Canadian banking matters afresh, proposing several new regulations "with a view to the security of the public." The focus was on the need to ensure that any prospective bank had the necessary subscribed capital before being opened for business; other requirements concerned limits on the amount of paper disseminated and the amount of borrowing by directors and officers, the prohibition on directors purchasing their bank's own stock, publication of twice-yearly reports, and the like.

The imperial government took a special interest in Upper Canadian banks. The pressure to create more banking capital in the upper province was more acute than it was in Lower Canada in the 1830s, resulting in the establishment of several new banks. The Bank of Upper Canada had been conducting business there since 1819 with a capitalization of £100,000. New legislation proposed by the Upper Canadian legislature, however, came under critical scrutiny, with the Privy Council for Trade threatening to disallow acts extending bank capital or creating new banks unless amendments were made imposing "double liability" on the Commercial Bank of the Midland District, which were accepted with great protest by the latter institution's management.[45] The insistence of the imperial authorities on greater safeguards against insolvency or instability included the threat of the use of the royal veto to disallow legislation not meeting these conditions. The imperial government's continuing oversight of and firm restraint over the Canadian banking system (especially as it was unfolding in Upper Canada) permitted that system to avoid the worst of the economic calamity that befell North America in the Panic of 1837.

Correspondence between the Bank and Commissary-General Routh in the early 1830s gives a good example of London's continuing and close interest in the development of Canadian banking, and specifically the Bank of Montreal's emerging approach and organization.[46] There is considerable correspondence detailing the workings of the bank, especially its primary business in dealing with bills of exchange, promissory notes, and bullion. In 1833, for example, Routh reported that the Bank's shares had reached an extraordinary value – "a premium of twenty percent [with] the annual dividend at eight percent, with a bonus, usually forthcoming of four percent, making an interest of twelve percent."[47] Governance was also a matter for comment, perhaps because the Montreal Bank held government accounts. Treasury officials were kept informed of Canadian public expenditures and the general state of government accounts held by the Bank of Montreal.[48] Bank officials also sent detailed memoranda to the Treasury about the constitution of the bank, its regulations, capital, and resources.[49]

State interest in the Bank extended to negotiating for expanded services for the broader public. In May 1831 Routh asked the president of the Bank whether it might be "disposed to afford to the Public" expanded services in the light of the large amount of funds entrusted to it by the Government.[50] The Bank replied that it would agree to cash government cheques in Montreal, Quebec, and Kingston without charge of commission. In spite of the policy of offering no interest to depositors, the Bank undertook to keep an interest account with the government at 3 per cent per annum if £50,000 were kept as a constant balance. The dialogue between imperial agents and bankers was an interplay of interest, a battle over position, and even at times a contest of personalities.

The commissary-general was much more successful in rebuffing attempts in the 1830s to transfer all financial transactions of the military in Canada to local banks. Such a move would have significantly benefitted the Bank of Montreal – indeed, Routh believed that it was the only bank that could undertake such a large-scale commitment. But he was also convinced that the directors of the Bank would then become the "real capitalists of the country at little personal risk." In addition, entrusting local banks with the army's financial business would, in his estimation, run the risk of compromising the ability of the military to act independently, as well as creating the possibility that intelligence about troop movement could fall into the wrong hands.[51]

Routh's careful supervision of government accounts and his views on the proper development of Canadian banking indicate clearly the interlocking nature of colonial banking with wider political and military imperatives in British North America. The fear that the Bank of Montreal's success and expanding capacity would cause excessive dependency demonstrates that point eloquently. Imperial interest in banking increased in the 1830s with the raft of legislation passed in 1836 and 1837. Lieutenant-Governor Francis Bond Head[52] reported to the Privy Council in April 1837 that the central problem in the colonies was "circulating medium" and the availability of specie in British North America. "The impression is very general," Bond Head wrote, "that it is requisite to prove means for an extension of the circulating medium, and for increased Banking accommodation," but opinions differed as to how to proceed. The question was whether more banks should be established or whether the subscribed capital of existing banks should be expanded. In essence, the issue was as much political as it was financial. The pressure to establish smaller banks in developing districts was constant. As Bond Head suggested, such banks "afford within each district or locality some little patronage and in the Officer that connects with them, and [since] Banking appears to be profitable, there is a natural desire that the profits ... should be spent within each circle" rather than going to the larger districts or cities.[53]

By contrast, the legislature's assent to the entry of the London-based Bank of British North America into colonial banking in the same session showed a desire on the part of the local government to "afford an opening introduction of British capital" without regard to the "narrow considerations that the profits immediately derived from its employment" would flow to investors and shareholders in England. Bond Head suggested that the "real state and resources of the colony" would become better known with the introduction of the London-based bank – something that is "of all things, most wanting." The banking discussions in the mid-1830s demonstrated to Bond Head at least that the "public are very much alive" to the business of banks and was willing to "try almost every scheme" to improve the banking situation in the colonies.[54]

The lieutenant-governor's own pet scheme, as we saw earlier, was a provincial bank of issue under the control of the legislature. Such a bank would serve, Bond Head wrote in 1837, to act as a safeguard and reserve in difficulty" and control the issuance of paper currency. The credit of the province could therefore be used to attract additional capital into the colony from England. "In point of climate, soil, free institutions, intelligent population and natural advantages of position and navigable waters," Bond Head concluded, Upper Canada was "prodigiously favoured and it is not to be wondered that an anxious desire is felt to keep pace with the astonishing progress of improvement which distinguishes the present age." The resources of the province were limited, however. Taxation would "bear hardly" on the emigrants and discourage settlement. The answer, according to both Bond Head and the legislature, was to "seek other means of adding to the resources."[55]

Banking regulation in the early 1840s, as already explained, established a series of stringent rules related to the business of banking in Canada. These included conditions on capitalization and requirements that banks could not start business until the whole of the capital was subscribed, that the capital should be paid up with a specified period of time, and that debts could not exceed the amount of paid-up capital.[56] The regulations of the 1840s also set down the principle that promissory notes be payable on demand and placed limits on possible suspension of specie payments. Importantly, the banks were prohibited from advancing money on security of lands, houses, or ships and confined to discounting commercial paper and negotiable securities and other "legitimate banking business." Specific and detailed reporting obligations, as well as provisions for election of directors and other elements of corporate governance, were also written down in law.

This period, then, witnessed the establishment of key safeguards in the financial system. The characteristics of the system also mattered: a small number of highly capitalized banks conducted business across an extensive territory. The shareholders of banks were doubly liable. The Canadian banks were typically prudent, pragmatic, and cautious in their approach to banking: regulation reinforced these characteristics.

Speed versus Safety

The emerging Canadian banking system was designed for safety, not for speed of response. The landscape featured large-capitalized banks with a relatively small number transacting business. The cautious, risk-averse approach of the chartered banks, moreover, would not allow the emergence of smaller banks in rural and small-town Canada. The tension continued, however, between the creation of a safe and productive banking system versus one that was more immediately responsive to the capital requirements of under-served areas. The legislative response to these pressures was the passage of the Free Banking Act of 1850. The concept of "free banking" facilitated the establishment of non-chartered banks in Canada. The "free" in "free banking" meant simply that anybody could open a bank if the group or individuals involved met the requirements. In the United States, most laws permitted quick entry without much sunk costs.[57] The concept was especially popular in Canada West, where the American experience with free banking was looked upon as a model of how to accelerate lending and capital flows in a challenging capital market – especially in an agricultural economy.[58] Molsons Bank, the Niagara District Bank, and the Zimmerman Bank, along with a few others, were established in the 1850s.

As Canadians obtained greater legislative and executive control over their own affairs, the imperial government's interest and influence began to decline. Yet, even as late as the 1850s, the colonial banking system was attracting some comment in Whitehall. An imperial government representative in the Canadas, C.E. Trevelyan, wrote to the lords of the Treasury in June 1851 to express some reservation about what he viewed as a major alteration to the Canadian banking system. The inspector-general's report on free banking legislation in the United Province observed that the "freedom of Canada from those evils which have attended the system of Banking followed in the United States" could be attributed "to the small number of Banks which have thitherto been incorporated in the Province and to the prudent manner in which they have been conducted."[59] Trevelyan noted that the colonial legislature had restricted the privilege of issuing promissory notes payable on demand to joint-stock banks with a certain amount of subscribed capital, and that it had also stipulated that the deposit of government debentures must be equal to the amount of the notes that the banks were authorized to issue. Such provisions were critical to "securing the ultimate solvency of the Banks of Issue."[60] Trevelyan pinpointed the kernel of the problem: "The great difficulty of legislators on the subject arises from the risk that in giving the facilities to commerce which are afforded by the issue of Bank Notes, the Country may be exposed to a derangement of its monetary concerns from speculative issues exceeding the legitimate demands of Trade."[61] The obligation to pay in specie on demand had not, in Trevelyan's view, been "sufficient to guard against this evil and ... competing Banks *with the unrestricted power of issue* are too often disposed at times when speculation is rife to extend their issues beyond the amount which would be practicable" [original emphasis].[62] Trevelyan added that the monetary system of Great Britain, which had been established by an act of 1844, had been based on *restricting* the amount of promissory notes "found on credit considerably within the lowest amount of the previous circulation of the country; and that all issues of notes exceeding that amount should be made only on the deposit of specie in the Bank of England."[63]

Trevelyan suggested that the Canadian Free Banking Act appeared to be defective on the point of guaranteeing a safe circulation of promissory notes. The solution had to take into account the prevention of losses from failure on the part of the banks – and that meant a deposit of public securities equal in amount to the notes found. "It appears to my Lords that the facilities for the indefinite extension of Banks of Issue cannot safely be conceded without some precautions of this nature."[64] Even the right of inspection would be of "little real avail if unaccompanied by any power to control the proceedings of the Banks in regard to the circulation."[65]

Trevelyan proposed that the lords of the Treasury approach the Canadians carefully, explaining that, "in making these suggestions," they "have no wish to interfere with the general management of the concerns of Canada which has now the advantage of a responsible Govt., but on the other hand they could not reconcile it to themselves to withhold from that Govt., the result of that wider experience which after many trials and difficulties has been obtained in this Country of the effect of introducing the circulation to competing Banks without adequate control."[66] Trevelyan reminded the lords that Canadians also had an obligation to the mother country – specifically, a "claim to require that no measure should be passed which may in its results have an effect on the public credit of Canada and thus possibly interfere with the arrangements for the repayment of those loans; and that, in that view, it is not less their interest than their duty to warn the Canadian Govt. of those consequences which they may apprehend from legislation of the character now before this Board."[67]

The report seemed to make an impression on the lords of the Treasury, who concurred with Trevelyan's analysis and hoped that the "Canadian Govt and Parlt. will not fail seriously to consider this most important subject & take precautions against the dangers to which the Province may be exposed."[68] In the event, by the end of the 1850s, more than a few Canadian banks had disappeared. In March 1857 a bill was introduced to discontinue the incorporation of joint-stock banks and the issue of registered notes. The "merchants and money men" of the province were generally in favour of the charter system which had proven itself resilient and stable during the economic cycles of the 1850s. The Free Banking Act was finally repealed in the 1860s. Indeed, the US experience with free banking generally failed to have a serious effect on growth, and the Canadian advocates of free banking seem to have been similarly let down.[69] The imperial perspective had prevailed.

In the end, the shaping of Canadian finance resulted in a banking system authored by legislators, lords, and bankers that took on specific historical characteristics. Before Confederation, four principal banking types emerged in the Canadian system: banks chartered by the legislature; banks operating under royal charter (such as the Bank of British North America); private or joint-stock banks without corporate power to sue; and free banks (after the legislation of 1850). As E.P. Neufeld notes, however, it was the chartered banks that dominated Canadian banking in this period.[70]

Canadian legislatures of the 1850s expanded the chartered banking system to include several new banks, including the Bank of Canada (1858), the Bank of Commerce (1859), and La Banque Jacques Cartier (1861). Between 1822 and 1867, seventy-eight charters were issued and fifty-six banks began business. Between 1841 and 1867, paid-up capital in banks in the United Province increased twelvefold, circulation of notes increased ninefold, and the average annual rate of expansion of chartered banks hovered around 12 per cent per year. By the time of Confederation, banking dominated the financial scene, and the Bank of Montreal dominated banking.

Conclusion

The relationship between colonial banks, especially the Bank of Montreal, the legislators of British North America, and the imperial government both shaped and defined the emergence of Canadian finance – its form, substance, and character; and its regulation, mandate, and deployment. The mid-nineteenth century was a testing time for banking, currency, and capital. The forms finance would take, the laws and regulations that would be put into place, and the limits that bank leaders would have to respect were all proposed, debated, defined, and codified into law and practice. Between 1817 and 1860, colonial legislators, imperial administrators, and merchant bankers sought to define their mandates, defend their prerogatives, and establish the boundaries of the possible in financial matters in Canada. More than any other factor, this triangular relationship defined Canadian banking.

The Bank of Montreal's central role in three areas – the colonial economy, intercolonial trade, and North Atlantic financial networks – made its operations and activities particularly important to colonial legislators. So did its rapidly developing links with the American market, especially New York. From an imperial perspective, the Bank's role as the standard-bearer for Canadian finance implicated it in matters both financial and military. The close, interlocking mature of financial, political, economic, and military activities in British North America meant that banking and security were not considered separate spheres, but rather ones that overlapped at various points.

As we have seen, the relationships between bankers, legislators, and lords were intense, consequential, and close. Canadian banking was in its formative stages: everything, or almost everything, was on the table. In the legislature, Bank of Montreal promoters sought a political and legal licence to operate. They also sought to put their stamp on an emerging Canadian regulatory regime. Within the councils of Empire, relations turned on three principal sets of questions: collaboration in the maintenance of order and imperial defence; the issue of safe operation of banking activities; and the twin systemic matters – of currency and the establishment of a state bank. The third subject – currency and state banking – elicited the sharpest disagreement. Rival arguments pitted Canadian colonial bankers intent on developing a profitable, cost-efficient, stable currency and banking system against imperial regulators and their desire to establish the pound sterling on a continent dominated by dollar-denominated economic activity. The Canadian banks, led by the Bank of Montreal, successfully rebuffed those plans not least because they ran counter to both Canadian trade interests in general and Canadian bank profits and activity specifically.

By the late 1850s, the triangular relationship of legislator, lord, and banker had produced several key outcomes. Canadian banking rested on a solid foundation, the product of public and private collaboration. The character and reach of the Bank of Montreal were increasingly well established as it grew in its first generation. The decisions taken by the Bank in this era solidified its preference for stability and caution in financial affairs. Finally, Canadian priorities and preferences, particularly with regard to currency and the idea of a state bank, were defended and prevailed.

By 1860, Canadian banking had emerged as a small and generally well-functioning system. Experiments such as free banking were attempted, then abandoned without much effect on the system. The motivation behind a more experimental or innovative approach to banking remained, however: the desire to stimulate economic activity, then have capital and economic activity follow. Frustration with the small size of the colony's capital market and the conservative approach of its most consequential banks continued to grow. The Bank of Montreal's role in this unfolding discussion was central. Its preference for stability was reflected in its nearly total immunity to appeals to adopt a more expansionist approach to its operations. The Montreal style of banking was forged partly through a generation of experience of Montreal bankers, and partly through the prism of the Bank's relationship with public power at both the centre and periphery of Empire. As we shall see, the 1860s would catapult the colony and its banking system into new, uncharted territory. But the fundamental character, tenor, and approach of Canadian banking had been, through a generation, bred in the bone.

CHAPTER FIVE

Risk, Return, Reward

As we have seen, in the 1820s and 1830s leaders of the Bank of Montreal were able to establish Canadian banking on a solid footing with a keen eye to generating, holding, and extending the kind of reputational capital required of the bank's ambitions to become the premier bank in British North America. Subsequently, between the early 1840s and the mid-1850s, an incipient Bank of Montreal branch network began to appear in the Canadas, especially in the western section of the territory – Cobourg, Guelph, and Hamilton in what is now southern Ontario. This combined with a gradual professionalization of the business of banking. Formal and informal networks of information and credit began to expand and mature, coupled with an increasing analytical capacity on the part of the Bank's personnel. Under the leadership of Benjamin Holmes, the chief cashier, and President Peter McGill, the Bank developed a professional and undeniably careful approach to banking operations in British North America. The language of the Bank's annual reports capture that spirit. Here is an excerpt from Peter McGill's address to the stockholders in the 1858 report: "As regards the future prospects of the Bank, no improvement in the general condition of commercial affairs is at yet apparent, and the contraction of business, together with the depression which pervades every branch of trade, have naturally an unfavourable influence upon the interests of the Bank, and interfere with the advantageous employment of its funds."[1] McGill also cautioned that the degree of prosperity enjoyed by Canada was "to some extent fictitious" and engendered a "spirit of speculation and over-trading." Those conditions had added greatly to the prosperity of the province and the progress of the country, of course, but the cautious tone is what strikes one the most.[2]

In the late 1850s, the Bank hired Edwin H. King to be its "inspector" or auditor. King was to become a central player in the Bank of Montreal's story in the 1860s. His appointment as inspector signalled that the Bank was putting its management on a much more solid, professional foundation. A contemporary, George Hague, offers this recollection of King: "I remember meeting him when on an inspection tour in an Ontario town, and hearing while there of the trenchant style in which his inspections were made, and how utterly regardless he was of the views and feelings or managers of the bank. In truth, the old style of inspection badly needed reform, for it was worse than useless ... He once told me that it took five years of hard work to get the Bank of Montreal into proper shape."[3]

This was in marked contrast to other banks, especially in the Toronto hinterland, which plunged into the funding of railway ventures. Competitors such as the Bank of Upper Canada invested heavily in the railway initiatives of the 1850s. For its part, even when the government of the province guaranteed aspects of the debt, the Bank of Montreal chose its deployments carefully and usually quite successfully – steering clear of ventures that did not meet its high standards. But it was the exception. The great railway promotions of the 1850s combined with the passage of the Free Banking Act to facilitate the establishment of a number of banks. The result was to create an intense burst of infrastructure building, with capital investment flowing from the newly formed banks.[4]

Throughout the 1850s, the Bank steadily increased its capitalization, which in 1855 reached £6 million. By 1859, that authorized capital had been fully paid up, making the Bank of Montreal one of the three leading banks in North America.[5] If its dividend-payment record was anything to go by, the Bank was indeed performing well, regularly returning dividend rates of 8 per cent annually. This was easier said than done in the late 1850s. The Panic of 1857 left the entire continent in "great difficulty and derangement in commercial and monetary affairs" and compelled American banks to suspend specie payments. Canadian banks, by contrast, were able to maintain their position.

By then, two elements had compelled the Bank to exploit its American links and establish an agency in New York. First, the continued bad harvests in the province were acting to "disturb and embarrass the commercial and monetary affairs of the country."[6] President McGill warned in 1859 that the directors could not lose sight of the fact that the "prosperity of the country depends upon its agricultural products, and that another failure of the crops must be attended with very serious consequences."

Second, competitive pressure in the domestic market, especially from western banks, was manageable but intense. This, along with lagging economic activity in the province, left bankers frustrated. "The Business of Banking," President T.B. Anderson wrote in 1861, "has been conducted during the last four years under disadvantageous circumstances. The profits have been diminished, and large appropriations have been required to meet the losses arising from bad debts."[7]

Accordingly, on 3 December 1858, the Bank established a New York agency under the directorship of Richard Bell. Three years later, in September 1861, another agency was created, this one at Chicago under E.W. Willard.[8] As President Anderson stated in 1861, "much attention has been recently directed to the importance of securing to Canada a portion of the great produce trade of the Western States." The new Chicago agency was established "with the view of affording increased facilities for that purpose" and anticipating "advantage to the community" and "benefit to the bank."[9] In 1871 the Bank intended to open a branch in Chicago, on the corner of Market and Madison streets, "as soon as the proper vault can be built."[10]

New Strategy

The period between 1860 and 1863 continued to be marked by difficult economic circumstances in Canada. The boom-and-bust cycle in Canada West resulted in a serious depression, especially affecting lumber and real estate values. In 1862–63 heavy losses were absorbed in the conversion of the Bank's US funds into gold. The depreciation of real estate values in the United States (which were held as security for old debts), combined with the choking of trade between Canada and the United States as a result of the Civil War, rendered a change in strategy urgent.

The Make-or-Break Decade

It is difficult to exaggerate the importance of the 1860s for British North America and in particular for its banks. Consider the landscape at the beginning of the decade and at its end. The economic cycles of boom and bust, often dependent upon agricultural production and terms of trade, were in full operation. The decade witnessed the union of the British North American colonies into the Dominion of Canada. The fluid regulatory and competitive environment of Canadian banking gave way to a permanent regulatory architecture codified into law which was destined to define the Canadian style of banking and its relationships into the twentieth century. For Canada's neighbour and major market, the United States, the 1860s saw both violent change (the Civil War) and far-reaching economic transformations in the banking sector (the National Banking Act and the emerging supremacy of New York as a financial centre).

Recent writing on the Canadian banking sector in this period has illuminated the ways in which political and economic pressures of the 1860s led ultimately to Canada's first Bank Act in 1871. In particular, studies comparing and contrasting the US and Canadian systems as seen through the Bank Act offer a comprehensive account of the intense pressure on the newly minted government of Canada to balance the regional, metropolitan and financial interests of the country within the ambit of the banking legislation of the early 1870s.[11] Canadian financial connections and links with the imperial centre of London are particularly relevant in this regard. On another front, Charles W. Calomiris and Stephen Haber have placed all banking within a conceptual framework that focuses squarely on political environments and the "banking bargains" they produce. Though they almost entirely neglect the weight of Canadian historiography on the subject, their conclusions about the national nature of banking are sensible. In particular, the conclusion that the "chartered banks represent a partnership between the parties in control of the government and the founders and shareholders of the banks" is undeniably true in the Canadian situation.[12]

Strategy and Leadership

Other chapters of this book have examined reputations, relationships, and networks, with a system-wide perspective trained on the role of the state in the making of the banking system. This chapter, by contrast, tries to pull the focus back to the operational context and strategy of the Bank of Montreal.

The Bank's leadership, organization, and strategy were essential in responding to the challenges of the 1860s. At the opening of the decade, the Bank was doing well but losing ground to competitors. It had slipped behind its main rival, the Bank of Upper Canada, in circulation, reserves, and capitalization. Ten years later, the Bank of Montreal had consolidated its leadership in Canadian banking and established itself as a small but strategic and undeniably profitable player in the New York and Chicago markets in the face of fierce competition and intense political pressure. It had done so by exploiting its superior organizational capacities, the strength of its networks, the growing ability of its agencies and branches in the business of banking, and the inherent soundness of its philosophy of banking – one that featured a much more conservative, rationalized approach to commercial credit and a focus on larger projects. Of course, strategy is nothing without the leadership to execute it successfully. The Bank's "crisis leadership" team proved to be an extraordinarily gifted group of men who used all the resources at their command – organizational innovation, experience, political and social links – to obtain the best possible result.

For a generation thereafter, the Bank built on the success it had secured in the 1860s, underwriting national economic development and becoming what Calomiris and Haber call the "coordinator in chief" of Canadian banking. In an important way, then, the 1860s were the decade that made the Bank of Montreal. Yet, in the aggressive pursuit of its strategy, and in its often-astonishingly successful outcomes, the Bank became a lightning rod for the financial, competitive, and economic anxieties and opportunities of the time.

Any attempt to examine strategy and performance should come with a warning most recently articulated by Philip Scranton and Patrick Friedenson: "The historical experience of nations and economies is surely nonlinear, peppered with unintended consequences, unacknowledged influence and expectations, accidents, failures and surprises." In other words, there is a tendency to "retrospectively rationalize" business strategy and performance, when in truth they were often contingent, reactive, and indeterminate. Narratives can unfold as a smooth sequence of logical steps leading to success, with the chaos and noise filtered out.[13] The historical dynamics of this story suggest that we need to understand that responses to emergent circumstances play a significant role in the story.

Bank Strategy

The early 1860s proved to be an inflection point for the Bank of Montreal. An audacious and bold strategy began to emerge from the Bank's leadership. That strategy comprised three central elements: 1) leverage the Bank's superior organizational capacities in banking to transform its operations, professionalize its lending policies by improving monitoring and screening processes, and maximize its profitability, focusing on large railway, lumbering, and industrial accounts and government business; 2) exploit the Bank's international networks and capabilities to expand its role in niche markets in Chicago (the grain/produce trade) and New York (foreign exchange and gold) as well as London (credit provision for banks, Canadian enterprise, government bonds); and 3) leverage the Bank's power and influence on all fronts – among economic and political elites, in the Canadian capital market, and so on – to secure government business and ensure that the Bank's interests were fully taken into account by any legal, policy, or regulatory changes.

That strategy emerged through the Bank's policies and actions through the mid- to late 1860s and was articulated through its senior managers. The Bank of Montreal's new "Differentiation Strategy" (leaving the Stability Strategy in its wake) was driven by a combination of factors: the intense competitive dynamics of the Canadian banking sector; a new and more rigorous approach to the bank's management of its capital and loan accounts; and a restless dissatisfaction with the status quo. It is important to note, however, that this strategy emerged not as a series of logical steps on the road to success but rather through the Bank's response to its political and market environment.

This strategy would, it was hoped, enable the Bank to respond to emergent circumstances and leverage its clear advantages – its social and political networks, its capabilities, and its capital power as the leading Bank in British North America. It put the Bank on the offensive against its competitors. It also put fully into play its reputational capital, which by then had been well and solidly established.

The Key Players

There were four key individuals who developed the Bank's strategy and were responsible for its execution in the 1860s. The new decade witnessed a changing of the guard, with the resignation of long-time Bank president Peter McGill. McGill had served from 1834 to 1860. Under his presidency, the Bank's reputational capital and the building of its network of financial infrastructure slowly emerged. A new generation of leadership took the reins of the Bank in 1860. They were, to varying degrees, leaders of exceptional strategic foresight and ability. From their extensive experience in an increasingly sophisticated Montreal metropolitan market, they were able to transform the Bank from an honourable but lacklustre performer to one of the leading banks – not only in British North America but on the continent itself. Five key architects stand out.

The Éminence Grise: Thomas B. Anderson

Thomas B. Anderson became president of the Bank of Montreal in 1860, succeeding Peter McGill. He remained in the post virtually all of the 1860s, providing guidance, support, and shrewd leadership.

Anderson was born in Edinburgh in 1796 and emigrated to Montreal in the 1820s. He had social and professional ties with the Bank's founders, especially John Richardson, his father-in-law. Anderson served on the Bank of Montreal board from 1830 to 1834 and again from 1835 to his retirement in 1869.[14] He worked closely with McGill to expand the Bank's operations, advocate strongly for a system of branch banking in the province in the 1840s, and generally defend the Bank's interests in the often-contentious precincts of the Legislative Assembly. As Carman Miller writes of him, Anderson was of the "old race" of Canadian merchants. Recognizing the urgency of putting the bank's operations on a more professional corporate footing, he spearheaded an expansion in the ability of branches to handle more business (such as insurance and other corporate interests). In his second year as president, he was the motivating force behind the creation of the position of general manager to deal with the growing complexity of the bank's business.. Anderson's selection of David Davidson in 1862 as the Bank's first general manager gave a strong indication of his commitment to managerial transformation. Davidson stayed but a year, returning to Scotland to become general manager of the Bank of Scotland. Anderson's subsequent promotion of Edwin H. King to the general manager's position was likely the most significant action in the history of the Bank.

The Fixer: Thomas Ryan

Thomas Ryan, vice-president of the Bank of Montreal from 1860 to 1873, was an Irishman born in 1804 in Ballinakill (County Laois) and educated at the Jesuit college of Clongowes Wood in County Kildare. He and his brother Edward emigrated to Canada in the 1820s and founded the firm of Ryan Brothers and Company. Over time, the firm's ties to the Baring Brothers grew strong, with Thomas assuming the office of chief commercial correspondent in the Montreal office of Barings. He was an important figure for Barings – as agent and source of on-the-spot analysis of financial and especially railway matters.[15] As Gerald Tulchinsky and Alan R. Dever note, his intimate association with Barings "must have enhanced his position in the Canadian commercial élite." That, and his extensive business ties and interests (including a mercantile firm), ensured that his service at the Bank as vice-president would be invaluable. Ryan's character – he was described by R.G. Dun and Company as "unmarried, queer and somewhat peculiar & inclined in his business intercourse to be opinionative and overbearing"[16] – must have made for some interesting conversations at the Bank in the 1860s between the key players, especially with Edwin King. Ryan's prominent standing in the community was reflected in his presidency of the Montreal Board of Trade, his service as a lieutenant-colonel in the local militia, and his term as consul-general in Montreal for France, Denmark, Lubeck, Bremen, and Hamburg. His election to the Legislative Council of the Canadas in 1863, and his later appointment to the Dominion Senate in 1867, allowed him to advocate strongly for commercial and bank interests. Ryan was also a devout Catholic whose championship of the interests of the Irish Catholic community in Montreal was outspoken and effective.

The Renaissance Industrialist: John Redpath

John Redpath, born in Earltson, Scotland, in 1796, was a vice-president of the Bank between 1860 and 1869. His ties to the institution, however, go far deeper. He was elected to the Bank board in 1833, a position he held until his death in 1869. He was also a large shareholder. Redpath was a major contractor and industrialist and a key figure in building the Lachine Canal locks – the most important public works of early-nineteenth-century Montreal – and a major investor across all segments of the Montreal economy: fire insurance, telegraphy, banking, transportation infrastructure, mining, and manufacturing. Most spectacularly, he became Canada's most prominent sugar refiner, with twenty new plants dotting the Lachine Canal. His philanthropic pursuits and charitable works were, as his biographer notes, "in the best Christian tradition."[17]

The "King of Canada": Edwin Henry King

Edwin Henry King was born in 1828 in Ireland, moved to Canada in 1850, and worked for much of the 1850s in the Bank of British North America. In 1857 he was hired by the Bank of Montreal as inspector of branches and shortly thereafter became manager of the important Montreal office. On 23 March 1863 he was appointed general manager of the Bank. From 1869 to 1873, he was the Bank's president; afterwards, he returned to England and served on the Bank of Montreal's London committee (1879–88). King has been called the "most striking figure in Canadian banking history"[18] and the "Napoleon of Canadian Finance"[19] by various historians down the years. He has been also derisively called the "King of Canada,"[20] "a little God who dares to treat the representatives of all other banks" in an insulting manner, "truculent and uncompromising." Even his allies described him as a "very peculiar fellow."[21]

King was quite possibly all of those things at the same time. What is certain, however, is that he was the most brilliant strategist and visionary in the history of the Bank. His experience in the 1850s at the Bank of British North America, his views on the proper running of bank branches – stemming from his days as the chief inspector for the Bank – and his opinions on the dangerous excess of commercial credit all found a channel directly into the Bank's 1860s strategy as it evolved. King's close relationship with Finance Minister Alexander Tilloch Galt was also an important element in the implementation of this strategy.

John Richardson (1754–1831) was the leader of the Bank of Montreal's founders. Although he never held a position in the Bank beyond his chairmanship of the founding committee, no other founder better captures the motivating spirit behind the establishment of the Bank of Montreal. ca. 1806–09. Painting by Gerrit Schipper. Image courtesy of McCord Museum of Canadian History, M969.53.1.

MONTREAL BANK, 7th Nov. 1817.

PROPOSALS in Writing from Applicants, to fill the office of MESSENGER, will be received at the BANK, on or before 10 o'clock on TUESDAY Morning next, addressed to the President and Directors ; at the same time naming the securities they propose.

R. GRIFFIN, Cashier.

(*above*) This advertisement from the *Montreal Herald*, published on 23 October 1817, was the first advertisement ever printed for the Montreal Bank. 1817.
(*opposite*) Augustin (Austin) Cuvillier (1779–1849) was an important business and government figure in Montreal and the sole French-Canadian founder of the Bank of Montreal. Undated (produced ca. 1900–24). Anonymous. Image courtesy of McCord Museum of Canadian History, M5205.

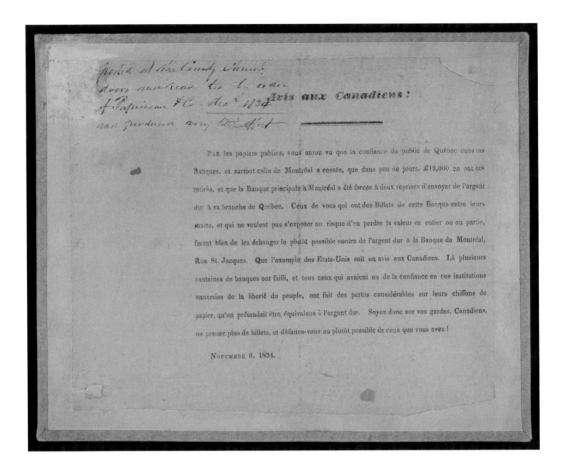

This "notice to Canadians" was posted on a church door, urging Quebeckers to exchange their bank notes for coinage. According to the handwritten message in the corner, the notice "produced very little effect." 1834.

The Bank of Montreal chose Place d'Armes, in the heart of historic Montreal, as the location for its headquarters, first constructed in 1819. In 1847–48, the site was enlarged with the addition of the classic Main Branch building that still stands today. This view is from the front of Montreal Main Branch. 1850. Library and Archives Canada/W.H. Coverdale collection of Canadiana [multiple media] Manoir Richelieu collection/c041453k.

Sir John Rose (1820–1888) was a director of the Bank of Montreal and chair of its London Committee. He served as finance minister under Sir John A. Macdonald from 1867–69. His tenure was dominated by a debate on the nature of the Dominion's banking system, with Rose (along with BMO's E.H. King) favouring a state currency backed by government securities. Undated. Library and Archives Canada/Topley Studio fonds/a025959.

George Stephen, 1st Baron Mount Stephen (1829–1921), pictured here in his mid-30s, served as president of the Bank of Montreal from 1876–81 and was instrumental in organizing the financing of the construction of the Canadian Pacific Railway, which he co-founded with his cousin, Donald A. Smith, 1st Baron Strathcona and Mount Royal. 1865. Photographer William Notman. Image courtesy of McCord Museum of Canadian History, I-14181.1.

Peter McGill (1789–1860) was the longest serving president of the Bank of Montreal (1834–60) and served as mayor of Montreal from 1840–42. Under his leadership, the Bank developed national ambitions. 1866. Anonymous. Image courtesy of McCord Museum of Canadian History, I-21029.0.

Sir Edward S. Clouston (1849–1912) (*second from the left*), pictured here with his cricket club, served as general manager and vice-president of the Bank of Montreal. 1869. Photographer William Notman. Image courtesy of McCord Museum of Canadian History, I-39938.1.

This image captures the influence the Bank of Montreal has had on the development of Canada. Pictured here is the CPR Bridge at Lachine, Quebec. Both the construction of the Lachine Canal and the CPR were funded by the Bank of Montreal and were of tremendous importance to young Canada. 1870. Photographer Alexander Henderson. Image courtesy of McCord Museum of Canadian History, MP-0000.892.6.

Donald A. Smith, later 1st Baron Strathcona and Mount Royal (1820–1914), served as president of the Bank of Montreal from 1887–1905 and held various senior government and diplomatic posts. Along with his cousin, George Stephen, he founded the Canadian Pacific Railway. 1871. Photographer William Notman. Image courtesy of McCord Museum of Canadian History, I-66959.

Sir Edward Clouston, later Bank of Montreal general manager, pictured during a costume party in Montreal. Clouston is seated in the middle row, third from the left. Clouston and his wife liked to entertain lavishly at their Montreal residence and at Boisbriant, their chateau at Senneville. 1875[?]. Photographer Wm. Notman & Son. Image courtesy of McCord Museum of Canadian History, II-149797.

Sir Alexander Tilloch Galt was Canada's first finance minister, serving from July–November 1867. He also served as a director of the Bank of Montreal. Through marriage, he was related to David Torrance, who served as president of the Bank of Montreal from 1873–76. 1876. Photographer Notman & Sandham. Image courtesy of McCord Museum of Canadian History, II-42813.1.

Gold Range Views - Driving the "Golden" Spike, b—
Summit, on C.P.R., Nov. 7, 1885, 9.30 a—

BANK OF MONTREAL CHICAGO TEMPORARY
OFFICE 145 RANDOLPH STREET AFTER GREAT FIRE 187
MANAGER IN DOORWAY WILLIAM RICHARDSON

(*above*) The temporary office of the Bank of Montreal on 145 Randolph Street in Chicago after the Great Fire of 1871. Standing in the doorway is branch manager William Richardson. 1871. (*opposite*) This image, taken either slightly before or after its more famous cousin, depicts Donald A. Smith "driving the last spike" on 7 November 1885. The tremendous occasion signalled the completion of Canada's first transcontinental railroad – a project with which Canada's First Bank and its executives were intimately involved. 1885. Library and Archives Canada/Topley Studio fonds/a209978.

(*above*) Montreal was the epicentre of Canadian industry and business in the late nineteenth century. Shown here is the ss *Durham City* in the midst of the busy port. 1896. Photographer Wm. Notman & Son. Image courtesy of McCord Museum of Canadian History, II-116749. (*opposite*) Sir Henry Vincent Meredith (1850–1929), shown here in costume in his younger years, served as president of the Bank of Montreal from 1913–27. 1885. Photographer Wm. Notman & Son. Image courtesy of McCord Museum of Canadian History, II-75991.1.

Sir Edward Seaborne Clouston held the position of general manager from 1890 to 1911. He was described in his day as "the epitome of Canadian banking" and as "shrewd, powerful and austere, although far from cautious or conservative in financial matters." 1899. Photographer Wm. Notman & Son. Image courtesy of McCord Museum of Canadian History, II-130515.

George Alexander Drummond (1829–1910) served as vice-president from 1887 to 1905 and as president between 1905 and his death in February 1910. During his tenure, he was instrumental in shifting bank policy to favour the Canadian industrialist community, allowing, for example, long-term loans against the collateral of warrants. Under his leadership, the Bank of Montreal also embarked upon a significant expansion that saw the opening of 110 new branches and a dramatic increase in staff. 1899. Library and Archives Canada/Topley Studio fonds/a028058.

Shown here is the Merchants Bank branch in Castor, Alberta, in May 1909. Standing in the doorway are branch employees F.R. Pike (*left*) and Short Riggs (*right*). The Bank of Montreal would take over the Merchants Bank in 1926, thereby dramatically increasing its number of branches across the country. 1909.

The personnel of the Bank of Montreal branch in Estevan, Saskatchewan, from left to right Ethel Medcof, Les Thompson, Athie Yardley, Herb Holmgren, Mr Williams, and Mr Mason. The interior is representative of bank branches of that time and place. 1910.
Bomac Photo Studio.

CANADIANS AS WE SEE 'EM

SIR EDWARD CLOUSTON
Vice-President and General Manager Bank of Montreal
Montreal

This cartoon by E.H. Hayes, part of a series called "Canadians as We See 'Em,"
depicts Sir Edward Clouston. As general manager, Clouston held the purse strings,
alluded to by him being seated on a giant chest labelled "Bank of Montreal Trust
Funds." 1910.

This series of cartoons was created by W.G.R. Humphrey. It depicts Canadian bankers in a variety of "stereotypical" situations and reflects a popular view of banking and bankers in the early twentieth century. ca. 1910.

Canada Cement Company was a Canadian industrial powerhouse and contributed to the crucial war effort in the First World War. Sir Edward Clouston's involvement in the company, and especially the business dealings of Max Aitken, led to Clouston's hastened retirement from the Bank in 1911. 1914–19. Library and Archives Canada/Ministry of the Overseas Military Forces of Canada fonds/a024443.

Alexander Tilloch Galt and John Rose were not directly involved in the execution of the Bank's operations during this period, but they were closely associated with the Bank through directorial or personal ties. Galt (born in 1817 in England) was an important exponent of Confederation and one of Canada's most brilliant and important politicians in the 1860s. His connections with the Bank of Montreal (as a director and confidant of King) meant that, in his role as minister of finance of the United Canadas in 1858–66 and later of the Dominion of Canada for a short time in 1867, King's vision of Canadian banking had a strong supporter in the councils of government.[22] His successor as finance minister in 1867, John Rose (born in 1820 in Scotland), was an extraordinarily gifted lawyer who entered politics in the 1850s and quickly became an important participant in the commercial and social life of Montreal. His stint as finance minister after Galt's short tenure in 1867 put him at the centre of the struggle over the new country's banking system.[23]

Consequences

The new strategy and the new leadership had some immediate consequences. In May 1863 long-time Bank cashier and senior executive Charles Smithers resigned from his position, citing differences with King and his operational methods. President Anderson departed from the usual comments in the 1864 Annual Report to declare that the directors had given "much consideration to the position of the Bank's business, and Banking prospects generally in Canada."[24] The strain involved in continuing to provide 8 per cent dividends while making provision for bad debt demanded a change in strategy. Advances on "accommodation paper" – mainly deployed in the western sections of the United Province – were to be targeted, reduced, and, if possible, eliminated. A "better system of advances" would ensure a "comparative freedom from loss" in future years." In addition, changes in branch and agency management had been put into place to streamline the Bank's operation. King's main goal here was to assure a more "faithful adherence to the conservative policy" that now reigned at the Bank of Montreal. As the Annual Report for 1865 remarked, the Bank had "steadily persevered during the past year in declining [accommodation paper] and in requiring payment or security for old obligations of this character."[25]

The banking theory behind these changes was sound. The system of loans via accommodation paper amounted to easy money obtainable in easy ways, and "often led both bankers and customers to lose sight of the legitimate functions of banking advances altogether." King and the Bank's management believed that bank capital should be deployed to facilitate commercial operations, aid manufacturing, and assist "in the transfer of the products of the country to home and foreign markets." Instead, it was often used to buy property and improve it, then requiring more borrowing to make it productive. Anderson wrote in 1865 that "the effect of this misapplication of banking advances would have been sooner felt, but for the large outlay upon railways and other public works which imparted a temporary stimulus and an appearance of great prosperity." People, in other words, spent borrowed money on imports and got into debt. The day of reckoning had been postponed by the railway boom and US demand, but it had now arrived.

The Strategy Unfolds

An important element of the Bank's overall strategy was its move into key international markets – in New York, London, and Chicago, in that order. The Bank had established representative offices in New York in 1858, making loans on commercial paper. Its Chicago agency was small but growing: by the end of 1861, for example, it had $121,985 of notes outstanding in the city. In early 1862, additional credits of $60,000 were granted on a temporary basis. The head of the Chicago agency, Richard Bladworth Angus, had established a strong presence in the Chicago market. His acumen in banking matters prompted the Bank to move him to the larger New York office after the departure of Smithers in May 1863. Angus would become an important leader in the Bank in the 1870s and beyond. The Bank had also participated in the establishment of the Chicago Clearing House in 1865.

The links between New York and Montreal had been consolidated by significant improvements in transportation infrastructure and communications in the 1840s and 1850s. The Champlain and St Lawrence Railroad (1836), telegraph links (1847), and the St Lawrence and Atlantic Railway (1853) all contributed to a marked increase in trade. Between 1840 and 1855, for example, the number of bushels of wheat exported to New York markets grew from two million to ten million.[26] The initial entry into the New York market was related to foreign-exchange trading. Thereafter, however, it soon took on greater significance. By the 1860s, sizable bank balances were maintained in New York and, as Ronald Shearer notes, "used to settle interbank clearings on account of domestic transactions, with surplus funds put out in call loans in the New York money market."[27] New York call loans became "the first line of secondary reserves, superior in liquidity to virtually any Canadian asset" and formed a business in which Canadian banks were a major player. As one observer remarks, "by about 1857 or a little later, the Bank of Montreal was larger than any American bank and probably the largest and most powerful transactor in the New York money market, where it maintained and employed immense sums."[28] But the King strategy was to exploit profitable niche markets in foreign exchange as well the market in gold.

The Civil War had transformed a growing market for the Bank in New York into a potentially very dangerous one. The *Trent* crisis of late 1861 – in which a renegade Union commander seized two Confederate agents aboard a British steamer – threatened to plunge Anglo-American relations into a diplomatic as well as financial crisis. As Jay Sexton writes, "securities plummeted on both sides of the Atlantic, contributing to a run on New York banks that resulted in the suspension of specie payments in the North on 30 December 1861" (the United States would not return to the gold standard until 1879).[29] Even before the possibility of Anglo-American conflict, British financiers viewed the ephemeral panic on the stock exchanges in the wake of the election of Abraham Lincoln as inaugurating a prolonged financial crisis. In other words, the New York market was full of perils and pitfalls as befitted the financial centre of a nation at war with itself. In this context, King's bold expansion of the Bank's operations in New York may have seemed visionary to some but dangerous to others.[30]

Circumstances had put gold to a premium, reaching at its zenith 300 per cent of average values. The Bank took full advantage of its plentiful gold reserve to profit from the demand in the New York market. The borrowers also offered US currency as security on the loans, which in turn allowed the Bank to employ that capital in discounting trade bills in the city. From one source, gold, emerged a double profit.[31] King's operations in New York were, it was said, of such a character as almost to make one's "hair stand on end."[32] Those bold moves ensured that the Bank of Montreal was a force to be reckoned with in the New York market – some even saying the most powerful factor in New York banking circles.

There were other strategic reasons to be in the New York market. New York City was emerging as the national wholesaling centre for banking. Financial instruments would gravitate to regional centres and increasingly New York, where they were traded and priced in secondary markets and mediated by note brokers, other private bankers, and commercial banks.[33] The Bank of Montreal's presence in this key market at this crucial time was important for its future development. As David F. Weiman and John A. James note in their study of the evolution of the US monetary system, the Civil War era constituted a watershed in the formation of a more integrated payments system and monetary union, with New York as the locus of these developments.[34] Indeed, the spread of deposit banking in New York City after the Civil War has been called nothing short of remarkable.[35]

In the spring of 1868, King paid a special visit to the Bank's New York offices to assess its prospects. Shortly thereafter, the New York agency was allocated a fourfold jump in its asset allocation, from $1.2 million to $8.8 million. Half of that new infusion was in gold acquired from Montreal to satisfy the voracious demand for specie on the New York market. In autumn of 1868, for example, gold commanded a 1 per cent per-day premium.[36] Canadian banks, in fact, had all participated in this gold bull market, but the Bank of Montreal was the prominent player, holding 78 per cent of the Canadian bank shares in that market. The Bank's overall share of the $20-million market for gold was about $7.8 million.[37] Its commitment to the New York market paid off in spades. By 1869, the Bank had moved to more prominent headquarters – at 59 Wall Street, renting its space for $5,000US per year.

In Chicago, the Canadian initiatives on the agricultural and financial front drew the favourable notice of the *New York Times*. In February 1863 the newspaper noted that Canadians were making "great efforts to secure the trade – at least a portion of it – of the West for several years past, and have been quite successful. The business relations between Chicago and Montreal, and other Canadian towns, has yearly been increasing."[38] In London, the Bank reorganized its operations and correspondent-bank relationships, while also renegotiating its agreement with the Bank of Liverpool. In 1870 it opened an office at 27 Lombard Street tin New York to encourage British and foreign trade with Canada.

Government Bankers

A further element of the Bank's strategy was to leverage its networks to procure government business. In November 1863, at the instigation of Finance Minister A.T. Galt and Montreal financiers, the United Province appointed the Bank of Montreal as fiscal agent for the government beginning on 1 January 1864. The Bank would replace its main competitor, the Bank of Upper Canada, which had long held the post. This represented an important victory. Independent of its close ties to the finance minister, the Bank of Montreal was an indispensable asset and intermediary. It was the only institution that could provide the sterling exchange the government required to maintain its credit in the London market.[39] As the banking historian Ronald Rudin states, the 1866 Provincial Note Act had been devised by King and Galt as the foundation of a single Canadian currency backed by substantial securities. The situation then obtaining in the province was that banks could issue notes without reserves up to the value of their unimpaired capital. The Note Act was intended to tame the beast of credit over-extension, put the currency on a sound foundation, and solve the pressing problem of the government debt.[40]

In fact, the Bank was instrumental in avoiding a government default in late 1864 with temporary and emergency loans amounting to $750,000. All told, by the end of 1864, government loans totalled $2.25 million, or about 16 per cent of the Bank's outstanding loans. Subsequent loans in 1866 and 1867 to finance government operations were substantial ($1.25 million in 1867 alone) and reinforced the central role that the Bank would enjoy as the principal banker to the newly formed Dominion of Canada. The shadow side of this arrangement, of course, was that the heavy government borrowing tied up the Bank's funds. Government securities were not the most profitable deployment of Bank of Montreal capital. Deliverance came in the form of the Provincial Note Act.

State Financing

The battle for position among the Canadian banks entered a new phase in the mid-1860s with the continuing struggles of the government of the province to finance its increasing debt load. Under the leadership of Finance Minister A.T. Galt, the government was compelled to float a loan of $5 million to meet its obligations – over and on top of what it already owed its banker, the Bank of Montreal ($2.25 million). One banker later recalled that the London creditors' letters to the finance minister were "written in exactly the same tone and to the same purpose as banks assume towards debtors whose bills are overdue ... a Canadian of the present day can hardly realise the position in which Canada was in at the time."[41] In 1864 the serious condition of the government's finances drew the notice of the *New York Times*. The *Times* underlined the dire nature of the government's reputation in London and the inability of the province of Canada to negotiate a loan.[42] The answer in 1866 came in the form of the Provincial Note Act of 1866 in which the government would issue its own currency up to $8 million, instead of borrowing or floating bonds on the market. The other major provision, that of retiring bank notes for government currency, was enshrined into law.

For the Bank of Montreal, the Provincial Note Act represented a quid pro quo of sorts: the Bank agreed to take $1.5 million of the 5 per cent debentures (the total assets locked up in government debt to that point was $2.8 million), and, in exchange, it would manage the accounts of the province. The position of the government was desperate: it could borrow no more on the London market, while the enormous debt to the Bank was increasing. The Montreal bankers were thus in a position where as much as three-quarters of their bank's whole capital was locked up in advances to the government. With the Note Act, the capital power of the Bank was brought into full force. Three things were at play here. First, the Bank was the government banker, and so the balances on account in other banks would typically be in favour of the Bank of Montreal. The Bank now pressed its option to compel payment in legal tender, and it had a direct interest in getting as many of those legal tenders circulating as possible. The Bank was able to compel its competitors into holding regularly at least $1 million of provincial notes. Banks that did not agree to the scheme were obliged to hold larger reserves and distribute them more widely, while having their power to discount diminished and impaired – either that, or restrict their business to the volume that could be covered by the old reserve. As one contemporary banker noted, all banks in towns with a Bank of Montreal presence were compelled to hold gold for settlement. As the Bank's general manager, King pursued the policy relentlessly, terminating all existing arrangements and instituting the new ones. By 1867, the Bank had secured most of the gold formerly held by the banks and instituted the system of holding legal tender notes.[43]

There was considerable opposition from Toronto interests to the legislation. That city's leading Liberal politician, George Brown, suggested that Galt had not exhausted every effort to renew the debt or provide for the debt in England. He also charged that the arrangement would be a profitable one for the Bank of Montreal. Galt replied that the impact for the Bank of Montreal was not the question. The "business of the Government and the Legislature was to enquire whether it would be for the interest of the country to enter into the arrangement."[44] Such an arrangement clearly was, from Galt's point of view.

The second major effect of the Note Act was more ominous for the Canadian financial system. The Bank of Montreal had been withdrawing its own notes from circulation and substituting for them the notes of the province. In this situation, the Bank's interest in maintaining an unimpaired system-wide credit network was broken. "The effect of that Act," a legislative committee report later suggested, "was to place the interests of the Bank of Montreal, the most powerful monied institution in Canada and the fiscal agent of the Government, in antagonism to those of the other banks."[45] Of course, many concluded that the general discredit of other banks would not only be desirable, but profitable, for the Bank of Montreal. The more provincial notes that were circulating as a result, the more the "Government Bank" – that is, the Bank of Montreal – would look attractive to depositors and merchants looking for a safe harbour and decent discounts.

There was more fallout to come. The fate of a prominent bank from Canada West, the Commercial Bank of Kingston, came to centre stage. Here was another major bank caught in a combination of bad luck and incompetent loan management. In 1858 and 1859 the Commercial Bank had invested £250,000 in the Detroit and Milwaukee Railroad, a sum that it was not able to recover;

the case ended up in the courts (which decided for the bank) in the early 1860s. Matters came to a head in 1867 when the bank made another series of errors, this time relating to its failure to sell the railroad's bonds at the right time and freeing up its locked-up funds. An emergency loan of $300,000 by the Bank of Montreal solved a temporary finance issue. By September 1867, however, a run on the Commercial Bank began which continued with redoubled force in October.

An emergency meeting of Canadian banks was convened on 21 October, with the Bank of Montreal offering to advance two-thirds of the money required to tide over the Commercial Bank's operations, and the British Bank offering the remaining third. When the other banks rejected the proposal, the Bank of Montreal withdrew from the meeting. A curious article appearing in the *New York Times* in October 1867 suggested that the Bank had been drawn into the political and railway "ring" after 1857 by Toronto capitalists. "The Bank had become of late years ... more or less a party political affair. It could generally be used ... [to] repel the legitimate patronage of business men."[46] The article also cited the new system of government finance, "which may be described as a cross between the Bank of England and our National Bank system here," as part of the problem since it created one predominant bank.[47]

Clearly, the Bank of Montreal held the upper hand. With its refusal to accept the responsibility for protecting the creditors of the Commercial on terms dictated by the banks of Canada West, the Commercial was left to its fate and on 22 October 1867 it stopped payment. The new government of Canada was anxious to avoid such a default, but it was so much indebted – literally – to the Bank of Montreal that it had no leverage in the matter. The Commercial later amalgamated with the Merchants Bank of Canada in a three-for-one share trade. All of the liabilities were redeemed in full, though the shareholders lost two-thirds of their investments. The bank's collapse was the major reason for Galt's resignation as finance minister the following month. The Bank of Montreal leadership under King had pursued its competitive strategy to the letter in the case of the Commercial Bank. Exploiting its advantage as the premier Canadian bank, the Bank of Montreal had prevailed over the "Western Banks" – those west of Montreal. In the judgment of the Bank, these banks had not followed the most sound banking principles, their management was second-class, and their prospects were not favourable. In late 1867 the Bank was rumoured to have telegraphed its branch managers to refuse the notes of several of the Ontario banks – specifically, the Royal Canadian Bank and the Gore. The effect was swift: there was a run on both – manageable runs, but runs all the same. King denied that the order was ever given to refuse notes, but there were complications to the story that ensured that the confidence in those banks would be rattled.

The results were clear in the assets and liabilities reported by the banks. While all other banks had suffered net decreases in circulation, deposits, and discounts, the Bank of Montreal registered increases in all three. In that critical month of November 1867, the Montreal gains were substantial: circulation +$389,184; deposits +$1.88 million; and discounts +$1.304 million.

Competitive Pressures

The Canadian financial market in the late 1850s was a very competitive one. As we have seen in the last chapter, experiments with free banking from 1850 were not generally successful. Between 1858 and 1864, several new banks were given charters: the Bank of Canada – later called the Bank of Commerce (1858); La Banque Nationale at Quebec (1859); and the Merchants Bank and La Banque Jacques Cartier (1861). Several more followed in the mid-1860s. The Bank of Montreal's biggest rival, however, was the Bank of Upper Canada. The BUC had grown steadily in the 1850s on the success of its activities in Canada West, especially in land speculation.[48] In the 1850s it also enjoyed the prestige of the position of government banker – a position it had enjoyed for fifteen years. The BUC's liberal loan policies led one contemporary observer to note its reputation of "honour and consequence" in that part of the province. "The bank had been the instrument of men of broad ideas and large purpose, ambitious, enterprising, hopeful pioneers."[49] Yet the BUC was also a considerable *debtor* to the treasury of the province. By the time the BUC had ceded the position of government banker to the Bank of Montreal, it was $1.15 million in debt to the treasury.

The collapse of real estate values in Canada West in 1857–58 (the same real estate that was taken as security on loans) doomed the BUC to further trouble – declining circulation, deposits, and capitalization, as well as no dividends – and in April 1865 the bank stopped payment. In the post-mortems on the failure of the Bank of Upper Canada, the actions of the government in the early 1860s came in for special scrutiny. As Breckenridge suggested a generation later, government members knew about the losses, had the bank at their mercy in consequence of its heavy indebtedness to the treasury, and therefore abused their position by compelling the BUC to take many financial decisions for political reasons, which resulted in making a bad situation worse.[50]

The lessons of the BUC's failure offered a "wholesome warning" to its competitors that they should pay attention to their "inner organization" and guard against any loans on real estate security. The leaders of the Bank of Montreal not only heeded the warning; they anticipated it much earlier by deploying their three-pillar Differentiation Strategy.

The politics over the banking and currency laws passed in the new Dominion of Canada between 1867 and 1871 has been told elsewhere. Andrew Smith notes quite rightly that the compromises made and the decisions taken in that period were fundamental in shaping the character, scope, and style of the Canadian financial system – from currency legislation to transcontinental branch banking. From the perspective of the Bank of Montreal, this period represented the apotheosis of King's "Differentiation Strategy." By then, the Bank had not only navigated treacherous political and economic shoals: by dint of its superior organizational capabilities and sound banking practices, it commanded by 1867 nearly a quarter of the total paid-up banking capital in Ontario and Quebec. One of every three notes in circulation or on deposit in the province originated from the Bank. It was also the government's fiscal agent.[51] The Bank had also seen two of its main competitors in Canada West succumb to their own banking mismanagement and the slings and arrows of outrageous fortune.

As general manager of the Bank of Montreal, King lobbied tirelessly to shape the legislation being drafted in Ottawa in 1867–71. The "bank of issue" system that he advocated was based on the National Banking System (NBS) of the United States. That system, the result of the US federal government's extraordinary intervention during the Civil War, linked the country's banks together through a reserve system that facilitated interbank transfers. It also restricted the growth of banking over large areas of the United States.[52] The appeal of the American system quickly becomes evident. The two major barriers to entry – minimum capital requirements and loan restrictions – represented key features of the Civil War banking laws. Minimum capitalization was to be strictly enforced under the American NBS.[53] That key provision must have been attractive to King, whose analysis of the Canadian banking system – and his experience with recent mismanagement – surely weighed heavily in his considerations. Another NBS barrier of great interest to King related to real estate. Real estate speculation, especially in Canada West, had seriously compromised the entire banking system in Canada from the late 1850s – so any mechanism that might bring such speculation under control was a good thing, at least in King's mind. Of course, this feature of the law, as Richard Sylla notes of the United States, had its "greatest effect on national bank entry in agricultural areas where land was the prime asset."[54]

King's advocacy of a "bank of issue," and the NBS model underlying it, was based on a variety of factors, not least the American system's perceived security and the best way to establish a Canadian currency system. For King and the Bank of Montreal, the NBS fit their situation perfectly. The Bank of

Montreal was the largest bank and the most agile, had an enormous capitalization compared to the others, its reserve was substantial, and it had no circulation of its own because of the Note Act of 1866. Of course, making the Bank of Montreal the "bank of issue" would also create a serious dependency on the part of smaller banks for rediscounting bills. One contemporary observer suggested that King's proposals would have raised the Bank of Montreal to the status enjoyed by the Bank of England in the United Kingdom.[55] In the event, the proposals met with vehement opposition, especially in Ontario, where the lack of any provision for the periodic expansion and contraction of the money supply was a crucial issue. That flexibility in the circulation of notes was absolutely essential for the farmers to "move the crops." As Breckenridge remarks, "the difference between the highest and lowest amount of notes outstanding at any time during the year was from twenty to fifty percent of the minimum."[56] The danger, it was suggested, was that capital, during the eight or nine months of the year when it was not employed in the high-return investments of the harvest-based trade, would find its way to more profitable pursuits, such as loaning at call on the New York or London markets, and thereby deprive Canadian trade of available credit.

The Toronto banks and merchant class mobilized, coalescing around Hugh Allan and William McMaster as their spokesmen. The press coverage was extensive – especially in those newspapers, such as the *Globe*, controlled by Toronto businessmen.[57] And its content was so furious and so negative that it contributed to the resignation of Galt as finance minister in November 1867.[58] "The Monetary King of Canada would not relent," wrote the *Hamilton Times*. "We fear the Bank of Montreal has the Government in its power and is disposed to play the tyrant not only over all monetary institutions in Canada, but over the Government itself."[59] "Every one acquainted with the commerce of Upper Canada must be aware that for many years the bank business has been of the most changeable capricious, fitful and arbitrary character," charged the *Globe* in 1867.[60]

In November 1867, the Bank of Montreal's Richard Bell, in a letter to the *Albion* that was reprinted in the *New York Times*, summed up the Bank's attitude regarding all the attention it was receiving:

DEAR SIR – With reference to our late conversation of yesterday on the subject of the Bank of Montreal, so fully alluded to in a late number of the *Albion*, on reflection, I think it not necessary to make any special reply, as intended, and merely add:

Prominent men and prosperous institutions must pay the usual penalty of success: and the Bank of Montreal and its general manager can well afford the enmity of rival and less successful corporations.[61]

Galt's successor as finance minister, John Rose, advanced a fresh series of proposals aimed at the stability of the system of circulation and featuring very stringent standards of entry. The plan also contemplated the establishment of a two-tiered system of banks: local banks, which would not be allowed to establish branches and would serve only the community in which they were located; and big banks, which would take care of national matters such as mercantile and foreign trade. But the critical issue – the issue that preoccupied Ontario and its farmers – was the elasticity and adequacy of the money supply. On this point, Rose's critics saw little to like in his scheme; in fact, his proposals were even opposed by members of the government party. Press accounts grew even more hostile. "MR. KING AND HIS BANK AGAIN! ANOTHER SHAM GAME!" screamed one headline in 1869.[62] Rose eventually withdrew his plan and resigned his post as finance minister that September.

The banking system envisaged by Galt and Rose clearly would have benefitted the Bank of Montreal. For Toronto businessmen, it would also seriously handicap the development of Ontario banks. Worse, it would expose Toronto and Ontario business to what was considered the tight-money policies emanating from Canada's largest bank. The Rose resolutions required the deposit of government debentures and specie against note issue and the control of the note issue by the Dominion government and its banker, the Bank of Montreal.

Rose was succeeded as finance minister by Sir Francis Hincks, who, in a third series of proposals set out in 1870, completely reversed the original banking policy of the government. The key was the retention of the bank-note issue against the general credit as opposed to gold reserve. This measure, as well as others respecting currency and note issue, was passed, but not without a protracted, acrimonious, and at times vicious struggle for advantage in Parliament and the press.

The biggest fallout for the Bank of Montreal was its loss of its power to issue and redeem provincial notes. Rather than paying the Bank of Montreal for that issue, the Dominion of Canada would assume the issue, as Dominion notes, of paper currency under $4. In addition, all banks, which would now be treated on an "equal footing," would be required to hold 50 per cent of their case reserves in Dominion legal tenders. "An Act Respecting Banks and Banking" was passed in April and given royal assent on 12 May 1870.

The Act of 1870, and the Bank Act of the Dominion of Canada of 1871, represented a defeat for the Bank of Montreal and its champion, E.H. King. The representations of Toronto banks – chiefly the Bank of Commerce and the Bank of Toronto – had successfully repelled King's forceful but ultimately futile attempts to tilt the playing field in favour of Montreal.[63] King's Toronto opponents in this contest were highly motivated to promote the interests of their emerging city and trade. At the Bank of Commerce, President

William McMaster (once connected to the Bank of Montreal) had graduated from dry-goods import to become actively engaged in finance. His circle included a broad section of Toronto interests, from hardware (H.S. Howland) to stockbroking (William Alexander) to saw and flour mills (John Taylor).[64] Their newspaper organ, the *Globe*, would carry their arguments in print and press the case that the relationship between the government and the Bank of Montreal could be summarized as follows: the monopoly of government business had enriched this bank at the expense of the public, and placed it in a position of financial power which was frequently exercised to the injury of weaker institutions.

In spite of the defeat, King collaborated with other banking colleagues to ensure that the implementation of the 1870 and 1871 acts proceeded smoothly. In fact, the influence of the Bank and its revolutionary general manager continued in full force.

The Balance Sheet

The 1860s proved to be a dangerous decade for the Bank of Montreal – but equally a daring one, full of opportunity. The balance sheet from the beginning of the decade to its end provided ample evidence that these years were transformative ones for the Bank in many ways.

In banking theory, economic growth is accelerated through bank lending and additional banks are needed to support locations that have experienced growth.[65] In the Canada of the 1860s, the expansion of financial intermediation through its greatest exponent helped stimulate growth of the nation's capital resources. Montreal bankers lived and worked in a city where in the 1860s, as David McKeagan reports, there were "six commission agents, 115 commission merchants and 52 brokers; 13 called themselves both brokers and commission merchants."[66] The emergence of the Montreal Stock Exchange in this period is also of note. The success of the Montreal bankers began to transform thinking on banking itself – particularly earlier nostrums about the salience of banking in a maturing industrial economy. In other words, the Bank pushed into new realms of finance and lending as it grew more prominent. A modern financial system and ample credit were undoubtedly of increasing importance to the financial future of the Dominion.

Abroad, the Bank of Montreal's international strategy provided a secure niche for Canadian banking in New York. Indeed, for much of the rest of the nineteenth century and into the early twentieth, the Bank provided a safe haven for depositors in New York during the major banking crises that occurred periodically. The placement of call loans in both the United States and Britain during times of banking crises could be completed as a result of the high reputation of the bank and the Canadian system of banking.[67] The Bank of Montreal enjoyed a predominant presence among its Canadian banking peers. Though it had, perhaps at most, a 2 per cent share of total deposits in New York, size was not the issue in this case. As Lawrence L. Schembri and Jennifer A. Hawkins suggest, "the primary function of the US branches of Canadian banks was not to solicit deposits of every size." Rather, they were focused on the large deposits. The fact that the Canadian banks were used as a safe haven "undoubtedly enhanced the reputation for stability that the Canadian banks enjoyed."[68]

A major impact of the Bank of Montreal strategy concerned the broader metropolitan struggle for financial hegemony. A generation ago, D.C. Masters wrote a seminal article on the struggle for financial hegemony between Montreal and its emerging rival, Toronto, in the 1860s. The "final stage of metropolitan development" required a mature financial system to take care of extended and hinterland trade and commerce. In other words, cities need banks and financial intermediaries to facilitate development. The battle within Canadian banking, therefore, can be situated as part of a broader struggle between competing metropolises.

The firestorm over the Commercial Bank in 1867, for example, is cited as a key moment in Toronto's desire to be free of Montreal's financial dominance. The story goes thus: here was an Ontario institution, the Commercial Bank, which needed a little more time and some coordination on the part of the Canadian banks. This may have happened but for the machinations of E.H. King, who was thoroughly vilified in the Toronto press. The incident both captured and magnified the resentment of the Bank of Montreal as an institution – as the government banker, as the top banking institution in Canada, and as a force to be reckoned with in British North America.

For the Bank of Montreal, the literal balance sheet over the decade was impressive. By 1871, with the call-up of the final $2 million in additional capital (to $12 million), the Bank possessed the largest paid-up capital of any colonial bank in the Empire. It was surpassed only by the much-larger banks – the Bank of England (BOE), the Westminster, the Royal Bank of Scotland, and the National Bank of Ireland. It was larger than any other English bank, and exceeded only by the Bank of Commerce in the United States.[69]

Bank of Montreal stock reached 117 points in 1860. By 1872, it had grown to 237 – double the value of the most banks and 40 points ahead of the Bank of Toronto in 1872.[70] The power and the influence of the Bank and its leaders would soon be directed to focusing on the transformation of the financial system and the country.

PART THREE

Fortune's Faithful Disciples, 1870–1918

*I hold it to be true that Fortune is the arbiter of one-half of
our actions, but that she still leaves us to direct the other half, perhaps
a little less. I compare her to one of those raging rivers, which when
in flood overflows the plains, sweeping away trees and buildings,
everything flies before it, all yield to its violence... it does not follow
therefore that men when the weather becomes fair, shall not
make provision ... in such a manner that, rising again, the waters
may pass ... and their force be neither so unrestrained nor so
dangerous. So it happens with fortune, who shows her power where
valour has not prepared to resist her, and thither she turns her forces
when she knows that barriers and defences have not been
raised to constrain her.*
Niccolò Machiavelli, *The Prince*[1]

One could not find a more apt summation of the genius, and perhaps also the limitations, of the Bank of Montreal in this half-century than the preceding quotation from Machiavelli. With a few exceptions, the Bank's leaders operated with a view to ensuring that the sphere of action within their control – in other words, the "other half" of affairs that fortune has left for us to control – would provide against the vicissitudes of fortune. When forces beyond their control prevailed, they ensured that the institution they guided would be sheltered from the passing storms in the political economy of the North Atlantic world.

In fact, the entire institutional makeup of the Bank was built to withstand outrageous fortune when it struck. This became, eventually, a characteristic of most Canadian chartered banks, famous for their conservatism. But the Bank of Montreal outshone all of them in this period as the model and example of how to navigate an institution of this size and importance through the perils of the late-nineteenth- and early-twentieth-century world. The greatest challenge and the greatest labour of the Bank of Montreal's half-century from 1870 to the end of the Great War was this: to build a resilient organization that could withstand fortune yet have the capacity to seize opportunities when they presented themselves.

The vision, strategy, and performance of Bank of Montreal in this half-century, as in no other period of its history, is closely intertwined with one major historical force: the rise of Canada to nationhood. The destinies of one and the other were linked by the people involved, the circumstances they faced, and the challenges they had to confront. Domestically, the Bank's challenges were at once defensive and offensive. On the defensive side, its primary mission included ensuring that Canadian finance could withstand the harsh and seemingly interminable periods of economic depression. The Bank's leaders also knew the value of a strong offence, becoming great protagonists of expansion into the Canadian west, the industrialization of the Canadian economy, and the participation of Canadian capital in the markets of the North Atlantic world through New York, Chicago, and London.

A Complex Story

The story of the Bank of Montreal in this half-century, covered in prolific documentary evidence running into the tens of thousands of pages, is crowded with events, circumstances, and personalities that defeat attempts at easy generalization. The Bank was at the centre of the political and economic action of a young and aspiring country. Its leaders were involved in politics, economics, and finance. They not only sought to build for the greater glory of the Bank of Montreal and their own prosperity, but also championed their city, region, and nation in the accelerating flows of capital, people, and activity in both metropolis and hinterland. The Bank itself went through several cycles of generational leadership in the period, complicating the process further.

Making sense of this foundational period and its connection to the overall development of the history of the Bank therefore runs substantial risks. Recounting every detail would be possible, but also be tedious or worse. Eliding over too much of the detail, by contrast, would strain credibility and hide from view some of the fascinating parts of this consequential period in the history of both bank and nation.

A Different Approach for a Consequential Era

This section of *Whom Fortune Favours* follows a different line and approach than what came before it and what will come after. First of all, the nearly half-century – forty-eight years to be exact – it covers is a period of paradox. There were long stretches of time, at least in banking, finance, and the economy, when exasperatingly little happened. In the days of wind, wood, and water, the nautical term would have been "becalmed" – used for sailing ships that would not be able to move as a result of little or no wind. Yet, at the same time, there were transformational developments rippling under the surface of Canadian economic history, even in the quietest moments – national economic development, industrial revolutions, the spawning of huge utilities in telecommunications, light, heat, and power, the large-scale movement of people, the growth of international trade – that made the era one of consequence in the life of the Bank and the country.

The years from 1870 to 1918, therefore, demand a unique treatment in this book. Accordingly, Part Three of *Whom Fortune Favours* features, following this Introduction, several thematic chapters. Chapter 6 is focused on offering an understanding of the internal contours of the Bank's development over time. Chapter 7 reaches beyond the walls of branches and head office to examine aspects of the unique role of the Bank of Montreal in the rise of Canada in the context of the North Atlantic world. Chapter 8 turns to the role of the Bank in the evolution of trade as well as in the wave of the mergers and acquisitions that occurred in the early twentieth century. Taken together, these examinations of internal and external trends offer a new perspective on the nature of Canadian banking at the beginning of the twentieth century.

The story of the bank in late Victorian times begins, really, at the end of the dangerous decade of the 1860s. This period witnessed the Bank achieve pride of place not only as the first Canadian bank but also as one of the most effective ambassadors of young Canada in the markets of the United States and in the councils of Empire. If Canada grew from colony to nation in this period, in the memorable phrase of Arthur Lower, then the Bank of Montreal had a lot to do with that.[2]

The Story So Far

The Bank emerged from the 1860s in a commanding position among Canadian banks. Under the leadership of E.H. King, the Napoleon of Canadian finance, the Bank vaulted into an enviable position as the undisputed leader in Canadian banking and one of North America's largest and most reputationally impeccable institutions. King and his associates did not waste any time in fully capitalizing on the Bank's performance by consolidating its place at the commanding heights of Canadian banking and attempting, and very nearly succeeding, to persuade the new Dominion government to enshrine its position in banking legislation and policy. As government banker at Confederation, the continent's "dangerous decade" of the 1860s, whatever its perils, proved to be a pivot point for the Bank of Montreal with respect to its competition. By the time E.H. King was headed for retirement, his achievements were undisputed. As the *Monetary Times* suggested in October 1872: "His annual balance sheets were well calculated to excite the envy of more timid bankers. Bold, resolute, energetic, and, as some say, unscrupulous, thoroughly versed in the theory and practice of banking, he has heaped up profits in a way that defies all precedent in this country."[3]

By 1867, the year of Canadian Confederation, the Bank had already reached its half-century mark, and its leaders enjoyed a prominence and a scale of influence that could not be easily matched. The protagonists of the Bank in this era – King, George Stephen, Donald Smith, and the rest – all captured by admiring painters of their day, together constituted a good part of the financial leadership of young Canada. Its leaders were not only leaders in finance but also helped to guide the destinies of a young underdeveloped country with visions of the future that would require careful financial consideration.

The period from 1871 to and 1918 forms, in the words of British historian Eric Hobsbawm, the tail end of the "long nineteenth century."[4] In the annals of the Bank's board minutes, the dates neatly frame concerns about the Franco-Prussian conflict at the beginning and the conclusion of the Great War at the end. In between, contemporaries in the North Atlantic world either witnessed or directly experienced cyclical economic fortunes, depressions, booms and busts, bank failures, and much else. The Bank's engagement with, and participation in, the flows of events powerfully illustrate that the preoccupations of its leadership were projected onto the broader stage of the North Atlantic world. Those preoccupations neatly symbolize two things:

first, the Bank's role in that wider world beyond banking; and second, how that relationship defined the way it viewed its place, its strategy, and its role.

The first two generations of Bank of Montreal bankers achieved the Bank's position of primacy in three ways. First, they built the organizational capacities of the Bank and its branches, in particular its risk- and market-intelligence functions, which were able to, in contemporary parlance, "execute" efficiently according to the standards of the time. Second, especially from the late 1850s, Montreal bankers pursued a strategically coherent set of policies which were flexible enough to respond to market opportunities, particularly in the New York gold market. Third, the institution could rely on a cadre of senior leaders whose talents, intuition, and vision represented the very best of Canadian business.

The power of the Bank of Montreal and its leading lights, the Bank's position in Canadian financial system, and its place in the economic and financial life of a country whose institutions were in the process of formation, all powerfully shaped the Bank's development over five decades and more. The Bank's plural roles as the largest bank in Canada, government banker, major issuer of currency, coordinator-in-chief of the Canadian banking industry, as well as fiscal agent for the government of Canada in New York and London, deeply affected its culture, planning, and performance. It would be wrong to say Bank leaders considered themselves governing a quasi-governmental institution – there was enough distance between public and private in both means and ends to ensure that such was not the case. But the objectives and projects that the Bank pursued and the roles it was expected to play in the financial structure of the new Dominion of Canada both at home and abroad put it in a position of substantial influence. In acting for, and on behalf of, government, the Bank of Montreal became a uniquely public-private institution in its outlook, strategy, and development. In effect, it acted as Canada's unofficial central bank. The bank leadership came to identify closely with national projects, and with national visions. That special sense of national purpose is the thread that unites these decades at the Bank, one that was shared by successive generations of leadership and executed in policy. This was a mutually beneficial relationship between bank and country, to be sure. On the one hand, it allowed the Bank of Montreal to enjoy the status and the economic rents that went along with the position. On the other hand, very few, if any, other banking institutions had the reach, the reputation, and the relationships required to successfully execute the demands of government. The privileges and responsibilities conferred on the Bank of Montreal by its relationship with the state had a marked effect on the strategies it pursued, the leaders it chose, and the decisions it made. Its position atop Canadian banking also influenced the culture of the Bank as it grew in prominence and influence into the early twentieth century.

Patterns Emergent

During the late nineteenth and early twentieth centuries, the Bank's strategy remained remarkably consistent. Indeed, that strategy for the entire period can be said to have consisted of two interrelated elements: responsibility and desire in the quest for prosperity. Responsibility was evident in the Bank's emphasis on stability and conservatism. This was partly an inheritance of the first half-century of the Bank's evolution. It was also imposed by its assumed roles and responsibilities not only to its shareholders and customers but also in its capacity as the country's principal commercial bank. Certainly, the need to manage risk in the frequently volatile economic cycles of the North Atlantic world was essential for its own survival and the profit of its shareholders. Yet it was equally for the benefit of the country as the Bank assumed a commanding position in both Canadian private and public/government finance.

The Bank had to balance this responsibility with the desire to search for profits in what was clearly a time of massive economic ferment. Mastering the balance between the two in a tough political and economic context was the Bank's central challenge. It would also be its central achievement. Without that ability to balance those two impulses effectively, the Bank would not have been able to ensure its place in the history of Canadian banking.

By the end of the 1860s, the Bank's leadership and organizational capacity had allowed it to achieve a strong track record of success in building, participating, and exploiting key North Atlantic financial networks. In other words, the Bank was uniquely positioned in this period to serve both imperatives over time – the responsibilities that came with its position in the firmament of Canadian finance, and the need to grow and expand.

The final element in understanding the experience of the Bank in this extraordinary period is to grasp the larger economic context. The details of this context will, of course, emerge in the chapters that follow, but it may be helpful now to provide a general picture of the challenges and opportunities facing the Bank's leadership between 1870 and the end of the Great War.

Economic Conditions

The economic landscape of post-Confederation Canada to 1918 is really the tale of two periods. The first stretches from 1873 to roughly the end of the nineteenth century; the second embraces the first two decades of the twentieth century, to 1918. Let's begin with the first. Economists refer to the

1873–1896 period in the North Atlantic world as the "Long Depression." More accurately, the era is bookended by two distinct depressions, one following the Panic of 1873, which lasted until 1879, and another following the Panic of 1893, which lasted until 1896.[5] Each panic had distinct underlying causes and do not necessarily share a common link. Generally speaking, however, between 1873 and 1896, countries in Western Europe and North America suffered from industrial overproduction, price declines, and high unemployment and experienced a prolonged period of general international stagnation. The economy of the United Kingdom suffered the greatest during this period, and the German Empire was able to catch up (though not overtake) the United Kingdom in terms of economic output.[6]

Canada also struggled. Historians acknowledge Canada's participation in the general economic cycles of the period. Those cycles were made worse by high unemployment and significant out-migration to the United States. At the same time, they hasten to add that the period was punctuated by long flashes of economic resurgence. As R.T. Naylor suggests, Canada experienced a boom from 1879 to 1883, when the Canadian economy flourished after the implementation of the National Policy tariff, the international market for Canadian staples (especially timber) improved, and investments in the Canadian Pacific Railway (CPR) stimulated growth.[7] The boom ended when "the bottom dropped out of land values in Winnipeg, financial difficulties beset the CPR, and industrial stagnation set in. Ontario, which had seen the greatest expansion, was hit hardest by the results of industrial over-expansion during the boom phase."[8] Gains made from 1879 to 1883 were surrendered, and growth in the 1880s and 1890s became a frustratingly distant and unattainable dream.[9]

The vicissitudes of the North Atlantic economy affected banking institutions as well. The period is littered with examples of bank failures in the North Atlantic triangle. To give the reader some sense of the precarious nature of the banking system, and the effects that this could have on the wider economy, one example will suffice. On 2 October 1878 the City of Glasgow Bank, one of the leading banks in Scotland, failed. The Glasgow Bank had a total capitalization of £12.4 million and a network of 133 branches.[10] While other Scottish banks agreed to honour the notes of the failed bank and offer banking facilities to its clients, the failure sent shock waves throughout the Scottish banking community as shareholders were called upon to make up a £5.4-million shortfall. When other banks, namely the West of England and South Wales District Bank, closed in December, the British banking system was a "hair's breath away" from a general panic.[11] This was the toll that a prolonged period of depression – especially of the industrial sectors in iron and coal – could take on the financial system of a country. Confidence in financial systems as a result of the sharp contractions and the depth of the crisis must have been a stern warning to the Bank of Montreal that prudence and overextension had to be avoided all costs, especially since the Canadian system had no Bank of England to act as a lender of last resort.[12]

By the end of the nineteenth century, long-awaited economic improvement finally materialized. The mineral potential of the west, specifically British Columba, was of particular excitement to the bankers at Montreal. The harvests in central Canada and the prairies were so good that it was "difficult to estimate the great boon the enhanced value of grain has been [to Canada.]"[13] Farmers were now able to reduce mortgage indebtedness and increase purchasing power. This stimulated trade, including railway traffic. "When business good, and the country prosperous, very little need be said," the Bank of Montreal's Annual Report noted in 1899.[14]

The upturn continued, producing a "universal prosperity, active trade, good crops and generally speaking satisfactory prices."[15] The Bank's 1900 half-year return provided "a pretty good indication of the state of the Dominion," showing the largest net earning on record for the Bank.[16] Significantly, the Bank now reversed itself on the desirability of call and short loans. Earlier, it had criticized other Canadian banks for lending large amounts on call in Great Britain and the United States. By late 1900, however, the Bank had begun to participate in this riskier form of loan because of record net earnings in that year.[17] The conservatism that had been the hallmark of the Bank's strategy began to be paid off in its performance in the early 1900s. The *Globe* enthused in 1901 that "the annual statement by the Bank of Montreal, issued to-day, is the most satisfactory in its history, and with such a conservatively managed institution shows the general trade of the country to be in the most gratifying condition."[18] The Canadian banking system's solidity and performance also attracted praise in the London financial papers.[19]

The reason for the upturn in Bank fortunes was simple: in the period between 1896 and the First World War, Canada experienced its single largest economic boom. On the international markets, its commodities, particularly wheat, fetched good prices, and the country created a truly transcontinental economic system. This system was a triumph as much for the Bank as for the Dominion broadly conceived, since its leaders were great champions of the CPR and the east-west integration of the country. Wheat was produced in the west, which was brought to larger cities via railroad. From there, it was loaded onto ships and exported globally (though mostly to the United States and Great Britain). In reverse, large ships brought imports to Canadian cities, which were transported across the country via the new railways. As part of this system, Canada's economy flourished, the west was settled (Alberta and

Saskatchewan became provinces in 1905), and the manufacturing industry in central Canada grew and diversified.

The period from the end of the century to the end of the Great War laid down the basis for the economic configuration of the country to well into the late twentieth century. Naylor suggests that that configuration included a "degree of American domination of its industrial base, the primary extractive orientation of its export sector, the relative growth of particular regions ... all logical outgrowths of the 'national policy,' and of the package of policies adopted by central Canadian capitalists to maximize the economic output (and their own positions) within the North Atlantic economy."[20] Indeed, some have called the first two decades of the twentieth century a "golden age of Canadian growth,"[21] citing massive influxes of migration to western Canada and an industrializing urban cluster in central Canada – Montreal and Toronto, of course, but also second-order cities such as Hamilton, London, and others in southwestern Ontario and southern Quebec. Finally, gross-fixed-capital formation began to consolidate Canada's economic position in the North Atlantic world, aided by what has been characterized as an "enormous net capital inflow from Britain."[22] Times were so good, in fact, that Canada was outstripping its peer group, and by a long shot. As Greg Marchildon puts it:

> These were good times for all, but no country enjoyed a faster rate of economic growth than Canada. Despite the fact that the 1870s and 1880s were sluggish decades, business had picked up sufficiently by the turn of the century that Canada's average growth rate for the decades in the second industrial revolution towered above that of every other country ... This remarkable growth rate reflected both high capital intensity and rapid technological innovation and adaptation. Starting from a relatively undeveloped industrialized position at the time of the birth of the country in 1867, Canada had grown into a vital manufacturing nation by 1914.[23]

The Canadian economy went into overdrive after 1896. Rising prices played their part, of course, as did the electro-chemical revolution and revolutions in light, heat, power, and communications, as well as the internal-combustion engine. Together, these spawned impressive economic growth as well as a series of significant technology-based utilities.[24] Forests, mines, hydroelectric power, and a succession of staples products put Canada firmly on the trajectory of prosperity.

Yet it must not be forgotten that, in the midst of this technological transformation, Canada's prosperity depended heavily on agricultural products, and, indeed, wheat remained king in the growth of Canada's GDP.[25] Grain elevators became a symbol of Canadian prosperity and wealth as well as of Canadian dependence on the terms of trade. Exports were the name of the game. Canadian banks were major beneficiaries and note circulation exploded in this period.[26] The dream of the west, so long dear to Montreal bankers, was realized, and this expansion meant massive new trade balances – which were in surplus after 1895 and then switched into an import surplus as business and population boomed in the west.[27]

Internationally, Canada found itself in the midst of a North Atlantic triangle pulsing with activity, situated between the surging republic to the south and the centre of Empire in London. This geography influenced its economic actions and outlook, most notably reflected in the country's tariff policies during the "Laurier boom." The story of the tariff policies need not concern us here, with the exception of a few points. First, the imperial preference on the tariff was notable for Canadians, underlining their country's aspirational role not only in trade matters but also within the British Empire.[28] To give the reader an idea of Canadian trade flows, consider that the United States was second to the British market in the area of exports, with the latter taking about half of Canada's exports and the former under 40 per cent. In terms of imports, the United States accounted for 60 per cent of Canadian imports, compared to the United Kingdom at 25 per cent.[29] But, in the realm of capital, Britain reigned supreme – Canada received almost all of its foreign investment from British sources. Empire capital outflows were almost exclusively directed to Canada, moreover. As Marchildon notes, "during the Laurier boom, Canadian finance became more closely linked with the mother country than ever before, with the securities of the largest Canadian enterprises trading almost as easily in London as in Montreal and Toronto."[30]

This, in brief brushstrokes, is the economic context in which Bank of Montreal bankers operated in this period. We now turn to an examination of the team, the players, and the key themes of the Bank of Montreal's remarkable half-century.

CHAPTER SIX

Players and Performance: Strategy and Organization

This chapter focuses on the key players and performance of the Bank of Montreal in the 1870–1918 period. The organization of the chapter follows the plan set out in the Introduction to Part Three, and the material has been presented in such a way as to provide a sharper angle of vision. We begin with life on the inside of the Bank – in particular, its leadership, strategy, and performance. The chapter also touches on some the broad organizational currents of the period.

We start with leadership.

Leadership: The Protagonists

The Bank's leadership consisted of four orders: the president, the vice-president, the general manager, and the board of directors (see table 6.1). In this period, the latter assumed more direct responsibilities of oversight and supervision – elements that over time migrated to the management of the Bank. Our focus here is on introducing the "Montreal Seven" that ushered the Bank, eventually, into a new and more prosperous era. The following sketches of the major players will allow us to consider the impact of personality and circumstance on the story of the Bank.

David Torrance's long association with the Bank of Montreal extended back to the founding of the Bank in 1817: his uncle Thomas Torrance had been one of the original shareholders and, later, a director of the Bank.[1] David was a New York City-born Lowland Scot whose family moved to Canada via

Table 6.1 | Bank of Montreal senior management

Presidents

Edwin Henry King	1869–1873
David Torrance	1873–1876
George Stephen	1876–1881
C.F. Smithers	1881–1887
Donald Smith	1887–1905
George Drummond	1905–1910
Richard B. Angus	1910–1913
Vincent Meredith	1913–1927

Vice–Presidents

Thomas Ryan	1869–1873
George Stephen	1873–1876
G.W. Campbell	1876–1882
Donald Smith	1882–1887
George Drummond	1887–1905
Edward S. Clouston	1905–1912
Vincent Meredith	1912–1913
Charles Gordon	1916–1927

General Managers

Richard B. Angus	1869–1879
C.F Smithers	1879–1881
W.J. Buchanan	1881–1890
Edward Clouston	1890–1911
Vincent Meredith	1911–1913
Frederick Williams–Taylor	1913–1929

New York at the turn of the century. After his birth in 1805, his family moved to Kingston in Upper Canada where young David came of age. Torrance relocated to Montreal in 1821 to work in his uncle's firm, John Torrance and Company, an increasingly important commercial house in the city. He eventually took over from his uncle in 1853, expanding operations to major interests in shipping and general merchandizing, and, significantly, becoming the first firm to deal directly with India and China. Torrance was a dedicated member of the Montreal community who, according to the *Montreal Daily Witness*, was a "diligent merchant, and did not meddle much in public affairs, though he was a consistent Liberal in politics throughout."[2]

David Torrance joined the board of the Bank of Montreal in 1853. In 1873 he became president after E.H. King's resigned and ranking senior director Thomas Ryan refused to take the post. He served in this capacity for barely three years, to 1876. His tenure coincided, regrettably, with the onset of a major depression, though, as his biographer suggests, "profits remained steady, dividends were held at 14 per cent and the bank entered the field of investment banking" by the joint underwriting of an issue of Quebec provincial bonds with Morton, Rose & Company."[3] His tenure was cut short by his death on 29 January 1876.

George Stephen was born in 1829 in Banffshire, Scotland, and emigrated to Canada in 1850 to work for his cousin William Stephen in dry goods. He eventually established a firm of his own in 1866 dealing with sale and manufacture of woolens and other cloths.[4] By the early 1870s, he had established a name for himself as a financier along with Hugh Allan and E.H. King. He turned his interests to the great dream of the era, railways, and became progressively more involved in railway investment.

He joined the Bank of Montreal in 1871 as a director. In 1873 he was made vice-president and by 1876 he had become president. His involvement in the forerunners to the Canadian Pacific Railway venture implicated the Bank in loans on easy terms and preferred rates – a rumour circulating in the day and confirmed by board minutes thereafter.[5] The story of the CPR has been told elsewhere, but, considering that the total cost was estimated at that time to be $100 million, one gets a sense of how massive the undertaking was.[6]

Charles F. Smithers succeeded to the presidency in 1881, on the heels of Sir George Stephen's resignation from the post, and served until his death in 1887. Smithers presaged the arrival of a class of professional bankers to executive positions in the Bank. After coming to Canada from London, England, Smithers joined first the Bank of British North America and then the Bank of Montreal, eventually serving as the latter's senior agent in New York City. From 1863 to 1869, he took charge of the Montreal branch of the London and Colonial Bank, after which he rejoined the Bank of Montreal to supervise its New York operations. A decade later, Smithers replaced R.B. Angus as the Bank's general manager for two years before ascending to the presidency.[7]

Richard Bladworth Angus was another key figure in the period. Born in Bathgate, Scotland, in 1831, he emigrated to Montreal in 1857, whereupon he almost immediately secured employment with the Bank of Montreal as a bookkeeper clerk.[8] In the words of his biographer, he "combin[ed] good looks with hard work and a mastery of figures and finance" and was promoted quickly to positions in New York and Chicago in the early 1860s.[9] He assumed the general managership of the Bank on 2 November 1869, succeeding E. H. King. He was to stay for a decade in that position, until 15 August 1879, joining George Stephen and Donald Smith (Lord Stratchona) in their ventures in mills and railway development, and using the Bank to offer Stephen and his syndicate favourable loans. Angus joined Stephen and Smith as vice-president of the CPR later that same year, "illustrat[ing] the allure of railways and the riches they offered," according to his biographer.[10] His involvement with both entities was vital in maintaining the close relationship between the CPR and the Bank of Montreal to the benefit of both, as the Bank grew in tandem with the railway's extension into the west. After resigning as the Bank's general manager, he pursued a successful business career in which he generated a huge fortune. Subsequently, he returned to the Bank as president between 1910 and 1913 and would remain a director until his death.

Sir Edward Seaborne Clouston occupied the position of general manager from 1890 to 1911, in the transition years when fortune once again began to favour Canada and its economic development. He would be described in his day as "the epitome of Canadian banking" – "shrewd, powerful and austere, although far from cautious or conservative in financial matters."[11] Along with Donald Smith and George Alexander Drummond, the history of the Bank of Montreal would bear his imprimatur in the late nineteenth and early twentieth centuries.

Clouston was born in 1849 in Moose Factory, Ontario, son of a chief trader of the Hudson's Bay Company (HBC). After completing his education at the High School of Montreal, he began working for the Bank of Montreal in 1864 at the age of fifteen as a junior clerk. His biographer remarks of him that his private and taciturn nature, energetic nature, and tactful manner all marked him for responsibility.[12] Between 1864 and 1875, he worked in the Brockville, Hamilton, and Montreal branches of the Bank, before moving to responsibilities in London and later New York. He returned to Montreal in 1877 to serve as assistant inspector for the Bank. Progressively promoted up the ranks, Clouston became general manager in 1890 and vice-president in 1905. He held these positions until 1911 and 1912, respectively.[13]

Clouston's competence and leadership qualities were very much in evidence to the leadership of the Bank in the 1870s and 1880s. His close ties to Donald Alexander Smith in particular were also helpful – in fact, Smith treated the young Clouston "like his son," since they shared not just personal affinity but also came from the HBC factor tradition.[14] Indeed, after Lord Strathcona became Canadian high commissioner to London in 1896, Clouston looked after his financial and philanthropic interests in Canada.

On a more personal level, Clouston was reputed to be a keen sportsman, active, as his biographer suggests, as a "snowshoer, fancy skater, curler, swimmer, yachtsman, golfer and motorist."[15] His interests indeed spanned the entire gamut of Montreal high society, from recreation to culture to horticulture. He and Lady Clouston entertained lavishly both at his Montreal residence and at Boisbriant, his château at Senneville. He was also particularly active in the promotion of health services and education. As well, he was a fervent proponent of the British Empire, supporting such causes as South African War charities and the creation of an imperial press service. In 1908 he was made a baronet.[16]

Clouston presided over a period of major consolidation and organization of the Canadian banking industry in what proved to be a variable period of turbulence and opportunity in Canada and in the North Atlantic world. At the zenith of his power, Sir Edward's personal and corporate power in financial circles was difficult to overestimate. As Carman Miller, his biographer, notes, he served as president, vice-president, or director of over twenty prominent firms.[17]

Donald Alexander Smith, 1st Baron Strathcona and Mount Royal, joined the Bank of Montreal as a board member in 1872, then serving as vice-president from 1882 to 1887, as president for a remarkably long time, from 1887 to 1905, and as honorary president from 1905 to 1914. While his involvement was in large part non-operational, he nevertheless had a substantial impact on the destiny of the bank.

There are very few Canadians who have had a similarly spectacular rise to prominence as Strathcona. He was born on 6 August 1820 in Forres, Scotland, and emigrated to Lower Canada in 1838, working for the HBC and rising to the rank of officer of the company by the 1840s.[18] He married Isabella Sophia Hardisty, whose mother was of native and Scottish parentage. His leadership experience with the Hudson Bay Company in various postings was distinguished by his enterprising and innovative methods to increase trade and manufacturing.[19] By the 1860s, he was frequenting Montreal on HBC business, and there, in 1865, he met his cousin, George Stephen. Stephen had already begun his ascent in the Canadian financial world, and Smith joined him in a number of partnerships which included Richard Bladworth Angus, Edwin Henry King, and other Bank of Montreal luminaries of the day.

Smith's superb business acumen was perhaps rivalled by his diplomatic skills, as evidenced in his intervention in the Red River Rebellion of 1869 to calm troubled waters on behalf of Prime Minister John A. Macdonald. He later served as president of the HBC's Council of the Northern Department and briefly as the governor of Assiniboia to oversee the negotiations between Canada and the HBC regarding the massive transfer of land and the reorganization of operations in the northwest on the part of the company. As his biographer notes, "as the HBC's executive officer in Canada, he would lead the firm's transformation into a land and colonization company."[20] In 1871 he was elected to the House of Commons as a Conservative MP, but Smith eschewed partisan politics and in fact voted to bring down the Macdonald government in 1873 in the wake of the Pacific Scandal. In 1887 he re-entered the Commons as an independent Conservative for Montreal West with the largest majority of any MP in Canada. His public service continued thereafter as he served as Canadian high commissioner in London between 1896 and 1914, a position for which he refused to accept the $10,000 annual salary.

Smith's business interests in the meantime were widening. In addition to his duties at the HBC, he was involved in railway promotions, banking ventures in Manitoba, and the Canadian Pacific Railway. The CPR venture, spearheaded in 1880 by George Stephen, was to be the most ambitious of the projects, and Smith was, in the words of his biographer, "a faithful financial lieutenant to Stephen," providing among other things moral support in the darkest hours of the CPR's construction.[21] Smith's business and corporate interests were multiple and intersecting across post-Confederation Canada: railways, milling companies, land companies, salt companies, real estate investments (especially in Vancouver), newspapers, and the Anglo-Persian Oil Company (forerunner to British Petroleum). Strathcona was also an extraordinary philanthropist, giving in excess of $7.5 million in donations and bequests.[22] As his biographer states, he was one of the leaders of society on both sides of the Atlantic. In London, his hosting of the annual Dominion Day festivities was a highlight of the social season, with over one thousand Canadian and imperial dignitaries in attendance.[23]

Another giant of the era for the Bank was Sir George Alexander Drummond. Born in Edinburgh in 1829, Drummond emigrated to Canada sometime in the 1850s. In 1857 he married Helen Redpath and quickly rose up the ranks of his brother-in-law Peter Redpath's firm, becoming partner in 1862. Drummond was an active industrialist and businessman, strongly favouring the union of the British North American provinces and a stiff protectionist trade policy.[24] Drummond emerged as a key commercial figure in Canada, serving as president of the Montreal Board of Trade, and, in spite of his party affiliation, he was a Liberal imperialist and member of the Reform Club of London, England.[25] His financial interests included mining development in Nova Scotia (the Drummond Colliery) and the Mexican Light and Power Company. He was also called to the Senate in 1888 as a Conservative, and in that parliamentary chamber he would act as a persuasive spokesman for banking interests.

In the 1880s, Drummond followed his brother-in-law, who was a major shareholder and key director at the Bank of Montreal, into the bank's upper echelons. Drummond served as vice-president between 1887 to 1905 and as president between 1905 and his death in February 1910. During his tenure, he was instrumental in shifting bank policy to favour the Canadian industrialist community, allowing, for example, long-term loans against the collateral of warrants. During the Drummond-Clouston administration, moreover, the Bank also embarked upon a significant expansion that saw the opening of 110 new branches and an increase in staff from 1,000 to about 3,000.[26]

These Bank of Montreal bankers were not only financiers: they were also Montrealers in an age when the city was coming into its own. Bankers from McGill to Strathcona and Mount Stephen to Drummond were at the heart of this remarkable time and left an indelible mark on the social and cultural life of Montreal. They were the protagonists in a Canadian gilded age when Montreal was the epicentre of Canadian wealth and power concentrated in the hands of a small English and Scottish industrial elite. They were members, sometimes founding ones, of the city's most prestigious clubs, including the St James Club and the Mount Royal Club, and voraciously supported the construction of hospitals, the endowment of universities (especially McGill), and the sponsorship of various cultural and social institutions that marked Montreal as Canada's great metropolis.

A brief story of the Mount Royal Club gives a good idea of just how exclusive and perhaps exceptional this Montreal elite really was. The club had been founded in 1899 out of the St James Club. Twenty members of that club had broken away because they felt that St James's membership had become too inclusive and they desired a more selective association.[27] The Mount Royal, which counted George Alexander Drummond, Richard B. Angus, and Donald Alexander Smith among its founders, immediately became the most exclusive club in the city, with membership being restricted to a tight-knit group of industrialists and other socially prominent figures, many of them directly associated with the Bank of Montreal.[28] The exclusivity of the club reflected the isolated nature of the Montreal social elite at the time. This isolation was further reinforced by a high-degree of intermarriage between Montreal's upper classes, which meant that the Bank of Montreal's top leadership was something of a family affair. To give only a few examples: John Torrance's brother-in-law was Alexander Tilloch Galt, finance minister and director of the Bank of Montreal; Sir Vincent Meredith's brother married R.B. Angus's daughter; George Stephen and Donald Alexander Smith were first cousins; and John Redpath's second wife was Jane Drummond, George Alexander Drummond's aunt. Drummond, in turn, married John and Jane Redpath's youngest daughter, Helen, in 1857. There is no question that the Bank of Montreal's senior leadership represented a golden branch of the emerging Canadian colonial establishment.

The Business Strategy of the Bank

Can we attempt to characterize almost half a century of strategy of an institution, let alone a Bank that is responding to changing economic and political conditions? The answer compels us to look at the long-run experience of the Bank, marking continuities and break points. First, let's focus on the continuities.

In the late nineteenth and early twentieth centuries, the Bank's strategy remained remarkably consistent and focused on three main elements: the support of commercial and agricultural interests, especially in the area of trade; the management of government finance both at home and abroad; and the expansion of networks of trade via the capital markets in New York, Chicago, and London.

The Bank's support of commercial and agricultural interests of the country, especially as Canada expanded to include the west beginning in the 1880s, was particularly pronounced during the construction of the Canadian Pacific Railway. Internally, the organizational capacities of the Bank at the head office and in the expanding system of branches were aligned toward the creation of deeper networks and greater flows of capital, whether to and from new regions of the country, or between capital centres such as London and New York.

What also emerges from the Bank strategy in the period was the continuation of its emphasis on stability and conservatism in its growth. This approach was not only an inheritance of the first half-century of the Bank's evolution, it was also imposed by its responsibilities to its shareholders and customers and by virtue of its capacity as the country's principal commercial bank.

The emphasis on stability marked the Bank's operations to the 1860s. Part of the approach was tied to the emergent nature of Canadian-style banking in the wake of the first Bank Act in 1871. That act set out the rules and regulations governing the configuration of banking in Canada. Yet underlying these bedrock requirements for stability was a palpable frustration about the opportunities to capitalize on an elusive prosperity in the post-Confederation era. That elusiveness would last roughly three decades, well into the late 1890s.

The push outward – championing of the transcontinental railroad and the extension of branches in the developing cities and regions beyond the Great Lakes – was an expression of the desire of Montreal capitalists to switch to a higher gear of economic development and opportunity. By the late 1890s, that push would lead the Bank's leadership to pursue new opportunities in Latin America and the Caribbean.

The key to understanding this long-run experience in the life of the Bank of Montreal is the recognition that its executives were not merely on some search for prosperity or greater economic opportunity, though they certainly were. Getting at the heart of the Bank of Montreal experience in this period means looking at the balance between structure and form on the one hand and dynamism on the other. The strategic nexus between order and opportunity lay at the heart of the Bank's story in the post-Confederation era. The demands of an ordered market and an approach demanded by tradition and statute was in tension with the aggressive pursuit of opportunities. Sacrificing order for opportunity was out of the question, but over time the Bank had to come to terms with finding a profitable equilibrium between the responsibilities it had and the greater economic opportunities and profits it sought.

Bank of Montreal managers therefore had to devise a strategy that balanced order and opportunity and maximized the possibilities of both. Exploiting the order and organization side meant capitalizing on the Bank's legacy advantages in the market, especially its size, relationships, and role as the coordinator-in-chief of the entire Canadian banking system. The challenge on the "opportunity" side was twofold. First, the Bank had to be prepared when opportunity would, in fact, materialize. Here, Bank of Montreal managers had a set of powerful advantages rooted in operational excellence that kept developing throughout the period. Second, the Bank's relationship with the Dominion government was an important element in perpetuating its position. The Bank's expertise and competence in national and international finance provided post-Confederation Canada with internal stability and external connections, especially in the absence of a central reserve bank.

Strategy and Change

An important part of strategy focuses on response to contingency. In this respect, the Bank had an established record. One or two stories might suffice to illustrate. The management of the Bank was severely tested in the aftermath of the Panic of 1873 – a contraction that initiated a long period of depression. At the annual meeting of the Grand Trunk Railway in London, England, its president, Richard Potter, offered this "handsome and just compliment" to the Bank: "For the whole of that month there was only one bank in Chicago – a city of 400,000 inhabitants – that was able to give free accommodation to its customers and the public." Potter continued:

> That was a Canadian Bank, our own bank – the Bank of Montreal – worked by Canadian capital and managed by Canadian men; and it is a fact that the whole of the movement of the crops in the west for some three or four weeks was indebted to the skill and the enterprise and the credit and the resources of that Bank. And I think it is something to say for Canada; and while the Americans themselves, in the utmost possible scare, were removing their deposits from their own banks, they were taking them across the road and lodging them in the hands of a Canadian bank, formed of Canadian capital, and worked by Canadian men.[29]

The adeptness of the Bank's management extended, always, to the management of its dividend. The capitalization of $12 million had in the early 1870s been received with some trepidation among observers who feared that the Bank was biting off more than it could chew. Yet those same skeptics observed in 1874 that the management were able, "without resorting to sensational banking," to keep up the dividends at the accustomed rate.[30] This strategy paid off in reputation and confidence. The Canadian banks in New York, for example (especially the Bank of Montreal and the Bank of British North America), had been by the 1870s "for years been quoted at the same rate as those of Brown and Belmont."[31]

The performance of the Bank in the 1880s was, by George Stephen's lights, respectable. Stephen informed the 1885 annual meeting that even E.H. King would have approved in the circumstances. "King once said that the prosperity of the bank was not ephemeral, that it was not dependent upon chance or hazardous profits, and the same is largely true of it today."[32] In fact, while the economy continued to struggle, the Bank went on to post solid results. The following year, 1886, saw the distribution of an 11 per cent dividend payment. Further, the Bank's board of directors decided at a meeting on 13 May to set aside $45,000 for the purpose of staff bonuses.[33] Success was to be rewarded.

What is remarkable in this period is the Bank of Montreal's ability to endure periodic domestic and international crises. The domestic cyclical movements were almost always related to the fortunes of the harvest. The international crises that erupted in the 1890s (Argentinean debt crises, Baring Crisis, and so on) were also a periodic challenge to the finances of the Bank. There were inevitable losses on each front – depreciation of assets, devaluation of securities, and so forth. But, as Donald Smith remarked in 1891, "all the losses and appropriations this year were to a considerable extent of an exceptional character." A dividend of 10 per cent was thus granted, since, he explained, "the earning powers of the Bank" were such that "we need not have any apprehension about it."[34]

Indeed, by the mid-1890s, Donald Smith could boast that, between 1871 and 1893, the Bank had doubled its capitalization to $12 million and doubled its reserve funds to $6 million. "We believe in no time during the last seventy-five years was the Bank of Montreal in a better position in every way for the purposes for which it is intended, that of giving the best dividend possible to shareholders, while properly safeguarding their capital, and promoting the material interests of Canada than it is at this time."[35] This enabled Clouston to announce in 1894 that in some cases "Canadian currency was actually resorted to for the purposes of commerce and the payment of wages in the United States."[36]

A revealing comment of Clouston at the 1894 annual meeting put the Bank's strategy and its connection to the overall management of the finances of the Dominion in perspective. In Canada, it was not a banking crisis or the silver question that endangered the country. Canada was in the possession of a strong currency and banking system. The greatest threat, according to Clouston, was the low cash reserves held by Canadian banks.[37] Banks in New York were mandated to hold 25 per cent in cash as a reserve as a minimum, while Canadian banking regulations allowed individual bank executives to exercise discretion in this matter, "leaving many banks with low cash reserves, making them vulnerable."[38]

Most of the 1890s matched the description offered by General Manager Clouston at the 1892 annual meeting: "The chief characteristics of the year have been dullness and disappointment. After a succession of bad years, it was hoped that the fine harvest, together with remunerative prices ruling for grain, would stimulate trade and relieve the existing depression, but we have experienced as dull, if not duller, year than those preceding."[39] Worse was to come. Clouston reported in 1893: "We have had a banking crisis in Australia of unexampled severity, a money panic in London and a very unsatisfactory condition of affairs in the United States, arising from the vexed Silver question."[40] "In Montreal, also," he continued, "we have verged on troubles in the Stock market, but these came at a period when a little judicious leniency and assistance on the part of financial institutions allayed apprehension and tied the crisis over without difficulty."[41]

By the mid-1890s, the measure of success was not massive progress as much as it was avoiding disasters. Clouston put it as follows: "It should be a source of great satisfaction to Canadians and the business community that Canada has come so well through the ordeal and with so few failures and disasters ... Indeed, it has been a great surprise to me how well we have stood it."[42] He continued: "It is too soon to say that we are out of the woods, but in the United States there seems to be no doubt that the corner has been turned, and as Canada must always be affected in small measure by the condition of affairs in that country, it is reasonable to suppose that here too the depression has spent its force."[43] Clouston's hopes were dashed the next year, "one of the most disappointing in my experience as General Manager of the Bank of Montreal."[44] Geopolitical events intervened to upset the best-laid plans, particularly a short, sharp, and bitter boundary dispute between the United States and the United Kingdom involving Venezuela and British Guyana that nearly boiled over into military confrontation.

The resulting massive and sudden withdrawals of capital from US money markets and the selling of US securities produced a panic on various stock exchanges in the North Atlantic world, as well as skyrocketing rates for liquid capital. An exasperated Clouston reported in 1897 that "each succeeding year seems to increase the difficulty of maintaining our profits, and when in addition we are obliged to provide for shrinkage in values naturally resulting from the prolonged depression in business, it is almost a matter of surprise that we are able to appear before you with so good a statement at present."[45]

A Booming Economy

By the turn of the century, the national economy had taken a positive turn. As early as 1898, recovery in the United States led to increased commodity prices, and General Manager Edward Clouston reported the following year that it was "difficult to estimate the great boon the enhanced value of grain has been," stimulating trade in all directions. "There is hardly a branch of trade that is not prospering. The farmers are receiving good prices for their products, the Governments show increased revenues, the railways increased traffic, stocks of all sorts have appreciated in value, while the future wealth which our mining and forest industries are expected to realize for this country is beyond computation."[46] Clouston concluded that in England, the United States, and on the continent "manufactories are taxed to the utmost capacity to meet the demands of commerce."[47]

By 1905, production in the west was growing apace, and, as Clouston reported to the Bank's annual meeting that year, "the railways were prospering, the second transcontinental line is on the eve of construction ... and in the progress of material developments, there is increasing belief that this country has entered upon an era of great and enduring prosperity."[48] Even in a period of temporary downturn after the banking panic of 1907, the Canadian economy endured the headwinds without much sign of a slowdown.

The tide had turned so decisively in Canada that by 1908 the Bank could report that Canada and the Bank of Montreal could "look to the future with renewed hope and satisfaction, and if people "continued the conservative policy which is at present animating their conduct of business, we will emerge stronger and better in every way."[49] Prosperity was still robust on the eve of the Great War. President Meredith remarked in 1913 that the "commercial condition of Canada is fundamentally sound. Business as a whole, as I have said, continues good. Our vast natural resources have scarcely been scratched. Immigration is large, railway construction active, new territory and new resources of wealth are being steadily opened, the confidence of British and foreign capitalists in our country is unabated. A temporary halt can only refresh Canada for yet greater achievements."[50] General Manager Sir Frederick Williams-Taylor informed shareholders in 1914 that this period was the most trying time in the Bank's ninety-seven-year history, but that the Bank's "conservatism" ensured that it was prepared to weather the storm.[51]

Table 6.2 | Capital-stock increases, 1872–1918

Year	Capital Stock Increase	Total Capital Stock
1872	$2,000,000	$8,000,000
1873	$4,000,000	$12,000,000
1903	$2,000,000	$14,000,000
1911	$1,600,000	$15,600,000*
1918	$4,000,000	$20,000,000

* There was a further increase of $400,000 at some point between September 1911 and June 1912.

Indeed, by 1916, the Bank's prospects seldom seemed brighter, with $60 million in new total deposits – $102 million greater than in 1914.[52]

Performance

The strategy that emerged from this balancing act between order and opportunity produced a Bank that was extraordinarily effective in maximizing its performance across both adversity and good times. The organization was therefore able to weather the languid decades of low growth of much of the 1870s to the 1890s, build a strong organization, extend and deepen its networks, and execute its responsibilities to the institutions, customers, and shareholders it answered to. The numbers tell the story. (See tables 6.2 and 6.3.)

The difficult times lasted, with some exceptions, from 1874 to 1899. The Bank's assets grew, on average, at about 3 per cent. Assets in 1871 were $29.1 million; by 1899, they had increased, modestly, to $71.5 million. What the "average" approach does not show are the frequent reductions in assets, sometimes as much as 11 per cent – an indication of just how difficult some years were. By the end of the century, the Bank's strategic patience was on the verge of paying off. A series of economic opportunities and upturns in the North Atlantic economy by 1899 were offering hope. Between 1899 and 1918, the Bank registered a 12 per cent growth in assets – to $558.41 million. (See figure 6.1.)

The Bank's long-run performance in this period was determined by its unwavering pursuit of a Stability Strategy that emphasized the accumulation of large reserves and the payout of consistent dividends. In the 1870s the Bank declared dividends amounting together to 8 per cent for the half-year, while the Bank of Toronto routinely registered 6 per cent and the other banks 4 per cent.[53] The issue with the Bank of Montreal, however, was that by 1875, for example, if the dividend had been lowered to 6 per cent – which would have

Table 6.3 | Dividend payments, 1870–1918

Year	Dividend (%)	Bonus (%)	Recurrence	Total (%)	Dividend Payout	Total Dividend Payout (including bonus if applicable)
1871	6	2	semi–annually	16	12/70: $480,000.00 06/71: $480,000.00	$960,000.00
1872	6	2	semi–annually	16	12/71: $480,000.00 06/72: $535,000.00	$1,015,800.00
1873	6	2	semi–annually	16	12/72: $630,300.00 06/73: $813,259.93	$1,443,559.93
1874	6	2	semi–annually	16	12/73: $936,402.55 06/74: $952,384.71	$1,888,787.26
1875	7	n/a	semi–annually	14	12/74: $836,437.46 06/75: $836,793.00	$1,673,230.45
1876	7	n/a	semi–annually	14	12/75: $837,808.00 06/76: $838,233.58	$1,676,131.58
1877	Variable Payment ("Varied")	n/a	semi–annually	13	12/76: $838,538.21 (7%)* 06/77: $719,574.15 (6%)*	$1,558,157.35
1878	6	n/a	semi–annually	12	12/77: $719,904.00 06/28: $719,904.00	$1,439,808.00
1879	5	n/a	semi–annually	10	12/78: $599,920.00 06/79: $599,960.00	$1,199,880.00
1880	Varied	n/a	semi–annually	9	12/79: $599,960.00 (5%)* 06/80: $479,968.00 (4%)*	$1,079,928.00
1881	4	2	semi–annually bonus: annually	10	12/80: $479,968.00 06/81: $479,968.00 Bonus 06/81: $239,984.00	$1,199,920.00
1882	Varied	1	semi–annually bonus: annually	10	12/81: $479,968.00 (4%)* Bonus 12/81: $119,992.00 (1%) 06/82: $599,960.00 (5%)*	$1,199,920.00
1883	5	n/a	semi–annually	10	12/82: $600,000.00 06/83: $600,000.00	$1,200,000.00
1884	5	n/a	semi–annually	10	12/83: $600,000.00 06/84: $600,000.00	$1,200,000.00
1885	5	1	semi–annually bonus: annually	11	12/84: $600,000.00 06/85: $600,000.00 Bonus 06/85: $120,000.00	$1,320,500.00
1886	Incomplete AR					

Table 6.3 | *continued*

Year	Dividend (%)	Bonus (%)	Recurrence	Total (%)	Dividend Payout	Total Dividend Payout (including bonus if applicable)
1887	5	2	semi–annually bonus: annually	12	12/86: $600,000.00 06/87: $600,000.00 Bonus 06/87: $240,000.00	$1,440,000.00
1888	5	n/a	semi–annually	10	12/87: $600,000.00 06/88: $600,000.00	$1,200,000.00
1889	5	n/a	semi–annually	10	12/88: $600,000.00 06/89: $600,000.00	$1,200,000.00
1890	5	n/a	semi–annually	10	12/89: $600,000.00 06/90: $600,000.00	$1,200,000.00
1891	5	n/a	semi–annually	10	12/90: $600,000.00 06/91: $600,000.00	$1,200,000.00
1892	5	n/a	semi–annually	10	12/91: $600,000.00 06/92: $600,000.00	$1,200,000.00
1893	5	n/a	semi–annually	10	12/92: $600,000.00 06/93: $600,000.00	$1,200,000.00
1894	5	n/a	semi–annually	10	12/93: $600,000.00 06/94: $600,000.00	$1,200,000.00
1895	5	n/a	semi–annually	10	12/94: $600,000.00 06/95: $600,000.00	$1,200,000.00
1896	5	n/a	semi–annually	10	12/95: $600,000.00 06/96: $600,000.00	$1,200,000.00
1897	5	n/a	semi–annually	10	12/96: $600,000.00 06/97: $600,000.00	$1,200,000.00
1898	5	n/a	semi–annually	10	12/97: $600,000.00 06/98: $600,000.00	$1,200,000.00
1899	5	n/a	semi–annually	10	12/98: $600,000.00 06/99: $600,000.00	$1,200,000.00
1900	5	n/a	semi–annually	10	12/99: $600,000.00 06/00: $600,000.00	$1,200,000.00
1901	5	n/a	semi–annually	10	12/00: $600,000.00 06/01: $600,000.00	$1,200,000.00
1902	5	n/a	semi–annually	10	12/01: $600,000.00 06/02: $600,000.00	$1,200,000.00
1903	5	n/a	semi–annually	10	12/02: $600,000.00 06/03: $620,000.00	$1,220,000.00
1904	5	n/a	semi–annually	10	12/03: $700,000.00 06/04: $700,000.00	$1,400,000.00
1905	5	n/a	semi–annually	10	12/04: $700,000.00 06/05: $720,000.00	$1,420,000.00

/continued

Table 6.3 | *continued*

Year	Dividend (%)	Bonus (%)	Recurrence	Total (%)	Dividend Payout	Total Dividend Payout (including bonus if applicable)
1906	2.5	n/a	quarterly	10	03/06: $360,000.00 06/06: $360,000.00 09/06: $360,000.00 12/06: $360,000.00	$1,440,000.00
1907	2.5	n/a	quarterly	10	03/07: $360,000.00 06/07: $360,000.00 09/07: $360,000.00 12/07: $360,000.00	$1,440,000.00
1908	2.5	n/a	quarterly	10	03/08: $360,000.00 06/08: $360,000.00 09/08: $360,000.00 12/08: $360,000.00	$1,440,000.00
1909	2.5	n/a	quarterly	10	03/09: $360,000.00 06/09: $360,000.00 09/09: $360,000.00 12/09: $360,000.00	$1,440,000.00
1910	2.5	n/a	quarterly	10	03/10: $360,000.00 06/10: $360,000.00 09/10: $360,000.00 12/10: $360,000.00	$1,440,000.00
1911	2.5	n/a	quarterly	10	03/11: $360,000.00 06/11: $360,000.00 09/11: $360,000.00 12/11: $360,000.00	$1,440,000.00
1912	2.5	1	quarterly bonus: semi–annually	12	03/12: $385,798.70 06/12: $400,000.00 Bonus 06/12: $160,000.00 09/12: $388,302.98 12/12: $400,000.00 Bonus 12/12: $160,000.00	$1,894,101.68
1913	2.5	1	quarterly bonus: semi–annually	12	03/13: $400,000.00 06/13: $400,000.00 Bonus 06/13: $160,000.00 09/13: $400,000.00 12/13: $400,000.00 Bonus 12/13: $160,000.00	$1,920,000.00
1914	2.5	1	quarterly bonus: semi–annually	12	03/14: $400,000.00 06/14: $400,000.00 Bonus 06/14: $160,000.00	$1,920,000.00

Table 6.3 | *continued*

Year	Dividend (%)	Bonus (%)	Recurrence	Total (%)	Dividend Payout	Total Dividend Payout (including bonus if applicable)
1914/*continued*					09/14: $400,000.00 12/14: $400,000.00 Bonus 12/14: $160,000.00	
1915	2.5	1	quarterly bonus: semi–annually	12	03/15: $400,000.00 06/15: $400,000.00 Bonus 06/15: $160,000.00 09/15: $400,000.00 12/15: $400,000.00 Bonus 12/15: $160,000.00	$1,920,000.00
1916	2.5	1	quarterly bonus: semi–annually	12	03/16: $400,000.00 06/16: $400,000.00 Bonus 06/16: $160,000.00 09/16: $400,000.00 12/16: $400,000.00 Bonus 12/16: $160,000.00	$1,920,000.00
1917	2.5	1	quarterly bonus: semi–annually	12	03/17: $400,000.00 06/17: $400,000.00 Bonus 06/17: $160,000.00 09/17: $400,000.00 12/17: $400,000.00 Bonus 12/17: $160,000.00	$1,920,000.00
1918	2.5	1	quarterly bonus: semi–annually	12	03/18: $400,000.00 06/18: $400,000.00 Bonus 06/18: $160,000.00 09/18: $400,000.00 12/18: $400,000.00 Bonus 12/18: $160,000.00	$1,920,000.00

been an entirely justifiable action considering the deepening economic contraction – the stock market would have taken a serious hit.[54] The number of shareholders varied from year to year, of course, but the 1882 annual report suggested that 2,012 shareholders held the stock. Given the fact that Bank of Montreal shares were among the few desirable stocks available, the wide shareholding should not surprise.[55]

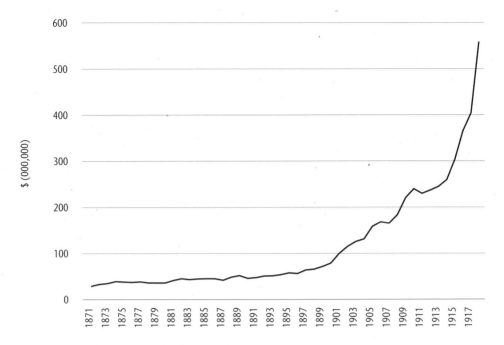

Figure 6.1 | Assets, Bank of Montreal, 1871–1918

Notes: 1871–1903: Assets measured at the end of April, discussed at annual meeting in June. 1904–1918: Assets measured at the end of October, discussed at annual meeting in December.

Source: Bank of Montreal Annual Reports, 1871–1918.

The twin policies relating to reserves and dividends came under periodic pressure from shareholders to decrease the former and increase the latter. As consistently, however, the Bank's leadership would typically resist such calls, with E.H. King suggesting that an inflated dividend might be "for the sake of momentary applause."[56] Toward the 1890s, the Bank of Montreal moved toward a more aggressive posture in its investment strategy. Its management was the first to complete a transcontinental system of branches to exploit the opening of the Canadian west. Similar to other Canadian banks at the time, it then turned to the financing of ventures of an industrial or commercial nature, especially outside of Canada.[57]

Capitalization

The capitalization of the Bank usually attracted a great deal of discussion at annual meetings. Here again, the voices against increased capitalization (this time to $12 million) were motivated by fiscal conservatism. One intervenor at the annual meeting in 1872 suggested that the Bank's past success "had been attributable in a great measure to the power of concentrating their funds at particular points where such concentration was desirable [e.g., New York and London]."[58] The routine increases in capitalization during the King era were later viewed with some anxiety as the North American economy descended into a long depression. The anxiety was borne of the dwindling possibilities to deploy capital in one quarter or another. "Montreal, Chicago, New York, and London," one contemporary observer noted, "afforded an ample choice of profitable business, while the practical monopoly of Government business then enjoyed by the Bank added immensely to its money-making power."[59] The Bank of Montreal effect in this instance was to "excite emulation and imitation" on the part of other, weaker banks which enlarged their capital as well. When the time came for a great contraction of loans, the results for businesses were noticeable. The easy-money period of Canadian banking, in hindsight, was seen as "little better than sowing thistles in a wheat field."[60] "And the worst of it is that a bad banker," one observer concluded, "like a bad farmer, not only injures himself but does a vast amount of mischief to his neighbours and to the mercantile community."[61]

When George Stephen was elected president of the Bank in March 1876, things continued to worsen. As Stephen commented on the economic circumstances in 1876: "Our commercial community is suffering in sympathy with the unprosperous condition of affairs in other countries more especially in the United States, and until an improvement is manifested there, we cannot expect a healthy demand for our lumber and other products."[62] Matters deteriorated to the end of the 1870s to the extent that even a temporary upswing in 1879 was viewed as "too uncertain to warrant the expectation of an early recovery."[63] Naturally, dividends were slashed and the rest fund was used to "meet the deficiency caused by the general depreciation of assets."[64] In fact, of the Bank's profits of $1.7 million, $1.1 million had to be diverted to bad or doubtful debts, or to allow for the depreciation of Bank assets.[65] To add insult to injury, in October 1879 the Bank had to set aside another $250,000 to meet additional obligations.

By 1880, Canada's economic situation had not improved markedly, and the Bank of Montreal was in much the same position. That year, its dividend was only 9 per cent. Even in 1881, C.F. Smithers summed up the year by quipping at the annual meeting that "there is no great deal to be said this year, [and] it is a generally good thing if there is not very much to be said."[66] Smithers vigorously pursued a policy of a steady of contraction of loans to get the books in proper order.[67]

It seemed, however, that the legacy of E.H. King would follow his successors in ways that must have been frustrating to contemporary management. "No one understands better than I do," Smithers remarked in 1884, "the great ability and success of Mr. King as a banker. He was generally considered a financial genius, and I am as ready as anyone to admit his claim to the distinction." He protested, however, that King "never paid a dividend upon twelve million dollars; he left before the increased capital was fully paid up, the average for that year being a little over $9 million." Smithers concluded that it was no mean task to employ the large amount of funds controlled by the Bank of Montreal, especially in Canada, "where the conditions are wholly different from what they are in London, or even New York."[68] The Bank's strong performance in spite of a struggling post-Confederation economy was a tribute, in management's eyes, to the bank's careful strategy. Again, the shade of King exerted itself in 1885, with Sir George Stephen quoting King's remark that "the prosperity of the bank was not ephemeral ... not dependent upon change or hazardous profits, and the same is true of it today."[69]

That confidence would be put to the test in subsequent years, as the North Atlantic economies failed to overcome their chronic underperformance. President Donald Smith captured the up-and-down mood of the Bank's leadership in his report to the shareholders in 1889: "At this time the prospects of an abundant harvest are excellent ... but you will recollect that at this time last year everything also looked very bright, but, unfortunately ... harvests both in the old provinces and the Northwest were a disappointment to all of us, and consequently the earning power of the Bank was curtailed because the capabilities of borrowing were not the same for the community as they would have been had the harvest as was hoped for."[70] Poor harvests would continue to plague the profitability of the Bank, even in otherwise good years. In 1889 bad and doubtful debts arising out of indifferent harvests and depressed prices were enough to decrease profits from the previous year.[71]

This languishing in the economic doldrums reinforced the idea in the late 1880s that there was great opportunity to be had in the west and on the Pacific Coast. Those areas were "small comparatively at the moment," President Smith suggested, but "growing so fast that we may expect in a very short time that they will be considerable factors towards enabling the Bank to increase its profits ... Calgary is the centre of ranching country. Vancouver, only three years old and now a city of some 10,000 inhabitants, and being the terminus of the Canadian system of railways on the Pacific Coast, cannot fail to become a place of very considerable importance in the immediate future, and we wish to be ready for whatever may offer itself to the Bank in both of these places."[72]

Organizational Change over Time

Leaders require effective organizations to execute strategy effectively. After Confederation, centralized control was an essential element in the function of banking, allowing the extension of authority and decision-making from city to hinterland, especially over a transcontinental expanse.

Two elements are illustrative of the kind of centralization that took place in this period. One is a relatively obscure artefact called the "Character Book"; the other is the system of branch development. The first is a simple book, while the second is an entire branch system. The symmetry is fitting, since the evolution of banking embraced the micro and the macro, so to speak.

The Character Book

The Character Book was created by the Bank of Montreal in 1885 and supplied to each agency of the Bank. The book contained rules and regulations by which the Bank of Montreal conducted its business and provided a clear example of the head office (centre) exerting a degree of control over the branches (periphery). Thus, although the archival name for this document is "Character Book," the document was officially, and more aptly, titled "General Regulations for Officers."

The book provided a standardized way for every conceivable aspect of business within the bank to be conducted, from the duration of book loans in branch libraries to the appropriate margins in office communications and memos. The attached appendix, moreover, included templates of how certain things should be recorded, thus ensuring a organized method that could easily be monitored and controlled and from the centre.

The Character Book also contained system of letters and numbers by which the Bank organized its customers into different categories. The letters and numbers were assigned based on "all reliable information regarding the standing and character of customers, from whatever source obtained, supplemented by the Agent's private opinion."[73] Using a combination of these letters and numbers, the Bank branches could communicate complex information about customers quickly and efficiently in an age when communication over long distances was slow and often cumbersome. Each branch recorded and kept this information in a subset of the Character Book, the so-called Reference Book, which contained an assessment of client's creditworthiness, character, assets, and any information that might be considered relevant. Any changes were immediately communicated to headquarters and other branches using this shorthand. Every week the agencies were supplied with a "change list" and the head agent would be responsible for seeing to it that "all changes [were] made in the Reference Book as soon as received."[74] The Bank furthermore stressed that all decisions regarding customers should be based on the information contained in the Reference Book: "Agents are cautioned against being misled by any

Table 6.4 | "Character Book" codes for estimated net worth and creditworthiness of customers

1	Less than $1,000	21	Perfectly good for engagements
2	1,000 to 2,000	22	Rich and out of business
3	2,000 to 3,000	23	Means large
4	3,000 to 4,000	24	Means sufficient for business
5	4,000 to 5,000	25	Means considerable
6	5,000 to 6,000	26	Good for small engagements
7	6,000 to 8,000	27	Means moderate
8	8,000 to 10,000	28	Means not known
9	10,000 to 20,000	29	Means small
10	20,000 to 30,000	30	Means not sufficient for business
11	30,000 to 40,000	31	Has no means
12	40,000 to 60,000		
13	60,000 to 80,000	*Credit Ratings*	
14	80,000 to 100,000	A	Credit undoubted
15	100,000 to 200,000	E	Credit high
16	200,000 to 300,000	I	Credit good
17	300,000 to 500,000	O	Credit fair
18	500,000 to 750,000	U	Very moderate credit
19	750,000 to 1,000,000	W	Very poor credit
20	Over 1,000,000	Y	No credit

Source: BMOA, Character Book.

statements of customers' affairs, verbal or written, supplied by themselves, or by outside reports or opinions regarding them. No information of any kind whatsoever coming to the Agent from outside sources, with regard to the standing of parties is equal to the evidence arising from actual transactions by or with those parties." (See tables 6.4 and 6.5.)

The imposition of this system to communicate complex information across branches and to head office provided the Bank with a degree of control it did not have before. James C. Scott explains in *Seeing like a State* that "the pre-modern state was, in many crucial respects, partially blind; it knew precious little about its subjects, their wealth, the landholdings and yields, their location, their very identity."[75] In some ways, the Bank of Montreal in the nineteenth century faced very much the same problem. It, too, lacked a comprehensive overview of its customers and its business, and this problem grew larger as the Bank extended over an ever-increasing geographical territory. The Character Book allowed the Bank to interpret locally complex information according to a common standard necessary for a synoptic view from the centre.

Table 6.5 | "Character Book" general characteristics of customers

Points of Strength		Points of Weakness	
I – Business Extent and Profitableness			
B	Business large	Bx	Business small
C	Business small	Cx	Business risky
D	Business profitable	Dx	Business not very profitable
F	Liabilities small	Fx	Liabilities too large
II – Business Ability and Management			
G	Good business ability	Gx	Not much ability
H	Has good judgment	Hx	Sanguine and visionary
J	Generally successful in his undertakings	Jx	Has not hitherto been successful
K	Business well managed	Kx	Business not very well managed
L	Conservative in management	Lx	Inclined to spread out too much
M	Cautions in incurring liabilities, and careful of his name	Mx	Endorses too freely, and not sufficiently careful of his name
N	Careful in giving credit	Nx	Giving credit too freely
P	Buys for cash	Px	Takes all the credit he can get
Q	Meets engagements promptly	Qx	Not punctual with payments
III – Character and Habits			
R	Considered honest and upright	Rx	Not over–scrupulous
S	Industrious and attentive to business	Sx	Lacks energy
T	Economical and saving	Tx	Extravagant tastes and habits
V	Habits correct	Vx	Habits irregular
Z	Property unencumbered	Zx	Property encumbered

Source: BMOA, Character Book.

Branches and Systems

The Bank of Montreal's branch system is the second element of organization that marks the period. The Bank's expanding branch system was far more significant than its geographical reach. In fact, it could be considered a foundational component in the creation of a transcontinental Canadian economy. For the Bank itself, the branch system was not just an extension of financial facilities, but an information network that allowed it to deepen its understanding of local and regional trends. It was also a key driver in increasing the Bank of Montreal's business, both commercial and private.

The development of the branch system had two phases. The first phase, running from 1870 to about 1900, can be seen as a period of slow growth.

Predictably, between 1900 and 1918, there is a remarkable expansion. This two-speed expansion mirrors the larger economic development of Canada, whose economy suffered from slow growth for the first three decades following Confederation.

The Bank and Its Branches in Broader Context

The Canadian branch-banking system, as its name implies, is a system of banks consisting of branches that deal directly with the public. The head office, in turn, functions as a unit of administrative oversight that does not generally deal directly with the public.

The Canadian branch-banking system was based on a British model.[76] It had its roots in Scotland, and it was the prominent Anglo-Canadian businessman Alexander Tilloch Galt who, as finance minister in 1860, proposed that the Canadian banking system should expand across the country "through the extension of branch networks of the existing banks rather than through the creation of new banks."[77] This approach was in sharp contrast with that of the United States, which adopted a banking system based on "unit banks," established under federal or state jurisdiction. The American system famously veered away from branch banking after the National Banking Act of 1864. Individual states passed banking statutes that controlled banks founded with state charters.[78] The situation is aptly summarized by one historian: "The United States had a large number of small banks, numerous bank failures, and many statutory restrictions on intrastate and interstate banking."[79] In the Canadian system, banks were greater in size but fewer in number.

The Canadian branch-banking system was codified in law with the 1871 Bank Act and was not substantially changed thereafter. At that time, the Bank of Montreal controlled 30 per cent of all bank assets in Canada.[80] The structure of Canadian banking gave the Bank of Montreal the resources and degree of safety and stability that could not be matched by small, regional unit banks typical of the United States banking system. Because their branches also covered a much greater territory, Canadian banks generally obtained a diverse asset portfolio and provided loans to economically diverse commercial ventures and industries, again providing increased stability. Historians of banking have pointed to these two factors – large resources and a wide diversification of loans and assets – as key in the safety of the Canadian banking system. That meant Canadian banks were larger, more diversified, and better able to diversify risk in their asset portfolios. The branch system functioned as a great diversifier as well as an efficient allocator of capital across what would become a transcontinental nation.[81] One snapshot from the Panic of

1893 will illustrate the point. In the United States, over six hundred banks suspended payment and shut their doors as a result of the economic downturn. Many never reopened. A Manitoba-based bank was the lone casualty on the Canadian side.[82]

Extending Canada

Two important facts stand out about the Bank of Montreal's branch system. The first is that the Bank's branches acted in their communities as a nationalizing institution. Having a Bank of Montreal branch was not only a sign of status for a town, city, or region: it tied communities to the larger project of the nation. As late as 1895, the Bank of Montreal was the only Canadian bank with a truly national, transcontinental system of branches. Its nearest rival, the Canadian Bank of Commerce, by contrast, was almost exclusively based in Ontario.[83]

The significance of the Bank of Montreal branch network – and of the Bank as a national institution – was recognized virtually from the moment of Confederation. The expansion of the bank-branch system quite simply helped to lay the foundations of nationhood across a very big country with very little capital. Thus, the new Dominion government asked the Bank to open branches in Halifax and Saint John "to act in conjunction with customs offices to be opened in those cities."[84] The expansion of branches was not only about capital allocation, but about the extension of governmental and systemic authority across the land, for both public and private ends. For example, by the time of the First World War, banks were used as outlets for the sale of War Bonds, since, extending as they did to the farthest corners of the country, they were an easy means by which the government could reach people quickly and efficiently.

Expansion of the Branch Network

As table 6.6 demonstrates, the period 1870–1918 saw a great expansion of the branch network of Canadian banks. Although the system demonstrated some growth from 1870 to 1900, this was nothing compared to the explosive growth in the first two decades of the twentieth century. Across Canada, the number of Canadian bank branches "between 1890 and 1920 ... grew from 426 to 4,676."[85] The Bank of Montreal alone acquired eighty-nine branches from 1900 to 1908.[86]

The Bank of Montreal expanded its network in two main ways: through the establishment of new branches, and through mergers with and acquisitions of existing banks that had established branch systems of their own.

Table 6.6 | Bank of Montreal domestic branches

Year	Number of Branches
1886	29
1895	38
1900	52
1908	142
1912	167*
1917	182
1920	319
1926	617

* This includes international branches.

Source: Data from Merrill Dennison, Vol. 2, pgs. 265, 272, 282, 341, 352–53. Data for 1912 from Kate Boyer, "'Miss Remington' Goes to Work: Gender, Space, and Technology at the Dawn of the Information Age," in *Professional Geographer* 56, no. 2 (May 2004): 201–12 at 210.

Expansion meant the extension of banking facilities across frontier territory, especially in the west. As Merrill Denison notes, "banking facilities played an important role in the orderly settlement of the Canadian west and the conservatively dressed bank manager with his black satchel was as much of an image as was the sheriff with his six-shooter south of the border."[87] The strategy was to focus on strategic branches in the key centres, and to avoid to the greatest extent possible the boom-and-bust towns that periodically popped up on the landscape.[88]

The Bank of Montreal's approach to branching was perfectly consistent with its broader conservative and capital-conscious approach to banking affairs. In the first years of the twentieth century, developments in the Canadian economy pushed banks in the Maritimes to seek mergers and amalgamations with their larger counterparts in central Canada. This wave of mergers and acquisitions resulted in a substantial reduction of banks in Canada – from fifty-one in the late nineteenth century to twenty-two in 1914.[89]

It was the 1901 revision of the Bank Act that gave rise to this cascade of mergers. The 1901 act relaxed regulations about bank mergers, and the Bank of Montreal subsequently acquired the Exchange Bank of Yarmouth in 1903, the People's Bank of Halifax in 1905, and the People's Bank of New Brunswick in 1907.[90] It also took over the branches of the troubled Ontario Bank in 1906. As a result of this period of mergers and acquisitions and a general expansion west and east, the Bank of Montreal had 167 offices nation-wide in 1912, "as well as branches in Great Britain, the United States, and Mexico, and affiliate branches in major cities in Asia, Europe, Australia, New Zealand, Argentina, Bolivia, Brazil, Chile, Peru, and British Guiana."[91]

After the First World War, the Bank of Montreal would acquire even more branches through mergers, increasing its number of branches from 182 in 1917 to 319 in 1920. Seventy-nine of these were as a result of the acquisition of the Bank of British North America.[92] In 1926, after the acquisition of the Merchants Bank, the number of Bank of Montreal branches rose to 617.[93]

Expanding Business

The expansion of branches was more than just a geographical endeavour. In addition to their importance in creating a transcontinental economy, the new bank branches brought the Bank of Montreal's financial expertise to all corners of the country. On the reverse side, the expansion of branches across the country gave the Bank a deep knowledge of local and regional conditions and diversified both its loans and its asset portfolio. It also was a valuable tool in forging new business relations. In fact, long-time General Manager E.S. Clouston noted that many new branches were unprofitable for the first few years, but that "the deciding factor in opening an office in a manufacturing district was ... the desire to protect head-office business, which might otherwise be tempted away by competing banks offering local amenities merely as a convenience to the manufacturer."[94] Branching was not limited to Canada; the Bank of Montreal expanded to wherever money was to be made. The Bank opened an office in New York less than a decade after its founding, and it crossed the Atlantic to open a branch in London by 1870.[95] These branches were intended to facilitate foreign business as well as to invest the funds of foreign investors.[96]

The Far-reaching Consequences of Branch Banking

The proliferation of branches did more than just geographically expand the Bank: in some ways, it changed its very nature. Branches brought Montreal to cities, towns, and provinces far afield from the head office. In so doing, they created a remarkable Canadian financial and intelligence network. The extension and proliferation of branches, moreover, imposed a more distributed leadership model within the Bank. Managers were expected to follow rules of engagement, but time and distance generated possibilities for the exertion of local leadership.

What is more, the expansion of branches slowly changed the nature of Bank of Montreal banking itself. In the early years, the Bank of Montreal had been a commercial bank first and foremost: it invested in businesses, industry, and government. As it acquired new branches across the country, it increasingly turned to private banking. This movement was a precursor to the 1930s and 1940s, when the commercial orientation of the Bank of Montreal changed to accommodate a more universal banking approach.

Branching beyond Banking

The Bank of Montreal's branch system represented more than just the extension of the Bank's financial network; its branches became the center of social life in many small communities through social clubs, sports programs, dances, and other trappings of the corporate associational life so typical of this period in large institutions. Perhaps a most shining example of the Bank of Montreal branches serving a role well beyond that of a "traditional" financial institution in this period comes, not from one of the Bank's Canadian branches, but rather its London, England, branch at Waterloo Place during the First World War. This branch became the hub of Canadian life overseas between 1914 and 1918. While the branch was, of course, a place for customers to deposit money and conduct a wide variety of financial transactions, it was also a very popular social spot for the soldiers serving in the Canadian Expeditionary Force (CEF). Additionally, the branch was a meeting ground for families who had accompanied Canadian soldiers, as well as for those families of enlisted Bank employees already living in London. Eager for news about the fates and whereabouts of their husbands, fathers, and sons serving on the front, family members flocked to the Bank's London branches for information, support, and consolation.

A Transforming Organization

The Bank of Montreal in this period confronted a varying set of challenges with a high grade of leadership, organization, and strategy that was, generally speaking, adaptive to circumstances and effective in ensuring that opportunities could be exploited when they presented themselves. The story of the Bank in this period can be told in four charts. The first chart shows the notes in circulation; the second, the profits of the Bank over time, to 1918; the third, the bank's steady share price; and the fourth, the dividend total payments of the Bank in the period to 1918. (See figures 6.2, 6.3, 6.4, and 6.5.)

These charts demonstrate how the Bank had to deal with two very different eras. In each, we see the strategic patience required by the Bank between the 1870s and about 1900. After 1900, everything changes.

How the Bank arrived there is the focus of the next two chapters.

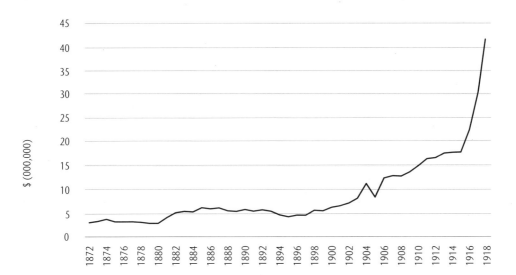

Figure 6.2 | Notes in circulation, Bank of Montreal, 1871–1918

Notes: 1872–1903: Notes in circulation measured at the end of April, discussed at annual meeting in June (except in 1886, 1887, and 1891, which used measurements from October, as April was unavailable). 1904–1918: Notes in circulation measured at the end of October, discussed at annual meeting in December.

Source: Bank of Montreal Annual Reports, 1872–1918.

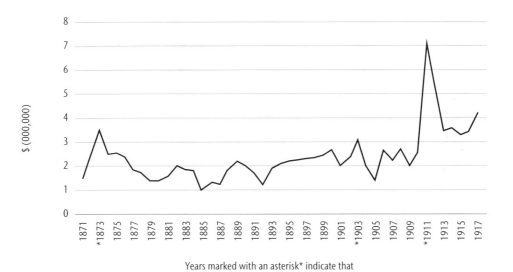

Years marked with an asterisk* indicate that
profits were artificially inflated by issuing new stock

Figure 6.3 | Profits, Bank of Montreal, 1871–1918

Notes: 1871–1903: Profits measured at the end of April, discussed at annual meeting in June. 1904–1918: Profits measured at the end of October, discussed at annual meeting in December.

Source: Bank of Montreal Annual Reports, 1870–1918.

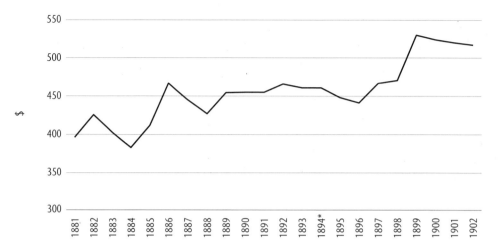

Figure 6.4 | Share price, Bank of Montreal, 1881–1902

Note: All years are recorded in April, except for 1886, 1887, 1891, 1892, 1895, 1899, and 1901, which use data record in October, as April was unavailable.

*No data available for 1894

Source: Bank of Montreal Annual Reports, 1881–1902.

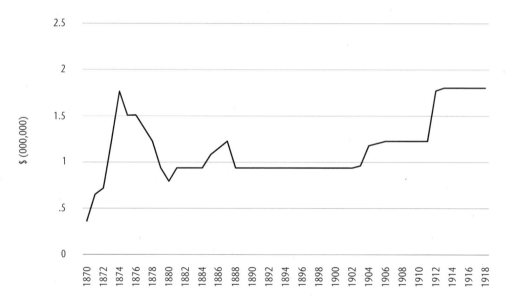

Figure 6.5 | Total dividend payments, Bank of Montreal, 1870–1918

Source: Bank of Montreal Annual Reports, 1870–1918.

CHAPTER SEVEN

Bankers and Nation Builders

This chapter examines the first of three major interrelated themes that came to define the Bank of Montreal experience in Canada's post-Confederation era: its relationship with Canada's rise to nationhood. As we have seen in previous chapters, the Canadian colonies seemed to live in a perpetual state of capital scarcity, extremely prone to the whiplash effects of the economic cycle. Its staples-based economy, focused on wheat and timber, was vulnerable to the terms of trade and the vagaries of geopolitics. The colonies – its governments and its public projects as much as British North America's private-sector industries – depended heavily on capital inflows from the New York and London markets. The uneven development of the financial infrastructure of the country put great pressure on the institutions with the networks, capabilities, and experience required to confront this challenging set of circumstances.

That, in a nutshell, is the context out of which the Bank of Montreal emerged as a key player in the economic and financial development of Canada in the late nineteenth and early twentieth centuries. Its close and symbiotic relationship to the development of Canadian national institutions, structures, and infrastructures grew deeper and more intensive over the decades. Canada's young national institutions required exactly the kind of networks of expertise, capital, and connection that the Bank of Montreal had developed over the previous half-century. Of course, other financial intermediaries were gaining ground and were increasingly able to move in similar capital and market circles of the North Atlantic. But the Bank of Montreal's networks, its experience, and its effectiveness conferred on it a prominent and unique role in the development of the young nation.

The close relationship between Montreal bankers and governments of the new Dominion was based on a highly sophisticated sense of mutual self-interest. As government bankers, as virtually de facto central bankers, and as the "men on the spot" representing Canadian municipal, provincial, and federal governments in the money markets of London and New York, Bank of Montreal bankers enjoyed privileged and handsomely profitable access to government business. That business in the late nineteenth century became a key element in the success of the Bank, especially in years of scarce national economic development. In other words, however inflected with altruistic motives their actions may have been, Montreal bankers put their comparative advantages as an institution to work – advantages of scale, scope, reputation, and networks – and reaped the rewards.

Bank of Montreal bankers both sought profits and vigorously exercised their influence and power to create the greatest possible liberty of action for themselves, shorn of close regulatory oversight. To leave the explanation there, however, is to miss the other half of the story. The leadership and workforce of the Bank of Montreal were also deeply vested in the dream of nation: of a prosperous and connected British North America that spanned the continent and could take its place within the Empire and among the nations of the world. Indeed, many of the Bank's officials were key protagonists in translating this vision into reality. Both elements – the advancement of the Bank and the development of the country it helped to build – must always be considered in analyzing this relationship.

Bank of Montreal bankers also understood that they did not only represent Montreal capital, they were ambassadors for Canadian banking. Frequently, they represented the government of Canada directly as its agents. Always and everywhere in the councils of the city of London or the offices of New York City, the reputation of Bank of Montreal leadership both reflected and refracted the overall presence of Canada in the Empire. A few examples will suffice. Sir John Rose, 1st Baronet, a director of the Bank and a member of its London committee, became in 1869 Canada's first diplomatic representative in the United Kingdom. Sir Alexander Galt, not only a director of the Bank but a key player in its strategy and destiny, was the first formal high commissioner for Canada, appointed in 1880. Lord Strathcona was high commissioner from 1896 to 1914, while simultaneously serving as the president of the Bank of Montreal. This is the same man who raised one of the last privately financed regiments in the British Empire, Lord Strathcona's Horse – the Royal Canadians – when he was both high commissioner and Bank president.

The nexus between Canada's national development on the one hand and its first bank on the other, therefore, involved capital, it involved projects, it involved people and communities, and it involved a shared sense of destiny as Canada developed. This chapter focuses on a broad range of developments and occurrences that shed light on the intimacy of the relationship. between bank and nation, between Montreal bankers and Canada itself.

The Banking System and Capital Markets

As we have seen in previous chapters, the Canadian banking system was essentially set into law by 1870–71. Attempts by Bank of Montreal leaders to introduce a system that would divide the banking world into a two-tiered system, with a class of large trade- and mercantile-focused banks with many branches, and a second tier of local banks, were ultimately defeated. The turmoil surrounding the first Bank Act had been a victory for the Toronto financial interests over the Bank of Montreal and its position in the shaping of the financial system. Yet, whatever its faults and missed opportunities (from the Bank of Montreal's perspective, at least), the Bank Act did enshrine a financial system based on oligopoly, branch banking, and stability.[1] The result was that the banking system and currency questions were issues of secondary importance to the politics of the era. As the *Monetary Times* suggested in July 1871, "the restrictions [the Bank Act] imposes materially change the former system but they furnish increased security to the public, and, although the circulation is limited by the Act, a profitable business can still be conducted under its provisions."[2]

The preference given to branch banking and the existence of a few large banks allowed for other advantages as well, including the establishment of branches in small or remote areas that would have been simply unsustainable for smaller banks. As the *Monetary Times* put it, the "necessity laid upon the banks to open branches in the, at present, more remote centers of industrial life, at places which bid fair to afford a good paying business in time, but which temporarily supply few deposits," was one that only large institutions could bear. In towns such as Orillia, Collingwood, and Orangeville, the *Monetary Times* concluded, "had the traders been compelled to wait for a local bank[,] their operations would have long restricted and the district kept without most valuable facilities and stimulus."[3]

The Bank's main importance to the financial system, however, was its contribution to the development of a securities market in Canada and the evolution of brokerages in the city of Montreal.[4] Still, as Ranald Michie notes, the securities market in Canada remained fairly restricted, centred around Montreal until Toronto vied for supremacy in the early part of the twentieth century.[5] As late as 1908, J.H. Dunn remarked that "the market is so narrow that one or two buyers can easily advance the price of securities two or three points on very small sales."[6] He explained that the situation was so under-developed that the "substantial buying or selling would both rapidly exhaust the market and greatly alter the price."[7] "The Bank of Montreal refused to make call loans to Canada, believing that they were not sufficiently liquid in time of crisis."[8] This was contrary to the Bank's policy in the much larger and better-developed New York market.

The industrial organization of the banking sector that was set into place by the 1870–71 legislation was essentially left undisturbed for the remainder of the century, with some minor amendments being introduced during the required decennial revisions of the Bank Act. Some of those amendments provoked consternation (such as the 1890 amendments on capitalization) or interest (the 1901 provisions created the Canadian Bankers Association), but generally speaking, the regulatory regime set in place by 1871 was left to do its work.

Banking on Government

The Bank's role as "government banker" started well before its official debut as Canada's official agent. Indeed, Montreal bankers were the bankers at Confederation; the Bank's control over comparatively large loan portfolios kept it as a central player for government finance. Starting in the 1870s, the Bank ramped up its involvement in the placement of government bonds for both the federal and provincial governments. Continuing its expertise, acquired particularly from the 1860s with the United Provinces, the Bank acted as agents of the Quebec government and the city of Montreal, in conjunction with Morton, Rose and Company, Sir John Rose's firm.[9] On 21 February 1879, for instance, the Bank's board of directors approved a $3-million loan to Quebec.[10]

The Bank's importance to the financial security of the Dominion was constantly in play in the 1890s. On 4 December 1891 the Bank granted the Dominion government a loan in the amount of $2 million.[11] In November 1892 General Manager E.S. Clouston reported to the board from London that his negotiations with Canadian Finance Minister Sir George Foster to acquire the management of the all-important Dominion Government Account in London (from Glyn, Mills, Currie and Company and Baring Bros. and Company) were successful.[12] In 1893 the Bank of Montreal was larger than any of its Canadian competitors and, according to historian Carman Miller, promoted itself as "being the world's third largest bank."[13] As fiscal agent to both the Dominion and provincial governments, the Bank of Montreal exercised immense influence within the London market. The Bank also extended its representation in London to a number of prominent Canadian cities: Montreal (starting in 1911), Calgary (1911), Quebec City (1911), and Regina (1913).

To quantify the Bank's role as banker to the federal government, a closer look at public accounts will be useful. Canada's direct debt rose from $292 million in 1900 to $389 million in 1910. Wartime changed this picture: by 1918, direct debt stood at $2.8 billion and indirect debt at $2.9 billion. To offer further context, the government of Canada's budgets in the 1880s typically hovered around $30–40 million, with some exceptions. The Dominion's ten-figure budget came only in 1907 ($110 million). At the end of our era, 1918, the figure jumped to $696 million. The increasing demands made on public expenditure – and the constant return to the capital market – made Bank of Montreal managers important players in public finance. The trend toward greater public spending and borrowing also meant that the state was acquiring powers and responsibilities that would eventually begin to rebalance the scales between public and private power – with consequences for key relationships such as the government-banker connection.[14]

The relationship of banks, and specifically the Bank of Montreal, to the federal government changed very little over the period. The decennial revisions to the Bank Act were largely inconsequential in terms of the architecture of the banking system.[15] But in 1910 the balance between public and private power shifted away from the banks and toward the federal government. While revising the Bank Act in 1910, Finance Minister W.S. Fielding, unlike his predecessors, declined any advice or assistance from finance-industry experts. As the *Globe* noted, "the Minister of Finance apparently wishes to be able to describe the bill when he brings it before the House as entirely the handiwork of Government, and in excluding the bankers he has at least saved himself from the necessity of listening to a vast amount of gratuitous advice from other quarters."[16] The provisions of the bill included requirements for an outside auditor if shareholders representing at least 5 per cent of a bank were to request it – a mild change, but one in a certain direction.

Canada's "Other" Department of Finance

The role of Dominion banker required the Bank of Montreal to use its professional and administrative capacities and networks in banking and the market as a virtually "other" department of finance, at least when it came to matters of financing of large loans and extension of credit facilities for the government. The Bank had, by the 1910s, developed a first-class set of facilities and deep networks where it mattered – New York and London – to push placement of loans and the maintenance of credit. This became even more

crucial in wartime, when such links and connections were especially important. Advice and analysis regarding stability of the system was an important
element in this relationship. So were placement strategies. One example of
each will illustrate this clearly.

The first example concerns the Newfoundland banking system. The Bank
of Montreal agreed, in the wake of a serious banking crisis in 1894, to offer
a $400,000 loan to the government of the Dominion of Newfoundland. All
Canadian banks had been "invited" into this bleak cash-poor market, but,
after some conferral on the part of the Canadian chartered banks, only the
Bank of Montreal accepted. Thus began a long and complex relationship between the Bank and the Dominion of Newfoundland in matters of finance
and government-capital requirements.

The second example involves strategizing between the Bank of Montreal
and the government of Canada. In May 1915 the Bank's general manager,
Sir Frederick Williams-Taylor, conducted a lengthy correspondence with
Sir Thomas White, the Canadian minister of finance, on the advisability of
floating a $40–50 million loan on the New York, as opposed to the London,
market. The latter was preferred, but the former was likely easier to be obtained. Williams-Taylor's analysis embraced the larger context. "In view of
the fact that so far as we can see London can take care of your requirements," he wrote, "it becomes more of a national question as to whether or
not you should go to the New York market. Your doing so would, I gather,
be quite agreeable to the Imperial Government and would temporarily
relieve London. Also it would not be seriously resented by the London
money market, though it would not be a popular step there."[17] As a veteran
of dealing with capital markets, Williams-Taylor knew the sensitivities of
London lenders. In a period of war, those sensitivities – about London's
position compared to New York, and about the ambiguities of the wartime
economic cycle – may have upset the usual loan placements for the next
time. New York simply offered a better deal, however: there was no taxation on the transaction and a low rate of interest was being offered. For his
part, Minister White was at first reluctant to accept the idea, "unless it appears clear from the reception of our next loan in London that the financial
community would prefer that we should obtain funds elsewhere." Over the
course of their correspondence, White relented on the idea of approaching
the American market, in spite of his preference for London.[18]

This example helps to demonstrate the extent to which the Bank of
Montreal and the government of Canada brought public and private power
together to manage federal credit requirements, loans, and fiscal policy in
general. Naturally, this arrangement circumscribed the power of government
in fiscal and monetary policy, since the levers of that power were either small

or did not exist. But the limited nature of government requirements and taxation made such an arrangement at first necessary, then desirable.

As already explained, the Bank of Montreal in this period acted as the coordinator-in-chief of the Canadian banking system, a role that it partially shared after 1901 with the Canadian Bankers Association. That role emphasized the fact, that in the absence of a central bank, Canadian monetary and fiscal policy was essentially run by the private sector. The Canadian banks, for their part, played their part as guarantors of the system, ensuring that any dysfunctions or failures would be dealt with inside the ambit of the bankers' fraternity. Indeed, the Bank Act of 1901 conferred upon the CBA powers of self-regulation that formalized its role in the Canadian banking system. As Michael Bordo, Angela Redish, and Hugh Rockoff wryly remark, "in many respects, the Canadian banking industry was a cartel backed by the federal government limiting entry and policed by the Canadian Bankers Association."[19]

News of the "cartelization," if you will, of the Canadian banks was met with general approval. The *Financial News of London* wrote the following about the Canadian banking system: "We think the Canadian banking system to be a sound one, particularly as it is now reformed." Significant, in this journal's view, was the safeguarding of "the new note circulation by the new by-law providing for a monthly return to the President of the Canadian Bankers' Association, showing the condition of each bank's circulation." The *Financial News* regarded the "devolution from the State to the associated bankers themselves" as moving in the "right direction" and that "better results will be achieved by giving the banks a large measure of local self-government."[20] Sir Edward Clouston remarked at the 1901 annual meeting of the Bank that the new provisions made the CBA practically "the agent of the government in the administration of the Act."[21] The key provision in the new Bank Act was the ability of other banks to purchase the assets of other banks, "thus overcoming the barrier which formerly existed to the amalgamation of banks."[22]

For the time being, the Canadian banking system was relatively efficient, not characterized by higher costs than those in the United States, and enjoyed similar rates of return on equity. Matters would begin to change only in the First World War. Ottawa's massive capital requirements with the advent of the war prompted government actors to think about establishing institutions that could act independently of private companies in order to achieve their objectives. In other words, the exponentially increasing economic demands of the wartime economy could not be sustained by the private sector alone. Officials in the federal Department of Finance began to open a debate about the necessity or desirability of Canada establishing a central or reserve bank. Canada was the only country in the North Atlantic world that did not have such an instrument at the disposal of government. The Canadian Bankers

Association argued, in fact, that there was simply no need for one.[23] From the presidency of the CBA, Sir Frederick Williams-Taylor argued strongly against such a move. Bank of Montreal President Sir Vincent Meredith reinforced the point with Dominion Finance Minister Sir Thomas White, arguing that any such scheme would "deprive Canadian banks of the present resources for extending credit without any advantages," adding that such an institution would not be immune from partisan meddling. On the crucial question of facilitating trade, Meredith pointed out that the Canadian banks already met the needs of state and enterprise.[24] The organization of Canadian banking, with a central head office and many branches widely distributed, formed "a most efficient Central Reserve and Clearing House for all its branches wherever situated through the country."[25]

The banks won the argument this time, but something was shifting in the relationship between the state and the chartered banks. Any shift, of course, would have the greatest impact on the Bank of Montreal since its relationships and responsibilities were deeply linked to facilitating the financial operations of the government. A second portent of this shift would come in January 1919 over the question of the servicing of the national debt. As the official government banker, the Bank of Montreal naturally offered its services to deal with this important element of fiscal policy. Finance Minister White, however, informed Sir Vincent Meredith that he thought it would be unfair "to give one bank which is in active commercial competition with all others the sole administration of the national debt with all the collateral advantage involved. This is undoubtedly the view of my colleagues also."[26] Governments, fortified by increasing economic arguments in favour of such a move, were already beginning to consider a larger role for the state in the shaping of economic policy.

The arc of the Bank of Montreal's relationship with government over time changed to meet new demands and circumstances. The story here, however, is not about change: it is about the remarkable continuity of the basic arrangements of the relationship. Any change proposed would have had to confront Bank of Montreal bankers arguing that their management of the financial affairs of the state both here and abroad had not only been successful but also exemplary – certainly well worth the cost to the national treasury. The quid pro quo – top expertise and professionalism in the service of Canada in return for the business – seemed to work just fine. To be sure, cracks were appearing in the old arrangements. In Canada, however, it would take a major and unexpected shock in the form of a stock-market crash or a sharp and crisis-generating contraction in economic output for the relationship between the Bank of Montreal and the national government to change significantly. Until that day, change would be registered only along the margins.

Infrastructure of an Emerging Nation: The Canadian Pacific Railway

The Bank's role in national development famously extended to the construction of the Canadian Pacific Railway. No other single undertaking before or since has better captured the relationship between the Bank and the development of the country, not least for the iconic images it produced for posterity. The announcement of the building of the Canadian Pacific Railway in October 1880 by the Dominion government was intended to signal that this was a project that would turn sagging Canadian fortunes around. George Stephen, Bank of Montreal president, was one of six financiers who would underwrite what eventually became one of the most celebrated public-work projects in the history of Canada. The Bank's involvement was extensive and consequential.

The historian Harold Innis called the contract for the construction of the CPR "an index of the growth of civilization in Canada," and stated that its details were "evidence of the extent and character of that civilization."[27] Whatever one may think of this judgment, Innis had a point when he described the capitalists undertaking the enterprise as "significantly representative."[28] It drew in, most prominently, the Bank of Montreal as the bank and the city at the centre of the action, railway interests, English capital, and European capital.[29] Of course, the largest partner in the enterprise would prove to be the Dominion government, which agreed to give a subsidy of $25 million and 25 million acres of land. An additional $37.78 million was allotted for completed sections of road from Selkirk to Lake Superior and from Kamloops to Port Moody.[30]

The Bank's involvement through George Stephen and Donald Smith had several dimensions. On 28 September 1880 the board authorized an advance to Stephen and Smith of $600,000 – an eye-popping sum undoubtedly destined to help in the financing of the CPR's incorporation on 15 February 1881.[31] For the next four years, Stephen would involve himself intimately, and expertly, in Canada's biggest public-infrastructure project. The Bank of Montreal, for its part, would be a major player in the financing of the project, providing the CPR's first major loan of $1.5 million on the company's promissory notes secured by stock of the St Paul, Minneapolis and Manitoba Railway.[32]

As Pierre Berton's popular history of the CPR noted, "there was only one conceivable place to get [the necessary] kind of financing, and that was from the Bank of Montreal."[33] The Bank's deep involvement with the CPR included a network of loans to the syndicate itself, as well as a $2.7-million loan to the Canada North West Land Company on 21 November 1882.[34] That was only the beginning, moreover: in 1883, for example, the Bank was drawn into a scheme to salvage the CPR's credit by depositing $15.9 million with the Dominion government to continue construction and cover the dividend on the issued capital of $65 million.[35] By 1884, the CPR had an outstanding balance of $1.95 million with the Bank, after the latter's board agreed to a temporary overdraft on the CPR account to $3.95 million, which came with the personal guarantee of President Donald Smith himself for the full amount. The Dominion government itself, of course, was in for much greater amounts: in March 1884 it granted a loan of $22.5 million of which $7.5 million was to be applied against the settling of debt already accrued.[36] In subsequent years, the Bank of Montreal made additional loans, often at critical points, to enable the CPR to make payroll. This was the case, for example, on 5 May 1885, when the Bank's board authorized an additional advance of $750,000.[37] The general manager in 1885 reported to the board that the CPR directors and the government would repay the $1 million loan by 1886 if the funds were made available immediately.[38] Smith and Stephen would frequently personally guarantee loans made by the Bank of Montreal to the CPR, as was the case, for instance, with the $1-million loan to build a bridge across the St Lawrence River at Montreal. Stephen and Smith promised in this instance that the loan would be repaid at the rate of 80 per cent by June 1887.[39] As Innis notes, the financing of the railway was every bit as difficult as its physical construction. "At every turn," he writes, "the company exercised and was obliged to exercise the utmost care in the conservation of its financial resources. That "care" passed through the Bank of Montreal and involved complex arrangements and incentives to complete the railway.[40]

The cross-pollination of interests, especially between the Bank and the CPR, and specifically Stephen and Smith, occasionally raised eyebrows. At the 1884 annual meeting, shareholders asked whether there was "in the bylaws of this bank any provision against a Director in this Bank being a Director or office holder of any railway corporation." The chairman replied curtly, "I am not aware of any," and closed the debate.[41]

The building of the CPR was a project that tapped into the Bank of Montreal's hopes for the potential of the Canadian west and that promised to provide some sort of deliverance from the lacklustre economic conditions of the 1870s and early 1880s. President C.F. Smithers summed it up at the 1882 annual meeting: "It has become increasingly difficult of last years to make money at banking in Canada."[42] The CPR was a "national undertaking" with which the "prosperity of the country in the immediate future" is "very much bound up" and thus deserved the Bank's urgent attention.[43]

The Bank of Montreal's vision of the economic opportunities that would be made available through the instrument of the CPR was finally realized with the railway's completion in 1885. As Donald Smith assumed the presidency on 27 May 1887, his inaugural address brought it all together:

Since the last Annual Report ... the Bank has been established in Calgary, and so far your Directors have reason to be satisfied with the progress of business there, and, looking to the growing importance of British Columbia and the greatly increased facilities afforded for communication between Eastern portions of the Dominion and that Province by the completion to is seaboard of the Canadian Pacific Railway, preparations are being made by opening an office in Vancouver, a growing town already connected with China and Japan by a regular line of steamers.[44]

According to Smith, the opening of branches in Calgary and Vancouver enabled the Bank to do business "in what may be called the great centres of the Northwest and the Pacific Coast."[45] In the coming years, Canadian prosperity would be underwritten by the massive and orchestrated wave of Canadian immigration to the west, where, between 1900 and the First World War, 1.5 million settlers sought homes.[46]

The Search for Prosperity

The Bank of Montreal's integral role in financing the construction of the CPR should be understood in the context of the search for prosperity on behalf of the Bank and the country in the 1880s. That prosperity would not come until the turn of the century, but it was considerable when it did. Between 1900 and 1920, Canada's gross-capital formation quadrupled from $1.28 billion to $4 billion.[47] Accordingly, by 1918, the total amounts Canadians had on deposit with the chartered banks, including government deposits, was $2.1 billion – for perspective, this was nearly double the amount deposited in 1913. Most of that ($1.9 billion) was non-governmental deposits. In terms of personal savings, Canadian banking system-wide had $250 million on deposit.[48] Unsurprisingly, the stock value of Canadian chartered banks by 1914 was remarkably high – double the average. Only utilities outperformed the banks.[49] For the Bank of Montreal, the long-awaited upswing in economic activity and prosperity in Canada showed immediate results in its own statements. In 1902 alone, for example, circulation of Bank of Montreal currency increased over half a million dollars; deposits increased $14.1 million to reach $86.8 million.[50] By 1903, the Bank had increased its capitalization to $14 million and subdivided its shares to a par value of $100 each.[51]

The opening of the CPR afforded the Bank of Montreal new opportunities for western expansion and in 1887, less than three months after Vancouver welcomed its first transcontinental passenger train, Campbell Sweeny arrived in the city.[52] Sweeny, who had been born in Phillipsburg, Quebec, in 1846, had worked his way up through the ranks of the Bank of Montreal.

He had started as a bank teller at age eighteen in Hamilton, Ontario, and had moved around the country, eventually serving as a manager in Winnipeg from 1877 to 1882 and in Halifax from 1884 to 1887. Between 1882 and 1884, he briefly worked at the Bank's head office, where he came to the attention of the senior leadership. His next assignment took him to Vancouver to establish the Bank's first permanent branch in British Columbia.[53]

Campbell established that branch on Hastings Street soon after his arrival. He quickly rose to become a key business figure in Vancouver society, spearheading the establishment of the Vancouver Club and serving on the board of governors of the University of British Columbia. Sweeny, along with his wife, Dorothy, belonged to the city's social elite, and newspapers of the era frequently announced the couple's social dealings and event attendance.[54] As the Bank of Montreal's key representative on the West Coast, moreover, Campbell exercised a great deal of influence on the shaping of provincial banking regulations. He regularly corresponded with Charles Wilson, who was not only the official counsel of the Bank of Montreal but had served as British Columbia's attorney general from 1903 to 1906 in Premier Richard McBride's first administration.[55]

From beginnings on Hastings Street, Sweeny expanded the Bank of Montreal's presence into the interior, opening up new branches in mining and lumber districts, including the booming Kootenay region.[56] In recognition of his outstanding services, he was promoted to superintendent of the British Columbia and Yukon district in 1912.[57] He served in this role until retirement in 1916, remaining a staple of the Vancouver social scene until his death in 1928.[58]

After 1887, the Bank of Montreal's western presence quickly expanded, not only in British Columbia but also in Alberta and Manitoba. The west became increasingly important to the Bank. As the Annual Report of 1904 stated, "production in the Northwest grows apace, the railways are prosperous, a second transcontinental line is on the eve of construction, the reports from the mining districts of British Columbia are more encouraging, a spirit of abiding confidence in Canada pervades our people; and despite temporary checks in the progress of material developments, there is an increasing belief that this country has entered upon an era of great and enduring prosperity."[59]

From agriculture to industrial production, Canada, in the late 1890s and early 1900s, was a land where, in the words of Sir Edward Clouston, "the symptoms of prosperity are in the ascendant."[60] His buoyant message in late 1899 set the stage for a remarkable run for the country:

There is hardly a branch of trade that is not prospering. The farmers are receiving good prices for their products, the Government shows increased revenues, the railways increased traffics, stocks of all sorts have appreciated in value, while the future wealth which our mining and forest industries are expected to realize for this country is beyond computation ... We are not singular in our present fortunate position, as there appears to be a universal wave of prosperity sweeping over most of the countries of the world and in England, the United States, and on the continent manufactories are taxed to the utmost capacity to meet the demands of commerce.[61]

The boom in business was reflected in the Bank's capital flows. Note circulation increased by $525,000 and total deposits reached a record $86.8 million. Notable also was the massive capital inflows of British investment into Canada. Between 1906 and 1913, British investment in Canada increased by £246 million, of which more than 50 per cent was negotiated by the Bank of Montreal.[62]

By mid-decade, Canada's economic performance was strong and sustained, underpinned by a strong financial sector. In 1907, in the midst of a US financial crisis, the Canadian banking system held firm. Clouston likened Canada's position to a "man living in a fireproof house with his neighbour's residence ablaze. He believes himself safe, but is naturally nervous as to the result."[63] Clouston's own nerves were being tested: Canada's banking system was strong, but it was not immune to external pressures and tensions. Indeed, the international financial crisis occasioned by the Panic of 1907 led to a very noticeable squeeze on credit in both the Canadian and European money markets. The timing of the crisis, moreover, was critical. Reaching its height in October, the crisis hit right during the credit-intensive time of year when the bountiful harvest in the Canadian west needed to be shipped east. Canadian Finance Minister W.S. Fielding expressed great anxiety at "the prospect of insufficient financial accommodation to move the crop."[64]

The response to the crisis of 1907, however, highlighted the strength of the Canadian banking system.[65] Starting on 20 November 1907, the Dominion government offered advances, through the Bank of Montreal, to finance the shipment of grain, against the collateral of high-grade securities.[66] The banks were authorized to circulate up to $10 million in additional notes, but in the end they borrowed just over half of that amount and repaid it by the end of April 1908.[67] The Bank of Montreal's role as a lender of last resort in the crisis of 1907 was critical in easing tight credit and allowing commodities to flow. As Joseph Johnson, dean of the New York School of Commerce, Accounts, and Finance, put it in 1910: "The bankers were right in their claim that they were fully able to take control of the western situation."[68] Although the Canadian economy did not escape unscathed – Canadian imports fell by about 2 per cent as a result of the crisis – Canadian domestic exports, partly thanks to the actions of the Bank of Montreal, stayed level.[69] "The solidarity of the Canadian banking system," the *Globe* suggested, "could not be more effectively demonstrated than by the steady confidence that is continued here through a time of panic ... in the financial center of the continent."[70] Moreover, even in this temporary but sharp emergency, the Canadian banks never suspended specie payments on demand – a further sign of the strength of the banks and the system.[71]

The role of Canadian banks in general and of the Bank of Montreal in particular in providing a safe haven for US deposits during the 1907 crisis – long before the establishment of the Federal Reserve – is worth emphasizing. Economists note that, even though the Bank of Montreal held at most an approximately 2 per cent share of total deposits in New York, the role that the Bank (and, to a lesser extent, more junior Canadian banks) played in the United States was much bigger than that number may suggest. The Bank of Montreal's deposit balances, for example, went up during banking crises, such as the one that struck mainly the New York market in 1907. In other words, Canada's first bank, thanks to its reputation and stability, was considered a secure harbour in stormy weather.[72] Remember that a significant portion of these deposits were "bankers' balances" that belonged to the network of US state and national banks.[73] In Chicago, the Bank of Montreal's importation of currency in that same troubled year, 1907, relieved pressure on midwestern US banks.[74] In 1907, therefore, the Bank of Montreal reprised the role it had played in 1890 and 1893 and provided a critical refuge for the US banking system.[75]

As Bank of Montreal President George A. Drummond noted in the Annual Report the following year: "A year ago business in the United States was staggering under a sudden collapse in credit and acute money stringency, while in Canada the brakes had been applied and the slowing down process had begun. To-day, the situation is much improved, confidence has been largely restored, credit is again good, [and] the money markets of the world are abnormally easy."[76] The key to success, according to Clouston, was the continuation of the "conservative policy" of Canadian business, with the result that the Canadian economy emerged "stronger and better in every way."[77] Though Sir Edward had not directly referred in his remarks to the stabilizing role that the Bank had just played in responding to the difficulties in the United States, the events of 1907 must have underscored to Bank management just how strategically important their institution had become in the North American financial system.

The strong performance of the Bank and its counterparts in the Canadian banking system in the face of cyclical credit crises in the United States was well timed politically. The Bank Act was due for another round of examination in 1909–10. Since it had been revised in 1901 and had "been found to confirm so admirably to the requirements of trade and the interests of a rapidly developing country," no material change would be contemplated in this round.[78] The following pre-war years were ones of prosperity and expansion, requiring capital-stock increases from $16 million to $25 million in 1912.[79] The profit picture by 1913 hit its stride with an $8-million increase in general assets and $2.6 million in profits.[80]

The economic prosperity of the age was captured by William S. Fielding during his budget speech in April 1911 when he announced that the Finance Department had recorded a surplus of $30.5 million, in spite of significant expenses for railway construction and public works. "We need new markets in all directions," Fielding remarked. "We need them for the surplus products of Canada as it is to-day, and we shall need them in even greater degree for the vaster surplus of Canadian products to come ... from the Great West in the near future ... With peace and progress and prosperity at home, with the friendliest relations with the great Republic lying alongside us, with the warmest attachment to the great empire of which we are so proud to form a part, the Canadian people can look forward to the future with every hope and every confidence."[81]

This was reflected in the Bank's performance as well. At the 1912 annual meeting, President R.B. Angus stated: "We have again to report a year of universal and almost unbroken prosperity throughout the length and breadth of the land."[82] The following year, the new president, Sir Vincent Meredith, was less optimistic, pointing to the deteriorating political situation in Europe. He maintained, however, that the Bank of Montreal's proven policy of conservatism would prepare it for this crisis as well:

> The finger of prudence points to a policy of conservatism. While the financial sky remains clouded over in Europe, we shall do well to hasten slowly. It is not a time to attempt enterprises of a speculative nature, nor to undertake new commitments prior to the financing thereof, and an accumulation of stock by merchants and manufacturers should, as far as possible, be avoided ... on the other hand, the commercial condition of Canada is fundamentally sound. Business as a whole, as I have said, continues good. Our vast natural resources have scarcely been scratched. Immigration is large, railway construction active, new territory and new resources of wealth are being steadily opened, the confidence of British and foreign capitalists in our country is unabated. A temporary halt can only refresh Canada for yet greater achievements.[83]

The First World War

With the advent of the Great War in August 1914, the Bank shifted its policy and thinking to the exigencies of wartime. General Manager Sir Frederick

Williams-Taylor suggested in 1914 that, though the times were perilous, the Bank was in a strong position thanks to its conservatism.[84] Similarly, echoing his speech at the 1913 annual meeting, Meredith summed up the Bank's approach again in 1915:

> The war in which the Empire is engaged to protect its integrity had made it incumbent upon Canada to assist the mother country in every way possible. We have already provided a large number of troops and more will follow. In the manufacture of munitions, clothing, and other requirements, we are doing our full share. This had brought profitable enjoyment to Canada when sorely needed, and at the same time rendered great service to the common cause. Let us, however, remember that the manufacture of war materials is a grim and transient form of so-called prosperity, that the cost thereof comes out of the national exchequer of Great Britain or of Canada, and from the blood of the flower of our manhood.[85]

The bank was quick off the mark in offering immediate assistance to the war effort, with a $100,000 contribution to the Canadian Patriotic Fund on 22 August 1914.[86] Yet the dangers that the war posed to the Canadian financial system were almost immediately apparent: the Monday after the declaration of mobilization of the armed forces in Europe, Canadian banks were faced with a possible run on the currency as depositors sought to convert paper money into gold. The Dominion government moved swiftly to suspend convertibility with the Finance Act of 1914.[87]

At the Bank's annual meeting in December 1914, Williams-Taylor emphasized the gravity of the financial situation:

> The outstanding result of the war on Canada has been the instantaneous stoppage of the supply of British capital to which we have become so accustomed. Money from that source flow[s] to us in such volume that during a considerable period it amounted in round figures to at least $25 million a month. Canadian public borrowings from the London money market for the seven months period ending July 31 last were $177 million dollars. Since the outbreak of the war the inflow of such capital has ceased. This monetary deprivation, coupled with the necessity of using earnings and income for the purpose of paying to Great Britain the interest on our indebtedness of $2.8 billion to London[,] has brought home to us the extent to which the London money market and the British investor have been our friends.[88]

The Bank of Montreal's adroit handling of Dominion finances during the Great War, especially as the federal government's agent in London, was not only important for the war effort; it provided the Canadian government with the expertise required to navigate the complex world of imperial finance.[89] The Bank also had an important hand in paying Canadian forces in Britain during the conflict. Furthermore, the Bank was concerned not only with government finance but also with borrowing in London "for the general purposes of the Dominion."[90] That meant making representations in regard to the maturing of debt of many Canadian cities. As agent for many of those cities, such as Prince Rupert, BC, the Bank had to make representations to the Dominion government on securing renewal of their loans (payable "on" London) in a time when war financing was taking priority. The danger, of course, was default. In the case of Prince Rupert, Williams-Taylor suggested that "the consequences to the credit not only to the City of Prince Rupert but to other Western Cities (Calgary for one) and in fact the whole of Canada, cannot be regarded but as a catastrophe."[91]

The Bank's contribution to Canada's war effort was commensurate with its leadership role in the Canadian banking system. In London and New York, the Bank's representation of Canadian financial interests meant that it was involved in complex and sometimes delicate negotiations involving Canadian financing of the war. This included the first issue of a $45-million loan in the United States.[92] President Meredith commented that the rise of the United States as a "great creditor nation" would adversely affect Bank profits, while at the same time being "of the utmost importance to Canada, as it has enabled the Dominion, our provinces, and our cities, and railways to finance their requirements to an extent that we could scarcely have hoped for a year ago," citing as evidence the fact that, between 1914 and 1915, the Canadian government had borrowed $142 million on Wall Street.[93] "It is satisfactory," he concluded, that "our credit is good in that market."[94] In 1915 the government, with the assistance of the Bank, negotiated domestic loans amounting to $200 million and a further loan of $95 million in New York.[95].

The banks' handling of Victory Bonds and their assistance in matters of wartime finance enhanced their reputation. "The advantages of Canadian banking have perhaps never been more strikingly shown than by the way Canadian banks quickly met the unprecedented situation arising out of the war and the manner in which they're now helping the country and the difficult period of reconstruction" remarked the *Globe* in November 1919. [96]

While the Bank's efforts were crucial in financing the Canadian war effort, its actions were not entirely altruistic. Over the course of the war, the Bank's holdings reached record highs. In the year 1916 alone, the Bank's total deposits increased by $63 million, and that year's Annual Report showed that total deposits had grown by a total of $102 million since 1914.[97]

The Bank's performance after a year of war was virtually undiminished. In fact, as the *Globe* reported in November 1915, the "total resources of the Bank of Montreal at the end of its fiscal year on October 30th last established a new high record in Canadian banking, amounting to approximately [$302,980,551], an increase of about $43,000,000 over a year ago."[98] According to Meredith, Canada's economy was "buoyant in nearly all lines of business" and, as the Dominion's unofficial central bank, the Bank of Montreal was able to take advantage of favourable economic conditions to reach new heights of prosperity.[99] The year 1918 saw particularly stellar results, with the Bank's assets jumping from $280.5 to $558.4 million. As the *Globe* reported in November, this dramatic increase was partly "due to the absorption of the Bank of British North America," but it was also attributable to the Bank's "large resources, which were placed at the disposal of the Imperial and Canadian Governments and Canadian municipalities and industries."[100] The growth in the Bank's business and assets prompted an expansion of executive staff. In November 1918 the Bank introduced four assistant general managers with different territorial assignments: Francis J. Cockburn (Quebec, Newfoundland, and the Maritimes), H.B. Mackenzie (supervision of the recently acquired Bank of British North America branches), G.C. Cassels (London, England, office), and D.R. Clarke (Ontario).[101]

The Bank, the Empire, and the Maple Leaf Club

The Bank of Montreal's representation of Canadian interests within the halls of finance and government in the United Kingdom reached its zenith in this period. Its influence as well as its importance as a representative of Canada in London can be neatly captured by the wartime history of one of the Bank's branches in the West End of the city, at Waterloo Place.

As indicated in chapter 6, Waterloo Place became a central rendezvous point for expatriate Canadians in London during the First World War. Of course, the branch was a place for Bank of Montreal customers (during this period, mainly members of the Canadian Expeditionary Force) to deposit pay, remit overseas, and otherwise conduct a variety of financial transactions. Indeed, of the 10,000 accounts registered with the Bank's Waterloo branch in May 1919, for example, 7,000 were military. As the war progressed, Waterloo also became a meeting place for Canadians, both soldiers and civilians.

As manager of the Bank's Waterloo Place branch, Dudley Oliver was a significant person in the lives of many Canadians stationed overseas. His most important role was to facilitate communication between soldiers and their families, and vice versa. Oliver remembered that "there were from

4 to 5,000 officers' wives in and about London. Letters for many of them were addressed to the bank and it was a rendezvous for hundreds."[102] Oliver also took it upon himself to personally inform families if a soldier had died in battle, in the absence of official communications. "We were frequently given the names of the next of kin," Oliver recalled, "so that the officers' loved ones would have the news broken to them in the most delicate manner possible." The Montreal head office not only approved of the branch's transformation into a social/service centre, but the general manager "encouraged us in every way and gave us wonderful support," Oliver recalled some years later.[103]

The success of Waterloo Place in establishing a home away from home for Canadians, Bank employees, and Londoners alike inspired similar initiatives. The Maple Leaf Club, the first official club to be established in London for Canadian soldiers overseas, had its origins with the Bank. Lady Grace Parker Drummond, wife of the late George Drummond (Bank president, 1905–10), visited London and lamented the absence of an official place of refuge for soldiers on leave from the front to rest or reconnect with their families. Hotels were often overcrowded and unsuitable, and, as a result, "these poor chaps had to sleep in the parks." Lady Drummond tried to remedy the situation and made several enquiries "for a large house that might be leased as a residential Club for Canadian Soldiers." She did not have to wait long. Wealthy Londoner Ronald Grenville, who had heard of the plight of many Canadian soldiers, offered a spacious mansion at No. 11 Charles Street, Berkeley Square, in Westminster, right in the heart of London. In the words of Oliver, "[Lady] Drummond and Grenville, [and] Mr. and Mrs. Rudyard Kipling were among [the Maple Leaf Club's] first friends and … subscribers, [and] they gave the club invaluable help throughout [the war]."[104]

The story of Waterloo Place was only a part of the story. A far greater sacrifice awaited Bank of Montreal employees who fought on the front lines during the Great War. Many never made it home. "I have seen a great deal of misery caused by this unfortunate war," Oliver wrote in 1916, "and it pleases me very much when I am able to do the smallest thing for anyone in connection with their dear ones at the Front."[105] As such, he often helped widows to return to Canada from abroad and wrote letters of condolence. One such letter to a grieving war widow captures something of the compassion offered in those dark times:

Please allow me to express my sincerest and deepest sympathy with you at the loss of your dear son who I knew for a number of years both at the Bank and at the Golf Club where we lived together. Everyone who knew "Mat" [a nickname for a Dr Matthews], as we called him, loved and respected him and there was no finer fellow in the Bank of

Montreal or a more capable officer for the time that he was a soldier. It was the custom of the officers of the 60th Battalion when they wanted to know anything to say, "Ask Mat." He knew every department of the game and spent all his spare time studying.[106]

Delivering news of Canadian soldiers' deaths took a toll on the branch manager. "I, personally, have a terrible time," Oliver wrote in 1915, "as I have had to break the news to several of the wives of the officers who are in London whose husbands have been killed. I have not been home until after midnight for the last five days and am really at my wits' end and almost at the end of my tether."[107] As the war intensified and the casualty lists grew longer, wartime exigencies consumed the bulk of his attention. "I had a very hard time last month," he reported in 1916, "owing to the extremely heavy casualty list. You have probably heard that since the Canadians went into the Ypres Salient they have lost from 18/19,000 [men]," he wrote in 1916.[108]

Oliver largely experienced the war from London. Occasionally, he would visit the actual front in France. The peril inherent in these forays is best described by the following excerpt from a diary entry in 1917:

> We have had six terrible raids in the past ten days; the most appalling part of it is the heavy fire from Artillery; we have Batteries practically all round our house and the shells keep whizzing over making the weirdest noise; occasionally there is a lull for a few minutes, when you will hear our machines attacking the German ones, machine guns, going for all they are worth. The last raid lasted for three hours; unfortunately, our little girl was ill and I had to take her out of bed four nights running the last time she caught a cold, and I have had to have a doctor several times during the last three days. We have no safe place in our house so I put my wife and baby behind the piano with the mattress and sofa as protection, but of course this would only protect them being hit by broken glass; if a bomb were to strike the house we would not have a chance.[109]

Oliver's many contributions to the Canadian war effort were rewarded by official recognition and, more to the point, the gratitude of the hundreds of families he managed to help along the way.

The Ties That Bind

The ties that bound the Bank of Montreal and Canada originated decades before this period and extended decades after. But it was in the late nineteenth and early twentieth centuries that the relationship reached its greatest intensity. The reasons, in retrospect, are not hard to spot. By the late nineteenth century, the Bank possessed the national and international prominence, the professionalism, the reputation, the resources, the capital, and the networks that no other Canadian institution possessed in quite the same combination and in the same way. The power and reach of the Bank were harnessed to the growing needs and demands of a fledgling federal government. Its capital was deployed to fund public-infrastructure projects, and its international networks and presence were exploited to stimulate capital inflows and ensure proper credit facilities for both state and enterprise. The expertise of its managers and executives was used to provide advice and analysis in ordinary times and in times of national emergency. In concert with the other major chartered banks, the Bank of Montreal as coordinator-in-chief and senior bank acted to safeguard the integrity of the Canadian banking system.

In many ways, the protagonists of the history of the Bank and the policymakers and politicians of the post-Confederation era had visions of economic development and prosperity that, if they did not always align, frequently intersected at multiple points – including the west, trade, and the broader place of the country in the Empire and the wider world. Indeed, Montreal bankers and federal politicians shared a broad common vision of the country and its direction, so much so that, between 1900 and about 1920, one could justly call this period one of "Canadian banking ascendancy." By every measure imaginable, Canadian bankers enjoyed remarkable success and influence.

Of course, as I have already stressed, even if the dream of nation was a shared one, the relationship between bank and state consisted of a set of mutually beneficial transactions. The Bank of Montreal reaped remarkable rewards from its privileged position in the Canadian banking system. The rewards were, of course, mainly monetary. But they also came in the form of enhanced prestige, of being considered, in many situations, a quasi-governmental organization and an ambassador for Canada in the markets of the North Atlantic world. The Bank enjoyed remarkable sway over the deliberations of government and influence over policy decisions. Bank of Montreal bankers were listened to and heard in the corridors of power: indeed, they often owned those corridors! Even if their positions did not always win the day, they were a force to be reckoned with. No other Canadian bank achieved this level of prestige or influence in this era – an era when the Bank and the nation were allied in the cause of national development, and in their own respective interests.

CHAPTER EIGHT

Capital Unshackled: Bankers, Mergers, Trade, and the Expansionist Spirit

This chapter focuses on two discrete themes key to the Bank of Montreal experience in the late nineteenth and early twentieth centuries. The first theme is the Bank's championship of Canadian trade. It is in this period that the Bank leverages its networks and capabilities in Canada and the North Atlantic world to become the Canadian trade bank par excellence. The second theme is the Bank's wave of mergers and acquisitions initiated as part of a broader consolidation of the Canadian banking system in the first two decades of the twentieth century.

At first glance, national and international trade on the one hand and bank mergers on the other seem to have very little to do with each other. The trade issue is a long-term phenomenon. It is outward facing and involves a significant number of actors, from governments, to investors, to agricultural producers and manufacturers. It is also about creating the kind of credit facilities and bank services that support Canadian trade at home and abroad. The merger phenomenon, by contrast, constituted a specific set of events beginning at the turn of the century and terminating in the mid-1920s. It is concerned with the evolution of Bank of Montreal market strategy and the organization of the banking sector in Canada.

Yet, together, these two subjects find a common connection through the Bank of Montreal experience. Each subject constitutes an important set of events for Canadian economic development. Each of them is also linked to the Bank's strategic capabilities and shows its strength and agility in different market contexts. Both trade and the consolidation of the banking sector provided Bank of Montreal leadership with the chance to exploit significant competitive opportunities and steal a march on their rivals. That, in brief, was the expansionist spirit which underlay the Bank's strategy on these two major fronts.

The subjects of this chapter, of course, intersect with the themes of the previous ones. Both trade initiatives and merger activity were important parts of the Bank's corporate strategy. Both had a significant impact, moreover, on the country's economic development and its financial arrangements. But I argue that they are sufficiently distinct – in other words, they stand out enough – to merit a closer look. First, we turn to trade.

The Evolution of a Trade Bank

The Bank's links with the financing and facilitating of trade extend right to its establishment in 1817. The funding of Montreal merchants and their activities was one of the prime motivations for organizing the Bank in the first place. The connections the Bank of Montreal generated with producers, manufacturers, and especially the New York and London capital markets positioned the institution well to exploit and direct developments in trade. Its commanding position in the Canadian banking system only underscored its influence.

Of course, the demands of an evolving trade bank always had to be balanced with the fundamental needs of the broader bank. Indeed, the Bank's loan policies from one year to the next would have an effect on trade and the movement of goods. When, for example, the Bank called in its temporary loans in the summer of 1871 to operate with more capital in the lucrative New York market, the move caused some anxiety in Canadian trade circles. Any curtailment of the usual accommodation at the banks, "coming at a time when all their funds are required for moving crops, and especially with so large a yield as we have this season," according to the *Monetary Times*, occasioned "inconvenience, not unmixed with an element of danger." The principal anxiety was that "monetary stringency" would tend to affect markets adversely and "aggregate results to the farmer" as it related to the harvest.[1] But the Bank also had to exploit opportunities in the New York and London markets, even if it meant ending the "easier condition of money" in Canada.[2] The practical effect was that borrowing jumped from the "easy money" days of 6 and 7 per cent to 15 or 20 per cent. The consequences were almost immediately felt, "a fact sufficiently proven by the sudden collapse in prices."[3] The discomfiture that resulted was primarily felt by stock speculators who, by certain press accounts, had found it "more convenient to remain in debt than clear up finally their account for share transactions on which losses have always been made."[4] As one commentator suggested, the Bank of Montreal's ambitions of being "to Canada what the Bank of England is to England" might have spurred it to imitate the Bank of England's less stringent loan policies.[5]

The strategy of capital deployment and its emphasis on stability was especially appreciated in the wake of the Panic of 1873. As the *Monetary Times* suggested after the Bank's annual meeting of June 1874, "the Bank itself has acquired so very prominent a position, not in Canada only, but also in the United States (for it has at times ruled Wall Street), it is well to consider carefully the line of policy therein sketched."[6] That policy's foundation was maintaining government business and trade and foreign exchange, not only in Canada but in New York and Chicago as well. The Bank's role in foreign exchange in particular, and its operations facilitating the business of mercantile houses trading into the East and West Indies as well as across the Asia Pacific region, were especially important.[7] Indeed, by the mid-1870s, the Bank had moved even further in the direction of merchant banking "to become," in the words of R.B. Angus, "as much as possible, the banker of other banks."[8] This refers to re-discounting, or lending to other banks, and provides particular thrust to the argument that the Bank had been influenced by English methods of banking, since that line of business "has for a long time formed a prominent feature of banking as carried on in England."[9]

As the principal merchant bank in the country, the Bank of Montreal was the object of much scrutiny and the subject of anxiety regarding any changes in loan or capital-deployment policies. The Bank's leadership, consistently throughout the period, favoured cautious expansion and strongly tilted toward a conservative approach. The Bank would promote trade and economic development, but not at the cost of its Stability Strategy. In the long term, the Bank's leadership believed that having the Bank of Montreal as a premier banking institution outweighed the short-term and riskier potential benefits of temporary trade gains. Instead, the Bank promoted development and trade through other means. It developed credit networks and facilities in the New York, Chicago, and London markets to facilitate capital flows. It also, of course, famously supported public-infrastructure projects like the CPR to stimulate the economy of the Canadian west and promote that region's trade with the countries of Asia, particularly Japan. The branch system, therefore, particularly in areas considered on the frontiers of trade such as the British Columbia lower mainland, was an essential part of its support and promotion of Canadian trade. Here, the Chicago and New York agencies could be considered important strategic outposts as well. Investments, moreover, in export-led staple-based industries such as lumber and forestry not only made good banking sense but also further promoted the Canadian capacity in international trade. When the conditions were right, as

they began to be in the late 1890s, and overall economic conditions permitted, the Bank moved swiftly to exploit opportunities in emerging areas such
as Mexico and the Caribbean.

Missionary of Canadian Capital and Trade

In the early years of the twentieth century, under General Manager Sir Edward
S. Clouston's direction, the Bank of Montreal began to connect its capital in
New York, and especially in London, to interests in Latin America and the
Caribbean.[10] Canadians were then establishing hydroelectric and traction
companies, a trend supported by investment interests. Under the leader-
ship of F.S. Pearson, an American businessman with close ties to Clouston,
Drummond, and James Ross, Montreal investors plunged into the world of
Mexican utilities.[11]

In this area, Clouston was building upon the Bank's deep involvement
in Canadian external trade from its very beginnings. Its expertise and connections in dealing in foreign exchange, as well as its role in the New York
call market, made the Bank's position especially powerful and relevant.[12] Its
track record as the once-largest and most powerful "transactor in the New
York market" gave it special advantages with regard to further expansion into
Latin America and the Caribbean. Other banks pushed into the region as
well: the Bank of Nova Scotia opened a branch in Jamaica in 1882; the Royal
Bank in Havana in 1898.[13]

As H.V. Nelles and Christopher Armstrong recount in their examination
of Canadian capital's "southern exposure," the work began in 1902 when a
Canadian syndicate bought the Necaxa waterpower concession, about one
hundred miles from Mexico City. The syndicate then incorporated the Mexican Light and Power Company, which, in due course, through mergers and
acquisitions, acquired monopoly control of electrical distribution in Mexico's
Federal District. In the meantime, the syndicate added a number of tramway and electrical companies in the region to its holdings, finally purchasing the Mexico City Street Railway.[14] "As if to dignify these foreign ventures,"
Nelles and Armstrong write, "the Bank of Montreal, Canada's most prestigious financial institution, announced it would open a Mexican branch" in
1906. Sir George Drummond was at the heart of the syndicate – an indication of the depth of Canadian capital's – and particularly Montreal capital's
– involvement in Mexico.[15]

For years after the opening of the Bank's Mexico City branch, the country
exploded in revolution and internecine conflict. Although the Mexico City
branch operated at a loss in the early years (averaging between US$50,000 and
US$100,000 per year), the investment was considered a long-term one, since

Canadian trade and capital were establishing themselves in the country.[16] The principal business there was in primary resources such as lumber and staples such as sugar and cotton. After 1917, the Mexico operations began turning a profit and posted significant returns in the 1920s.[17]

Beyond the opening of official bank branches, the Bank of Montreal was deeply involved in other Mexican ventures through substantial loans – for example, $500,000 to the Rio de Janeiro Tramway, Light and Power Company and $1.8 million to the Mexican Light and Power Company.[18] General Manager E.S. Clouston was also personally tied to many of these ventures, particularly the Mexican Light and Power Company of which he was a principal shareholder and a member of the board of directors.[19] His interests further included Rio de Janeiro Tramway, Light and Power, the Mexican Electric Light Company, the Mexico Tramways Company, and the Demerara Electric Company.[20]

The convergence of interests in the Mexican ventures between the Bank, its leaders, and the Canadian financial community sometimes generated conflict. In 1908 Clouston attempted to lease the Mexican Light and Power Company to Mexico Tramways. The result was a falling out, at least initially, between Clouston, as general manager, and Sir George Drummond, as president. The disagreement was notable for its exceptional nature: the two leaders of the Bank were typically in perfect alignment. Gradually, the two men's differences waned, and by the time Clouston had come around to Drummond's plan for defeating the proposal, they lost control of Mexican Light to Toronto, British, and American interests.[21]

The Bank's Mexican involvements under Clouston and Drummond were, in retrospect, founded on a misguided confidence in the political stability of the country. When the Mexican dictator, General Porfirio Díaz, was overthrown in 1911 after twenty-seven years in power, the Bank incurred considerable losses. Bank of Montreal President R.B. Angus noted at the annual meeting in 1912 that "in Mexico, politics have been a very disturbing element, but there are indications of an improvement which will allow business to resume its usual course."[22] While business continued, it would take several years for normality to return to the Bank of Montreal's Mexico operations, with the Bank's only operative branch in Mexico City operating at an annual loss.[23]

The controversy and subsequent loss of Mexican Light to rival interests, on its own, would not have been a career-ending calamity. Clouston's involvement in a venture closer to home, however, almost certainly hastened his retirement from the Bank in November 1911. The story centres on Clouston's ill-fated support of Max Aitken's (later Lord Beaverbrook's) action in forcing the Western Canada Cement and Coal Company, owned by Sir Sandford Fleming, into bankruptcy, and that company's subsequent transformation into the

Canada Cement Company in 1909.[24] As a result of Clouston's involvement in the venture, the board of directors, after an unprecedented five months of deliberation and reflection on the matter, chose Richard Bladworth Angus as president, passing Clouston over despite his contributions and qualifications for the position.[25]

The championing of new trade and economic opportunities in this period came with great potential rewards, and also a high degree of political risk. Perhaps one of the ablest – and certainly most powerful – bankers of his day, Sir Edward Clouston was a dramatic case in point of the latter. The accession of Angus to the presidency over Clouston was an unmistakeable, and also very rare, rebuke by the directors of their president – the consequence of his having the Bank dragged into the unsavoury business wrought by Beaverbrook. It is to be recalled that the Bank leadership was extremely jealous of its sterling reputation for probity, propriety, and conservatism, even at the cost, as it later emerged, of innovation and adaptation. This perhaps suggests why the directors named R.B. Angus, the famous, but almost prehistoric, hero of the 1870s Bank and the 1880s CPR, to the presidency. It was an effort to restore order to the pantheon.

The Secret Life of the Bank in London

The Bank of Montreal's connections with the imperial centre are virtually as old as the Bank itself. The Bank's first half-century was fundamentally shaped by its relationship to the area of London confined to Whitehall, Westminster, and the city of London. It may have been a small area, but it had a big impact on the fortunes of the Bank. As we have seen in previous chapters, the Bank established clear relationships with the lords of the Treasury in Whitehall, the Colonial Office, and the business centres of the London capital. It was only in 1870, however, that the Bank's relationship with the city acquired a more prominent dimension, as Canadian state and enterprise began to acquire relevance and stature. On 6 April 1870 the London committee (or London "board") of the Bank was formed, with perhaps the most influential Canadian financial figure of his generation, Sir John Rose, as chairman. Later, in the 1870s, the London committee would be run by E.H. King after his retirement as president of the Bank in 1873.[26] Though he disappeared from the Montreal scene, King would remain very active in the Bank's business in London. (Throughout its existence, the London committee offered a forum for former Bank of Montreal executives, as well as high-ranking Canadian political, business, and military figures, to continue to serve Canada's oldest bank.) He would guide the Bank's affairs in London until October 1888, succeeded by Sir Robert Gillespie.[27]

From that committee, the Bank's relationships in London would be largely governed, capital flows arranged for, and credit facilities developed. The committee would, with rare exceptions, meet every Wednesday for seventy-seven years. When Bank leaders were in London, they would join the proceedings as ex officio members (at least from 1893).[28] The London committee became the Bank's international hub for the placement of stocks and bonds and the raising of capital for the Canadian state and Canadian enterprises. By the late 1870s, the London committee had been able to transfer £6,873 to the head office in Montreal.[29] Its investments grew in size over the years, especially in connection with the acquisition of railway stock put on the London market. In August 1906, for example, the committee agreed to participate in a £1-million flotation of the CPR Perpetual Consolidated Debenture Stock.[30] Many other Canadian corporations used the Bank's London facilities for letters of credit and issuance of stocks, bonds, and debentures, especially of Canadian municipalities. But the committee also participated in activity outside of Canadian placements, such as a city of Moscow 5 per cent loan in March 1908.[31] It was also a frequent participant in the underwriting of loans to governments in Australia, Belgium, India, Japan, Kenya, and South Africa.

The business of the London committee included self-regulation when matters required it. In April 1908, for example, after a formal complaint had been made to Frederick Williams-Taylor about the practice of "stagging" issues by officers of the Bank, the committee took action. Stagging was a speculative activity in which the stag – bank officer – would purchase large quantities of a stock for short periods of time and then sell for quick profits. "As this is in defiance of Section 338 Rules and Regulations in addition to being most discreditable in every way," the London committee minutes recorded on 9 April 1908, "the Staff of this Branch is hereby notified that any officer of the Bank who should at any time, either directly or indirectly, subscribe for issues made by us or by any other Bank, for the purpose of speculation, renders himself liable to instant suspension and dismissal." The admonition, signed by Strathcona, further noted that taking "emoluments or perquisites on commissions [was] strictly forbidden."[32]

The placement of Dominion government loans, as well as the arrangement of loans for Canadian enterprises seeking financing, typically dominated the London committee's business. Such transactions show the patterns of British capital flows as they began to multiply by the 1890s and early 1900s to finance an increasingly wide spectrum of Canadian enterprise and projects. Indeed, the Bank's London committee was a vital conduit in the channelling of much-needed capital to a Dominion that by the end of the nineteenth century was on the verge of a massive expansion.

As we have seen, in both the pre- and post-Confederation periods, the Bank was deeply involved trade and exchange activities. That involvement grew even more in the latter part of the nineteenth century, when the Bank sought to provide facilities across the North Atlantic world to ensure that capital would follow the flag. Until the later 1890s, however, when a booming economy returned, the Bank ensured that its expansionist ambitions were contained within the ambit of its overall strategic imperative of stability and conservatism that had become its hallmark, its brand, and its guarantee against the tempests that periodically swept across the economies of North America and Europe.

The Spirit of Expansion in Banking

The second major theme of the Bank of Montreal's story in this period was its acquisition of a number of other banks. Revisions to the Bank Act in 1901 changed merger requirements for Canadian chartered banks, which set off a wave of consolidation that extended to the mid-1920s. While the wave extended beyond the era we are considering in this section of the book, it has its roots in the years before the First World War and thus deserves a closer examination here.

Mergers and consolidations were the most prominent element of the history of banking in this period. After 1918, they reached an intensity that reduced the number of banks from eighteen in 1920 to eleven in 1929.[33] Of the thirty-six amalgamations, many involved imminent or actual failures of banks, prompting the economist E.P. Neufeld to comment that the large number is rather surprising "in view of the Canadian banking system's reputation for solvency."[34] In some ways, moreover, the instrument of merger was the key weapon in the maintenance of the Canadian banking system's reputation for integrity.

The motivations of the Bank of Montreal leadership in embarking upon this acquisition strategy were complex. The Bank began its run of acquisitions in 1903, when it obtained the Exchange Bank of Yarmouth, and terminated it with the purchase of the Molsons Bank in 1925. In all, seven banks were merged into the Bank's operations in this period. Its list of acquisitions, listed in table 8.1, were part of a broader strategy to reinforce the Bank's ascendancy, especially in relation to its nearest and most serious competitor, the Royal Bank.

The competition between the two, especially over who would wear the crown of the Canadian banking in terms of assets and circulation, was fierce and protracted in this period – and would continue for some decades. Let's now take a look at the wave of mergers that happened in the first decade of the 1900s.

Table 8.1 | Bank of Montreal mergers, 1903–25

Bank	Year Acquired
Exchange Bank of Yarmouth	1903
The People's Bank of Halifax	1905
The Ontario Bank	1906
The People's Bank of New Brunswick	1907
The Bank of British North America	1918
The Merchants Bank of Canada	1924
The Molsons Bank	1925

The Bank of Montreal and First-Decade Mergers

Mergers involving the Bank of Montreal in the early 1900s included the Exchange Bank of Yarmouth, the People's Bank of Halifax, the Bank of New Brunswick, and the Ontario Bank. In the latter case, in 1906, the Bank took over the assets of the Ontario Bank and guaranteed its deposits after the management had engaged in "unfortunate" investments.[35] "The immediate absorption of the Ontario Bank by the Bank of Montreal," the *Globe* suggested, "is a most gratifying proof that our banking system and banking institutions are too strong to be shaken by even the worst effects of personal or corporate delinquencies."[36] The newspaper went on to add that "instead of alarmed depositors and panicky noteholders who crowd to the closed doors of embarrassed banking institutions under less stable conditions, we witness the simple transfer of the accounts to the largest and strongest of our chartered banks. The injurious disturbance of commerce and finance which elsewhere attends and follows the forced closing of a banking institution is thus entirely adverted, and the business goes smoothly on without a loss or inconvenience to the general public."[37] The *Globe* believed that "the highest praise should also be accorded to the president and directors of the Bank of Montreal for their prompt action and assuming all the Ontario Bank's liabilities to depositors and noteholders." While the Bank of Montreal had no legal obligation to act,

> all chartered banking corporations also feel a responsibility to the business community for the general stability of the fiscal system under which they operate, and are directly interested in maintaining that stability and sustaining unshaken the confidence of the public. The Bank of Montreal has risen to all the demands of this broader responsibility by promptly assuming the liabilities of the Ontario Bank before

the nature of its impairment could be known to the general public, and even before the story of its difficulties could obtain general circulation. Simultaneous with the story of personal mismanagement and recklessness has come the announcement that all the liabilities have been assumed, that accounts will be transferred to the Bank of Montreal, and that all obligations will be liquidated with open doors.[38]

The Bank of Montreal and the Bank of British North America

The Bank of Montreal's acquisition of the Bank of British North America is a particular case in point of the importance of reputation to Bank of Montreal bankers. The UK-based board of the BBNA found it increasingly difficult to manage the intricacies of Canadian banking from across the ocean, and as early as 1915 it had begun approaching the Bank of Montreal about a possible merger.[39] Finance Minister White initially poured cold water on the suggestion, informing the Bank of Montreal that the country would not be friendly to further bank amalgamations. Then, however, Lord Beaverbook, whose reputation as a cunning and ruthless financial dealer was well established in the halls of the Bank of Montreal, entered the picture. Beaverbrook's threatened takeover of the BBNA posed a definite reputational risk for Canadian banking.[40] By the spring of 1917, the situation had deteriorated so much – from the Bank of Montreal's point of view at least – that Sir Vincent Meredith wrote to White to express his concerns. He began by recalling that in 1915 the "feeling of the country was strongly opposed to such Bank amalgamation[s] unless the Bank to be purchased was nearing financial straits." Now, however, the circumstances were different. As Meredith explained, the reputations of the Bank of Montreal, the Canadian banking system as a whole, and the country itself were at stake. "You will readily understand how important it is to this Institution that it should be well to the fore in increasing its influence, and it would be a shock to us to think that Beaverbrook's plans might be carried to completion ... I hope you will be able to say something to me that may relieve my mind in regard to the possibility of your consent being given to the proposal I have mentioned."[41]

In a letter to Meredith the next day, White did not relieve anything, remaining non-committal as to the government's intentions in the matter.[42] The Bank forced the matter, proceeding without further advice from the minister and concluding terms in October 1917. White's response to the action was clearly irritation.[43] But Meredith was firm: "In this connection, I feel compelled to say that I think we are doing the country a service by our action and making it impossible for a bank acting under an English charter, with broad powers and certain disabilities, to enter the Canadian field of banking; also to say to you that it is not now our intention to call upon our shareholders for subscriptions for additional stock and that no money need necessarily be sent out of Canada in settlement of the transaction."[44] Meredith returned to the matter in subsequent correspondence, describing Beaverbrook's character as incompatible with the reputation of Canadian banking. As such, "the Directors [of the BBNA] were willing and anxious to turn the institution over to such an old friend as the bank of Montreal, who, being on the spot, could provide for the needs of their customers and look to the welfare of their staff better than they could do themselves from London."[45]

Meredith's representations did not, at first, have the desired effect, since White postponed consideration of the matter for several months; his position was that the proposed merger had to await a new government, whose election was imminent. This was to the consternation of the Bank, which had made all the arrangements for transfer. Ultimately, however, the merger was allowed to proceed.

The merger movement was driven by multiple, independent factors. Banks with "superior organizational technology and economies of scale" were relied upon to take over smaller, more unstable banks, as a way to avoid collapse of the entire financial system.[46] The costs of failure, both to the Canadian banks and to the government, in terms of reputational and political capital respectively, would outweigh negative elements of merging. While some argue that the initiative for the mergers appeared to come from the struggling institutions – smaller banks aware of their approaching insolvency – there is little doubt that the maintenance of the reputation of the Canadian banking system was a factor in the decision-making of the larger banks themselves.[47]

Analysis

From a strategic point of view, the Bank's acquisition of other Canadian banks from the turn of the century on made good sense. Increasing returns provided the capital necessary to "go shopping." The supply of second-tier Canadian banks was reasonably plentiful, and many of them were vulnerable – struggling with issues of generational change and a continuously transforming financial landscape. Some of the banks were also increasingly ill-equipped to handle unexpected fluctuations in the market. A few were plagued by bad management or worse. Sitting at the commanding heights of Canadian banking, Bank of Montreal managers looked out upon a target-rich environment that offered opportunities for immediate expansion in certain markets such as the Maritimes, southern Ontario, or British Columbia. As our examination has shown, moreover, the senior Canadian chartered banks exercised a serious fiduciary responsibility for the stability of the entire banking system.

In this era, regulatory guarantees, including such exotic features as deposit insurance, were years in the future. Government regulation was exercised in the lightest of possible ways through the Bank Act.

In other words, the power and authority the banks exercised over the banking system was massive. But with power and authority came responsibility for the system as well. Individual bank troubles and failures became the business of all Canadian chartered banks. In that scenario, moreover, as the senior bank and the coordinator-in-chief of Canadian banking, the Bank of Montreal held a special position as guardian and guarantor. In banking, reputation could mean everything. In Canada, the Bank of Montreal was both the model and example of the vital strategic and institutional importance of reputation.

A failure to protect Canadian banking from unfortunate circumstances, bad luck, or unscrupulous managers would not only result in reputational damage. It would also very much threaten Canadian bankers' freedom of action – to say nothing of their "ascendancy" in society – by giving rise to the threat of greater government regulation in their affairs. Industry consolidation in banking – in other words, big banks buying up smaller, struggling banks – was already raising concerns in Ottawa. Politicians and policymakers felt a growing unease with the rapid growth of the big Canadian chartered banks and the power they possessed over Canadian economic fortunes.

So, for the senior banks, there were many reasons to act, and all fell within their control. In the case of the Bank of Montreal, it played the part of the senior bank to perfection in this period by harnessing its considerable powers to ensure that its acquisitions were fully aligned with its competitive strategy, and that it met the high standard of trust that had been so hard-earned in its century of operation.

Coins of the Realm

Both the realms of trade and the acquisition wave of the early twentieth century provide us an opportunity to witness Bank of Montreal operations, strategy, and calculation in action. While, as noted earlier, trade is outward-facing and acquisitions are inward-facing, each illuminates the Bank's strategic calculations and networks of intelligence and knowledge, as well as the broader social considerations. In each instance, Bank of Montreal leaders had to exercise prudential judgments about balancing dynamism and form – what to risk and what to preserve. What is also striking about both subjects is how deeply the Bank's actions were implicated in the wider context that embraced markets and economic development as much as the political economy of the era. Those two issues placed the Bank at the centre of the action – in the unfolding story of Canadian trade in the one case, and in the evolution of Canadian finance in the other. Its leaders were primarily committed to the success of the Bank, of course. But, by applying their expertise so that the Bank could prevail, they also helped to ensure that the country to which they were so deeply committed also prevailed. Here again, we see successive generations of Bank of Montreal leadership stepping up to the challenges and opportunities the world created for them.

In each of these cases, moreover, we see very clearly how Bank of Montreal leaders were ready to seize the moment, advance the cause, and exert as much control over Fortune as destiny and circumstance permitted. In the late nineteenth and early twentieth centuries, the times called for an expansionist spirit. Subsequently, in the 1920s and 1930s, a wholly different set of circumstances and fortunes would challenge the Bank's leadership once again.

In the Introduction to Part Three, we placed the Bank's experience within the larger frame of Fortune – how, specifically, leaders and institutions can exert control over some of their environment roughly about half the time, if *The Prince* is used as the guide. Fortune's raging river can indeed overflow the plains with violent force.

But, if fortune favours the bold, it also favours the prepared, and especially those who make careful, intelligent plans to endure disruptions and exploit opportunities. In the case of the Bank of Montreal, leadership, strategy, timing, flexible regulatory frameworks, and organizational capacity all proved to be decisive in the success of its operations. To begin with, these elements allowed the Bank to endure the vagaries of Canadian and North Atlantic economic cycles. The results were significant first and foremost for the Bank but also for the development of Canada as a nation, for the evolution of its banking system, and for the changing terms of national and international trade.

Banking and the Natural World

This concluding chapter of Part Three seeks to reflect on some of the broader themes of the Bank of Montreal experience in the late nineteenth and early twentieth centuries. To begin, let me introduce a different, but complementary, metaphor than the ones we have used so far: a biological one. This is not as far-fetched as it may seem. One only has to read Andrew W. Lo's *Adaptive Markets*, where the point is made succinctly: "The short answer is that financial markets don't follow economic laws. Financial markets are products of human evolution, and follow biological laws instead. The same basic principles of mutation, competition, and natural selection that determine the life history of a herd of antelope also apply to the banking industry, albeit with somewhat different population dynamics."[48] Indeed, because the financial and natural worlds have several shared features, a biological framework provides remarkably effective explanatory power when applied to the experience of the Bank of Montreal in this period and beyond.

Forever in (Blue) Genes

The first shared feature of the financial and natural worlds is "genes." The role of genes in biology allows information to be stored and passed on from individual to individual. In the case of the Bank of Montreal, the developing corporate culture of the Bank acted as the repository of its organizational memory so that that memory could be stored and passed across the organization in time. Here, the evolution of the way of doing things, the experience of banking, its organizational forms, its regulatory context, its intelligence and financial networks, its assumptions about its role in the larger system and for the country, and its developing relationships all came together to constitute a particular corporate cultural context. It was this specific corporate culture that allowed the Bank of Montreal to flourish in this period. The developments in technique and head-office administration and coordination, as well as the growth of a transcontinental system of branches, both shaped and were shaped by this emerging corporate culture.

Mutation for a Change

The second shared feature is the potential for spontaneous "mutation." In the case of the Bank's experience in this period, stability was preferred and conservatism in banking was in the genes. But when opportunities presented themselves to exploit new opportunities, especially in international investment and trade, the Bank's leadership did not hesitate to act. In the financial world, mutations are more typically conceived along technological lines – that is, technological innovations can change the nature of the business. In this period, however, the transformations were much less about technology and more about the ability of financial institutions to achieve stability and growth by altering strategies to meet opportunities in local and national markets, in emerging sectors such as light, heat, and power-based utilities, in developing markets, in capital markets, in imperial-colonial government financing ... and the list goes on.

The Competition for Resources

Yet another shared feature of the financial and natural worlds is competition. In biology, there is competition for resources between individuals within a species. Similarly, in finance, the Bank of Montreal was especially strong in terms of its ability to survive and thrive through the persistence of effective business practices. In addition, the ability of the Bank's leadership to use its power as the largest and most consequential Canadian bank, not to mention its reputation in international markets, to the greatest possible advantage set it apart from its rivals.

Other elements of competition worth mentioning in this conceptual framework have more to do with the broader Canadian financial system. Two in particular stand out. The first one is "speciation," or biodiversity through the creation of new "species" of financial institutions. This was certainly the case in late-nineteenth-century Canada with the development of other forms of financial intermediaries such as life insurers, brokerage dealers, and trusts. The last element, "scope for extinction," when certain species die out altogether, can be seen in the disappearance of several mid-sized Canadian banks.

Networks of Performance

One of the most interesting but least understood elements of the Bank's history in this period is its successful participation in an increasingly complex international financial system. That system was made up of a growing number of network components operating within the North Atlantic financial world.[49] Even though it was Canada's principal bank, the Bank of Montreal was but one of an expanding number of banks and financial intermediaries vying for position, influence, and attention. The increasing complexity of the financial system, moreover, put an additional burden on its leadership to exercise careful judgment in their operations. Here, the emphasis on progressive conservatism, if one may use such a term and unmoor it from its political origins, may be apropos. In the Bank of Montreal context, the term encompasses an adherence to conservative banking principles that guaranteed a significant margin of safety, a healthy reserve fund, cautious expansion, and the general approach of the Bank to expansion and investment opportunities.

As the chapters in Part Three demonstrate, the Bank's performance in this nearly half-century was borne of a patient long-run strategy that defended the Bank's position in the long years of scarce opportunity and accelerated its growth in the period where, finally, it could exploit the advantages of scale, size, and scope.

Performance and Consequences

The Bank's performance, as we have seen, also held far-reaching consequences for Canada's position in the North Atlantic world. Its role in this period as banker, lender, and financial agent for the Dominion government as well as a host of other provincial and municipal governments on the New York and London markets provided critical capital flows for local and national development. No other Canadian bank could offer the depth and breadth of those facilities connecting British and American capital to Canadian state and enterprise. Massive tides of immigration to the west, an agricultural boom, and the rapid growth of new technologies in light, heat, power, communications, and transportation, as well as the changes wrought by the electro-chemical revolution of the late nineteenth and early twentieth centuries, needed a strong banking system to undergird development and ensure allocation of capital flows.

In each decade of this period – from the 1870s to the end of the Great War – the Bank of Montreal, at its best, maximized its comparative strengths to positive effect. As government banker, the Bank deployed its expertise in the capital markets of the North Atlantic world. It also worked in tandem with other major banks to ensure an orderly management of the Canadian banking system. As bankers to enterprise, Bank of Montreal managers supported a range of key industries from agriculture, forestry, and other resource industries in the west to the development of the industrial heartland of central Canada. As the trade bank par excellence, the Bank had deep and enduring links with the financial networks of the United States and London, and increasingly Latin America and the Caribbean, that created new, strong areas of opportunity for Canadian enterprise. Those enterprises would be assured of strong backing, while the Bank would be assured of reaping substantial profits as its power and influence grew.

To the Greater Glory Of

The first two decades of the twentieth century rewarded Fortune's faithful disciples to the greater glory of the institution they served. The leadership of the Bank of Montreal capitalized, through the evolution of strategy and organization, upon what I have called elsewhere the "Canadian banking ascendancy." This period appears in retrospect to have been a golden age for bankers, especially Bank of Montreal bankers. Growth in business was remarkable; consolidation favoured the larger, more established banks; Canadian banks more or less made the world as they pleased, at least from the regulatory point of view; and consistently high dividends made shareholders wealthier and wealthier. National and international expansion, development, acquisition, and consolidation all combined to put Bank of Montreal bankers even more at the centre of the action in a booming young Dominion. The influence of the Bank's senior executives everywhere – on government and enterprise alike – was profound. The Great War did little to diminish that influence or power, even as the power of government scaled up to coordinate the massive demand for capital, men, and materiel required to wage war. The powerful capabilities of the Bank and the financial connections and managerial expertise of its key leaders were deployed for the Canadian war effort. Those faithful disciples, in other words, found themselves at the very top of Fortune's wheel by 1918, but only after long years of hard work and patience.

Reputations and the Making of the Bank

There is another element that deserves attention in this era – reputation and prestige. The period from the turn of the century to the end of the 1920s was one in which the power and authority of Canadian banks reached their zenith. Whether individually (as in the case of the Bank of Montreal) or collectively (through the Canadian Bankers Association), Canadian bankers enjoyed a period of untrammelled prestige and influence that was never to be repeated thereafter. That reputation was hard-won, and hard-earned, and it was built on several key drivers: strong performance, prudent management, and a host of other positive attributes. The high standing of senior Bank of Montreal bankers and their reputation both at home and in the North Atlantic world was important for Canada as well as their own banking operations.

Reputation: Its Strengths and Its Limits

An important element in bankers' power in this era was social capital. Senior Canadian banks were places where not only Montreal anglophone elites, but Canadian elites in general, were very much in control. The management and directorships of the Bank of Montreal had the broadest possible cross-section of Canadian financial and industrial elites at the helm. In the most important branches in the cities across the Dominion, branch managers and local boards reinforced the importance of social networks to the Bank. These elites also formed a close-knit circle with the Canadian political class. They were in close contact professionally as well as socially.

The maintenance of that reputational capital, even if bankers did not call it that explicitly, was a key factor in the maintenance of their power within the Canadian financial system. Bank of Montreal bankers in particular understood this connection instinctively for a century of banking. Its status as Canada's first bank, the "premier banking institution in the Dominion," the representative of Canadian finance capital abroad, the Dominion banker, the centre of a massive information network on the financial and economic life of the country – all shaped its approach to how it conducted business.

Conclusion

This chapter ends our discussion of a remarkably diverse era in the life of the Bank of Montreal, from just after Confederation to the end of the Great War. Part Three as a whole has attempted to examine an important period in the history of Canadian banking from a new framework and perspective, incorporating new evidence and a more nuanced approach to business history. I would like to conclude by shedding light on a small but symbolic milestone that happened near the end of this remarkable era. The milestone to which I am referring was the 100th anniversary of the establishment of the Bank of Montreal. As the Bank reached the summit of its influence, authority, and prestige, it decided to celebrate its own centenary in 1917. The slim but handsome volume *The Centenary of the Bank of Montreal 1817–1917* was the result.

This was no ordinary occasion: "A century old career such as ours is unique in this country," General Manager Sir Frederick Williams-Taylor wrote Victor Ross in 1916, "and so the work in question would not have been undertaken at all unless we can secure someone who can do the subject justice."[50] In fact, justice was apparently not being done in the first drafts of the work, at least according to the Montreal bankers, and so the manuscript underwent a major rewriting after the first author did not meet the Bank's standards.[51] There then followed the most exacting scrutiny by Sir Frederick and his office – so much so that the exasperated replacement author accused them of being "hypercritical" after engaging in an abstruse and altogether overextended discussion of English-language usage in the first paragraph of the book. In any event, Sir Frederick's assistant G.W. Spinney ensured that the volume would be in every sense satisfactory to the bank. The care taken by the general manager and his deputies in sweating the exacting details of the work signalled that the book was to be treated as a precious artefact that would place the Bank's experience in its proper context for a wider public.

One would expect any self-respecting institution to exercise care and consideration in producing its own history for several reasons: reputation, communications, public relations, and employee morale, as well as a range of other, lesser objectives. The surprisingly deep involvement of Bank executives in the production of a corporate history – in both what is ultimately produced and what happened behind the scenes – can often reveal the motivations, anxieties, and aspirations of the participants. It can also shed light, retrospectively, on the strengths and weaknesses of the institution, its conception of itself, and its fidelity to the historical record as it attempts to explain itself and its experience to the wider world.

In the centenary volume of 1917, the Bank of that year reveals itself to be an institution at the very height of its powers, confident in its strategy and pleased with its performance. The leadership and workforce of the Bank understood their role in the Canadian experience, and, even in the crucible of war, they moved with the assurance of skilled navigators of the country's economic waters. Not surprisingly, then, they used the occasion of the centenary of the Bank to remind Canadians of the Bank's role as "the oldest bank in British North America and one of the largest in the British Empire."[52] The book's closing chapters were devoted to the few years leading up to 1917, during the flood of prosperity and speculation. Here, a cautionary tale was offered. The irrational exuberance of the years leading up to 1913 in Canadian markets had "aroused suspicion and distrust of Canada's economic position in the money markets of the world, followed by a close scrutiny of [the Bank's] securities and a curtailment of money supplies so essential to our development."[53] The Bank's position as a sentinel and guardian of orderly Canadian economic development was under a spotlight. As Sir Vincent Meredith suggested in 1914, the events of these years "brought us to realize the fact that unproductive expenditures must of necessity cease for a while, and our efforts be directed towards development of natural resources, accelerated by a large flow of immigration. The situation was pregnant with economic danger."[54] The warnings were heeded in time for the Great War, when prudent policies led to a substantial increase in national wealth.[55]

The Bank's self-image – its understanding of the role it played in the life of the country, and its sense of responsibility to shareholders, depositors, governments, and national well-being – was a vital part of its character. It desired to "rise to the height of any emergency, however great."[56] Sir Frederick Williams-Taylor believed that, in 1917, it was not so much the "impregnable position of the Bank" that elicited the greatest pride, but rather the staff who had answered the call of duty and had gone to do "battle for the safety of their race and the freedom of the world."[57] Two-thirds of male staff of military age enlisted. By 1917, 51 were killed, 107 wounded or missing or taken prisoner. Speaking for his generation, Williams-Taylor saw the Bank not only as a vital strategic financial institution but also as one that stepped up to meet its obligations to the nation.

The multifaceted sense of duty – to king and country, to the financial system, to employees, to shareholders, to depositors and borrowers – deeply informed the culture of the Bank as the Great War, as well as this epoch in the history of the Bank, drew to a close. This is how these faithful disciples of Fortune understood banking and how their business overflowed the regular channels of commerce to incorporate the development of the nation at large. Bank of Montreal bankers had reached the summit.

PART FOUR

A Changeful Fortune, 1918–1945

*It is clear [that] Bank of Montreal crowd feel they have been
beaten and are down on their knees[,] as they well may be.
It is a new day when that crowd begin sending their emissaries
direct to plead for mercy.*
Prime Minister William Lyon Mackenzie King,
Diaries, 4 November 1925

*Quicquid erit, superanda omni fortuna ferendo est.
[Come what may, all bad fortune is to be conquered by endurance.]*
Virgil, *Aeneid*

*I therefore conclude that, fortune being changeful and mankind
steadfast in their ways, so long as the two are in agreement men are
successful, but unsuccessful when they fall out.*
Niccolò Machiavelli, *The Prince*, Chapter 25

On the threshold of the post-war era, the Bank's leadership had every reason to feel that their establishment was at the top of its game: the Bank's performance was strong and its assets had grown substantially from the beginning of the decade. The Canadian banking system, with the Bank of Montreal at its head, had delivered vital financial assistance in the war effort. It also had provided national financial stability during the entire span of the Great War. The Bank's organization was mobilized for the war effort, its credit networks and its relationships in the financial market pressed into service both in Canada and abroad. The Dominion government came to rely on the Bank of Montreal for wartime financing as Canada's official agent in the financial markets of the North Atlantic world. Throughout wartime and the post-war period, prime ministers, and especially finance ministers, worked in close concert with Bank of Montreal bankers to navigate the massive financial and material requirements of wartime emergency. For 1,414 Bank of Montreal personnel who enlisted in the Canadian Expeditionary Force, the contribution was intensely personal. Hundreds of Bank of Montreal bankers across the Dominion "went forward at the call of their King and Country to save the British Empire from the ruthless domination of a foreign foe,"[1] with 230 making the ultimate sacrifice.

That would only be part of the story. As we saw toward the end of Part Three, the Bank's conspicuous presence at its Waterloo Place branch (and a subagency in Trafalgar Square) in London provided a popular hub for Canadian businessmen, travellers, and especially the hundreds of thousands of Canadian soldiers of the CEF. Remember that this was before the establishment of the Canadian High Commission residence in Trafalgar Square which subsequently became the natural rallying point for Canadians after 1925. By 1919, the Bank had 14,100 accounts in the Waterloo Place and Trafalgar branches combined, with about 9,000 being military accounts held by CEF personnel.[2]

In the estimation of its leaders and in the eyes of its countrymen, the Bank of Montreal represented a fundamental part of an emergent Canadian nationhood in the realm of finance. Its vital role in the development of Canadian trade and the expansion of Canadian capital – especially into the Canadian west – was one element of the equation. Its role in the Canadian financial system was another. The Bank's status as government banker, moreover, conferred a unique status and prestige upon its operations. It was both perceived as and acted as a quasi-governmental institution. The membership of its board of directors was a who's who of the Canadian financial and political elite of the day.

General Manager Sir Frederick Williams-Taylor's 1918 address to the annual general meeting captured something of that spirit: "The ease with which financial Canada has met the stress of work conditions has been favorably commented upon abroad. At home one hears no expression of surprise at the stable financial conditions in the Dominion. The real basis of that stability is a banking system that has proved most efficient in peace times and, with the facilities accorded by the Minister of Finance, has withstood the severe test of war times. The system as it stands is without doubt adequate to meet any possible demands arising during the reconstruction. And for years thereafter."[3]

Send Them Victorious

Nowhere is the Bank of Montreal spirit of that bygone age more neatly captured than in the American artist James Earl Fraser's sculpture *Victory*, a nine-foot marble statue commissioned by the Bank to honour the "many members of the staff who made the last great sacrifice in the cause of liberty and civilization."[4] It was unveiled in the atrium of Montreal Main Branch in December 1923 and has kept vigil in the same spot down to contemporary times.

As the historian Maureen Miller reminds us, objects tell a story: they act as "sources of human actions and ideas."[5] *Victory*, too, tells a story. It tells us more than meets the eye, or even what was intended by the bankers who commissioned it. The Bank ran an international competition and from all the contestants it chose Fraser, considered an inspired exponent of the Beaux-Arts tendency in sculpture, whose monuments in Washington, DC, *Contemplation of Justice* and *Authority of Law* at the Supreme Court of the United States, are universally recognizable symbols. *Victory* would have august company in the Fraser pantheon.

How *Victory* was born, the details of its commission, and what it represented offer us a glimpse into the Bank of Montreal's managerial mind of the generation of 1918. The depth of feeling at the Bank's loss of so many people to military conflict is a key element. It is, however, in the less conscious choices made that another, subtler story gets told. The Bank's actions and choices reflect an understanding of itself as an important and prestigious national institution. Institutions of the pedigree of the Bank of Montreal had an obligation to their institution, their country, and their posterity to allow its monuments – whether sculptures or buildings – to telegraph the values and relevance of the institution across time and distance. The fallen were "those to whom we looked to fill the highest positions in the service,"[6] Bank President Sir Vincent Meredith remarked at the dedication of the wall of remembrance at which *Victory* maintains her vigil. The service to which he was referring was in a bank that had become, by tradition and experience, a powerful protagonist in the governance of the country. *Victory*, therefore, is not merely a monument to the fallen but in some sense a symbol of the Bank of Montreal's ascendancy in this era.

The Canadian historian H.V. Nelles once observed that "art involves willful deception. The artist creates illusions; the audience suspends disbelief."[7] So it is with *Victory*, in two ways. First, her elegant, stately figure, keeping vigil beside the fallen, cloaks the raw, searing consequences of war for humanity. Second, the prestige and sense of command she projects is in some ways a self-portrait – a moment in time of an organization in time. In her splendor, *Victory* stands as the Bank's self-expression of its place in the country and the world, of solemn experience born of a century of successful operations and leadership.

To the men and women gathered at the unveiling ceremony in Montreal Main Branch on the Sunday before the Christmas of 1923, *Victory* must have been a breathtaking sight to behold. Beyond its obvious purpose, it projected the prestige, permanence, and possibility of the Bank of Montreal. This was a marble manifestation of the Bank's enduring prominence in the unfolding narratives of city and national life, of economic prosperity and development. Its position in one of the great neo-classical banking halls of the North Atlantic world, barely two decades old, rendered the scene complete. That the Montreal branch resembled an architectural tribute to the Roman pantheon invited reflections from classical times. The bankers of the twentieth century, of course, did not see themselves as gods, but they undoubtedly regarded themselves as protagonists and guardians of Canada's destiny who were worthy of such surroundings.

Yet *Victory* shielded some of the deeper and increasingly fast-moving currents of Canadian finance and political economy in the quarter-century after the Treaty of Versailles. Those changes – those currents and cross-currents – would forever change the Bank's fortunes and its role as the twentieth century unfolded.

Transformations

In any era, any single transformation offers a challenge to business management. Markets, adverse economic conditions, or serious changes in the political economy are the usual suspects. When the transformations are multiple, however – and when they threaten an institution's operating environment – that institution's entire universe can shift.

Between 1918 and 1945, the Bank of Montreal found itself exactly in that position. The challenge to its position and its authority came slowly, incrementally. It emanated from multiple quarters, but nowhere was it more sustained and at times acute than it was in the changing political economy of Canada in this period. Some trends were slow to manifest themselves, while others, hastened by the First World War, had more acute and immediate repercussions. Metropolitan rivalry between ascendant Montreal and fast-gaining challenger Toronto played its part. Regional rivalries and tensions also had a role to play. The Bank of Montreal was an eastern bank in the west, closely identified with Montreal capitalists and the Canadian Pacific Railway – connections that were frequently admired and, more often than anyone cared to admit, reviled when times got tough. Prime Minister William Lyon Mackenzie King poured scorn in his private diaries on the "Montreal interests," foremost among which were the Bank of Montreal and the CPR. The antipathy arose in part because of King's judgment that the Bank was hostile to the Liberal Party, though he also had a special animus for the Bank of Commerce, which, in his estimation, had "tried to destroy Sir W[ilfrid Laurier] & were not my friends."[8] These tensions would often be converted into actions squarely aimed at challenging the Bank of Montreal's perceived monopoly in government business and its preponderant influence in Canadian financial life. The fraught relations between Mackenzie King and the Bank, however, did not preclude important professional relationships, between the Bank's leadership on the one hand and King and his small cadre of confidants on the other, from resuming when national need arose.

Bankers of the era, down to the local branch managers across the country, were in demeanour, perspective, and approach worlds away from the comparatively soft, compassionate, and professionally friendly bankers of today. Bank of Montreal managers and executives of early-twentieth-century Canada were influential, respected community leaders who wielded significant financial power. Their reputation depended upon risk aversion, absolute probity, and the exercise of responsible local leadership. In fact, their social and economic status in the communities the Bank served was often second only to the mayor's. Those Bank of Montreal men staring out from journals, annual reports, and the pages of *Who's Who in Canada* knew who they were and they knew their place. Men such as Sir Vincent Meredith, Sir Frederick Williams-Taylor, F.J. Cockburn, and a cadre of other bankers belonged as Montreal bankers to a quasi-military structure with a clear chain of command. They were overwhelmingly drawn from the English Canadian Protestant elite of central Canada. They had a very clear sense of their position and standing in the order of things, and what was required of them – the responsibilities and the burdens. When the status quo was challenged or under scrutiny, the parts they played in the Order of Things came under pressure to change.

Even though the lion's share of Bank of Montreal operations were in Ontario, its Toronto competitors – the Commerce and the Toronto Bank, for example – often attempted to highlight its Montreal (i.e., not-Toronto) roots. At the same time, the labour-socialist, farmer-worker critique of banks and capitalism, growing especially intense in the last years of the First World War, became a more permanent feature of the political landscape. These critiques manifested themselves not only in broad challenges to the capitalist system, and who benefited from that system, but also in conflicts over more pragmatic matters such as loan accommodation and note circulation.

The Arrival of the State

By far the most consequential challenge to the authority of banks was the growing power of the state in public finance. Wartime finance was successfully conducted without a Canadian central bank, but a growing number of influential Canadian economists and senior Dominion public servants were convinced that Canada should join the ranks of the United States, Great Britain, and most European countries and establish a bank of Canada. Concurrently, the Department of Finance's increased regulatory scrutiny of mergers and acquisitions after 1914 reflected a growing concern about the concentration of financial power in banking. Beginning after 1918, moreover, public power began to flex its muscle and challenge existing political and economic arrangements. The advent of the Great Depression in Canada in the 1930s accelerated these trends to the tipping point, prompting far-reaching changes in the structure of Canadian banking. Depression and wartime emergency after 1939 consolidated the trend toward greater powers for government over a broad range of financial and economic initiatives.

Competitive Pressures

Bank of Montreal bankers were not the only bankers to be affected by the rise of a powerful bureaucracy and political class, but their influence as representatives of Canada's coordinator-in-chief of banking, the unofficial central bank, and the country's first bank would mean there would be major adjustments to their influence once those roles were no longer required.

The Bank's emerging rival, the Royal Bank, moreover, eclipsed the Bank of Montreal by assets by 1925 as a result of merger and acquisition activity. The loss of primacy was more symbolic than real, but it had psychological consequences for the Bank of Montreal as it struggled to maintain its position and authority in a more competitive world. Sir Vincent Meredith, the Bank's president, was so annoyed by the Royal's overtaking his institution that he refused to speak to the Royal's president, Edson Loy Pease, for two years. Pease's advocacy in favour of the establishment of a central bank – a position tenaciously opposed by the Bank of Montreal – undoubtedly contributed to the frigid relations at the top of Canadian banking in the 1920s.

Complexity and Contingency

The period between 1918 and the end of the Second World War was a remarkably complex and transformational one for government, for business, for banking, and for the country. Focusing merely on the headlines and outcomes, as this Introduction must, cannot do justice to the messy, open-ended, and indeterminate character of events.

When Bank of Montreal management was confronted with a changing operational environment or changing rules of the political or regulatory game, they did what any institution has done since antiquity: they sought to exercise their influence and sway outcomes. Yet the landscape was no longer the same. Following the First World War, a century after the Bank's establishment in 1817, Bank of Montreal bankers were confronted with an unprecedented set of challenges to their authority and position which set their institution on a new historical trajectory. They remained influential, important protagonists in the financial life of the country, but in ways that had to accommodate other significant players in a mixed private-public economy. In a way, this was the era in which the Bank of Montreal fell to earth.

The quotation that opens Part Four, a diary entry by Prime Minister William Lyon Mackenzie King in 1925 – at a particularly intense moment in the political life of the country, and in the relationship between politics and Montreal bankers – captures beautifully the idea that personality and relationships can play surprising and unexpected roles in the historical record. In other words, bankers, businessmen, ministers, politicians, and public servants were not cardboard cut-outs. They were (and are) people who faced contingent circumstances, massive responsibilities, enjoyed little if any clairvoyance, and wielded variable access to power. King's exclamations show that finance, economics, and politics inevitably exist in close collaboration and contact in this period. The men of the inter-war generation understood the interlocking nature of their relationships – personal, political, professional – very well indeed.

Part Four of this book continues our examination of the Bank of Montreal's long-run experience. It analyzes what this section's title suggests – the nature of the Bank of Montreal's changes of fortune in the post-First World War period, and its energetic and strategic responses to these changes. It is a remarkable story. The Bank's history in this period primarily unfolded in the arena of political economy, so it is a very much a story of business-government relations. But the chapters of Part Four also study the development of a complex twentieth-century financial organization managing regional, national, and international financial flows and networks and confronting unprecedented social, economic, and geo-political upheaval. At its heart, Part Four recounts the story of how the Bank faced the challenges before it and how it endured and adapted to a changing world – war, post-war, boom, crash, depression, and war once again.

There are five chapters in this section. The first, chapter 9, covers the key themes of the 1918–29 period. Chapter 10 continues the story, covering the decade of the Depression to 1939. The following two chapters, 11 and 12, focus on two key historical events in the life of the country and the Bank: first, the Bank's role in attempts to salvage public finance in the Dominion of Newfoundland in the early 1930s; and second, the struggle to establish a central bank in Canada. The final chapter examines the Bank's involvement in the Second World War, to 1945. The overarching theme is the Bank's effort to come to terms with new challenges, new situations, and new roles.

CHAPTER NINE

The Boreal Winds

The period from 1918 to 1929 represents roughly a decade of increasingly transformational shifts in the operational environment of Canadian banking. In these years, the "B of M," as it was increasingly referred to, experienced growth, competitive pressure, and major change in its relationship with the Dominion government. The focus of this chapter is on the Bank of Montreal's response to these developments – and how it fared in the multiple arenas in which it competed.

A Post-war World Dawning

The period following the Armistice of November 1918 was a turbulent one for Canada. An economy shaped by the demands of wartime emergency was compelled to readjust to uncertain post-war economic and political conditions. The legacy of the Great War was complex and in many ways contradictory. On the battlefields of Europe, the Canadian Expeditionary Force fought with exceptional bravery and resolve. The Canadian contribution in blood and treasure earned the country a place, although a limited one for the time being, in the international diplomatic order. If "colony" became "nation" after the sacrifices of Ypres, Passchendaele, and Vimy and elsewhere on the battlefront, Canada would have to await further developments to acquire its seat at the table. On the home front, social and economic relations had been strained almost to the breaking point. In 1917 the issue of military conscription divided the country and reignited both English-French tensions and east-west antipathies, with many French Canadians and western farmers deeply resenting the call to arms. Dramatic political events followed: Conservative Prime Minister Sir Robert L. Borden entered the 1917 election with a Union coalition of pro-conscription Conservatives and Ontario Liberals and won a secure majority. That victory, however, came with enduring and damaging consequences for Canadian politics. Relations between labour and capital were also stretched to the breaking point, most acutely symbolized in a confrontation at Winnipeg, where a general strike called in May 1919 was suppressed by police action near the end of June.[1] Post-war economic conditions of high unemployment and inflation added to Canada's difficult transition to a peacetime economy. In fact, any significant recovery was painfully slow in materializing: only in 1924 were there signs of a return to relative prosperity.

This was the complex and fraught environment that Bank of Montreal bankers entered in 1918. In the immediate post-war period, however, the Bank's performance seemed to exist in another economic reality. Fuelled by an initial post-war optimism, the Bank's loans and discounts rose from $162 million in 1918 to $238 million in 1920 – a 47 per cent increase.[2] The Bank's strategic acquisition of a number of banks in the 1900s continued with a major move, discussed in the previous chapter – the purchase of the Bank of British North America in 1918, adding seventy-nine branches to its network. The BBNA acquisition also established the Bank of Montreal's presence on the US West Coast, in San Francisco. Together with new branch openings, the Bank by 1920 had 319 branches across the country.[3]

The immediate post-war growth in business led to an expanded organization and command structure, with four new assistant general managers and the creation of several departments and divisions based on function – Foreign Department, Foreign Exchange, Routine Efficiency, Bank Premises, and Special Debts. Later, the Securities Department was formed – a recognition of the Bank's long-standing role in underwriting bond financing.[4]

The view from the Bank's Place d'Armes headquarters, however, was positive but characteristically careful. Sir Vincent Meredith lamented the prevalence of labour unrest – "strikes and disorder" – not least because of the "decreased efficiency, lessened production and greater cost of output" that resulted. The "abnormal nervous strain of the Great War"[5] undoubtedly had played its part in giving rise to these conditions. On top of that, a sharp recession made worse in Canada by the US imposition of the Fordney-McCumber tariffs on agricultural and dairy commodities sent the Canadian economy into a tailspin. A few statistics will suffice. In October 1919 Canada shipped $28.6 million in agricultural exports. The same month a year later, the figure was $7.32 million. In five months, the tariffs had reduced overall exports from Canada from $62.1 million to $17.3 million.[6]

The economic and political convulsions of the 1919–20 period contributed to an exceptionally challenging operational environment. Meredith's view was that the 1920 banking year had been one of "unremitting anxiety, entailing constant vigilance in order to avoid serious losses." Bank General Manager Sir Frederick Williams-Taylor added for good measure that 1920–21 was the "most troubled period in [the banking world's] history." Only by mid-1922 did the Canadian economy, led by an upswing in exports, begin to show signs of strength.[7]

The difficult and often-unpredictable economic circumstances of post-war Canada seemed to vindicate the Bank's twentieth-century version of its Stability Strategy, which heavily favoured large cash reserves and a cautious and conservative approach. "Our cash reserves should be kept exceptionally strong," Meredith declared in 1923, "to enable us to lend aid if and when called upon to do so."[8] The Bank of Montreal's role as key guarantor of the banking system demanded nothing less. The fact that Great Britain and Canada abandoned the gold standard at the outbreak of the First World War, and did not return to it until 1926, put an even greater onus on established financial institutions to ensure monetary stability.

Canada's Banking Magisterium

In strategy and outlook, the post-war Bank of Montreal looked a lot like the pre-war Bank of Montreal. It was, in almost every sense of the term, Canada's "Establishment Bank." Its outlook, strategy, brand, and reputation mutually reinforced that deeply rooted reality. Its role as the largest bank, and especially as government banker, and in many ways de facto central bank, cemented that notion in the managerial mind of the early twentieth century. Certainly, its unique role as guardian and guarantor of the Canadian banking, in the absence of stringent regulation or a central bank, strongly influenced leadership's approach to banking and national economic affairs. In some ways, the Bank of Montreal could be called Canada's banking magisterium – the repository of Canadian banking orthodoxy, its teaching office, its deposit of banking "faith."

Leadership and Organization

That banking "faith" was strongly rooted in both the Bank's experience and its traditions. Its organization, capabilities, national networks, and links to economic development and the growth of enterprise reinforced these notions in the minds early-twentieth-century Bank of Montreal management. The Bank's actions in protecting the Canadian banking system by absorbing or merging with failing banks were seen as uniting shareholder interest with the broader interest of the Canadian banking system and, by extension, the national interest as well. Bank of Montreal directors of this era – among them, Edward Beatty, J.W. McConnell, General Arthur Currie, and F.W. Molson – were the *ne plus ultra* of the Canadian financial and economic elite.

The two men who most guided the destiny of the Bank in the 1920s, Sir Vincent Meredith and Sir Frederick Williams-Taylor, were in every sense of the term "traditional bankers." Born in London, Ontario, in 1850, Vincent Meredith had joined the Bank in 1867, rising through the ranks. He became general manager in 1911 and served as president from 1913 to 1927 – a position his training and temperament had made it seem he had been born to.[9] Meredith personified the establishment banker of his day: a man of "erect, military bearing" with a character that "epitomized the values of Canadian banking: integrity and meticulousness."[10]

Sir Frederick Williams-Taylor, Meredith's general manager, was also a career banker. He joined the Bank at the tender age of fifteen in 1878 and would stay for the next sixty-seven years, until his death in 1945. He was promoted to manager at the age of twenty-eight, thereby becoming the "youngest officer in the service" to occupy such a position. He managed the London office from 1905 to 1913 and served as general manager from 1914 to 1929.[11] Williams-Taylor was also a bit of a dandy. A former Bank employee recalled that Williams-Taylor requested new bank notes every week, and his portrait prominently featured bank notes as he removed them from his wallet.[12] Where Meredith was quiet and patrician, Williams-Taylor was voluble and free-wheeling in character – "urbane and outgoing," according to one observer.[13] The two sometimes clashed over approach and on specific issues but they were united in espousing a deeply, perhaps compulsively, conservative perspective on banking and economic questions undisturbed by more contemporary notions about changing roles for government or new approaches to the economy.[14]

Meredith and Williams-Taylor were not alone, by far, in their leadership of the Bank. Sir Charles Blair Gordon, a native-born Montrealer, began his professional life as a clerk before forming his own business selling shirts.[15] From a roaring success in that business, Gordon joined the syndicate in 1904 that put the Dominion Textile Company together, becoming its managing director and eventually president. Gordon achieved "millionaire status" by 1911 and by 1913 was a director of the Bank of Montreal. His brilliant business sense was recognized by an important wartime appointment – the vice-chairmanship of the Imperial Munitions Board in Canada in 1915, followed by an appointment as the deputy to Lord Northcliffe, the head of the British War Mission in Washington from 1917 to the end of the war in 1918. It was a job Gordon confessed to have disliked and endured, since his British superiors were both inexperienced and enormously condescending, "ignoring Gordon's years of experience in munitions supplies."[16] By the time he joined the Bank of Montreal as a vice-president, he was considered, according to his biographer, "a leader among the elite of the city's business community."[17] Gordon's presence on the Bank's executive was absolutely key, given his experience and strategic insight into the complex world of North Atlantic finance. "Perhaps there is no other man in Canadian business life," one newspaper enthusiastically reported in 1917, "whose career so aptly illustrates the reward of conscientious business energy as that of Chas. B. Gordon."[18] By 1927, he was elected president (with a salary of $25,000) as Meredith moved to the position of chairman.[19] Gordon would hold that position unto death, in 1939.

These leaders depended upon an increasingly important second tier of executives and an expanding array of managers such as H.B. Mackenzie (eventually general manager), Huntly R. Drummond, Clement Hamilton Cronyn, and Francis Jeffrey Cockburn to manage the growing operations of the Bank. Mackenzie was a southern Ontario-born banker who entered banking life through the Commerce and the BBNA, where he acquired a distinguished reputation in banking circles. Drummond was the son of Sir George Drummond of Bank and Redpath fame.[20] The Calcutta-born Cockburn was a life-long banker who entered the Bank's service in 1879 and worked his way up the ranks to the post of assistant general manager, which he held from 1918 to 1929 at a salary of $17,500 and an allowance of $2,500.[21] Most of the executives were career banking professionals with decades of experience in the Bank of Montreal. On the board of directors, Major-General S.C. Mewburn, a former minister of defence in the Union government (1917–20), was particularly active as a member of the executive committee – a new entity that had been created in December 1927 to deal with the expanding business of the bank. From these able bankers the institution could draw a deep well of experience in banking and enterprise; in command of a network of branches, staff, and information, they were ready to formulate strategy atop the largest and most influence bank in Canada.

By the 1920s, the Bank had become a large bureaucratic organization with a powerful head office and hundreds of branches across its territory. The institution produced a distinct working and operating culture in the regional and head offices, complete with extracurricular activities.

The major bureaucratic expansion of the head-office operations in this period reflected both the Bank's growth and the greater complexity of operations. It was in this era that, under the supervision of C.H. Cronyn, a number of new departments, including advertising, were established alongside the traditional divisions handling routine bank business. By the end of the decade, the growth in the sheer number of staff required new methods to reach them: and thus the staff magazine was born.[22] In April 1926, under Cronyn's supervision,[23] the Bank began to publish a monthly "Business Summary" – a digest of "information received by the Bank of Montreal from its branches throughout Canada and from its offices abroad."[24] The summaries provided detailed information and analysis of government finances and public policy, the foreign trade of Canada, and in particular agricultural production both at a national and a regional and provincial level, as well as in the Dominion of Newfoundland, Mexico, Great Britain, France, and the United States.[25] The summaries acted in a dual role: as important information for managers and clients, and as a reminder that the Bank, in its capacity as fiscal agent on behalf of "Governments, Municipalities and Corporations," was "in constant touch with security markets at home and abroad."[26]

On its face, the Bank's approach paid handsome dividends. In Meredith's tenure from 1913 to 1927, assets tripled to $831.5 million. Shareholder dividends were remarkably generous, even in some of the lean years (see table 9.1). By 1925, Canadian banks could point to the fact that Canada had one branch bank for every 2,100 people, compared to 3,780 for the United States and 3,000 for Australia.[27]

The Benefits of Conservative Banking

The Canadian banking system taken as a whole also benefitted from the Bank's strategic and operational conservatism. One study found that interest rates paid on deposits were generally higher in Canada than in the United States, as was interest income received on securities. Loan rates were comparable, moreover, in Canada and the United States. The more conservative Canadian system, with its branch system, economies of scale, and emphasis on stability, had undeniable advantages.[28] Indeed, the reputation of the Bank of Montreal as the "premier banking institution in the Dominion" enabled it to pass through periods of "unusual conditions without any impairment of its traditionally strong position."[29]

The Bank's major loan activities in the late 1920s demonstrate the extent of the Canadian economy's activity and consolidation. The Bank's involvement in company reorganizations was one such measure. The Bathurst Company's reorganization committed the Bank of Montreal to $16 million in advances to finalize the deal through Nesbitt, Thomson and Company.[30] Other major loans included Canadian National Railways ($5.9 million and $22.5 million), Greenshields and Company ($1.725 million),[31] and Royal Securities Corporation ($4 million).[32]

Table 9.1 | Bank of Montreal dividend payments, 1913–27

Year	Dividend	Bonus	Recurrence	Total %	Total $
1913	2.5%	1%*	quarterly *bonus: semi-annually	12%	$1,920,000.00
1914	2.5%	1%*	quarterly *bonus: semi-annually	12%	$1,920,000.00
1915	2.5%	1%*	quarterly *bonus: semi-annually	12%	$1,920,000.00
1916	2.5%	1%*	quarterly *bonus: semi-annually	12%	$1,920,000.00
1917	2.5%	1%*	quarterly *bonus: semi-annually	12%	$1,920,000.00
1918	2.5%	1%*	quarterly *bonus: semi-annually	12%	$1,920,000.00
1919	3%	n/a	quarterly	12%	$2,372,250.00
1920	3%	2%*	quarterly **bonus: annually	14%	$2,960,000.00
1921	3%	2*	quarterly *bonus: annually	14%	$3,080,000.00
1922	3%	2%*	quarterly *bonus: annually	14%	$3,657,500.00
1923	3%	2%*	quarterly *bonus: annually	14%	$3,815,000.00
1924	3%	2%*	quarterly *bonus: annually	14%	$3,815,000.00
1925	3%	2%*	quarterly *bonus: annually	14%	$4,161,671.00
1926	3%	2%*	quarterly *bonus: annually	14%	$4,188,388.00
1927	3%	2%*	quarterly *bonus: annually	14%	$4,188,388.00

* Variable payment.

Source: Data taken from Annual Reports, 1913–1927.

The Bank's loans operations also extended far afield. In 1928, for example, the Republic of Mexico approached the Bank for a $5-million loan "to be used for carrying out a programme relative to roads, irrigation and schools, repayment to be made $500,000 monthly from assigned taxes."[33] The Bank advised that it was "foreign to our practice to make loans abroad other than for commercial purposes." However, if the Mexican government would obtain an endorsement on the certificates it had intended to issue for covering the loan "in a form that would obligate the mining, textile and other companies to retire a certain proportion each month and the total within ten months," the Bank might consider the proposal.[34]

The Bank's returns in the late 1920s give some indication of its prosperity: between April and July 1928, the Bank netted $2.43 million in profit, in comparison to $1.78 million for the same period in 1927.[35] By 1929, the Bank was anticipating a $10-million profit.[36]

On Conditions of Investment in Canada in 1928

The later 1920s were very active ones in the capital markets of the Dominion. In 1927 Canadians repurchased foreign securities in Canadian enterprises, and when the purchase of foreign securities and bonds is also taken into consideration, total Canadian investment exceeded $100 million in the United States alone. Canadians were also repurchasing industrial concerns that has passed in to foreign hands – Goodyear Tyre, Windsor Hotel, Hiram Walker, Acadia Sugar, National Steel Car, Montreal Piggly-Wiggly Corporation, and many others.[37] The balances of the Canadian chartered banks abroad were impressive, too: a total of $238 million – 60 per cent of which was in the United States, 20 per cent in the United Kingdom, and 20 per cent elsewhere.[38] Insurance companies topped the banks, with $285 million in investment. Canadian investment abroad, in total, was $1.579 billion.[39] By contrast, British and foreign investment in Canada was comparatively larger. In 1928 British investments were $2.2 billion, while US investments were $3.2 billion. The largest UK investments were in public utilities, while the US investments were mainly in government securities.[40]

By the late 1920s and early 1930s, Canadian chartered banks were in decent shape, as tables 9.2 and 9.3 show. Yet the Bank of Montreal continued to display its characteristic caution. Even when conditions markedly improved, they were declared "reasonably satisfactory" and typically came with a caveat that "we cannot hope for substantial and permanent betterment until worldwide conditions show a marked improvement, and this is likely to take time."[41] The prescriptions, moreover, were characteristically blunt. Conditions would never improve until Canada succeeded in balancing its budget. "For the time being," Williams-Taylor suggested in 1924, "we are handicapped in three distinct respects ... high cost of living and high taxation ... [and] lack of adequate population."[42] The perennial problem of national railway debt was also a constant subject of concern. "I am persuaded that, of our national problems," Meredith suggested in 1926, "none presses more urgently for solution upon Parliament than that of the railways." Only in 1927 would Meredith suggest that Canada had "emerged from the shadow of restricted business, unsatisfactory earnings and indifference balance sheets – "so much so that the future could be finally

Table 9.2 | State of Canadian banking, 1929

Deposits – Demand	$689 million
Deposits – Time	$1508 million
Notes in Circulation	$154 million
Gold	$92 million
Dominion Notes	$183 million
Call Loans on Securities – Canada	$263 million
Call Loans on Securities – Abroad	$302 million
Current Loans in Canada	$1320 million
Percentage of Current Loans to Time Deposits	87%
Gold – Held By Banks	$92 million
Gold – Held By Government	$59 million
Percentage of Gold to Notes in Circulation	86%
Percentage of Gold to demand Deposits and Notes in Circulation	17.5%

Source: BEA OV 58/1 430, "Office of the High Commissioner of Canada (Natural Resources and Industrial Information Bureau) Special Bulletin (J.L. Fisher)," 24 July 1929.

"viewed with confidence."[43] The Dominion's return to the gold standard in 1926 was a sign of that returning confidence.

The Bank closely identified its own destiny with the national one. "The interests of your Bank," Williams-Taylor stated in 1925, "are more closely bound up with those of Canada than ever before, and unless Canada prospers the Bank cannot expect the prosperity it should enjoy."[44] By the late 1920s, the Bank could point to its full participation "in the general prosperity." Investment was buoyed by major improvements in trade and industry, as well as a bountiful harvest in the prairies, not to mention "higher rates for call money in New York."[45]

There were additional advantages to the cautious approach. As the Canadian economy heated up in the latter half of the 1920s, the Bank warned its managers about "the increasing tendency on the part of the public, including many of our customers, to speculate in mining shares, some of which appertain to Mines which are as yet in the development stage."[46] Those shares "could not be regarded as constituting acceptable collateral for bank loans."[47]

Again in 1927, the head office began to sound notes of caution about valuations in the stock market. Managers in June 1927 were advised that, although head office had "no reason to believe that setback is imminent," "should any weakness in prices develop there is always the danger of widespread financial difficulties."[48] Williams-Taylor added in 1928 that "speculation is now so much in evidence … speculation, like fever, is not a disease but a symptom, and like many a fever, will probably cure itself." However,

Table 9.3 | Branch presence of Canadian banks, 1933

Name of Bank	PEI	NS	NB	QB	ON	MN	SK	AB	BC	YK	Total
Bank of Montreal	1	14	13	120	216	36	51	55	52	2	560
Bank of Nova Scotia	9	36	37	23	134	7	22	9	6	–	283
Bank of Toronto	–	–	–	15	104	12	27	13	9	–	180
Banque Provinciale du Canada	4	–	13	107	14	–	–	–	–	–	138
Canadian Bank of Commerce	7	19	6	67	300	43	91	67	65	2	667
Royal Bank of Canada	6	62	22	82	253	72	118	68	55	–	738
Dominion Bank	–	–	1	8	99	12	4	5	4	–	133
Banque Nationale	–	–	–	213	15	8	7	6	–	–	249
Imperial Bank of Canada	–	–	–	4	122	8	39	23	12	–	208
Barclays Bank Canada	–	–	–	1	1	–	–	–	–	–	2
Total	27	131	92	640	1,258	198	359	246	203	4	3,158

Source: BEA OV 58/1, "Encl. To Letter 27/9/33 from Peacock, 'Memorandum by Mr. JA McLeod, President, the Canadian Bankers' Association on the Present Working of the Canadian Banking System,'" 7 August 1933.

"experience suggests the wisdom of guarding against possible set-backs, whereas over-optimism carried with it the ever-present danger of a rude awakening."[49] As he explained:

> There seems to be a somewhat widespread idea that Canadian banks have transferred large amounts of money to New York for employment in call loans. That notion is wholly erroneous. The policy of the Bank of Montreal, and, I may say, I believe this applies to all Canadian banks, has long been to carry in New York a substantial proportion of ready reserves of quick assets. No funds, however, are ever transferred to New York or London to be loaned on call until every legitimate need of our own country has been carefully examined, and, if at all possible, complied with.[50]

In fact, the amount of "time money" on loan by the Bank in New York was about $10 million – a substantial amount but not large in comparison to the overall picture.[51]

Capitalization Increases

One of the clearest signs of the Bank's health was its capitalization. The mounting capitalization of the Bank in the 1920s continued throughout the decade. In 1922 a $5.25-million increase raised the capital stock to $27.25

million, as part of the Merchants Bank acquisition.[52] In 1925 another $2.66 million was added as a result of the Molsons Bank acquisition, bringing the capital stock to $31.17 million. It was in 1929, however, that the largest and most significant capital-stock increase occurred: $18.82 million to bring the total to $50 million. The move was not without its internal opponents, who had warned against such an aggressive capitalization.[53]

Canada's economic activity in 1929 seemed to warrant such an increase. Bank returns had shown further expansion in commercial loans. In August 1929, for example, these loans exceeded $1.3 billion – an increase of $179 million over the corresponding period in 1928. New note circulation also went up $19.53 million, "an exceptional increase" in the Bank's view.[54]

International Expansion: Mexico and France

The Bank's international presence was restricted, by policy, to areas where the Bank could assist Canadian capital and enterprise with banking facilities. Typically, however, the Bank preferred to focus on developing relationships with corresponding banks rather than developing long-term extraterritorial branches. The two exceptions in this period were Mexico and France, for different reasons.

Mexico

The Bank of Montreal first entered the Mexican market in 1906 when it opened a branch office in Mexico City, following Canadian capital and in some ways the aspirations of its own early-twentieth-century leaders such as Sir Edward Clouston. In 1910, as we have seen, the country collapsed in revolution and civil war, which lasted until a new constitution was signed in 1917 although violence continued until 1920. The year 1917, however, "may be taken as the beginning of [Bank of Montreal] operations after the revolutionary period," as Mexico returned to the gold standard and relative economic stability was achieved.[55]

Unsurprisingly, the Mexico City branch operated at a loss in these turbulent times. Between 1911 and 1915 the Mexico City branch losses averaged between US$50,000 and US$100,000 per year. After 1917, it began turning a profit, a trend that continued into the 1920s as the effects of revolution subsided. (See table 9.4.)

In that decade, the Bank also opened a number of new branches in Mexico: Veracruz (1922), Puebla (1923), Guadalajara (1924), Monterrey (1924), Tampico (1926), and a second Mexico City office (1926). A 1926 memorandum sent to Bank of Montreal Managers H.H. Davis and G.E. Howard highlights the

Table 9.4 | Bank of Montreal in Mexico, 1918–23

Year	Profit (in USD)
1918	$60,000
1919	$130,000
1920	$275,000
1921	$225,000
1922	$175,000
1923	$250,000

Source: BMOA, Mexico, Memos & Precis, 1926–1927; Mexico – Report on
Accounts, "Mexico, D.F. Managers – H.H. Davis – G.B. Howard,"
11 May 1926.

progress made by the Bank of Montreal in Mexico: "Our business in Mexico continues to increase. The largest increase is the loans in the account of *Cia. Comercial Comisionista* (Sugar Pool)[,] approximately $2,100,000 secured by warehouse receipts for sugar. The balance is spread over a number of accounts. 30% of our loans may be classified under the head of 'Sugar' and 20% 'Cotton.' The balance is fairly well spread among commercial accounts. [The Bank] continues to hold first place in clearings."[56] The memorandum also shows that most of the corporate accounts at the Bank's Mexican branches were primary-resource-oriented (sugar, cotton, lumber, etc.), playing to the Bank's strengths and also adhering to the more trade-oriented, lucrative, and secure parts of Mexico's economic productive capacity.

At its height of activity in the late 1920s, the Bank of Montreal operated seven offices in Mexico. Following the collapse of world markets in 1929, however, business turned sour. In response to the worldwide economic downturn, the Bank of Montreal slowly withdrew from the Mexican market. By 1935, its operations in Mexico had ceased and by 1938 the last legal hurdles for withdrawal had been cleared. After official closure of business, the Bank of Montreal faced a storm of complaints, inquiries, and even lawsuits from former corporate and private clients. The Bank enlisted the services of a solicitor, J. Vera Estanol, to deal with the legal aftermath of its complete withdrawal from the Mexican market.[57]

Although the Bank of Montreal's venture into Mexico was limited and ill-starred, its leadership continued to be attracted by the country's opportunities. As early as 1946, less than ten years after the Bank's exit from Mexico, management contemplated a potential return. One internal Bank memorandum put it this way: "Inflation is rampant in Mexico at present. This would have to be borne in mind. There will probably be little opposition; in fact the Government would likely welcome our return for the prestige. However, once we were in we would have to be prepared for the usual aggravating laws and bleeding to which we would be subject. Mexico will not have changed in this respect."[58] The Bank had also learned lessons from the legal complications that had followed its withdrawal from Mexico in the mid-1930s. Should the Bank re-enter the Mexican market, the memorandum stated, it would do so under a different legal status: "Should it be decided to reopen a branch in Mexico City, consideration might be given to the desirability of forming a separate corporation similar to San Francisco ... If this were done it is assumed we would be on an equal footing with local banks as regards to all operations. This would also get away from any liability the Bank of Montreal [might be exposed to] in Canada by way of suits, et cetera, which would have to be in instituted against the local bank."[59]

In the event, the Bank would not re-enter the Mexican market until three decades later, in 1963. The *Financial Post* of that year captured the Bank's reasoning for returning and sheds some light on why it had established a presence in that country in 1906 in the first place:

> The new Mexico City office of the Bank of Montreal, open nearly a year, is one source of commercial and credit information for Canadians doing business in Mexico. This is the only Canadian banking office in the country. Canadian banks were once widely represented in Mexico, but most closed their offices in the mid-1930s, fearing the political climate then existing there. B of M opened its first branch in Mexico in 1906 and had seven branches when it pulled out in 1934. The new office, run by Dr. Luis Gonzalez and William J. Carr, is, like other foreign banks, not permitted to engage in the Mexican banking business. B of M President Arnold Hart says the office was set up to help further trade and other business ties between Canada and Mexico and to help Canadian businessmen develop their Mexican interests.[60]

The re-entry into the Mexican market in the 1960s was conducted under markedly different conditions than in earlier decades. While the Bank had been allowed to operate as a regular bank with branches in the 1930s, this was no longer possible during the 1960s. Banks were nationalized in Mexico in the 1930s. This meant that the Bank could operate only a representative office in the Mexican market.

The fact that the Bank of Montreal entered and withdrew from the Mexican market three times over the course of the twentieth century suggests the enduring appeal of that market as an international opportunity. The other international adventure for the Bank of Montreal in the 1920s happened across the Atlantic Ocean, in France.

France

In 1918 Bank directors agreed to establish a branch in Paris, a move designed, in the words of Vincent Meredith, "not for the purpose of loaning Canadian funds, but to supply necessary banking facilities to Canadians travelling abroad and to further the interests of Canada generally in France."[61] Like Mexico, this decision was somewhat of an exception from the Bank's policy of "strengthening and extending our relations with foreign banking houses and to retain their good-will, thereby conserving our resources for the assistance and encouragement of home trade."[62]

The opening of the Paris branch was part of a much larger international expansion. The Bank's powerful and well-connected London committee not only dealt with a long list of banking and business clients and the placement of Canadian, Empire, Commonwealth, and other bonds and loans.[63] It also continued its heavy involvement in the underwriting of colonial government loans across the Empire – South Africa, Australia, Western Australia, New Zealand, the government of Victoria (Australia), Kenya, India, and the like.[64] At the same time, the Bank's networks and governmental contacts in the Dominion allowed it to acquire similar business in the North Atlantic; for example, with respect to the UK government, the Bank of Montreal acted as the official agent of the secretary of state for India in the post-war period for the purpose of receiving tenders for telegraphic transfers in rupees on Calcutta.[65] By 1927, the Bank of Montreal could report a total of £10.68 million in capital deployed by the London branch. An additional £1.2 million was invested on account of the head office, yielding an average profit of £295,000 per annum between 1924 and 1927.[66]

The establishment of a Bank of Montreal branch in Paris was intended to help with these efforts, promoting Canada and Empire.[67] Operating as a subsidiary of the Bank of Montreal under the name of the Société Anonyme Bank of Montreal (France), the Paris branch, as it was more colloquially known, opened on 1 July 1919.[68] The new subsidiary was controlled from London and was headed by Sir Vincent Meredith as president, Sir Charles Gordon as vice-president, William Fish Benson (an old hand at the head office and joint assistant manager of the London office between 1912 and 1919) as manager, and Edward Pope as assistant manager.[69]

Mirroring its Mexican counterparts, the Bank of Montreal's Paris branch bloomed in the early 1920s. It turned a healthy profit of £69,000 in the first half of fiscal 1921 and £73,000 in the same period for 1922.[70] The Bank of Montreal's presence in London and Paris made it a significant player in interwar continental affairs. One small example of this influence and significance can be seen in late 1931, when the Bank of Montreal's London committee discussed the question of the German 5½ per cent "Young" Bonds, which were held by the Bank's Paris branch.[71] The "Young" Bonds referred to the renegotiations of the German war reparations with the 1929 Young Plan, and the Bank of Montreal's subscription to these loans demonstrates that the Bank's Paris office was a significant player on the continent.

The onset of the Great Depression halted the Paris branch's prosperity and, just as in Mexico, operations in France ceased by 1935. On 9 March 1935 the final meeting of the Bank of Montreal (France) was held in London at which the accounts of liquidation were approved and the closing of the books authorized.[72] The branch shut its doors on 15 June 1935 and, by the middle of September, C.D. Kerr, assistant manager of the former Paris office, had left Paris.[73]

With the closure of the Paris branch, another international adventure of the Bank of Montreal came to an end. It was not until 1956 that the Bank would re-enter the French market, with the establishment of a representative office in Paris. The opening of branches in both Mexico and France in the early part of the twentieth century was sabotaged by the onset of the Great Depression and the unwillingness of the Bank's leadership to stick with the international offices in times of hardship. The Bank's presence in both Mexico and France was well founded – this explains why the Bank returned to both countries during the post-war period – but the economic unpredictability of the 1930s doomed the Bank's international presence until after the Second World War. And even after 1945, perhaps soured by its inter-war experience in Mexico and France, the Bank of Montreal was a reluctant player in world markets, setting it apart from its rivals, particularly the Bank of Nova Scotia and the Royal Bank, which embraced international expansion wholeheartedly.

Strategy and the Instrument of the Merger

Domestically, however, the Bank of Montreal met with more long-term success in the inter-war period, thanks in part to a series of mergers and acquisitions which were a vital feature of its conservative growth strategy in the first part of the twentieth century. Between 1918 and 1924, the Bank acquired the Bank of British North America (1918), branches of the Colonial Bank (1920), the Merchants Bank (1921), and Molsons Bank (1924).[74] The mergers in this period allowed the Bank to grow and acquire market share without changing its core approach to banking itself. Therein, perhaps, lay the advantage and the disadvantage of the strategy. While mergers added to branch totals and asset figures, they were bound up in a number of competing objectives at the Bank.

Mergers represented the strategic instrument most suited to the Bank's approach to growth, expansion, and competitive response in the market. They were a straightforward and relatively simple way to expand and add to the

Bank's assets. Through mergers, the Bank was using its market power and highly seasoned managerial capabilities to the greatest extent, and it pursued such opportunities with vigour as they arose. Between 1918 and 1924, there were plenty of opportunities, generated by failing or weak institutions ready to give up the fight.

Mergers, as we saw in the previous chapter, were the most prominent element of the history of banking in this period. These mergers not only represent a major pillar of the Bank of Montreal strategy but also point to a key set of developments in Canadian banking in the 1920s. Some scholars have argued that mergers and consolidation in Canadian banking were straightforward market processes that transferred assets from weak to strong management and were functions of efficiencies of scale.[75] Others, by contrast, suggest that they functioned as an implicit government and industry guarantee of deposit.[76] The weight of the evidence suggests that the mergers and consolidations had two important dimensions to them that tend to be overlooked. The first is that mergers do, indeed, have a systemic dimension to them, one that reflects the Canadian banking system's ability to protect its reputation nationally and internationally among shareholders. In the case of the Bank of Montreal, it had excellent market reasons for merging with other banks. But these reasons were also part of a broader strategy to reinforce the Bank's ascendancy, especially in relation to its nearest and most serious competitor, the Royal Bank.

The Merchants Bank Acquisition and Its Aftermath

In the post-war era, one case in particular underlines the strategic importance of mergers to the Bank. In 1921 the Merchants Bank's questionable decisions began to catch up to it, resulting in an imminent failure. That autumn, after "wild days of rumors, much excitement on the stock market, and some concern among financial men generally," the Bank of Montreal officially announced that it was taking over the Merchants.[77] The failure of that institution under the presidency of Sir Montagu Allan was ascribed to "adventurous banking carried on by the General Manager and transacted without the knowledge of the Directors." The immediate cause of the collapse was a large loan to Thornton Davidson, a failing investment house.

After much due diligence on the part of its management,[78] the Bank of Montreal purchased the Merchants Bank for $1.05 million, equal to $10 per share.[79] The Bank was granted a stock increase to meet broader capital requirements in the wake of the acquisition, and it also had to deposit $5.9 million with the minister of finance under the provisions of the Bank Act of 1914 to cover the excess of the paid-up capital of the stock of the purchasing bank.[80] A reluctant Dominion government acquiesced to the deal, in spite of its growing concern about bank concentration, simply because there was no other choice.

The Bank's view, one expressed to the minister of finance, was that "no legislation that can be devised" would act as a complete safeguard against the "consequences of mismanagement which, besides being incompetent, is also ambitious and optimistic."[81] The directors and management of the Merchants were exactly that combination of adjectives, and more, according to the Bank of Montreal. If nothing else, the episode underscored the fact that sound bank management was not to be taken for granted in Canada, and that even Canadian banks, contra their reputation, could falter if not properly looked after.

The Merchants Bank affair illustrated the value of the Bank of Montreal's Stability Strategy and its emphasis on conservative banking principles. In December 1921 Finance Minister Sir Henry Drayton noted that the "painful impression on the public mind" made by the Merchants' troubles could be alleviated only by vigorous action on the part of the Department of Finance.[82] Apart from regulations to ensure the "probity and stability of the banking business in Canada," the Bank of Montreal's swift action ensured that the depositors would be protected. "The Bank of Montreal is in a strong financial position," Drayton concluded, and "will be fully able to handle the situation."[83] The move added 400 branches to the Bank of Montreal network.[84]

The acquisition of the Merchants Bank fed into the increasingly prevalent perception that the Bank of Montreal and its chief rival, the Royal Bank, were engaged in a struggle for supremacy, with the Royal as the challenger and the Bank of Montreal as the incumbent. "Canada's two largest banks, the Montreal and the Royal," the *Globe* reported in 1921, "have been running a neck-and-neck race for supremacy during the past year or two, but the action of the Montreal in absorbing the Merchants will give it a lead which scarcely will be overtaken in all ordinary probability, except by a similar stroke of amalgamation by the Royal."[85]

In 1924 the Bank then acquired the Molsons Bank's 125-branch network, principally but not exclusively in Ontario and Quebec.[86] "This announcement does not come altogether as a surprise in local financial circles," suggested the *Globe*. "The proposed merger will remove the only 'family' bank in Canada from the list of chartered banks of the country, and, incidentally, will reduce that list to 12, as compared with 18 at the beginning of 1922."[87]

The press could not resist returning once again to its theme of mergers-as-horseraces. "The record for mergers is even between the Canadian Bank of Commerce and the Bank of Montreal, each having absorbed six other institutions," the *Globe* reported in 1924, while the Royal and the Bank of Nova Scotia each boasted four.[88] The prize for the largest one, however, went to the Bank of Montreal for its acquisition of the Merchants Bank, which involved

$32.5 million in capital. By the end of 1924, the Bank of Montreal had assets of approximately $750 million, with the Commerce and the Royal at $500 million and the Scotia at $200 million.[89] Less than a year later, the Royal was closing in, becoming the bank with the "most widespread activities," with over 800 branches in Canada and over 100 branches in the Caribbean and South America. The Royal's purchase of the Union Bank of Canada in 1925 put it within striking distance of the Bank of Montreal, and it would eclipse Canada's first bank by the end of that year.[90]

In the merger race, banks with "superior organizational technology and economies of scale"[91] did indeed press their advantage. The costs of failure both to the Canadian banks as well as to the government were high – in terms of reputational and political capital, respectively. There were a number of factors at play in these mergers, but in the case of the Bank of Montreal, the key ones were the desire for asset accumulation and the determination to preserve the reputation Canada's oldest bank. In the wake of the Home Bank failure in 1923, reputation was a precious commodity indeed.

The Home Bank "Wreck"[92]

By far the worst failure to occur in this period was that of the Home Bank of Canada, which, with $21 million in deposits and 71 branches, closed up shop in 1923. The closure led to civil actions pursued, and ultimately damages were awarded for "misconduct, malfeasance and negligence." The result, as noted by A.B. Jamieson, was that only the strongest and most solid banks escaped the suspicion that the banking business rested on shaky foundations.[93] While the Bank of Montreal was not directly involved, the failure of the Home Bank indirectly affected the operating environment of the entire banking sector.

The potential reputational damage of the Home Bank's failure for the banking system as a whole became that much greater when it was revealed in 1924 parliamentary hearings that Sir Thomas White, minister of inance in the Borden administration, had on two occasions, in 1916 and 1918, received information that the returns of the Home Bank had been seriously misrepresented. But White was satisfied with the explanations and assurances of management that their affairs were in order.[94] When the matter became public, the Canadian Bankers Association informed the minister that, even had the Home Bank failed during the war, the Canadian banking system would not have suffered. Between the government of Canada and the CBA, "47.3% of the deposit liabilities of the Home Bank were paid."[95] Of course, this was in an era before public deposit insurance, which Canadian banks argued against on the basis that such moves were impractical and "undesirable on efficiency grounds."[96] The American system again provided an example of how adverse incentive effects had been the unintentional result of such schemes south of the border. Both in 1913 and in 1924, Canadian policymakers concluded that the guarantee of bank deposits had proven unworkable in the United States and only encouraged the "venturesome banker" who would "feel free to incur risks he would not take with the knowledge that confidence in his institutions rested upon the personnel of the bank."[97]

The Home Bank failure had a variable impact on the reputation of governments and banks. For the government of Canada, the reputational damage was potentially significant: Was the government overseeing, supervising, and regulating properly? For those smaller banks operating regionally in Canada in the 1920s, increased scrutiny followed the Home Bank failure: Were they big enough, was their management smart enough, and were their assets strong enough to weather any storm? In the case of the Bank of Montreal or some of the other senior chartered banks, the reputational risk was minimal, at least in the short term. The responsibility for the reputation of the Canadian banking system was carefully differentiated. Taking responsibility in a larger sense had to align carefully with the duty of individual Canadian bankers to their own institutions. Collective responsibility, it was believed, could not embrace an actual obligation to save weaker banks. Senior Canadian bankers such as those at the Bank of Montreal pursued prudent and conservative management practices that focused first and foremost on the health of their own institutions. There could therefore be no statutory guarantee for depositors in the Bank Act. Similarly, the Canadian state suggested the limits of government responsibility in the wake of the Home Bank failure: the state would concentrate on exercising due care in the operation and administration of the Bank Act and in auditing banking functions via an inspector general of banks. Mergers "reassured depositors and stabilized the banking system."[98] This was a system, however, that preserved depositor risk. That risk provided incentives for prudence by bank managers and adequate vigilance by the depositors themselves as well as government regulators. In this system, the individual reputation of banks mattered a great deal.

Mergers and Reputation

The first three decades of the twentieth century in Canadian banking were a time of high reputational capital for senior Canadian banks. In the case of the Bank of Montreal, this reputation was something that was complex and intricately linked with strategy, performance, image, and identity. The maintenance of that reputational capital, even if bankers did not call it that explicitly, was a key factor in the maintenance of their power within the Canadian financial system. Bank of Montreal bankers in particular had understood this connection instinctively for over a century.

A similar dynamic was in operation in the broader Canadian banking system, as we have seen. The Bank of Montreal's post-war merger strategy was successful on a number of fronts. It added substantial assets to the bottom line. It played to the strengths of a powerful, financial institution.[99] It was not especially challenging, though the political economy of banking could put senior executives through their paces in terms of exercising influence and letter-writing. They used the tools at their command to do what they needed to do and reaped the rewards.

At the same time, the strategy came with a shadow side. It gave Bank executives a false sense of security in the infallibility of their institution and in the place of their Bank in the larger society. As Meredith's biographer suggests, amalgamations did "little to extend the bank's reach, merely adding branches where the bank was already well rooted."[100]

The Achilles Heel: Innovation and Adaptation

The Bank of Montreal and the other senior chartered banks were regarded as high-trust entities. That reputation, and their success, obscured the need for Canadian bankers in the 1920s, perhaps especially Bank of Montreal management, to understand two things: the the changing nature of money, and the advancing power of the state that would ultimately compel them to accept sweeping changes to their industry and their status in the 1930s. In other words, a healthy balance sheet and careful tending of its overall reputation was not enough to insulate Canadian banking from criticism or the need to change. As a result, the bankers lost one of the more consequential battles of the twentieth century in monetary thought.

One of the limits of the banks' reputational triumphs in the early part of the century was a type of intellectual rigidity on the subject of monetary theory and, perhaps more importantly, the impact of that rigidity on monetary policy in Canada. As Irving Brecher noted in the 1950s, among economists, bankers, politicians, and businessmen in the North Atlantic world, the workings of monetary and banking systems became a lively subject of debate after 1918. This followed on the experience of industrialized countries with the techniques and dangers of large-scale financial operations experienced as a result of the First World War.[101]

The Canadian monetary system in that period had several characteristics that were to come under scrutiny. First, the Canadian currency comprised legal-tender Dominion notes (government issued) and the notes of the chartered banks. Those notes were issued in a limited uncovered issue and a covered issue with 100 per cent gold backing. Bank notes were allowed to be issued to the extent of the capital of the bank in question. Some exceptions were allowed during harvest seasons, but the rules were generally adhered to.

The most dominant feature of the Canadian banking system was the gold standard, in force from 1853 until 22 August 1914, when heavy withdrawals of gold in large urban centres forced the Canadian government to abandon the standard. This action allowed the Dominion government to make advances on Dominion notes to the banks, as long as they had satisfactory collateral.[102] The gold standard was then resumed on 1 July 1926. The "gold standard mentality," a term coined by J.H. Creighton in the 1930s,[103] was deeply entrenched Canadian monetary orthodoxy. That orthodoxy was so entrenched, in fact, that only a series of unfortunate events in domestic and international finance forced Canada off the gold standard once again at the close of the 1920s.

The key battleground in the struggle to prevail in monetary thought was over the credit system – or the process of expansion and contraction in the mechanism of commercial credit. The principal combatants were not politicians or economists or even businessmen, but two opposing groups: bankers and a radical fringe.

Canadian bankers, much like their counterparts elsewhere in the North Atlantic world, believed three main things about the credit system: first, that demand deposits withdrawable by cheque were not part of the money supply; second, that bank credit could not be simply "created" – in other words, the volume of circulating money could not be raised or lowered arbitrarily; and third, that individual banks and the banking system as a whole had to follow the same rules and regulations for the issue of credit. In other words, each individual bank could lend only what it received minus the amount of its required reserves. Standard bank doctrine now recognizes that the system itself can make loans and investments that are multiples of any addition to its reserves in a fractional-reserve credit system. Sir Henry Drayton, minister of finance in the Arthur Meighen administration, recognized this dynamic in 1920 – that credit expansion has more to do with buying power than currency circulation.[104] In other words, the idea was that the banking system itself creates credit.

This was an idea that found significant support among labour, radical, and progressive groups in the post-war period. The argument, of course, came as a complete package, along with other monetary objectives: the establishment of a central bank and the nationalization of the banking system in Canada. It was also assumed, incorrectly, that the banks could by fiat simply create credit without referring to a corresponding increase in cash reserves, and a host of other significant conditions.

The battle lines over the future of monetary policy were drawn. On one side stood the uncritical, radical-based proponents of a version of the quantity theory of money espoused by Irving Fisher and John Maynard Keynes. On the other were bankers and policymakers within the precincts of government. The Bank of Montreal's Williams-Taylor quipped to MP William Irvine: "I am just a plain banker, and you are a student, I should judge, with a technical knowledge of things that I do not happen to possess."[105] He may have added, "or care to possess" either! Bankers in Canada adhered to the "banking principle" as an article of faith – the principle that the monetary supply is passive and adjusted to the needs of trade automatically. As Brecher notes, Canadian bankers "stressed only the demand side of credit, that is, the state of business determined the amount of credit and therefore made it impossible for control to be exercised from the supply side."[106] The fatal flaw in this argument, of course, was the fact that the relationship between the volume of credit and the volume of business was complex, dynamic, interactive, and both cause and effect. The failure of Canadian banks in this period was, in the words of one of their harshest critics, William Irvine, that they were "good bookkeepers ... they know the mechanics of banking, but they do not know what money is and they do not know what money should do in the industrial system."[107]

"Eppur, Si Muove" [And Yet, It Moves!]: Galileo

Part of the reason for this complacent attitude on the part of Canadian bankers was simple and powerful: the system worked. Its banks were held in high regard in international banking circles. If necessary, the Finance Act of 1914 could help banks in need of temporary assistance. Williams-Taylor of the Bank of Montreal, Sir John Aird of the Commerce, and C.E. Neill of the Royal all concurred that the system was in no need of repair or reform. The balance sheets of those banks bore witness to the assertion. And the bankers were not alone: Inspector General of Banks C.E.S. Tomkins and Assistant Deputy Minister of Finance G.W. Hyndman agreed that the "banking system as it prevails meets the needs of the country adequately ... there is [not] anything radically wrong with it at the present time."[108] Even professional economists shared a reluctance to recommend change. Dr Adam Shortt, one of the most eminent authorities on banking in Canada at the time, sided with the banks on a variety of issues, including the question of a central bank. There were exceptions: the redoubtable Queen's University economists W.A. Mackintosh and W.C. Clark, and W.W. Swanson of the University of Saskatchewan. W.C. Clark would, in the 1930s, work hard to reverse the tide of prevailing opinion and establish expanded state powers in banking through a reinvigorated Department of Finance as well as the creation of a central bank for Canada.

Near the end First World War, the Bank of Montreal campaigned aggressively to forestall the idea of a central bank. In correspondence with Finance Minister Sir Thomas White, the Canadian Bankers Association signalled the Bank's opposition to the creation of a central bank in Canada or even a US-style federal reserve system, though their competitive rivals at the Royal were favourable to at least the idea of a central reserve bank. In December 1918 Sir Vincent Meredith wrote to White to express his strong opposition:

> The proposal to establish a Central Bank, in Canada, must be considered in relation to the banking conditions at present existing in Canada, and to the reasonably anticipated requirements of our commercial community. The argument in favour of the adoption of a Federal Reserve System in the United States, does not apply in Canada, where, under our branch bank system, the Head Office of each bank, with its widely distributed branches, forms a most efficient Central Reserve and Clearing House for all its branches wherever situated through the country.[109]

Fearing additional contemplation of the matter, Meredith wrote to White once again in January 1919: "I am not going to remind you of what you know so well – that our banking system meant enhancement to this country during the trying times through which it has passed, but I should like to say to you that, in my opinion, it would be a hazardous venture ... with the probability of an entirely changed conditions within a year, to introduce fresh measures now which maybe open too much adverse criticism later."[110]

Retrospectively, the effects of this rigidity of thought in Canadian banking – and not just among the bankers themselves – served to intensify the dangers in the business cycle. The mini-boom of 1920 and the collapse of 1922 are good cases in point. Many factors, such as export-market instability, outdated methods of inventory accumulation, and lack of price control all contributed, but monetary policy tended to make matters worse. Governments and banks expanded the supply of money and credit, which ballooned from $4.4 million in 1916 to $116.5 million in 1918 and $123.7 million in 1920 – mostly powered by an increase in loans.[111] Between 1928 and 1929, the banks used the facilities of the Finance Act for call loans, expanding credit and indirectly upsetting the Canadian balance of payments, since most of that credit was required to purchase securities in New York by Canadians. This precipitated a significant export of gold from the Dominion treasury to the United States to meet increasing Canadian demand for funds in New York, and caused, ultimately, an abandonment of the gold standard (unofficially) in 1928.

In some ways, the carefully cultivated and preserved reputation of the Bank of Montreal and other Canadian banks had a paradoxical effect. Their success in managing the Canadian banking system through periodic turbulent times, and their effectiveness at ensuring that the main measures of their reputation were strength, size, stability, and prudential management, overshadowed their inability to slowly transform their role to embrace a more expansive view of the credit function and the system's role in contra-cyclical finance. Yes, the system in which they operated likely encouraged that kind of thinking, but Canadian banks were perhaps made too complacent by their successes in other areas. As it stood, they were not only unwilling to entertain new and innovative ideas; they also believed that any such ideas were far-fetched or the product of a theoretical mindset that had no purchase in the real world. The following decade would put those assumptions to the test.

Nonetheless, the Bank's performance in the 1918 to 1929 period was strong. The growth in assets over the period averaged 6 per cent, from $558.4 million in 1918 to $965.3 million in 1929. Dividend payments, as we have seen, were 14 per cent per annum over those years, with the exception of 1919 (12 per cent).[112] In dollar terms, the Bank in the 1920s distributed between $3.5 and $4 million in shareholder dividends. It could point to a thriving business in Canada and the expansion, where warranted, of its operations in Europe and Mexico. It had also acquired a number of banks, expanded its capital stock, and increased its reserve to $38 million. Heading into the 1930s, the Bank of Montreal had every reason to feel confident about its prospects.

Sir Vincent Meredith retired from the presidency in the autumn of 1927, but, for some time before then, he had been increasingly restricted in his duties. His death in February 1929, when he was serving as the Bank's chairman, marked the end of an era. As A.E. Phipps, the chairman of the Canadian Bankers Association, lamented, "his was a dominating personality for nearly fifty years in Canadian banking ... his services at the outbreak of the war and throughout the conflict are too well known to require comment. But it was, perhaps, in the post-war depression that his gifts of constructive and conservative finance were best exemplified."[113]

A Complicated and Changing Relationship: Bankers and Politicians

As we have seen throughout its history, the Bank's presidents, directors, and managers were deeply engaged at the highest levels of the political process on a vast spectrum of issues related to public finance, banking regulation, and economic development. The Montreal Bank's prominence in the councils of power was undeniable. Together with other Montreal capitalists, bankers, and industrialists, they were a political force to be reckoned with in post-Confederation Canada as they pursued expansion and sought to generate opportunities at home and abroad for economic development. The modest size and limited conception of state power prevailing among Canadian elites up to the early twentieth century encouraged a reliance on the expertise, organizational capacities, and reach of the Bank in capital markets and for financing of projects. Those arrangements conferred an extraordinary power and influence upon the leaders of the Bank of Montreal. Of course, the Bank of Montreal was still a bank, but it had, over time, by will, circumstance, and competence, acquired a much greater status as a quasi-government institution. That status, and its privileges, would come under increasing scrutiny as times changed, new players asserted their rights, and governments began to acquire greater power and prestige.

The Bank had long been Canada's principal banker and financier – a responsibility and a privilege that was jealously protected and defended from the depredations of other banking interests, particularly the Royal Bank. Up to the Great War, the Bank's relationships and privileges had not been seriously challenged, not least since its responsibilities were carried out professionally and with probity. After 1918, however, the impetus for change was clear. In this respect, the diaries of William Mackenzie King offer a remarkable backstage look at players and relationships in what evolved into a complex political battle for position among political and financial elites. That struggle involved the key politicians and banking figures of the day fighting over questions of public finance and political appointments. These conflicts were a forerunner of what was to come in the tumultuous 1930s.

One of the first orders of business between the Bank of Montreal and the newly elected King government in 1921 was not about banking at all but rather about the naming of a new Canadian high commissioner to London. That diplomatic posting was the highest and most prestigious within the power of the Dominion government. The two short-listed candidates were Peter C. Larkin and Sir Charles Gordon. Larkin was a remarkably successful businessman, founder and owner of the Salada Tea Company,[114] and a close confidant and unwavering supporter of Sir Wilfrid Laurier. Gordon was vice-president of the Bank of Montreal and a prominent Montreal businessman. The latter's candidacy was being strongly pushed by Senator Raoul Dandurand on behalf of the Montreal interests, not least because of Gordon's assistance in getting party financing for the 1921 election. King explained to Dandurand that it was "Sir Wilfrid's wish" to have Larkin "recognized." The debate, however, continued, with Dandurand urging Gordon even if for "only one year." King remarked that "it is Bank of Montreal and CPR influence [at play] again."[115] But CPR president and Bank of Montreal director Edward Beatty "disapprove[d] strongly of [the idea] of having Gordon go to England," since it would mean the Bank would lose one of its key strategic thinkers.

In the event, Larkin's candidacy prevailed, and he became Canada's high commissioner in February 1922. Gordon later admitted to King that Sir Vincent Meredith would have regarded him as disloyal to the Bank if he left Canada at this time – and so Gordon "had begun to worry over [the] prospect & felt relieved it had been settled otherwise," though "he would like to be remembered in this connection later on when Larkin retired."[116] Gordon did, however, accept the post of Canada's representative at the Genoa Economic and Financial Conference of April-May 1922,[117] where the financial reconstruction of Europe would be discussed. He rendered "good service" there to the Dominion government as its representative, since he was one of the country's leading experts on trade matters and was "against Canada granting further credits to European cities" – a position that pleased King.[118] "Gordon is an able man," King later enthused.

This episode reveals a few interesting aspects of the Bank-Dominion relationship. First, in spite of protests, the prime minister well understood the implications of the power and influence of Montreal business. He therefore had to find a way of, in his words, "reconciling [their] expectations" with their "disappointment in not getting the High Commissionership."[119] In other words, he needed to tread lightly, irrespective of his party-political views. Second, the Bank-Dominion relationship was close. It was also an asymmetrical one in favour of the Bank – for the moment, at least. Third, the networks and webs of influence underpinning the traditional Bank-Dominion relationship were showing early signs of unravelling, as hinted at in King's developing suspicions about the motives and intentions of those "Montreal interests" to which he frequently referred.

Yet it is important to remember that the Dominion-Bank relationship throughout the period was, by any measure, close by necessity. The Dominion government depended heavily on the expertise, advice, and capacity of the bankers. It did so to ensure that the capital and borrowing requirements of the state were met. Governments also relied on the main Canadian banks, principally Bank of Montreal, to ensure the health of the Canadian banking system. Consider one example among many. On 27 December 1921, in the immediate aftermath of the elections, Prime Minister-elect King noted that Sir Frederick Williams-Taylor, the general manager of the Bank of Montreal, "rang up to say that unless the Bank National [sic] could get a loan from the Gov[ernmen]t of one million dollars at once, it would fail." King had his finance minister, W.S. Fielding, phone Sir Frederick and sort the matter out, with Williams-Taylor opting to wait until King was actually installed in office in Ottawa.[120] Of course, in the coming years, much more contact and

Sir Vincent Meredith served as president of the Bank of Montreal from 1913 to 1927. He led during the turbulent years of 1914–18 and redirected many of the Bank's resources toward the war effort. Under his leadership, the Bank encouraged employees to serve their country and continued to pay their salaries for the first six months of military duty. 1915. Anonymous. Image courtesy of McCord Museum of Canadian History, II-264794.o.

BANK OF MONTREAL
HEAD OFFICE BUILDING
MONTREAL

In 1917, to celebrate its 100th anniversary and reflect on those years in business, the Bank published *The Centenary of the Bank of Montreal, 1817–1917*. 1917.

LORD MOUNT STEPHEN
VICE-PRESIDENT 1873-1876
PRESIDENT 1876-1881

LORD STRATHCONA & MOUNT ROYAL
VICE-PRESIDENT 1882-1887
PRESIDENT 1887-1905
HON. PRESIDENT 1905-1914

C. F. SMITHERS, ESQ.
GENERAL MANAGER 1879-1881
PRESIDENT 1881-1887

HON. SIR GEORGE DRUMMOND, K.C.M.G.
VICE-PRESIDENT 1887-1905
PRESIDENT 1905-1910

The leadership of the Bank of Montreal – from left to right, Lord Mount Stephen, C.F. Smithers, Lord Strathcona and Mount Royal, and George Drummond – as captured in the Bank's 1917 centenary publication. 1917.

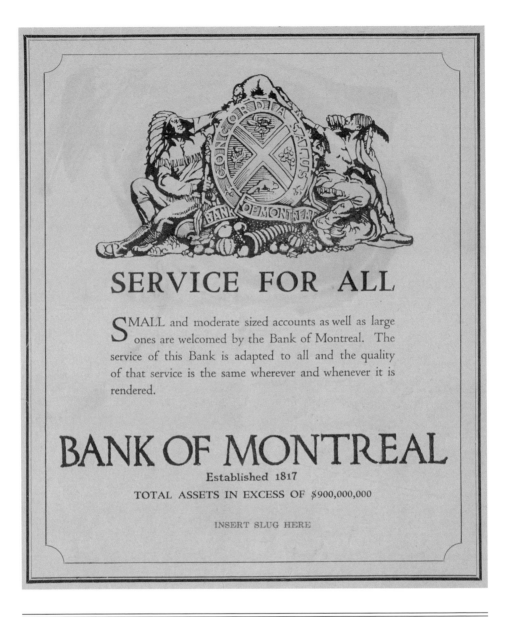

SERVICE FOR ALL

SMALL and moderate sized accounts as well as large ones are welcomed by the Bank of Montreal. The service of this Bank is adapted to all and the quality of that service is the same wherever and whenever it is rendered.

BANK OF MONTREAL

Established 1817

TOTAL ASSETS IN EXCESS OF $900,000,000

INSERT SLUG HERE

This advertisement features the Bank of Montreal's original coat of arms with the "kneeling supporters" on either side. As noted in the advertisement, at this time the Bank's total assets stood at $900 million. 1920s.

BANK OF MONTREAL LADIES' HOCKEY TEAM, 1920-1921

The Bank of Montreal Ladies Hockey Team, pictured in the 1920–21 season, included, from left to right: (*front row*) Miss N. Kennedy, Miss C.L.A. Wheeler, Miss M.E.R. Boon, and Miss K.I. Richey; (*back row*) Miss L.E. Grant, manager Mr J.S. Hughes, Miss D.A. Adams, Miss F.S. Cooke, Miss I.R. Harper, trainer Mr W. Galipeau, Miss I.V. McKyes, and Miss M. Scott. 1921.

HAROLD KENNEDY
Director, Bank of Montreal

This cartoon of Harold Kennedy, director of the Bank of Montreal, is part of a series by Arthur George Racey that depicts the Bank's executives. In the background is a cartoonish depiction of the "Old Lady of St James Street," the long-standing nickname of the Bank of Montreal. 1922. Image courtesy of McCord Museum of Canadian History, M20111.31.

This cartoon by Ernest Le Messurier, entitled "A Bored Meeting, or Ourselves as We've Never Seen Ourselves," was published in 1924 and depicts a Bank of Montreal board of directors meeting. Seen in the cartoon (with their tenure on the board of directors in brackets) are, clockwise, beginning with (*standing*) Sir Vincent Meredith (1910–29), Sir Frederick Williams-Taylor[*] (1929–45), General S.C. Mewburn (1924–54), F.E. Meredith (1923–41), James Stewart (1922–30), Sir Arthur Currie (1920–33), Sir Lomer Gouin (1920–29), Sir Edward Beatty (1919–43), Henry Cockshutt (1917–44), G.B. Fraser (1917–33), H.W. Beauclerk (1917–25), Harold Kennedy (1916–34), Herbert Molson (1916–38), William McMaster (1913–30), D. Forbes Angus (1912–43), H.R. Drummond (1912–57), C.R. Hosmer (1908–27), and Sir Charles Gordon (1912–39). Each director signed his respective caricature. 1924.

---

[*] Sir Frederick Williams-Taylor was not a director at the time; it is possible that he was replacing J.H. Ashdown (1917–24) who is not seen around the table.

Sir Frederick Williams-Taylor liked to entertain and frequently hosted dinners at his estate in Montreal. Pictured from left to right are: (*front row*) O.R. Sharp, Jackson Dodds, Sir Charles Gordon, Sir Vincent Meredith, Sir Frederick Williams-Taylor, F.J. Cockburn, and W.A. Bog; (*middle row*) G.W. Spinney, W.M. Bancroft, T.E. Merrett, C.H. Cronyn, E.P. Winslow, W.H. Hogg, J.W. Spears, J. McEachern, D.R. Clarke, C.W. Chesterton, A.E. Nash, A.S. Minnion, W.R. Chenoweth, and J.T. Stevens; (*back row*) W.W. Bruce, H.B. Mackenzie, J.H. Gillard, G.G. Adam, S.C. Norsworthy, W.T. Oliver, R.E. Knight, W.R. Creighton, O.R. Rowley, and F.G. Woods. 1926.

Bank of Montreal subagency in Glenwood, Alberta, in 1926–27. Arthur George Clandfield, manager (or officer in charge), is standing in the doorway. The note in the window reads: "open Tuesday and Saturday." 1927.

Sir Charles Gordon took over the reins of the Bank of Montreal in 1927, shortly
before the Great Depression. Seldom has a Bank of Montreal president faced
a more difficult start to his tenure. By the end of his term, in 1939, the Bank of
Montreal had recovered from the lows it had experienced in the early 1930s. 1929.
Anonymous. Image courtesy of McCord Museum of Canadian History, II-292627.

Unveiled in 1923, this statue at the Montreal Main Branch honours the 230 Bank employees who died in the First World War. It still stands in the branch foyer today. 1930.

(*above*) This advertisement, with the tagline "Ambition makes successful men out of barefoot boys," reads: "Turn your visions into realities by means of a Bank of Montreal savings account, as thousands of Canadians are doing." 1930.

(*opposite*) This advertisement ran in the *Canadian Geographical Journal*. The image depicts the entrance hall to the Main Branch in Montreal. The text reads: "A Bank half a century older than the Dominion itself – equipped through experience, resources, organization, and connections to serve helpfully all Canadian business." 1931.

A Bank half a century
older than the Dominion
itself—equipped through
experience, resources,
organization, and
connections to serve
helpfully all Canadian
business

BANK OF MONTREAL

Established 1817

As GOOD *as* GOLD
~wherever you go

TRAVELLERS' CHEQUES

A round-the-world cruise — a two weeks' holiday jaunt into the country — on whatever trip you may be planning … don't burden yourself with the risk of carrying rolls of bills when Travellers' Cheques afford you such convenience and safety.

Travellers' Cheques are sold at every Branch of the Bank.

BANK OF MONTREAL
Established 1817
TOTAL ASSETS IN EXCESS OF $800,000,000

This "As good as gold wherever you go" advertisement was printed in the *Canadian Geographical Journal.* The text reads: "Around-the-world cruise – a two weeks' holiday jaunt into the country – on whatever trip you may be planning … don't burden yourself with the risk of carrying rolls of bills when Travellers' Cheques afford you such convenience and safety." Note that, at the height of the Great Depression, the advertised total assets of the Bank of Montreal stand at "in excess of $800,000,000," rather than the $900,000,000 advertised in the 1920s. 1931.

Despite the Great Depression, construction continued on the Bank's premises in Canada's capital, Ottawa. 1931. Library and Archives Canada/Clifford M. Johnston fonds/a056609.

The Bank of Montreal's London locations at Waterloo Place (pictured here) and Threadneedle Street were of tremendous importance, not only for international business dealings across the North Atlantic but also for the Canadian war effort in both world wars. 1931.

Head Office: Montreal

"I Feel That The Bank of Montreal Has A Distinct Personality"

Said an old customer of the Bank recently: "In my opinion a bank has a personality just as positive and distinct as that of an individual."

The personality of the Bank of Montreal, created by its founders and perpetuated by their successors, is reflected in the substantial character of the clientele the Bank has drawn to it, and expresses itself through more than 600 Branches, which are so many points of contact with the people and the commercial life of Canada.

The elements which have gone into that intangible but very real thing —the personality of Canada's oldest bank—include the Bank's unwavering strength and conservatism, its helpful, efficient service, and its thorough knowledge of local conditions wherever it is represented.

BANK OF MONTREAL

Established 1817

TOTAL ASSETS IN EXCESS OF $750,000,000

This advertisement, which ran in the *Canadian Geographical Journal*, speaks to the Bank of Montreal's "unwavering strength and conservatism" at the height of the Depression. The Bank's assets, which had been listed as "in excess of $800,000,000" earlier in the year, have now slipped further, to "in excess of $750,000,000." 1931.

A Fourfold Organization
for Efficient Banking Service

THE organization of the Bank of Montreal includes these four features:

1. The local Branch and Manager

2. Provincial Headquarters and Supervision.

3. A Nation-wide Institution with over 600 Branches.

4. An International Bank with offices in the world's leading financial centres and world-wide banking connections.

Each individual customer enjoys the full benefit of this well-rounded organization. Notwithstanding its great size and scope, the Bank of Montreal welcomes small accounts as well as large, and extends to all the same high quality of service.

BANK OF MONTREAL
Established 1817

(*above*) Mexico was an alluring target for the Bank of Montreal throughout the twentieth century. The Bank opened its first location in Mexico in 1906, only to leave in the 1930s. Further attempts to expand business into Mexico were made in the 1960s and 1990s. Pictured here is a Bank of Montreal location in the Aragon district of Mexico City. 1932. (*opposite*) This advertisement from the *Canadian Geographical Journal* highlights the Bank's "fourfold organization for efficient banking service," which includes local management, provincial headquarters and supervision, nationwide coverage, and international connections. 1932.

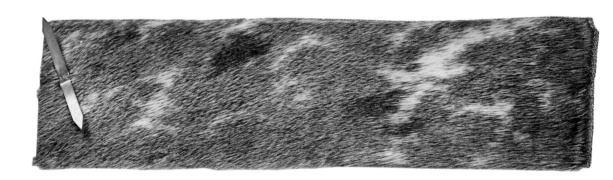

This highly unusual cheque was issued on a piece of sealskin. The customer, Lieut. R. Greenwood, used it to purchase furs from a trapper in Spitzbergen, Norway, when no other cheque forms were available. The payee is the trapper's Norwegian agent. 1933.

The armorial bearings of the Bank of Montreal were submitted to the College of Arms in London in 1933. These were henceforth the bank's official armorial bearings. 1933.

This Bank of Montreal location, in the wilderness of the Canadian west, shows how the Bank was at the forefront of the Canadian frontier. 1937.

Canada played a pivotal role in the Allied effort during the Second World War. A streetcar passing by the Bank of Montreal main branch in Winnipeg features a sign that reads: "Let's be good hosts to our American visitors." 1940s. Library and Archives Canada/Ronny Jaques fonds/e010980684.

During the Second World War, twenty-three senior officers of the Bank took leaves of absence to assume administrative and advisory roles in the government. BMO President G.W. Spinney served as chairman of the National War Finance Committee. Pictured here is Spinney giving a speech on behalf of the committee. Behind him, left to right, are: Paul Earle, Jackson Dodds, Adélard Godbout, U.S.N. Captain Arthur Purvis, Colonel Frank Knox, and Huntley Drummond. 1941.

discussion was to come over a variety of issues that included bank amalgamations (in particular, the Bank of Montreal's purchase of the scandal-ridden Merchants Bank).[121]

Thus far, there is nothing that seems out of the ordinary. But something is clearly moving under the surface. An issue that continually emerges in King's diaries is the Bank of Montreal's monopoly on government business. As incoming prime minister in 1921, King reported on 2 September 1921 of his dinner with C.E. Neill, the managing director of the Royal Bank: "I spoke later when alone of intention not to permit monopoly in any line, Banking included, said the Bk. of Commerce had tried to destroy Sir W. & were not my friends. Neill said they were much against me. I sd. I felt differently towards Bk. of Montreal, tho' had no desire to see them monopolize Govt. business. Neill said the Bk. of Montreal ought not to be overlooked. It should receive Govt. recognition. I told him I believed in sharing of business of Govt. as well as all else."[122] Again, on 24 January 1922, King reported another encounter with Neill and reiterated his desire to transfer of "some of Govt. business to other banks."[123] His finance minister, Fielding, however, was for "holding to the Bank of Montreal monopoly," which King thought was wrong. "Govt. business should be distributed. Here again, 'old men' are hard to change and difficult in a reform cabinet."[124] But it was not the Bank of Montreal alone that was in King's sights; on the contrary, he reserved special venom for the Bank of Commerce, which was "too closely identified with Mackenzie & Mann & has done all in its power to destroy the Liberal Party."[125]

The matter of government banking business kept on being raised around the cabinet table, leading to a stand-off of sorts between a prime minister intent on breaking the Bank of Montreal monopoly on government business and a finance minister resisting strongly. King wrote on 8 April 1922: "I have urged Mr. Fielding to change his policy … but he becomes almost panic stricken when I suggest it." He continued: "Today most of the members of Council were of my view & if matters had been pressed far I think Mr. Fielding would have collapsed. He looked very frail & almost broken down in standing for what 'has been the custom for 40 years.' I told him I thought this was a reason for change now. His only argument is that it will lead to pressure from other banks for Govt. business. Why should it not? If they are sound institutions[,] better have public monies distributed than in hands of wealthiest interests."[126]

Anti-Bank of Montreal voices were gathering momentum. Dr William Pugsley, the lieutenant-governor of New Brunswick and a canny Liberal machine politician, Major-General Robert Rennie, a Liberal stalwart and failed Liberal candidate in Toronto, and Toronto investment dealer J.H. Gundy reported to King that Fielding had been in Montreal dealing with J.P. Morgan

Bank "through Bank of Montreal, instead of thro' Royal Bank which is friendly to Morgans and to us." King concluded from this episode that "Fielding's conservatism & stubbornness in this is not fair to his colleagues."[127]

Fielding's biographer, Carman Miller, offers a clue as to the finance minister's disposition: "In his old age he refused to make concessions to the new era," opposing among other things Canada's representation with Washington and signing its own treaties. "His world," Miller concludes, "remained the world of pre-war Canada."[128] When J.A. Robb took over responsibilities at Finance in 1924 because of Fielding's failing health, the government moved quickly to negotiate better terms on treasury bill sales with the banks. King noted in September 1924 "how Bank of Montreal grabbing for more than 4½ [points of margin] had lost all, with Robb able to negotiate 4 and 20% commission with a rival bank."[129] "I like the way he has stood up to the Bank of Montreal," King concluded. "Fielding never would have done so in like manner."[130]

Robb's tougher stand on negotiating maturing loans with the Bank of Montreal was the clearest sign of a new, emerging set of arrangements. In late 1927, when half of a $45-million maturing loan was being negotiated, Montreal bankers held out for 4 3/8ths instead of the usual 4 per cent. Robb promptly called New York and got the Royal to come in as well to pressure the Bank into accepting the lower margin. King remarked at the time that the Bank of Montreal "gets about $280,000 interest free & Royal about $80,000 on monies allowed to remain with them."[131]

Government business was one thing: elections and the formation of governments was quite another, and riskier, arena. The federal election of October 1925 had produced a constitutional and political crisis over which party was to govern – the incumbent Liberals under King or the challenger Conservatives under Sir Arthur Meighen – in spite of the Liberals' clear loss. King held on for nine months with Progressive Party support, after which the governor general dissolved Parliament, new elections were held, and the Liberals were returned.

The electoral outcomes of 1925 and 1926 are not our major concern here. The point, rather, is how risky political involvement was, even for powerful bankers, in such a febrile atmosphere. King confided to his diary that J.W. McConnell, a newly minted Bank of Montreal director, and Sir Frederick Williams-Taylor, the Bank's general manager, had made strong public declarations against King and in favour of the Conservative leader. McConnell's motive was clear: he was tipped to be the minister of finance in a possible Meighen government. Taylor's motive is more opaque, but it seems evident that he was hoping for a Meighen victory.

The interventions infuriated King, and he threw a scare into the Bank of Montreal leadership – so much so that, on the night of 4 November 1925, the

Bank's assistant manager, F.J. Cockburn, went to see the prime minister at the insistence of Bank president Meredith. Cockburn assured King that the "Bk. of Montreal were not in politics," that what McConnell had done was on his own behalf and that, moreover, he "had been a director of the Bank for only a short time, they cld. not control him." Cockburn's description of his colleague Williams-Taylor was much more devastating: "[Williams-]Taylor was a fool, with a foolish wife." Sir Vincent had told Williams-Taylor to "restrain himself," and that "no one regarded him seriously, that he had only got the position [his noble title] from entertaining people in Eng. who ate his meals without thanking him for them."[132]

It is worth pausing here for a moment to absorb that extraordinary scene in the prime minister's residence on that particularly frosty autumn night.[133] The Bank's emissary, F.J. Cockburn, not only apologized; he also managed to throw overboard both McConnell and Williams-Taylor as part of an effort to defend the Bank's relationship with a thin-skinned prime minister. The dismissal of Williams-Taylor is particularly surprising for its vehemence and personal nature. Perhaps the story underlines the stakes believed to be at play.

In any case, King's conclusion after hearing Cockburn's declaration, quoted at the opening of Part Four, was telling: "It is clear [that the] Bank of Montreal crowd feel they have been beaten and are down on their knees, as they well may be. It is a new day when that crowd begin sending their emissaries direct to plead for mercy."[134] Obviously, he felt, the Montreal interests, the Bank included, had backed the wrong horse in Sir Arthur Meighen's Conservatives, some of them had done so rather blatantly, and the Bank's leadership was now in full damage-control mode.

The prime minister's suspicion of the "Montreal interests" continued. The next day, his Quebec lieutenant, Senator Dandurand, telephoned from Montreal to suggest that some kind of national-unity government be proposed with neither King nor Meighen at the helm. "I spoke pretty firmly to Dandurand about any such idea – it meant handing over govt. to Montreal interests after they had done all they could to destroy the Liberal Govt. It would be a betrayal of the Liberals who had fought the recent battle, and it was not in accordance with constitutional usage, a sort of repetition of Union Govt., with all the attendant evils of a coalition. I was amazed at Dandurand getting into that frame of mind. It reveals what 'atmosphere' does."[135]

King was convinced that he had lost the 1925 election because of Liberal losses in Ontario. "The main factor in our reverse in Ont was the money from Montreal," he concluded, and that "the battle was one of financial interests there to gain control of prlt. [Parliament]." He told Liberal insiders Percy Parker and Andrew Hayton at lunch on 15 November that "if the Toronto men really wished to put up a fight I was willing to help them against the St. James St. the Bank of Montreal, the CPR, McConnell & his crowd. Something of this kind is needed to get these men to act, self-interest is their dominating impulse."[136]

The events that unfolded in Bank's relationship with the Dominion government in the 1920s formed a troubling pattern, at least from the Bank's perspective. Bankers, especially Montreal bankers, still exercised a preponderant influence in Canadian public finance. But the marked asymmetry between bankers and ministers began to tip in favour of the latter as governments started to assert public power in the management of public finance. The Bank of Montreal's leadership could point to its long and careful management of capital provision and its excellent stewardship of the Canadian banking system, as well as the senior banks' technical and professional competence. The Canadian banking system was highly admired and highly regarded – both inside and outside of Canada.

But that was not the point: what mattered increasingly was control over public finance, over banking and currency, by government. That struggle for control inevitably descended into the political arena. Prime Minister Mackenzie King was determined to bring his political adversaries, the Montreal interests, mainly Conservative in orientation, to a reckoning. The 1920s offered a foreshadowing of the events to come when radical circumstances would transform the politics of incremental change into the politics of transformation. The twilight of the all-powerful Montreal banker had begun.

CHAPTER TEN

The Montreal Banker's Paradox

"Well, the way of paradoxes is the way of truth. To test Reality we must see it on the tight-rope. When the Verities become acrobats we can judge them."
Oscar Wilde, *The Picture of Dorian Gray*

The late 1920s were good years for Canada and for the Bank of Montreal. "Never was there a time in the history of Canada," Bank President Sir Charles Gordon enthused, "when business as a whole has been at a higher peak than during the year under review." He assured Bank shareholders in 1929 that "[never before were] the developed sources of our wealth ... more wide and varied than they are to-day, and never [was there] a time when the earning power of our people was sustained in so many channels of production."[1] The stock-market crash, he concluded, was "the result of a collapse in a purely speculative orgy in the stock markets," which ought not "unduly to distort our view."[2] Gordon's views were reinforced by General Manager H.B. Mackenzie, who stated:

> For several years we have been living under the menace of the rising fever of stock speculation. The collapse brought painful consequences to many individuals and its effects will no doubt be felt in diminished spending in some directions, but it is well that the crash is behind us rather than still ahead of us and it is also well to remember that there has been no destruction of prosperity. The real national wealth of the United States and Canada remains what it was. That may not give much comfort to the losers, but is important from the standpoint of

national welfare and prospects. Business will perhaps be somewhat quieter while we are getting back to realities, but the realities in both countries afford firm basis for healthy optimism.[3]

Mackenzie was not the only finance official in North America to get it wrong so spectacularly: almost everyone did.

As we have seen in the last chapter, the warning lights were flashing throughout the Bank of Montreal branch network that stock speculation was beginning to show signs of overheating and generating intolerable risk. Few, however, were expecting the extent of the collapse in the wake of the October 1929 crash. Even fewer could predict the duration, severity, and transformational nature of depression that lay ahead for the country and for the Bank.

The Banking Paradox in Play

The Bank's experience as a premier Canadian financial institution in the Canada of the 1930s would complete the transformations that began as subterranean currents in the 1920s in the political, market, and financial realms. Too often, however, we look back at these processes and perceive their apparent historical inevitability: the force of destiny. In fact, what the evidence points to instead is the fact that these changes were neither predestined nor automatic: they were filtered and influenced through leadership, luck, will, personality, and circumstance. Bank of Montreal leaders used every tool at their disposal at every turn to influence the course of events to safeguard the Bank's interests.

In the 1930s, the Canadian banking system worked well and proved resilient. Bank of Montreal bankers remained influential and, at key points in the financial life of the country, provided professional advice to business and government. To be sure, the influence of Montreal bankers in the 1920s was greater than it would be in the 1930s, but the Bank of Montreal still held much of the power and cachet that it had previously enjoyed. Still, something important had clearly changed. The Bank's influence in the corridors of power was legendary, but on the key issue of the day – a central bank – it was destined not to prevail.

Its strategy and approach, in a few quarters derided as too conservative or risk-averse, was not only a saving grace during the most turbulent times; it was also a necessary precondition for institutional survival and system stability. The Bank of Montreal represented the key anchor of Canadian financial life – government banker, foundation of Dominion finance, bondholder, lender, enterprise financier. Its senior leadership also represented the finest in Canadian banking. Yet the Bank's status was both an obvious blessing and a subtle curse, since it reinforced the need to perpetuate banking conservatism. By becoming a large national institution and quasi-governmental enterprise, the Bank of Montreal had acquired the prestige and privileges attached to that status. It was, in other words, responsible for something greater than itself.

By the 1930s, the Bank's emergence as a large, bureaucratic institution reinforced the default-conservative or risk-averse outlook of its most senior bankers. It had also seemed to acquire many of the complex bureaucratic "tendencies of organization" famously identified by German sociologist Max Weber in classic twentieth-century organizations – centralization, officialization, impersonalization, careerization, formalization, and standardization. Those tendencies were key managerial tools – and necessary ones – to manage the increasingly voluminous information and capital flows, offices, branches, personnel, policies, and procedures required for the bureaucracy to run at all. The same tools were a way for bankers to help manage the uncertainty of the world around them. But tools can also shape the users: they can become iron cages. The emergence of a large bureaucratic, rule-bound institution tended to promote an overweening caution in outlook and decision-making. The system would also impose progressively powerful constraints on innovation and the ability to accommodate alternative perspectives on changes in strategic direction, even if such voices were present.

The Bank's strengths were therefore its weaknesses. In its strengths lay its limitations; in its apparent solidity and unchangeable banking virtues, its vices. What rendered its operations so resilient against headwinds also made it resistant to change when change came knocking. Its position and capacities conferred powerful competitive advantages but also transmitted a more ambiguous, tenacious, and enduring inheritance. That was the Montreal Banker's Paradox, and it was one of the main features of the Bank of Montreal's experience in the Great Depression.

If the entire, collective experience of the Bank of Montreal in the 1930s – from coast to coast, in businesses and boardrooms across the Dominion, in the branches of the small towns and metropolises, in the departments across the institution – is taken into account, a highly complex mosaic emerges. The stories and evidence tell of thousands of loans and mortgages, of human hope, suffering, and perseverance. The subcultures of the Bank thrived in their local, regional, and functional manifestations, brought together under the aegis of a common institution, set of rules, and leadership. Being a Bank of Montreal banker meant something important to the leadership and workforce of the Bank, but it also contained a spectrum of different and rich experiences. Those experiences cannot possibly be captured in this book, for reasons of space. But they are central to the Bank's story.

Cometh the Hour

The Bank of Montreal senior management team responsible for dealing with what ended up being the greatest protracted economic and political crisis since Confederation comprised a well-prepared group of seasoned, senior bankers and directors at the top of Canadian financial and economic leadership. Sir Charles Gordon became president in 1927 and would remain in office until his death in 1939. Huntly R. Drummond served as a vice-president (1927–39) and would eventually succeed Gordon. Sir Frederick Williams-Taylor would also serve from 1929 to 1932. Major-General Sydney Chilton Mewburn would serve as a vice-president and on the executive committee of the board from 1927 to 1950. Originally trained as a lawyer, Mewburn was a former minister of militia and defence in the Union government. He possessed a remarkable number of directorships – even for the era.[4]

Key to the navigation of this era would be the Bank's able general managers. H.B. Mackenzie's appointment in 1929 was cut short by his untimely death in 1930. The Ontario-born William Alexander Bog, his replacement, would serve as general manager to 1936 and then as vice-president from 1936 to 1944, rounding out sixty-three years in the service of the Bank. Lauded for his "high character and unswerving integrity,"[5] Bog, by the time he became joint general manager at the starting salary of $25,000,[6] had served across virtually the Bank's entire territory.

Bog's co-general manager was Jackson Dodds (1930–42). Dodds would assume a critical role in many of the political and financial contests that unfolded in subsequent years. The Montreal banker dreamed of by central casting, he was "a Londoner born and practically speaking a banker born."[7] He served in the British Army during the Great War, fighting in France and being mentioned four times in dispatches. By war's end, he had earned the rank of lieutenant-colonel and been awarded the Mons Star and an OBE. He joined the Bank of Montreal in 1918. By the time of his retirement in 1942, Dodds was considered a "leader in Canada's financial affairs" and "a leader also in social and philanthropic movements and enterprise and one of Montreal's most public-spirited citizens." His work in the Scout movement earned him the highest awards in international scouting – the Bronze Wolf and the Silver Wolf.[8]

George W. Spinney was another protagonist in the events of the era. Spinney entered the service of the Bank in 1906, in Yarmouth, Nova Scotia. Between 1915 and the early 1930s, he was promoted to progressively more important positions. His responsibility for the newly formed Securities Department in the late 1920s was a sure sign of his increasing influence within the Bank firmament. "This phase of banking brought him into close and confidential touch with government and corporate finance," one account of the era noted.[9]

He was appointed assistant general manager in 1928 and joint general manager in 1936 for a salary of $35,000; in 1942 he vacated the latter position for the presidency of the Bank. Spinney earned a stellar reputation in Canadian financial circles – so much so that Prime Minister Mackenzie King reported in June 1940 that Bank directors Beatty and McConnell strongly recommended him as the "best appointment that could be made" to the post of Dominion minister of finance.[10] King agreed, adding that "he is a very honourable man, a Liberal, and in Finance would be a great strength to the government."[11] In the event, Spinney declined on the grounds that he "really could not handle the parliamentary end of it" and was "simply interested in banking."[12] The determining factor, however, was that Spinney's "heart from early youth had been in the Bank of Montreal."[13]

The 1930s would be a testing time for the entire senior executive, but that was especially true for these general managers (or chief operating officers) who were faced with what was often a troubling climate for banking: loans under pressure, skyrocketing defaults, clerk dissatisfaction at rates of pay, and social and political unrest all contributed to a challenging landscape. For Bank of Montreal leaders, the stakes were especially high. In the market, the Bank was no longer the largest Canadian bank by assets, having ceded that position to the Royal in the late 1920s as a result of merger and acquisition activity. The dramatically changed economic conditions generated ever-more insistent calls for state intervention in fiscal and monetary policy – particularly through the creation of a central bank – that could not be ignored. The entire banking system was scrutinized as never before for its role in economic development and growth. At the same time, the failures of capitalism in Canada and abroad took on a new and more urgent tone with the emergence of political and economic movements – and governments in some provinces – hostile to the status quo.

The trouble, famously, started over a number of days in late October 1929. On 23 October 1929 the New York stock market plunged to record lows, dragging the world economy into one of the most severe economic depressions on record. Canada, heavily dependent on exports, was one of the countries most affected by the crash.[14] In the four years following 1929, the country's Gross National Expenditure (GNE) fell by 42 per cent, national income by over 50 per cent, income in agriculture by almost 80 per cent, and domestic investment by almost 90 per cent – to only 11 per cent of its 1929 level.[15] At the height of the Great Depression in 1933, almost one-fifth of the country's labour force was unemployed.[16]

Despite these trying conditions, however, the Canadian financial system held together. Canada experienced no bank failures during the Great Depression, compared to the nearly 5,000 US banks that failed in the 1930s.[17] Explanations for the stability of the Canadian financial system vary. Some of the factors that scholars consider include national branching, which made the Canadian system more diverse and therefore stronger in the face of local and regional shocks; the existence of the Canadian Bankers Association, which played a coordinating role in times of financial crisis in the absence of a central bank; and the government's encouragement of mergers between stronger and weaker banks, which eliminated weak players before the Great Depression hit.[18]

Even with deteriorating economic conditions throughout 1930, the Bank's leadership remained at least publicly optimistic. In 1930 one bank publication acknowledged that the "unemployed have appeared in a larger number," but it immediately explained this away with the statement that big cities were always the places where the unemployed gathered.[19] In fact, the Bank's "business summary" suggested that "business in Canada can best be described as marking a time in a between-seasons period. There has been less activity both in manufacturing and merchandising than a year ago, and trade cannot yet be said to have emerged from the slough into which it was thrust by the stock market slump and the storing of a short wheat corp. Bank clearing, for example, indicate[d] a shrinkage in volume of turnover, practically all reporting centres having returned decreased clearings during the last few weeks."[20] Thus undeterred, the Bank still paid out a 2 per cent bonus on dividends in December 1930.[21]

President Gordon pointed to the Bank's long-term experience as an important point of reference – and competitive advantage. "We have one advantage in the Bank of Montreal possessed by few business institutions," he suggested in 1931. "We have the advantage of an intimate record in our own annals of the course of trade in this country for the past 115 years. Looking into that record, we see reflections of periods when conditions and outlook, not only in Canada but throughout the world, were blacker than any we have experienced during the past two years ... Yet, even under greater disadvantages than the present, conditions have always righted themselves."[22]

As the 1930s progressed and adverse conditions began to entrench themselves, the realization dawned that this was no ordinary contraction. "There is still an abnormal degree of unemployment, commodity prices slowly decline, buyers operate cautiously and less money is in circulation than last year," one circular observed in the summer of 1930.[23] President Gordon added the following year that "business throughout the Dominion has experienced a general recession more severe than recorded in our last report, and the basic industries of the country have suffered correspondingly."[24] The environment was not promising: as the months wore on, the analysis grew more sober: "The clouds have not yet been dispelled ... Few nations have balanced budgets, without which credit is impaired. Taxation is high everywhere. The wheat situation ... is beclouded by the reappearance of Russia as an exporter, and the disposition of other European countries to grow their own requirements ... Then, the pressure of competition in world-markets is intense, as in the case of fisheries (an industry that Japan is actively developing), lumber, copper, and other commodities indigenous to Canada."[25]

One of the saving graces for Canadian banks was the Canadian prohibition on lending on real estate and other "unproductive extensions as has been the case in the United States." As a result, the Bank of Montreal and other Canadian institutions did not have their resources "tied up in frozen loans."[26] The Bank's policies and procedures, as well as its general conservative approach to banking, protected the institution to some extent.

The Bank's 1931 performance could have been much worse, but that did not mean it was by any means good. The Bank's assets shrank by $25.3 million to $769.2 million. "This decrease, I think you will agree, is a moderate one," General Manager Bog reported, "in view of the state of domestic business, the large decline in foreign trade and the low levels to which all commodity values have fallen."[27] The Bank closed thirty-two branches across Canada (while opening five), preferring to focus on urban centres. As a further measure, the Bank sold its stake in Barclays Bank's Dominion, Colonial and Overseas (DCO), of which it had been an original shareholder.[28] Even in these difficult circumstances, the Bank turned a profit of $4.7 million in 1932.[29]

The Depression also compelled the Bank to repatriate much of the profits generated from its long-standing London operations. The London committee reported in early May 1932 that the head office had withdrawn £448,000 from London in that month alone. Over the following two weeks, a further £639,000 was withdrawn.[30] That May, therefore, over £1 million had been withdrawn from the London operations. The London committee continued to search for new ways to generate business, and it found one opportunity when the New York gold market closed in the spring of 1933 and the Dominion government turned to London as an amenable outlet for raising funds.[31] Indeed, the London committee's activities remained an important node in the Bank's financial network. The Bank, moreover, continued to act as the Dominion government's fiscal agent in London.[32]

The difficulties of the Canadian banks paled in comparison with those of their counterparts in the United States. In 1932 a run on banks, starting in Michigan, eventually led to the "unbelievable situation of every bank in the United States temporarily suspending payment."[33] Many banks, and their customers, placed all their hopes in the ability of the new Roosevelt administration not only to stabilize the banking situation but also to restart America's economic engine – a turn of events whose effects would, in the view of the Bank of Montreal, "radiate to Canada and ... the world at large."[34]

The deterioration in economic conditions continued unabated. By 1932, the scrutiny on any loans, especially to provinces and municipalities, was redoubled. In May 1932 the Bank issued instructions to managers to "analyze carefully all loans in this category now on our books, and to investigate thoroughly all fresh applications for credit, either for current expenditures, unemployment relief, capital expenditures, et cetera," in order that the Bank might escape "being saddled with additional borrowings which will add to an already heavy burden."[35]

Trouble in the City

The Bank of Montreal was involved in the fate of many public entities from the national to the municipal level. One of the most serious cases involved the city of Montreal and its inability to meet its loan obligations in the late 1930s. The debts were held not only in Canada but also in England, which generated consternation on both sides of the Atlantic.

By 1939, the creditor banks – the Bank of Montreal prominent among them – took a firm stand and, together, served notice that "no further capital advances will be made unless a source of repayment is definitely assured."[36] The banks had loaned the city of Montreal over $30 million. The city struggled to meet its obligations regarding relief as well as the interest-repayment schedule on the loans it had secured over the decade. The banks demanded that the repayment schedule be adhered to, and they also called for the appointment of a "Controller of the Budget and a business-like management of the city's finances."[37] The situation was complicated, however: if the banks refused to advance funds, the city would be obliged to cut relief, "and in the present state of unemployment in the city, there is a likelihood of serious unrest," Bank of Canada official Donald Gordon reported. "Naturally, in such an event, the banks will be blamed and it is possible that they will, in consequence, weaken on their stand."[38] This situation, in the eyes of one banker, "has come about through a succession of weak administrations, which by reason of ignorance and incompetence have been unfit to administer the affairs of the City, with the result that Montreal has lost the confidence of the local securities market."[39] In the event, as G.W. Spinney informed the Bank of England on 25 May 1939, a crisis was avoided by the intervention of provincial authorities who had promised action "in co-operation with banks."[40]

In 1940 Montreal defaulted on part of its debt, and control of the city passed to the Quebec Municipal Commission (QMC). The QMC had been formed in 1932 and vested with sweeping powers to take over municipalities "unable, or in danger of becoming unable, to meet their financial obligations."[41] The matter had seized the attention of the Bank of Montreal network in England, where much of the city of Montreal debt was held. On 13 August 1941 W.A. Pope informed the Bank of England that plans were being prepared to deal with Montreal's debt. By then, the debt had ballooned to £60 million (about CA$268 million). The sterling issues were £13.5 million, most of which were Bank of Montreal-issued. The next day, Sir Montagu Norman, governor of the Bank of England, cabled his counterpart at the Bank of Canada, Graham Towers, to express his wish to "avoid any unfavorable repercussions on Canadian credit whether Dominion or Provincial in London; and b) to ensure that sterling bondholders have a fair opportunity of judging the merits of the position."[42] News of the rescheduling was urgently broadcast across the Bank of England's network.

The Bank of England was greatly worried that a "leading Dominion City" might take measures to reorganize the debt, with a resulting negative effect on Dominion and UK government credit. "British stockholders, are of course, vitally interested: an approach by the City to British holders would normally have been expected but the Bank of Montreal are privately afraid that stockholders may be presented with a fait accompli," lamented one Bank of England official.[43] English holders on the Bank of Montreal, London, register alone numbered 15,000.[44]

The bankers, however, were loath to allow Montreal to borrow outside of the Empire. "However badly this City has behaved – and I understand that its behavior has been intolerable – I do not believe that it pays in the long run to drive such a City out of the Empire for the purpose of satisfying its inescapable needs," one Bank of England official remarked in 1939.[45] "I believe that if ructions are to occur within the Empire they should be smoothed out there and not evaded by going to foreign countries." The Bank of England banker added that their experience with New South Wales in that regard was instructive. The government of New South Wales had threatened a rescheduling of payments and negotiation on loans outside the Empire (to the United States). London "thought to teach them a lesson" by refusing their requests and ignoring their threats. "The only lesson they learned was to cock a snook at us and go to the USA, much to our discredit and discomfort: and to our inconvenience since, because we have had to transfer the service of the loan there."[46] In the event, a Dutch bank loaned Montreal $4 million as an initial loan, with another equivalent amount to come.[47]

The issue dragged on into the mid-1940s, with conferences between the bankers and the bondholders committee and the city ongoing, until a reorganization involving the city, the province, and the Bank of Montreal was reached in 1944.[48]

An Insider's Look at Canada's Economic Crisis

The minutes of the executive committee of the Bank of Montreal's board of directors in the 1930s reveal the extent to which the Bank held in its hands the fate of countless businesses and enterprises. The committee functioned as the core decision-making deliberative body for the board, taking on the day-to-day decisions and preparing positions for the larger board to consider when appropriate. It was chaired by Sir Charles Gordon as president; the other members were S.C. Mewburn, E.W. Beatty, W.A. Bog (general manager), and C.H. Cronyn as secretary. Jackson Dodds was also frequently in attendance as the joint general manager. The committee considered advances in excess of $100,000. What the minutes reveal is a Bank carefully weighing the fate of a large number of companies, sometimes in concert with the Royal Bank or other banks.

A few examples offer the flavour of these voluminous documents. In September 1930 the president and general manager advised the committee on the case of Greenshields and Company, which sought earnestly to "avoid embarrassment to the Company" as a result of a "large amount of undigested house securities on hand for the financing of which they have used clients' cash and securities on deposit with them," leaving the company an eye-watering $1.8 million short. The solution was for the Bank of Nova Scotia, the Royal, and the Bank of Montreal to each advance $620,000 to a subsidiary company, taking as collateral house securities of the company not held by other banks.[49] Dodds informed the committee that the banks were accepting these loans in spite of the risk of "a possible loss of say $2[00,000 to] $300,000 in the interests of avoiding a general situation."[50] As ever, the loan came with specific conditions imposed on the borrowers and on Charles Greenshields himself to liquidate securities and repay as soon as possible.

The dire conditions facing the pulp and paper industry were the subject of multiple meetings of the executive committee. Numerous companies found themselves adrift in a sea of red ink. On 17 December 1930 Bank of Montreal President Charles Gordon called a special meeting of the committee to discuss advances to the Canada Power and Paper Corporation. Bankers C.E. Neill and M.W. Wilson of the Royal had met with Gordon, Dodds, and Bog to discuss a situation that had emerged from the amalgamation of several paper companies into Canada Power and Paper. The bought-out companies had been "satisfactory accounts" of the Bank of Montreal. After amalgamation, however, there was a dramatic reversal of fortunes. The Bank noted that the company's working capital had evaporated in the course of its offering "pre-paying" commissions to William Hearst instead of paying shareholder dividends, debenture interest, and recompense for fixed assets. Gordon insisted to C.E. Neill that those obligations – to shareholders and lenders – had to come first. Neill conceded the point, but there was no escaping the legal obligation to pay the outstanding commissions. The banks simply had no choice in the matter. "If we had to stand on our own security," Neill warned, "we would lose $2,000,000 and it was therefore imperative that all payment should be met in January, after which all the things Sir Charles had mentioned, with the exception of the Hearst payment, should be postponed; this payment, he said, would have to be met."[51]

What was at stake was a loan of $7.5 million from the Bank of Montreal and an equivalent amount from the Royal, along with a complex arrangement of bond holdings. The Bank of Montreal agreed to make advances up to $7.5 million, take one-third of the bonds, and get back as many of the remaining bonds as possible from the company's major promoters.

When made public, these actions, as well as the size of the loan, could pose a danger to the Bank's reputational capital. But even that angle had been considered. "It was pointed out," Dodds wrote in a memorandum, that "the only criticism that can come of our action would be from people who might say that the bank has taken steps to secure itself whilst other people were not being looked after. On the other hand, it was suggested that we could say that the bank was giving time to enable the difficulties to be ironed out."[52]

The Bank of Montreal, in concert with the Royal, also moved to save the likes of Montreal Power, National Breweries, Shawinigan Power, and Dominion Bridge – when required through the market by "buying shares" at predetermined prices. Gordon added that he did not want Dominion Textile, in which he was involved, to receive any special help because "it could look after itself."[53]

The Bank entertained a considerable number of requests for extensive loans in the 1930s to protect its own long-standing clients and to permit them to consolidate their own positions, as was the case with Distillers-Seagram and B.C. Distillers. In 1931 the executive committee reviewed a rather length list of loans that required "special attention" – in other words, from companies in "embarrassing situations." The list is an impressive cross-section of enterprises and firms hard hit by difficult economic times. The names and the amounts outstanding, set out in the following table, give a good idea of how much was at stake.

The executive committee also considered protecting the shares listed on the Montreal Stock Exchange after considerable discussion with W.E.J. Luther, the exchange's president. It was decided that the general manager should study the advisability of approaching other banks and/or trust companies about acting in concert and agreeing not to call loans should the pegged prices be removed.[54] The banks were in a powerful position to keep things

Table 10.1 | Large loans requiring special attention
of executive committee, 31 October 1931

Company	Sector	Loan Amount
Canada Steamships Lines	Shipping	$1.275 million
Greencoy Corp. Ltd	Investments (Greenshield)	$943,000
Hudon, Hebert, Chaput Ltd	Food merchandising	$1.539 million
T.B. Macaulay Securities	Sun Life President Personal	$1.041 million
Newsprint Bond and Share Co.	Pulp and Paper	$1.136 million
Bonaventure Pulp & Paper Co.	Pulp and Paper	$998,000
F. Lyall and Sons Construction Co.	Construction	$1.026 million
Tetrault Shoe Co. Ltd	Consumer	$663,000
Madawaska Corporation Ltd	Pulp and Paper	$3.311 million
Quebec Fisheries Ltd	Fisheries	$427,000
Quebec Investment Co.	Investments	$1.092 million
John Perkins	Individual	$547,000
Canada Power & Paper Co.	Pulp and Paper	$8.119 million
Howe Lumber Co. in Liquidation	Forestry	$491,000
Acadia University	Education	$406,000
BC Packers	Agriculture	$689,000
Canadian Fishing Co. / New England Fish Co.	Fisheries	$2 million
Western Provincial Governments	Government	"Guarantees of Large Amounts"
Government of Newfoundland	Government	$2 million

Source: BMOA, "Executive Committee of the Board Minutes, 5 Dec. 1927–13 Feb 1953," 8 December 1931.

rolling. Had they called every loan, the effect would have been a serious run on the exchange, with dire consequences to follow.

The banking relationships that are chronicled in the records reveal the extent to which the banks intervened to keep innumerable enterprises afloat and how they acted, at critical points, in tandem. The two most consequential banks, the Bank of Montreal and the Royal, emerge from these pages as wary competitor/collaborators united in the necessity of saving some of the country's most important businesses – and with them, of course, their own massive loan and investment portfolios.

Occasionally, however, the competition "ying" would overcome the collaboration "yang." On 6 October 1936 Gordon called a special meeting of the executive committee. The sole agenda item was the shocking loss of the government of Quebec account – one of the cornerstones of the Bank's government business – and to the Royal Bank of Canada, no less. The news must have incensed the Bank of Montreal executives. Indeed, they were so exercised that there was talk of withdrawing from the Canadian Bankers Association altogether in protest. The loss of business, however, prompted the directors to reflect on whether the "general rate structure of the banks to borrowers is, in view of the competition from sources other than the banks in Canada and from abroad, too high."[55]

The travails of the 1930s demanded that Bank of Montreal decision-makers confront the full range of challenges facing Canadian enterprise. Those challenges took their toll. The Bank's assets were reduced by more than $200 million between 1929 and 1935. The Bank's share prices, moreover, declined from $425 in 1929 to a mere $150 in 1933.[56]

The persistence of economic adversity forced the Bank of Montreal to make some tough decisions. First, the Bank had to re-evaluate its entire asset portfolio. At his annual address to shareholders in 1932, President Gordon reminded people that "our banks welcome borrowers to whom they can safely lend, and as trustees of depositors from whom their loaning resources are derived, banks ought not to lend on any other conditions."[57] Indeed, with dwindling deposits and a lack of creditworthy borrowers, the directors switched the Bank's portfolio toward low-yield bonds, which were more secure but also less profitable.[58] The Bank also drastically reduced the number of branches and shuttered much of its international division. In 1932 it closed thirty-six branches, including three in Mexico.[59] In 1934 a further one hundred branches were closed. Despite the closures, the Bank did not lay off any employees, instead finding them employment in other nearby branches.[60] In this regard, the approach toward branching foreshadows some of the changes that the Bank would adopt after the Second World War – closing branches in remote towns and villages as the automobile made it easier for people to reach branches that were more centrally located. As Jackson Dodds pointed out in 1931, there was "less need for branch banks in hamlets which formerly justified the opening of offices within a few miles of other branches of the same institution or of another bank."[61]

Competitive pressures from American lenders added to the concerns of Canadian banks. American bank and trust companies and other institutions had idle funds in Canada and had "invaded the Canadian field by offering to make loans to Canadian borrowers at extremely low rates." In the case of the vital grain trade, loans were made for three, four, or five months "against pledge of Terminal Elevator Receipts for grain and the rate quoted covers a hedge against exchange risk." The Bank of Montreal told its superintendents in 1936 that it had "lost a considerable volume of this class of business last season to American sources."[62]

The major reorientation of the Bank's asset portfolio and the contraction of the branch network ensured that the Bank fared relatively well during the war, even if more secure bonds ate into the traditional and accustomed-to margins. These decisions ensured that the Bank never had to touch its emergency rest fund to make ends meet, never posted a loss, and, notably, continued to make dividend payments consistently. In 1929 and 1930 the Bank paid out a dividend of 12 per cent plus a bonus of 2 per cent.[63] This was after accounts for all losses had been made and a considerable sum had been contributed to the Bank's rest. With the Depression lasting longer than expected, however, by 1931 Gordon acknowledged that while "the profits for the year have proved sufficient to provide payment of the customary dividends ... the bonus of 2%, paid for several years past, the Directors have deemed it advisable to omit," adding that this cautious approach was "a manifestation of the traditional conservative policy of the Institution."[64]

The Last Years as Government Banker

If the Bank's final five years as Dominion banker – between 1930 and 1935 – were among the most challenging ones in its entire experience, its leadership also showed the full capabilities of their institution in handling financial and economic emergencies of the sort that followed the crash of 1929. The continuous flow of loans into the government's consolidated revenue fund was more important than it had ever been since revenues from tax and customs were drying up along with economic activity. The Bank's strong cash position, moreover, provided a pillar of security for both itself and the country at a precarious time when Canada was flirting with economic catastrophe. The following chapters on the Bank of Montreal's role in Newfoundland and the creation of the Bank of Canada offer a closer look at the stakes, the struggles, and the nature of the government-Bank relationship. But, even outside those remarkable episodes in banking history, the routine business of government illustrated the intimate nature of the relationship, the extraordinary lengths the Bank would often travel to accommodate requests – and the tensions that could result.

Two examples are illustrative of this point. In one exchange at the beginning of the Depression, Sir Charles Gordon reminded Prime Minister R.B. Bennett, who had succeeded Mackenzie King in 1930, of the "unusual service" the Bank had provided out of its ready funds to cover Dominion financial obligations in the New York market – to the extent of $25 million in government obligations. "So as to relieve the Government of the necessity of actually remitting such a large amount to New York within a short space," the Bank took the step of selling the Dominion government the $25 million at par as of 1 August 1929. "As a means of compensating us, the Government agreed to pay us in Canada, in June for the funds, but the risk of the market was ours and on the 1st of August we were obliged to put up the $25,000,000 in New York."[65]

The events of 1930 and the Bank's extraordinary measures to secure Dominion credit were raised again in 1932 when the government decided to drop the Bank's name from the cheques of the receiver-general. Gordon wrote to Bennett: "I realize that this is past history and am reluctant to make reference to it, but I feel that in the crucial matter under discussion, I would not be doing my duty to the Bank if I failed to draw such matters to your attention."[66] What is more, Gordon explained to the prime minister, the strong cash position held by the Bank was a critical element in backstopping Dominion credit. This matter "may not mean very much to the public generally, as they do not examine the bank statements carefully, but it means everything when some crisis occurs and we are called upon to do something which helps the credit of the country."[67] Gordon elaborated: "Had this Bank not been in the position it was, we could not possibly have converted such a large amount of short date bonds into long date bonds, as it was bad banking to do so, and it was only because of our strong cash position, and for patriotic reasons, that we felt justified in giving this lead to other people and thereby taking the risk of a potential loss which has turned into a real one."[68]

Gordon's emphasis in his note to Prime Minister Bennett on "patriotic service" merits a closer look. The remark underlines a certain frustration with changing government attitudes toward banking and with the lack of appreciation of the efforts made by the Bank of Montreal in securing the credit of the country. This frustration was evident again in May 1933 when Finance Minister Edgar Rhodes elected to take a loan with the Chase Bank in New York, rather than going through Bank of Montreal facilities. Gordon laid out his case as follows:

> With reference to the temporary loan which the Government required in New York on the 1st May and which you secured from a New York bank at a lower rate than that offered by us, I should like to point out to you that we have always kept in mind the possibility of such temporary loans being required by the Dominion Government and for this reason we have maintained funds at New York at most unremunerative rates in the shape of United States Government bonds, Call Loans and Bank Balances, which we otherwise would not have done. You will appreciate that our position in regard to actual cash balances in New York is different from that of a local bank ... Under such circumstances we obviously cannot compete as to rates with a local Bank. If the position in New York had been that the Government could not have borrowed from a local Bank, and in these times this is not a remote possibility,

we feel that you would have expected us to assist you and that when this is in view it should not be a mere matter of rates that should have influenced your action in the present instance.[69]

The Bank's frustration with the Dominion government's actions in New York illustrate the sometimes-exasperating nature of its position as government banker. That responsibility required the Bank to deploy its investments in a certain way, with an emphasis on availability of funds and security. As Gordon explained, this was something the Bank would not otherwise have done. Hence the objection about the government seeking the lowest rates available without considering the larger picture.

Within twenty-four months of this exchange, the ups and downs of the Bank of Montreal's position as government banker would be solved once and for all with the establishment of the Bank of Canada. A new era had opened.

Conclusion

The financial story of the Bank can be told in four simple charts (see figures 10.1, 10.2, 10.3, and 10.4). The story in terms of assets is dramatic in the first years of the Depression, with a year-by-year loss from the peak of 1929 to the trough of 1934. Thereafter, the trend line begins to climb back up, and by 1939 the Bank's assets surpass the 1929 peak. Profits and dividends steadily declined, but much more gently than the broader economy. The final chart, depicting the Bank's vaunted rest fund, stayed level, however. In 1930 the rest stood at $38 million, climbing to $39 million over the course of the decade.[70] The preservation of the rest fund, even in conditions of unprecedented economic challenge for Canada, is both a remarkable accomplishment and a telling reminder of the Bank's markedly conservative approach to the management of its affairs.

The 1930s proved to be a transformative decade for Canada's first bank. A protracted economic emergency summoned its leadership to a set of unprecedented challenges. When the Bank was put to a series of tests, the efficacy of its financial networks and the quality of its decision-making were on full display. The Bank never faltered in its role as Dominion banker and guardian of the Canadian banking system. Its leadership took the decisions required to safeguard core operations and extend credit and conflict in complicated times. The long struggle to maintain dividends and reverse the decline in assets was ultimately successful, even in the depths of the most severe economic contraction any banker in the 1930s had experienced in living memory. Bank of Montreal leaders never once resorted to their institution's reserve fund, and this fact was a tribute to the professionalism and

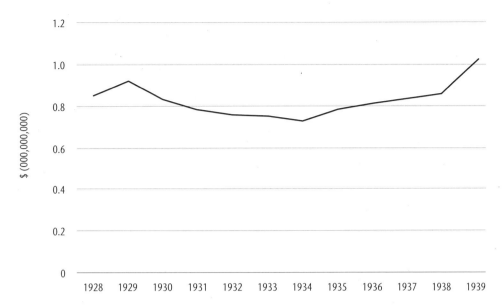

Figure 10.1 | Assets, Bank of Montreal, 1928–39

Source: Bank of Montreal Annual Reports, 1928–39.

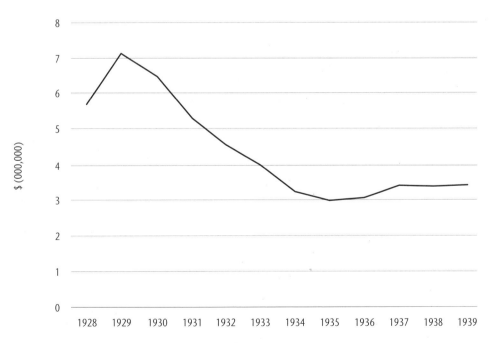

Figure 10.2 | Profits, Bank of Montreal, 1928–39

Source: Bank of Montreal Annual Reports, 1928–39.

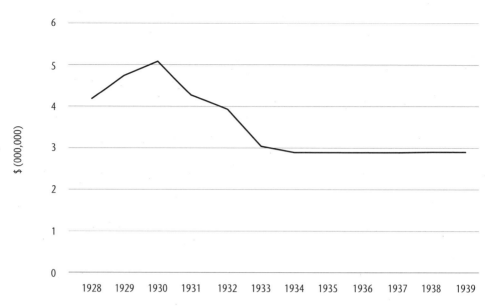

Figure 10.3 | Total dividend payments, Bank of Montreal, 1928–39

Source: Bank of Montreal Annual Reports, 1928–39.

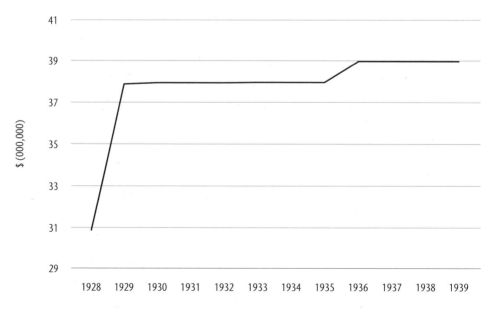

Figure 10.4 | Rest fund, Bank of Montreal, 1928–39

Source: Bank of Montreal Annual Reports, 1928–39.

A CHANGEFUL FORTUNE, 1918–1945

discipline of that generation of bankers. They took the tough decisions the times demanded to preserve their institution, while also holding the fate of scores of industries, enterprises, and even governments in their hands.

The 1930s also produced a series of political, social, and economic earthquakes that shifted and transformed the entire Canadian financial landscape. Desperate times produced a range of public-policy responses that resulted, as we will see, in the establishment of a central bank, and with it, the arrival of governments more willing to acquire the fiscal and monetary instruments needed to shape economic activity and achieve public-policy outcomes. In the west, farmer-labour movements produced devastating critiques of capitalism, governments, and the chartered banks. A socialist political party, the Co-operative Commonwealth Federation (CCF), was formed in Calgary in 1932 and it adopted what came to be called the Regina Manifesto at its first national convention in Regina in July 1933.[71] The manifesto proclaimed the group's objectives to replace capitalism with a system characterized by economic equality – a new social order based on the "proper collective organization of our economic resources such as will make possible a much greater degree of leisure and a much richer individual life for every citizen."[72] The party declared that "the chartered banks must be socialized and removed from the control of private profit-seeking interests; and the national banking system thus established must have at its head a Central Bank to control the flow of credit and the general price level, and to regulate foreign exchange operations."[73]

The thunder rolled right across the Canadian prairies, where the Bank of Montreal had forty-seven branches in Alberta and thirty-four in Saskatchewan. In Alberta, the United Farmers, which had assumed power in the election of 1921, governed to 1935, when the Social Credit movement under William Aberhart took the reins. Social Credit "tended to focus their attacks on the financial institutions."[74] Those attacks were both popular and effective, since many constituents across the province considered themselves victims of a monopolistic and exploitative system that included banks and railways. The pages of the *Social Credit Chronicle* bristled with anti-eastern, anti-capitalist, and especially anti-bank sentiment.[75] The Aberhart government stoked this hostility, suggesting that the banks had control over the "one thing which alone can relieve the distress of the masses, 'Money.'"[76] It passed sweeping interventionist legislation – the Reduction and Settlement of Debts Act in 1936 and the Home Owners' Security Act of 1938 in particular – that sought to give the power to provincial boards to unilaterally reduce the interest rates on loans that financial institutions charged homeowners, farms, and small businesses. The legislation put the Alberta government on a collision course with the Dominion government under Mackenzie King (back in power after 1935), which asserted exclusive federal jurisdiction over banking and currency. The legislation was disallowed by the courts, but the political atmosphere would not change for years to come.

In this environment, the nature and reach of Bank of Montreal banking changed, sometimes dramatically. The Bank was indeed compelled to make adjustments in the wake of the Bank of Canada's establishment. After 1935, however, its expanding commercial business served to "offset any decline in its activity on Government account," prompting one observer to concluded that "no ground has been lost in relation to the other banks" as a result.[77] Its competitors had their own specialisms as well. The Bank of Nova Scotia was heavily involved in savings deposits and acted primarily as an investment bank. The Canadian Bank of Commerce, echoing its predominantly agricultural roots, was particularly focused on financing wheat movements and grain dealers.[78] The Royal was ahead of the other Canadian banks in international business, with a larger network of foreign branches than any other competitor bank. Its focus in Canada was pulp and paper in Ontario and Quebec, as well as Quebec power companies. Its extensive security business also distinguished it from the other major banks.

All Canadian banks in the 1930s expanded their business but managed to maintain their relative positions, with the exception of the Bank of Toronto, which was, according to one overseas observer, "the most aggressive of the smaller banks and unpopular with the others."[79] The competition was severe, leading frequently to over-banking – particularly in cities. "If, e.g., one chartered bank opens a branch in a new suburb, the others general follow suit," one banker observed, "whether the available business justifies it or not."[80]

The response to these changes would have to wait, since, by the late summer of 1939, the country and its people were again thrust into a global military conflict. For the second time in a generation, Bank of Montreal bankers would once more be enlisted to put the full powers and capacities of Canada's first bank at the service of the national war effort.

CHAPTER ELEVEN

No Banker's Dominion: Montreal Bankers and the Financial Fate of Newfoundland

Nowhere was the severity of North America's economic contraction more dramatically experienced than in the Dominion of Newfoundland. As Canada's government banker, the Bank of Montreal was instrumental in formulating the response to this crisis. Moreover, precisely because of the Bank's status as a quasi-government institution, the troubles of Newfoundland could have a direct impact on Canadian public finance – especially in the United States bond market, whose practitioners often thought of all of North America, including the "not-United States" part, as one undifferentiated jurisdiction. The unfolding of the events in Newfoundland sheds light on one of the most telling financial chapters in the Bank's Depression-era experience. The story also provides us with a glimpse of the complex and consequential role that the Bank of Montreal played in the financial system of the North Atlantic world in general, and in the realm of Canadian public finance in particular.

The Bank's involvement is this saga was complex. The Bank acted as banker to the government of Newfoundland. At the same time, it was Canada's principal banker. Also, as the leader of the "Syndicate Banks" – the Bank of Montreal, the Royal Bank, the Canadian Bank of Commerce, and the Bank of Nova Scotia – that provided bailout relief to Newfoundland, it coordinated the response of the Canadian banking system to the crisis. And then there still other layers to the story. In London, the Bank of Montreal was the principal standard-bearer for Canadian banking and finance. And, of course, the Bank had its own interests to safeguard both on the Island and on the Canadian mainland.

President Charles Gordon was an infrequent but influential participant in the negotiations. A more pivotal role was played by Jackson Dodds, Gordon's general manager, who acted as lender, loan syndicator, adviser, intermediary, and guardian of the banking system and creditworthiness – both in Newfoundland and in the North Atlantic world at large. Finally, Sir William E. Stavert, a former Bank of Montreal banker, was as a key and trusted figure in St John's throughout the period.

Precarious Public Finance

The Bank of Montreal's relationship with Newfoundland began in 1894 in the aftermath of the failure of the colony's two principal financial institutions – the Union Bank of Newfoundland (est. 1854) and the Commercial Bank of Newfoundland (est. 1858) – leaving a small government-owned savings bank as the only financial institution under local control.[1] The Bank of Montreal established a branch in St John's in 1895 and soon thereafter was appointed as the Newfoundland government's official banker in the depths of the depression of the 1890s.[2] The Bank extended its first loan to the government of Newfoundland in 1895 to ensure that the government could meet its obligations.[3]

Even in prosperous times, governments in Newfoundland had some difficulty in meeting their obligations. The most serious challenges were kept in abeyance for a while. By the 1920s, however, governments increasingly resorted to loan flotation to cover persistent revenue shortfalls. Each year between 1921 and 1932, a loan was raised, ballooning the debt from $43 million to $97.5 million in just twelve years. The debt was exacerbated by a succession of capital projects that were likely necessary and undoubtedly expensive to complete. As a later report put it, "among the projects ... financed [with loans] may be instanced the construction of a dry dock, the building of high roads, the taking over and improvement of the railway, the expansion of the telegraph and telephone service, the provision of steamers for coastal services, and the construction of numerous public work buildings. Unfortunately, none of these projects has proved remunerative."[4]

The stock-market crash in 1929, coupled with the erection of protective tariffs and the subsequent collapse of international markets after 1930, created harsh conditions for a Newfoundland economy based on export staples – fishing, forestry, and mining. The result was that the existing debt, already on a narrow margin, spiralled out of control: between 1929 and 1933, Newfoundland debt rose by almost 24 per cent.[5] As revenue fell, debt servicing as part of Newfoundland's government expenditure also rose at a troubling pace. In 1929–30 debt servicing represented 35.9 per cent of total government expenditure; by 1932–33, it accounted for almost two-thirds (63.2 per cent).[6]

As the historian Peter Neary notes, faced with this deterioration of public finances, the Newfoundland government resorted to "a series of increasingly desperate measures."[7] With assistance from the Bank of Montreal, Prime Minister Richard Squires's government raised $5 million in 1930 to meet the Dominion's debt obligations.[8] Future loans would be much more difficult to procure. To meet obligations due on 1 July 1931, the government of Newfoundland authorized new debts to the amount of $8 million. In a sign of what was to come, however, there were no buyers for the new debt. Newfoundland faced a crisis. The Squires government put the sale of Labrador on the table in the hope that Canada would consider its purchase. The asking price was $110 million – a potential magic bullet that would erase the entire debt.[9] Unfortunately, the state of Canadian public finance ensured that any such deal would never be seriously considered – even at the reputed bargain price.

The deepening crisis prompted Squires to make representations to Canadian Prime Minister R.B. Bennett and Canadian Trade Minister C.H. Cahan. He urged the federal government to persuade the big Canadian banks headed by the Bank of Montreal to agree to another loan for Newfoundland: "In view of the fact that the government of Newfoundland finds itself unable to see a bond issue of $8,000,000 recently authorized by the Legislature, the Government will be unable to meet the interest on its funded debt due 30th June and 1st July next, unless it receives substantial assistance by way of short term loan."[10]

The spectre of a Newfoundland loan default haunted all the principal players in the drama. The Canadian government feared its possible reputational impact, to say nothing of how a default would affect Canada's ability to meet its obligations. The UK government was similarly concerned about the impact on the credit of Britain's colonies. The banks were anxious to avoid losing money and losing face, considering how deeply they were implicated in Newfoundland's loans.

After Squires contacted Bennett for help, the prime minister approached the Bank of Montreal's general manager, Jackson Dodds. Dodds was also the leader and spokesman for the Syndicate Banks involved in the Newfoundland bailouts. On 19 June 1931 Bennett appealed to Dodds on the basis of protecting Canada's creditworthiness: "It is the opinion of this government that it would be very injurious to Canada if Newfoundland should make default at this time, and therefore we would appreciate the Banks taking such action as would make this event impossible."[11] Dodds obliged, organizing the other Syndicate Banks to agree to another loan to Newfoundland. The following day, 20 June, Dodds sent a telegram to A.A. Werlich, Bank of Montreal branch manager at St John's, laying out the details of the proposed bailout:

> Syndicate composed of Bank of Montreal, Bank of Nova Scotia, Royal Bank of Canada, Canadian Bank of Commerce, has agreed to make advances to government of Newfoundland against temporary debentures in proper legal form passed by your solicitors drawn at two, three and four months following[,] amounts of Bank of Montreal $838,481, Nova Scotia, $700,000, Royal $450,000, Commerce $125,000[,] to enable Government to pay interest on funded debt around end of month amounting to $2,085,740, and a sinking fund $27,740. Total $2,113,481.[12]

The total amount was well short of the $8 million originally floated by the Newfoundland government, but it was enough for the Dominion to meet its 31 July obligations.

The money came with strings attached: the Syndicate Banks insisted that the British Treasury appoint a special commissioner to investigate the financial condition of Newfoundland and make recommendations to rehabilitate government finances.[13] The UK government obliged, appointing Sir Percy Thompson, the deputy chairman of the Board of Inland Revenue, to look into the situation.[14]

To the banks, Sir Percy's appointment was intended to push the Dominion of Newfoundland down the road toward financial solvency. Indeed, one of the loan conditions was that Newfoundland *was obligated* to accept any recommendations made in Thompson's report. Speaking for the Bank of Montreal and the other Syndicate Banks, Jackson Dodds took pains to inform Prime Minister Squires that, in the event that Thompson's proposed remedies proved insufficient to stabilize Newfoundland's public finances, the banks were under no further obligation to extend new loans to Newfoundland to cover interest payments: "If the plans recommended by the Commissioner do not provide enough money for the interest-payment of next January, the matter will be reopened by you; there was no commitment as to the future on the part of the Banks."[15] Dodds's message was clear: as far as he was concerned, the Banks had done their duty and, from this point on, Newfoundland would have to work out its own salvation.

By the autumn of 1931, the Newfoundland economy had lurched toward an even greater crisis. In October 1931 there were signals that the government would not be able to meet its January 1932 obligations. A desperate Squires told officials at the Bank of Montreal that "the imperative need for the Government was $1,500,000 for relief purposes and if this was not forthcoming many people would die."[16] At a meeting of the Bank of Montreal's executive committee, Jackson Dodds advised the members of the state of Newfoundland finance "as conveyed by confidential communication from Sir Percy Thompson to our St. John's Nfld., Manager." The committee decided that Thompson was to be informed that "he should not count upon the Canadian banks advancing further sums to the Government of Newfoundland either to meet interest commitments on 1st January or for other purposes."[17] Dodds and the other Bank officials would not budge, emphasizing that the Syndicate had reached the end of the road.

With no further aid forthcoming from the Syndicate Banks, Squires was forced to appeal to Canada once again. The day after Christmas 1931, Sir Percy Thompson, Bank of Montreal President Sir Charles Gordon, and Prime Minister R.B. Bennett met to discuss Newfoundland's situation.[18] Swayed by Squires's pleas, Bennett urged the Syndicate Banks to make another advance to Newfoundland. During the meeting, Gordon discussed the situation with his general manager, his senior executives, and especially the Bank's directors. Two days later, Gordon wrote Bennett that the Bank of Montreal, along with the other three Syndicate Banks, had agreed to throw Newfoundland yet another lifeline on the same conditions as those of the July 1931 loan:

> You will be interested to know that at your urgent request and on your assurance that you will take a convenient opportunity to bring before your Cabinet and, if necessary, before Parliament, the matter of your having urged the Canadian Banks, in view of the Empire and international importance of the matter, to advance the money necessary to pay interest due on the 31st December and 1st January thus preventing a default on the part of Newfoundland, our Board agreed to the advances made. We have since heard from the Bank of Nova Scotia, the Royal Bank of Canada, and the Canadian Bank of Commerce that they will take their shares of the business on the same basis as in July last.[19]

The Squires government's deliverance came less than twenty-four hours before the default deadline of 1 January 1932. The Bank of Montreal's branch manager in St John's, A.A. Werlich, shared the news with the government of Newfoundland:

> I have the honour to enclose copy of telegram in duplicate from our General Manager with further reference to conditions under which the Syndicate Banks will lend the Government of Newfoundland $2,200,000 to meet the interest on the Public Debt at this time.

Bank of Montreal	–	$863,500
Bank of Nova Scotia	–	$733,700
Royal Bank of Canada	–	$471,900
Canadian Bank of Commerce	–	$130,900
		$2,200,000[20]

The appeal to the "Empire and international importance" of the Newfoundland bailout proved to be a determining factor in extending the lifeline.

The year-end loan agreement was loaded with further conditions concerning the circulation of currency and gold exportation. Accordingly, the Newfoundland legislature passed a Currency Act that made the currency notes of the four Syndicate Banks legal tender in Newfoundland and prevented the export of gold from the country. These conditions "put the country on the brink of receivership."[21]

The Bank of Montreal and the other Syndicate Banks seemed to be caught in a trap, lending substantial sums against their better judgment. "Banks, if left to themselves[,] are averse to making loan," John H. Penson – Thompson's second-in-command – noted in December 1931.[22] Dodds echoed this sentiment, reminding Bennett in April 1932 that "the loans made in July and December last have been renewed from time to time and it seems likely that we shall have to carry them along for more or less indefinite term, awaiting a time when a surplus from revenue will enable the Government to make repayment."[23]

The Nightmare Scenario: 1932

In June 1932 Frederick Alderdice succeeded Sir Richard Squires as Newfoundland's prime minister. Alderdice was confronted with a nightmarish choice: maintain the Dominion's interest-payment obligations or feed "the growing army of the poor."[24] Meanwhile, the Syndicate Banks had realized their own impossible predicament months before, signalling that they could not be relied upon to extend new loans indefinitely. Indeed, a communication between the Bank of Montreal and the other three Syndicate Banks noted in late 1931 that the banks "do not expect to be asked to loan any further amounts to help meet interest payments due next July [1932] and January 1933, it being understood that the Government will be able to provide these themselves."[25]

With new debt obligations looming on the horizon, Newfoundland was running out of options. Fresh interventions by Canadian Prime Minister Bennett on behalf of Newfoundland were increasingly unlikely, as the Canadian attitude was hardening. Instead, Bennett urged Newfoundland to take the legislative action required, or "otherwise we are placed in very embarrassing situation, and position of our banks unnecessarily subject to criticism."[26]

To meet its obligations in July 1932, Newfoundland was compelled to consider alternative means, including an unprecedented and radical action: a unilateral rescheduling of outstanding interest payments.[27] The emergency plan had been developed by E.N.R. Trentham, who had been sent over from the UK Treasury presumably to forestall the very action he was recommending, and William R. Stavert, a career banker who acted as adviser to the Alderdice government. Even Trentham himself was unhappy with the plan.

The proposals were roundly condemned by J.H. Thomas, secretary of state for Dominion affairs, who resorted to the by-now familiar line that the "credit of all parts of the Empire would be damaged by any such action." Indeed, if the scheme were adopted, not only would it involve the "direct violation of terms on which money was lent to Newfoundland," but it would have a "risk of serious repercussions on financial and economic relations of the whole world." In the face of such dire warnings, the plan was abandoned.[28]

Instead of turning to the Canadian or British governments, or even the Syndicate Banks, Newfoundland floated the so-called "Prosperity Loan," which called for subscriptions from private companies and individuals. The total loan, issued at $2.5 million, was indeed taken up by a variety of companies and individuals: Imperial Oil took up $1.75 million of the loan in return for a monopoly to import, manufacture, and place on market all petroleum products in return for a minimum annual payment of $300,000[29]; the Anglo-Newfoundland Development company took another $250,000; the general public subscribed to the tune of $592,000[30]; and Newfoundland's Reparations Fund took $158,000.[31] It was an unconventional approach, but it did allow Newfoundland to meet its obligations. It also showed, however, that the government was reaching the end of the line: it had no future options left to consider. No outside help would be forthcoming from either banks or national governments, and this latest round of financing drained any remaining internal resources as well.

Well-nigh Desperate

The Alderdice government went to extraordinary lengths to stabilize the situation in the hope that Newfoundland's $10,170,000 budget could be maintained. The Treasury Control Act of 30 April 1932 created the post of comptroller of the treasury and ensured that no expenditure could be undertaken without the comptroller's explicit approval.[32] Public-service salary reductions alone were intended to shave $1 million off the deficit each year.[33] The verdict from the Bank of Montreal boardroom was bracing:

"There is little or no prospect of its [Newfoundland's] being able to do so, further advances should not be made by the banks, which would mean probable default in interest payment due 1st January next. No decision was reached, the matter being left open pending discussion with the other banks interested."[34] This was prescient, for, though they were ambitious, Newfoundland's cuts came too late to have much of an effect. As a 1933 memorandum later suggested, "it was soon manifest ... that [the] hopes [of a balanced budget] were not to be realized. It was found impossible to keep expenditure within the estimate owing to the necessity for continuous payments in respect of able-bodied relief while revenue showed a sharp decline owing to the decreased purchasing power of the people."[35]

The desperate situation in which Newfoundland found itself is reflected in an exchange between Prime Minister Alderdice and Bank of Montreal General Manager Jackson Dodds on 27 September 1932. Alderdice wrote:

> You fully understand our position. It seems to me it is getting well nigh desperate. So far as retrenchment is concerned, we are doing our best and shall continue to do our best. Unfortunately, retrench as we may our economies do not keep pace with the shrinking in revenue ... Without provoking an absolute revolt, I do not see how we can further econo-mize, and, on the other hand, without further retrenchment, I do not see how we can hope to balance the budget by the end of the financial year ... [Neither] I, nor any of my colleagues[,] are competent to decide which course would be best calculated to work out for the ultimate welfare of the country ... Believe me, it hurts me to write you in this strain. It looks almost like a confession of failure on my part to bring this country back to a stabilized condition. I hope you will excuse my writing you in this way. I am of opinion, however, that you should know exactly how I feel in the unfortunate position we are now placed.[36]

Alderdice also asked Jackson Dodds for his opinion on a new financial ad-viser. He wanted to dismiss Thompson because of the latter's association with the Squires government, writing that "Sir Percy Thompson, either through his own fault or through an unfortunate combination of circum-stances, has ceased to be helpful to us in our situation. The Government and Sir Percy are out of sympathy with each other. There cannot be any hope of working together in harmony."[37] The new financial adviser, furthermore, had to be somebody nominated by the Syndicate Banks. Alderdice believed that they alone would be able to lift Newfoundland out of its predicament: "If you could manage to spare one of your outstanding officials, a man upon whose judgment you can depend and upon whose opinions you can place reliance, to come here so as to form a first-hand opinion of our affairs, I believe it would help matters very materially …The situation is very largely in the hands of the syndicate [banks] and for that reason it seems to me we require a man to survey the situation on the spot, so that all the side issues may also be taken into account."[38]

Dodds advised Canadian Prime Minister Bennett of the request: "You will note that Mr. Alderdice requests the Syndicate Banks to select a man to go down and take charge of the situation, and he suggests that one of the officers of the Banks be chosen." Dodds suggested shrewdly that the person so nominated should not be a Syndicate banker, reasoning that "it would be better for all concerned that the choice should be a man outside of this sphere." Dodds noted that the banks had come up with the name of none other than William E. Stavert, an ubiquitous presence in Newfoundland's public-finance drama.[39] R.B. Bennett enthusiastically agreed on the Stavert nomination, adding that "I trust Mr. Alderdice appreciates the efforts the Canadian banks are making to be of assistance to him and that he will, so far as may be reasonably possible, be guided by their recommendations."[40]

Sir William E. Stavert was a life-long banker from Summerside, Prince Edward Island, who had worked for several banks in the region – the Summerside Bank, the Merchants Bank of Halifax, the Bank of Nova Scotia, and the Bank of New Brunswick. While at the Bank of Nova Scotia in the late 1890s, he had established the bank's branch in St Johns.[41] From 1905 to 1912 he had also served as the Bank of Montreal superintendent of branches for the Maritime provinces.[42] As a Bank of Montreal banker, Stavert was a close associate of its celebrated general manager Sir Edward Clouston. Unfortunately for him, his involvement with Clouston and Arthur R. Doble in the infamous Canada Cement merger orchestrated by Max Aitken compelled him in 1912 to give up a "promising executive career … with the Bank of Montreal."[43] Stavert quickly found another opportunity with a new investment bank called Corporation Agencies, set up in part by C.H. Cahan (a future Bank of Montreal director and Canadian trade minister).[44] The intervening two decades between 1912 and the onset of the Great Depression evidently gave Stavert a chance for rehabilitation of his reputation.

While the Banks were happy to put forward Stavert as a successor to Thompson, they were unwilling to extend further loans. As Dodds explained to Bennett in October 1932: "You will understand that with the finances of the Government of Newfoundland in such a precarious state, the Syndicate Banks cannot permit further increases in advances and that the Government must finance on revenue as best they can, making additional cuts in current expenditures if necessary."[45] Against this backdrop, Sir Percy Thompson's final report was published in early October 1932. In it, Thompson concluded darkly that "the Government of Newfoundland will be forced to default, at least in part, in payment of the interest due on their external debt at the end of the year."[46]

With the banks unwilling to extend further loans and no other options available, Alderdice's government announced unequivocally that Newfoundland would default on its debt payments – which by then had reached $100 million – by the end of 1932.[47] The frank admission shocked both the Canadian and the British governments, whose long-held concerns about the disastrous effects of a Newfoundland default once again came to the fore.

Jackson Dodds also worried about the effects a Newfoundland default could have on Canada in particular, fearing that American audiences might mistake Newfoundland as part of Canada. In October, shortly after Alderdice's announcement, Dodds wrote Bennett and urged the prime minister to make a public declaration emphasizing, for the benefit of the American capital market in particular, that Newfoundland was not part of Canada: "Should Mr. Alderdice decide to default, it seems to me that he should first give you an opportunity to intimate to the public in the United States that Newfoundland is not part of Canada. I think Newfoundland owes this to you in view of what you have done for them."[48] He underscored his request two weeks later, writing: "As suggested in my letter of 12th October last to you, no doubt you have in mind the effect which default on the part of the Government of Newfoundland will have upon Canadian securities and that the necessity of making suitable announcement in the press when the time is opportune will receive your consideration."[49]

Fearing a domino effect following on a Newfoundland default, both London and Ottawa vaulted into action. The Canadian and British governments jointly agreed to the Loan Act of 1932, which extended an emergency loan of $1,250,000 so Newfoundland could meet its debt obligations.[50] As ever, there was a catch, this time the appointment of a royal commission into Newfoundland's financial difficulties

> Of this loan ½ will be advanced by His Majesty's government and
> Great Britain, while His Majesty's government in Canada will arrange
> the advance of the other half. His Majesty's government in Newfoundland on its part has agreed to the appointment of a Commission
> consisting of two members nominated by His Majesty's government
> and Great Britain (one of whom will be appointed in consultation with
> His Majesty's government in Canada) and a third nominated by His
> Majesty's Government in Newfoundland. The purpose of the commission will be to examine into the future of Newfoundland, and in
> particular to report on the financial situation and prospects and what

measures may be necessary to secure its financial stability, with a view to the decisions being made before the debt interest due on 1st July, 1933 matures.[51]

With the Loan Act of 1932, the stage was set for this royal commission to begin its work. All the members would be appointed by Whitehall. The British appointee was Scottish Labour peer Lord Amulree, who was to act as chair. Canada's choice was Charles A. McGrath, while Newfoundland chose none other than Sir William E. Stavert, who had been appointed financial adviser a few months prior. The commission assembled in early 1933 and performed a thorough analysis of Newfoundland's financial situation.

In its final report, published in November 1933, the commission recommended the suspension of responsible government on the Island, along with a number of other provisions. A special Commission of Government was to be created and given full legislative and executive authority. The governing commission would be composed of six members, exclusive of the governor, three of whom would be drawn from Newfoundland and three from the United Kingdom – and all appointed by London. It would be subject to supervisory control by the secretary of state for Dominion affairs in the UK government. That government would assume the financial obligations of the Island "until such time as it may become self-supporting again,"[52] and would, in particular, "make such arrangements as may be deemed just and practicable with a view to securing to Newfoundland a reduction in the present burden of the public debt." Responsible government would return when "the Island's difficulties are overcome and the country is again self-supporting,"[53]

The Newfoundland government, left with very little choice, accepted the recommendations in November 1933, and the following February the new Commission of Government took the reins of power. It was destined to govern until 1949, when the country joined Canadian Confederation as the tenth province.

Montreal Bankers and the Dominion of Newfoundland

The financial collapse of Newfoundland in the early 1930s had a dramatic finale. The suspension of democratic, responsible government in the country for fifteen years was a high, and in the context of the 1930s, necessary price to pay in an increasingly desperate time. The establishment of the Commission of Government at the very least prevented the country from defaulting on its crippling debt and causing an even more dire set of circumstances.

As Newfoundland had moved further and further into an inescapable debt-interest trap, Canadian banks had to make tough decisions about whether to continue financing governments one last time before drawing the line. The political and human costs of so doing were getting higher by the month in the early 1930s. The evidence is clear, however, that politics would determine the ultimate outcome of this drama. The direct and multiple interventions of Canadian Prime Minister R.B. Bennett and the UK government in London were driven by their awareness of the implications of a Newfoundland default for Canada in the US capital market and for the Empire as a whole. Bank of Montreal bankers, along with the other Syndicate banks offering loan relief, acted in the national and imperial interest, and, it seems, with considerable reluctance, since loan repayment looked as if it would be many years away. These were events over which the Bank of Montreal had influence but not control. Refusing to extend the Newfoundland loans was only theoretically possible because it would mean, in effect, an abdication of the Bank's role in the guardianship of Canadian credit at home and abroad, especially in New York. A default was too high a risk to take. Protecting the bondholders was paramount.

The Bank's experience in Newfoundland shows that banking had both political and financial dimensions. Navigating the complexities of Depression-era public finance required bankers to exercise their professional expertise in extraordinarily difficult circumstances. But that was only half the equation. As the Newfoundland case shows, the situation demanded a high degree of political acuity and judgment. The foundations for action in this case were based only partly on banking principles; also at play was a network of close relationships between bankers, politicians, and governments in the North Atlantic sphere.

Where bankers could and did exert greater control was over conditions and consequences. The protagonists in these events from outside Newfoundland – the banks, the Canadian and UK governments – imposed progressively stricter conditions, thought necessary, over Island finances in exchange for loans and guarantees, a process that culminated with the establishment of the Commission of Government. Peter Neary writes that "in the last resort [Newfoundland] was dependent on what Richard Squires ... would call in one moment of nervous hope 'that thin red cord of sentiment and of blood' that tied the British empire together."[54] The "thin red cord" to which Richard Squires referred in 1929 did indeed tie Newfoundland to the Empire. The Empire ultimately acted – from Ottawa, Montreal, and London – to salvage the situation. Yet the Empire also struck back, exacting a very high price for its help. It bound Newfoundland to years of severe financial retrenchment and the loss of its representative government. For a decade and a half, Newfoundland would not be run by Newfoundlanders. Island politics and finance would never be the same.

CHAPTER TWELVE

Winners, Losers, and Bankers: The Making of the Bank of Canada

The establishment of the Bank of Canada as the country's central bank in 1935 was the most important development in Canadian banking in the twentieth century. It came decades, and in some cases centuries, after every major nation in the North Atlantic world had established their own central banks.[1] The absence of a central bank did not, however, prevent Canada from creating a strong, stable, and successful banking system of chartered banks, maintaining price stability, and avoiding systemic failures. Canada's senior bank, the Bank of Montreal, acted as government banker and the Canadian treasury acted as lender of last resort while the Canadian Bankers Association served as a coordinating body alongside the Department of Finance.

This chapter examines the struggle in Canada to establish a central, public banking institution. Previous chapters have examined the changes in the political economy of Canadian banking in the 1920s which were in a direct way a prologue to these events. The Bank of Montreal was one of several players in this unfolding drama – and the one that had the most at play as the premier banking institution in the country, as well as the government's central banker.

The Depression brought on its wings a number of sweeping changes to the status quo. In the early 1930s, the idea of establishing a central bank gathered momentum both domestically in political circles and internationally through such bodies as the International Financial Conference in Brussels in 1932 and the World Monetary and Economic Conference (July 1933).[2] Canada's decision to move off the gold standard in 1928 was another factor. In 1933 the Royal Commission on Banking and Currency formally recommended the establishment of a central bank. Then, the government of Canada drafted the necessary legislation and a central bank was established in 1935 as a shareholder-controlled, privately owned institution. In 1936 a second phase of legislation put the Bank of Canada exclusively in the control of the Canadian government, with the Finance Department as the exclusive shareholder.

From about 1932 to 1938, the players in Canadian banking engaged in a complex game of strategy involving moves, counter-moves, and shifting alliances. The intensity of the debate on the establishment of a central bank revealed the 1930s to be a highly competitive and contentious period in the history Canadian banking. This chapter will focus especially on the players with the most to lose: the Canadian banks themselves in the face of almost certain change in their industry.

The establishment of the Bank of Canada involved at least two distinct contests: the contest of politics, and, beyond mere politics, the contest of elites – public and private, Canadian and British. Politics did indeed fuel the intensity of arguments over a Bank of Canada. Party political differences over the proper role of the state in the economy divided Conservatives from Liberals, and Liberals from Progressives and the CCF. Yet there was more to the conflict than that. Sharp metropolitan, regional, and class differences often redrew the fault lines so as to make them run within, and not just between, parties. Within the Canadian banking fraternity, too, a united front presented through the Canadian Bankers Association masked divergent interests between the banks, not least their leader, the Bank of Montreal, and the Royal Bank, the powerful challenger. The debate over the central bank also revealed divisions among and between financial elites and public servants. Finally, the involvement of Bank of England bankers actively promoting imperial interests highlights a key, but not well appreciated, Anglo-Canadian dimension to the story.

The Context of Canadian Banking

Prior to the Bank of Canada's creation in 1935, private institutions assumed the typical functions of a central bank. Following Confederation in 1867, the Bank of Montreal acted as Canada's fiscal agent and would remain so until the creation of the Bank of Canada.

A summation of the state of Canadian banking in the 1930s is in order. By the early part of the decade, ten chartered banks operated in Canada, with the Royal Bank, the Commerce, and the Bank of Montreal leading the branch count (738, 667, and 560 branches respectively). In total, there were 3,158 branches across the Dominion.[3] According to one Bank of England observer, this meant that there was not the same necessity to provide executive ability in numerous centres "as is necessary but rarely found ... in unit banking."[4] The paid-up capital of the banks in 1932–32 was roughly $144.5 million with an additional reserve of $162 million.[5]

The Canadian banks were generally managed by conservative-minded officers with an established track record for good banking as well as stability. The bankers of the 1930s attributed Canada's success to five foundations: a single legislative authority; the straightforward, simple nature of regulation; the prescription of minimum size; the "systematic and progressive" training of bank executives through the branch system; and finally, the smooth, orderly distribution of banking capital according to local needs, another feature of the branch system.[6] Thus did the banks acquire a reputation in Canada for careful and orderly development of the Canadian financial system in both domestic and external trade financing. This was especially, but not exclusively, true of the Bank of Montreal.

The Canadian banks also maintained a steady rate of interest for time deposits (3 per cent per annum) and first-class commercial loans (6 per cent). The object of that policy was to exert a steadying influence on savers and borrowers and, most importantly, eliminate fluctuations in periods of cyclical economic uncertainty. As Bank of Montreal General Manager Jackson Dodds noted in 1933: "It [interest policy] has been an important factor in creating and maintaining the feeling of confidence in their banks by the public generally."[7] The Depression forced a slight alteration of the rate to 2.5 per cent for deposits and 7 per cent for loans.

From 1929, Canadian banks had been focused on effecting "an orderly retreat in the face of declining world prices and prosperity."[8] The resulting contraction in bank loans led to a vicious spiral of recall of loans and contraction of credit. Canadian bankers lamented the investment bankers' effect on the massive expansion of credit, which not even the "restraining influence" of the chartered banks could counter.[9] There was clearly no love lost between the chartered banks and the investment bankers.

Canadian banks were regulated by the decennially revised Bank Act. They could issue notes, deal in gold and silver, and generally carry on the business of banking, except lending on the security of real estate. No specified cash-to-reserve ratio was specified by law, but banks generally held 10 per cent of their reserve in cash. The provisions for expanding capital were originally limited to harvest or crop movements before the war. After the war, however, the power of credit provisions expanded significantly.[10]

Several other features of the Canadian system should be noted. The supreme importance of the harvest and the wide variation in climate made for regularly recurring seasonal fluctuations that had to be provided for on a massive scale, capital-wise, resulting in a 5 per cent swing in assets.[11] The banks had a right of bank-note issue, a feature that the bankers asserted enabled them to provide a lost-cost medium of exchange to pioneer communities and to open a larger number of new branches across the country; on average, there was one branch for every 3,350 people in 1933.[12]

The Control of Credit

Banks had control of credit in the Dominion even without any formally constituted body to do so. So tight was the Canadian banking fraternity, however, that the policy of one bank would be found to be the policy of all. "If the Board and Executive of one institution formed an impression – after the most serious consideration" – that credit expansion threatened the stability or health of the system, "that bank gradually would proceed to reduce its advances and restrict fresh applications for credit."[13] Once that happened, the other banks would likely confer, and even if there were divergence of views, "one view or the other would shortly be felt by all to be correct."[14]

Most Canadian bank reserves were centred in the New York market for reasons of proximity as well as the undeveloped nature of the Canadian stock and exchange markets. In addition, Canada's external obligations were predominantly in the United States, as well as its trade.[15]

The largest and most influential Canadian chartered bank was the Bank of Montreal, followed, in rough terms, by the Royal and the Commerce. The Bank of Montreal's position as Canada's first bank gave it pride of place, as did its status as government banker and the Dominion's agent in London, even if by other measures the ranking was more competitive. The Bank of Montreal's general manager in London, W.A. Pope, actively corresponded with the Bank of England on such questions as the need to widen the direct London-Canadian market in Canadian dollars, exchange controls, and excess reserves.[16] The issue of money markets was an important one, not least because Pope advocated a turn to London, since the Canadians "had had a bad deal from the Americans" and he hoped that they would "learn their lesson from it."[17] The New York market had offered "violent rate fluctuations" and it was a hard there even to obtain cover for £5,000 at a reasonable rate.[18]

Beyond individual banks, the Canadian Bankers Association was incorporated by statute in 1900 to act as an umbrella organization of the chartered banks with an educational and inspection function. Its other duties included receipt of deposits of gold and Dominion notes in the Central Gold Reserves. The CBA also had power to impose binding by-laws on the banks for specified duties. In the event of the failure of any bank, the president of the CBA was empowered under law to appoint trustees for the management of the failing bank.[19]

The Finance Act of 1923 allowed the banks to discount certain securities for which they received an advance of Dominion notes, and which were to be repaid in same. This allowed banks to obtain a discount of, say, 4.5 per cent and then extend credit and lending in the call-money market in New York at considerably higher rates. The Banks realized that this was not only obviously profitable: it made the existence of a central bank unnecessary. It did so by conferring the power of credit control on the Finance Department to check undue expansion.[20]

Opposition to the idea of central bank was a natural one for chartered banks, for the reasons stated as well as because such an institution would eliminate their own note issues. A central bank would also make unproductive branches even more so because of the cash-on-hand they were compelled to retain. The Bank of Montreal stood the most to lose from the development of a central bank by virtue of its position as government banker.[21]

International Currents and the Canadian Dollar

The Canadian financial system effectively abandoned the gold standard as early as 1928, though the appearances of adherence, if it may be so put, were maintained into the early 1930s. After the full onset of the Depression, parity between the Canadian and American dollars was lost. The Canadian dollar was, moreover, at a premium over sterling. Canada was not on a gold standard in the "full sense of the term." One BOE memorandum suggested in 1931 that, even if Canada returned to the gold standard, the stocks of the country would be dissipated without a permanent improvement in the exchange rate having taken place.[22] Maintaining the pretense that Canada "is in fact upon the gold standard when the exchange on New York stands at a considerable premium" was relatively futile. The memorandum further suggested that the Canadian chartered banks be encouraged to transfer their existing Canadian gold stocks to the Dominion government in return for government notes to stabilize the currency situation somewhat. Taken together, the chartered banks held, in 1930, $72.7 million of gold reserves. It was also to the advantage of the Canadian banks not to "encash" their own notes in gold, but to pay out Dominion notes and force the gold seekers to acquire it elsewhere.[23] Still, even with no central bank, the Department of Finance had powers under the Finance Act of 1923 to manage the currency and gold situation, including compelling banks to ensure sufficient remittance of gold reserves and purchase of Dominion notes (which was never a real issue). Expert opinion within government circles began to suggest that the legislation governing note issue needed an overhaul.[24]

The country owed large sums in the United States.[25] The shift in the Canadian balance of indebtedness from favourable to unfavourable after 1930 was also a matter of concern, as was the possibility of having to borrow abroad on a large scale for the Canadian National Railway and the refinancing of the burgeoning provincial debt. Canada, in other words, found itself heavily indebted to foreign countries for net investment and other purposes.

The main lever available to the Canadian government in influencing the situation was the ultimate control of purchasing power – and therefore of prices in Canada. The Department of Finance's ability to increase the total volume of purchasing power in the country could be done by borrowing from the banks (increasing the debt to the banks). Still, the Australian experience pointed to the dangers of "uncoordinated borrowing" and the situation in the New York money market underlined the desirability of cooperative action in order "to avoid a drastic rise of rates."[26]

By late 1932, the Canadian exchange situation had deteriorated markedly. The Canadian dollar had depreciated substantially against the sterling and the US dollar, a situation a well-placed Toronto observer called "very unsettling" in that it tended to focus the attention of the public on the whole question of exchange.[27] Canadian external-funded debts (Dominion, provincial, municipal, and corporations) added to the downward pressure. Capital flight from Canada, especially in the form of Americans' liquidation of their considerable investments in the Dominion, was a risk. The campaign for the depreciation of the dollar had also been advocated by both agricultural exporters and banking figures in the country.[28] The Banks, especially the two largest ones, the Bank of Montreal and the Bank of Commerce, did not take a position on the currency.

The Royal Commission on Banking and Currency: 1933

The Great Depression in Canada produced an increasingly catastrophic economic situation which multiplied calls for a government response. The Bennett government originally resisted the idea of more energetic intervention in the economy and specifically the notion of a central bank in the early 1930s because the country – by which the prime minister presumably meant the major chartered banks – was "not prepared to make the change."[29] By 1933, Bennett was ready at least to study the matter and so established the Royal Commission on Banking and Currency.

The royal commission was empanelled by order-in-council on 31 July 1933.[30] It was to be led by Lord Macmillan, a banker from England who had sat on the committee which formulated the Macmillan Report on UK banking in July 1931. Sir Charles Addis, another banker from England, had considerable experience in banking matters and been a member of the Cunliffe Committee and the Indian Currency Commission, was a director of the Bank of England, and had served as vice-chairman of the Bank of International Settlements.[31] The Canadian members included Sir Thomas White, former minister of finance during the war, and Beaudry Leman, of the Banque Nationale, described as a "Banker of the old school."[32] The fifth member was former premier of Alberta J.N. Brownlee.

Hopes for the commission varied. John C. Reade of *Saturday Night Magazine* suggested that the "Canadian Macmillan Commission will lay the foundation of a new Canadian state or will merely mix a bucket of whitewash to cover up the mildew and a little plaster to fill in the more obvious cracks. Which it is to be depends upon whether its members can refrain from sighing for the good old days – which mercifully are behind us – and embark on their work in the spirit of a Twentieth Century Renaissance."[33]

The commission held hearings across the Dominion during the summer of 1933, maintaining a gruelling pace by train from Halifax to Vancouver. It drew scores of submissions from every conceivable corner of the country, but especially from organizations in banking, finance, industry, and export trade, farmers, chambers of commerce, and municipalities. Representations were made by desperate exporters. The export trade, upon which the country relied so heavily, suffered badly in the early years of the Depression. Depreciated competitor currencies from Australia and large parts of the British Empire were seriously disrupting trade flows.[34] The Retail Merchants Association of Canada declared in favour of a central bank. "There is no intention in this Memorandum to place blame on the Banking Institutions, or on any other Organization under the present system ... the intention is to suggest rather that the difficulty must be met by the State as a whole and it is hoped that this can be done without too great a departure in the direction of socialization."[35] The present financial system had "fail[ed] to respond in the right way ... where purchasing power in the hand of the consumer begins to fall off."

The Investment Dealers Association of Canada urged the royal commission to reign in the banks, their powers, and especially their "encroachment on other business which are not proper banking functions."[36] The chartered banks had entered the bond business in 1923, a move that investment bankers greatly resented. They were particularly incensed by the Bank of Montreal's establishment of the Montreal Company of New York, an investment house, in 1926, and by its close alliance between Royal Trust and the Bank.[37]

Farmers were divided in their proposed remedies but united in complaining that the Canadian banks were "very stingy" with their facilities. One farmer suggested that the banks were like people who gave one an "umbrella when the sky was clear and then took it away when it began to rain."[38] Others blamed the banking system itself for the difficult economic conditions in the west, particularly Alberta.[39] A central bank controlled by bankers was "not enough" in the eyes of Alberta's farmer press.[40]

The newspaper magnate W.M. Southam believed that "with the exception of our friends, the members of the Canadian Bankers' Association, most thinking Canadians believe that we should round out our banking system with a Central Bank. Though the banks are unanimously opposed to such an institution for obvious reasons, I feel that the proposed monetary commission will endorse the proposal."[41] The Economic Reform Association also favoured strongly a central bank with muscular powers, but it conceived this institution as part of a larger overhaul of the Canadian economic system, including commodity-price movement and foreign-exchange relationships.[42]

Considerable anti-bank sentiment emerged at the hearings. One Toronto correspondent wrote to Conservative Senator Arthur Meighen to suggest a renewal of the bank charters only for a year to ensure that "we should know how our Central Bank now to be established is to work into the Financial structure before we give these Burglars the Banks another 10 year lease of life. The public are thoroughly aroused by the Bankers Methods, viz. the amount of money of the Royal Bank which [Herbert] Holt diverted to the Montreal Trust to support his investments in the late Crash."[43]

In a similar vein, a "Toronto Businessman" wrote to the *Globe* March 1934:

> Can bankers truthfully say that they have not in many instances been ruthless in putting established businesses to the "wall" and at times unscrupulously so? Can bankers say they have not been so ruthless in demanding too drastic reductions in commercial and industrial loans [and] that [in so doing] they have not seriously and severely hampered the ordinary daily running of many a good business? Can bankers say they have not, beyond ordinary reason, compelled their business loan customers to make uncalled-for and unnecessary sacrifices of private and personal investments for the so-called beneficial reduction of such business loans?[44]

The news of the commission hearings had some immediate effects along the Canadian border. The Bank of Montreal reported that its Windsor branch had experienced a large number of withdrawals by American depositors after a *Detroit News* Article of 7 March 1934 suggested that the Canadian banks were facing an inquiry. "We do not anticipate a serious turn on our office but the publication of news of this kind coupled with the fact that deposits in United States Banks up to $2,500 are now guaranteed by the Federal Deposit Insurance Corporation may result in continued downward trend in our deposits."[45]

Groups such as the Economic Reform Association of Canada and the League for Social Reconstruction (LSR) presented extensive briefs on the existing banking system and the urgency of change to that system for the national welfare. The LSR, in particular, viewed state control over the banking system as part of a new economic order. For that group, a central bank and state control of all existing banking institutions and a "majority of other financial institutions" were required for Canada to emerge from the Depression.[46]

Bankers' View

In such an environment, Canadian bankers opted, shrewdly, for carefully measured public statements on the issue of a central bank. Bank of Nova Scotia executive H.J. Coon testified to the commission that "the banks have had to keep in view on the one hand the representations made to the Commission in favour of this step and, on the other hand, the imperative necessity of avoiding any action which might adversely affect the financial structure of the country."[47] The banks took pains to stress that the banking system's strength in Canada was partly due to the fact that it had grown up with Canada and "has not been the subject of experimentation." Coon cautioned the commissioners to "avoid innovations which are imitative rather than essential or which might tend to weaken a banking system that has been a partner in the great development of this country during the past one hundred years."[48] His analysis was that the Canadian banking system worked because a small number of strong banks with multiple branches facilitated "a great mobility of loanable funds, a highly developed experience in the use of those funds for the purpose of commercial banking, and a bank note currently automatically responsive to the country's requirements."[49]

Yet Canada's chartered banks also realized that the creation of a central bank in Canada was one possible response to the financial crisis besetting the North Atlantic world. Indeed, the assistant general manager of the Bank of Montreal, G.C. Cassels, had been part of the Canadian delegation to the International Financial Conference in Brussels in 1920 which recommended the establishment of a central bank of issue, though Canada obviously did not consider itself bound by the conference's conclusions.[50] But the Canadian banks underlined the fact that even those countries with central banks were not able to take counter-measures to control the boom that had led to the bust. Though a central bank would operate to enlarge the credit structure of the country, it was but one solution, and that solution, moreover, required that the management and board of such an institution possess the "very highest qualifications."[51]

The banks further argued that a Canadian central bank would play only a minor role in international relationships. Its role would also be circumscribed by local conditions. The actions of the Bank of England and the Sveriges Riksbank (Sweden) in stabilizing commodity prices were laudable, but these were exceptional successes due to local conditions – in the case of England, the close control of the fluctuations in credit, and in the case of Sweden, by means of operations on the foreign-exchange market. Neither situation would remotely have been possible in Canada, since the country had no money market to speak of (in the sense of the size and consequence of New York and London banking organizations). There were no facilities in Canada for open-market operations. Canadian reserves were maintained in New York. The central bank solution, in other words, was not a one-size-fits-all answer to Canada's national economic challenges.

Canadian bankers, according to W.A. Pope of the Canadian Bankers Association, had "never found particular favour in the public eye." In a telling admission, Pope suggested that "bankers have acquired a mythical reputation for an absence of understanding or sympathy; they are supposed to be devoid of souls and brains as well. Such convictions as these supply the critics with a standing reserve of ammunition for their attacks, but when on top of that is piled three years of depression, it is perhaps little wonder that they herald, with exceeding joy, the long awaited opportunity to journey to Ottawa and lay their case before the government."[52]

The CBA wrote to the prime minister that it was "not desirable or necessary to establish a central bank in Canada at the present time."[53] The workings of the Finance Act were sufficient to ensure the operation of the business of Canadian banking in terms of credit and circulation and in meeting all other reasonable requirements. If a central bank were to be given the sole privilege of note issue, the CBA warned, "the crippling effect upon the present banking system of such a change, when the banking carried on in pioneer sections of Canada by the chartered banks is considered, needs only to be mentioned to be appreciated by anyone familiar with the operation of Canada's banking system."[54] As figure 12.1 shows, the notes in circulation of the big four chartered banks were considerable in amount, with the Bank of Montreal leading the pack until 1935 – and hence having the most to lose from the loss of the right of bank-note issue.

The banks conceded that a central bank, under the leadership of someone of high reputation and authority, might exercise moral suasion in the market. It could also purchase and sell bonds and foreign exchange and adjust the rate charged on advances.[55] Yet the instruments would be "somewhat crude,"

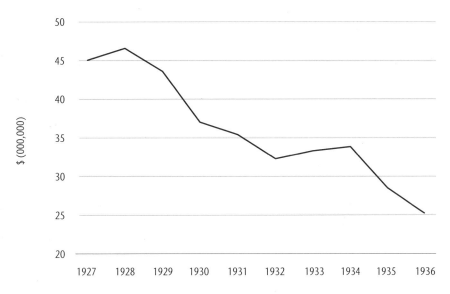

Figure 12.1 | Notes in circulation, Bank of Montreal, 1927–36
Source: Bank of Montreal Annual Reports, 1927–36.

and it would be "visionary" to hope that a Canadian central bank, no matter how wise or strong, would be able to force its will merely by the means available to it.[56] The benefits, moreover, would be "dearly purchased" if they involved any weakening of the existing banking structure or resulted in the commercial banks being able to give the public a less adequate banking service than before.[57]

Gold and Notes Spell Trouble

For Canadian banks, there were two troublesome aspects to the idea of a central bank. First was the question of the "sole right of note issue" – depriving the commercial banks of their note-issuing privileges. The note-issue privilege permitted banks to be maintained in small communities, and a single central note issue, in place of the inexpensive currency that the banks currently provided, would make the continued maintenance of all those branches too costly. Earnings would also suffer.[58] One CBA member told the prime minister that the loss of issue might cost as much as $40 million.[59] The second troublesome aspect of the central bank proposal was not as serious but still significant: the banks objected to the duty to be laid on the banks of keeping a reserve against liabilities with the central bank at all times.

Nonetheless, for all their meticulously argued objections, the banks also realized that the writing was on the wall: the movement was toward the creation of a central bank. As a result, they attempted to ensure that this institution would be free from political influence and limited to using persuasion more than the devices at the command of the chartered banks for controlling the domestic market. "We must emphasize with all the seriousness at our command," H.J. Coon noted, "the vital importance of the experience, intelligent and conservative management of any central institution which may be set up. A central bank can be no better than the men who manage it." If that were accomplished, "we might hope to retain the virtues of the present regime, without the defects which have been apparent in the centralized credit systems of other countries."[60] This would put a prospective Bank of Canada in line with the tenor and attitude of the Canadian banking system as it had long functioned – successfully.

The Banks and Commissioners behind Closed Doors: The Private Sessions

A private session of the royal commission with the Canadian banks, on 8 August 1933, offers a revealing insight into the different perspectives of the British commissioners and Canadian bankers. An exchange between Lord Macmillan and Bank of Montreal General Manager Jackson Dodds is especially telling. On the subject of the central bank's power to take coordinated action, Macmillan lauded the Bank of England for its ability to exert pressure to control the credit position of the country. "There is nothing comparable to that here?" he asked.[61]

> MR. DODDS: No. We have been rather afraid after what we have seen cross the border of adopting any such action because we do not consider it has been very successful.
> THE CHAIRMAN: Conditions here are so very much more like conditions in England in this respect, that you have a group of large commercial banks, ten banks, carrying on a general banking business ...[62]

The differences between the Canadians and the British commissioners were most pronounced on the subject of how policy should be made. The Bank of England exerted its powers through informal suasion and influence, direct consultation, and raising or reducing the interest rate.[63] Sir Charles Addis explained that "when the general policy is indicated ... the banks are asked so far as they can to make their transactions conform to that general policy." S.H. Logan of the Canadian Bank of Commerce explained in turn that the Canadian system relied on direct access to the minister and prime minister. "There is one thing which is very important from our point of view and that is that we are directly under the Prime Minister and the Minister of

Finance ... and in the event of any crisis ... we can come down here and sit around the table with the Minister of Finance and the Prime Minister and can arrive at a decision quickly. I have always felt that this is very important from the point of view of safety of the whole country and the position of the banks themselves."[64] When the banks were asked to lend to government or borrow under the Finance Act, they complied willingly. When Macmillan suggested this might be seen as political influence, the Canadian bankers responded that they never saw the transactions as political. Logan of the Commerce argued that "when it suits a government to step over the heads of the banks, a government will do it. That would apply to the Bank of England." Macmillan replied that central banks had to exist to curb irresponsible governments. "Of course, every government can propose experiments. *It is a question of exercising executive control over them*" [emphasis added].[65] This statement was very much in line with contemporary thinking on the role of the technocrat in the execution of public policy. But Canadian bankers, for their part, respected the political sphere, perhaps because they were typically used to getting their own way – at least until the 1920s.

The other matter that divided British commissioners and Canadian bankers was that of a money market. London, of course, had the "world's flow of money in and out" whereas Canada did not have that flow at all and so, in the view of the Canadian banks, did not require a central banking institution. Macmillan suggested that "you cannot get [a money market] unless you have some method of central banking and you cannot operate a central bank except through a money market." Dodds retorted that "that is a good many years ahead."[66] He further suggested with some justification that the "Federal Reserve System has proved to be no better than our own [system] ... We would much rather use our own judgement in the matter rather than have a ready-made judgement provided by a Federal Reserve bank such as that across the line."[67]

There followed a frank discussion about the differences between Canadian and British banking. The Canadian bankers pointed to their warnings in late 1928 and 1929 about the overheated speculation in the market, and particularly the fact that most of the banks did not lend any money to purchase stocks throughout 1929 "because we foresaw what was likely to happen."[68] The astonishing fact was, according to Logan, that "all the banks over the line, from Buffalo straight through to the New England states[,] were lending money on Canadian securities."[69]

Jackson Dodds put the question of a central bank this way:

MR DODDS: We will have to show you or try to show you that as far as this country is concerned we believe we are just as well off without the

central bank. In fact, we hope to show you that we are better off without having a central bank, that we have got along very well without it
and the time is not ripe. On the other hand, you may in the course of
your travels secure so much evidence that you will come to the conclusion that something different is needed. I do not say that we do want it
yet, but I do say that we will have to produce what you want when you
return and try to put up a debit and credit to you.

THE CHAIRMAN: That is only what I had in mind.[70]

On the question of note issue, the bankers warned that a state monopoly over
note issue would lead to the closure of many smaller branches. Dodds supposed that several branches had less than $6,000 on hand. Logan suggested
that it would cost the bigger banks each about $750,000 per year "if we had to
buy other notes instead of our own throughout our various branches."[71] The
note-issue privilege was one of the reasons why the Canadian banks were
able to carry on a banking business in the west "to the extent that we have,"
added J.M. McLeod of the Bank of Nova Scotia.[72] "There would certainly be
… branches close[d] because they would be in the red," Dodds explained.
"If some of the people in some parts of Canada had any idea that we lost as
much money as we did in that particular part of the country they perhaps
would not be as critical."[73]

In fact, the banks had already started closing a number of western branches,
prompting considerable protests in the rural parts of Alberta as well as a
steady stream of telegrams to the prime minister.[74] In the end, though, the
argument that won the day was advanced by W.C. Clark, the deputy minister
of finance, who told the commission that the control of currency and credit
would, if left alone, "be wholly in the hands of private interests. Personally
I would prefer an independent party not motivated by the profit motive,
to exercise that particular function."[75] Clark believed that the absence of a
Canadian central bank was not only embarrassing but also raised questions
about the propriety of having a political department in charge of administer-
ing the Finance Act. With an independent central bank, such concerns would
be resolved.[76]

The Public-Relations Strategy of the Banks

After that private session, the CBA, sensing which way the winds were blow-
ing, set to work devising its public-relations strategy. E.A. Peacock forwarded
a memorandum prepared by G.E. Jackson, the association's economic adviser,
to the Bank of England in September 1933, which revealed the banks' understanding that a central bank was inevitable – whether they liked it or not. In

order to get the best terms for the chartered banks, therefore, the banks themselves, Jackson argued, should set out their own vision of a central bank.[77]

The CBA memorandum presented a strategy for the Canadian banks that can be summarized as follows:

1 A central bank is a likely outcome of the commission hearings, "no matter what views we take."
2 The banks should insist on following the British tradition.
3 "Take the initiative" in creating a "private, Central Bank like the Bank of England, and not an official Central Bank like those of the United States."
4 Interfere as little as possible in the drafting of the legislation.
5 Ensure that the gold reserve and deposit for the security of note circulation were left with the chartered banks; that the central bank would take over receiver-general duties and clearing-house duties[78]; that central bank representation was not politically or territorially based; that reserve requirements were lifted; and that the privileges of note issue would be maintained.[79]

The Bank of England's R.N. Kershaw commented that the Canadian banks' strategy would be "unlikely to be received with great favour by the Commission."[80] Yet the CBA strategy acknowledged some political realities, not the least of which was the momentum in Parliament and in the country in the direction of the establishment of a central bank. There was, moreover, a "very strong body of non-partisan opinion" in favour of the idea, which was sufficiently widely held to "command recognition" in Ottawa sooner or later. G.E. Jackson admitted that current situation was not "from all points of view satisfactory."[81] Though conceding that one or two countries with central banks had "recently proven their ability *under present circumstances* [emphasis in original] to stabilize their own domestic price levels within narrow limits," he remarked that "this power has been exercised mainly through the manipulation of the value of the currency concerned on the foreign exchanges, in a time of wild confusion."[82]

There were two major threats to the chartered banks. The first was the loss of gold reserves by compulsion (that is, selling the reserves to a central bank). The chartered bank holdings of gold were in the neighbourhood of $40 million. They feared, rather presciently, that their institutions would be compelled to sell their gold at a non-market rate. Others would later argue that the profit on the gold was "fortuitous and the result of a national and international situation from which the banks have no reason to expect any profit."[83] The second, and even greater, threat, as already explained, was considered to be the loss of the right of bank-note issue. The stakes were high: the banks together were set to lose $1.5 million of annual banking profits.

In the meantime, the banks agreed that it would undesirable to adopt a stance of absolute opposition toward a central bank project. If a central bank was designed "in accordance with the best *British traditions* of banking, and in accordance with the *peculiar needs of Canada*, it might at least be found acceptable to them, even if they were not disposed to greet it with enthusiasm" [emphasis in original].[84] Such a central bank should be free from political control and be privately owned, not a state organ.

Bank of England officials greeted the CBA strategy paper warmly. J.A.C. Osborne, who would later become the deputy governor of the Bank of Canada, remarked to E.R. Peacock in October 1933 that it was very satisfactory to "find how weak the opposition of the Commercial Banks to the establishment of a Central Bank has become, even to the extent of their proposing to set one up themselves ... No doubt windfall profits are those people least enjoy surrendering, but any profit (or loss) on the Commercial Bank gold holdings will doubtless be for account of the State, not for that of the central Bank."[85]

Meantime, Lord Macmillan actively lobbied Liberal opposition leader Mackenzie King on the necessity of a central bank and urged him to go even further and embrace the idea of a central bank that had one shareholder – the government: "You must be bold and go in for a centralizing policy that will sho[re] up the national finances."[86] He admitted, however, that the actions of the banks in the early 1930s in the international market had served to maintain international-exchange stability. This was a vital service to the credit of the Dominion, not least because Canada was a debtor country and exchange fluctuations impaired its credit and "exert[ed] a random and disruptive influence" especially on those institutions needing to make interest payments."[87] The policy of the Canadian banks, "although not primarily directed to that end," had been in effect to accumulate abroad the proceeds of favourable balances of trade (visible and invisible).

The Old Lady's Chess Game

One of the most extraordinary facets of the events leading up to the creation of the Bank of Canada was far-reaching and aggressive involvement of the Bank of England. Lord Macmillan and Sir Charles Addis were not only active lobbyists for the central bank idea; they also kept in close contact with the BOE's senior leaders on strategy and tactics during and after the commission hearings. J.L. Fisher reported on 13 August 1933 that the Canadian bankers on the commission were on the whole "easy to get on with" although some could not see the forest for the trees. Speaking of Beaudry Leman of the Banque

Nationale, Fisher suggested that he is "in favour of a controlling authority but feels that a fully-fledged Central Bank is neither possible nor desirable yet"[88] and that it would be too expensive to run (a cost that would be borne by the bankers).[89] Sir Thomas White was said to live "partly in the time of his office as Minister of Finance" during the war and "sways from one opinion to another." It was said of White: "One doesn't talk to Sir Thomas White, one just listens while he goes on and on in a very courtly way and repeats himself with great skill."[90] J.L. Brownlee, by contrast was a sympathetic character of simple tastes who "will be wholeheartedly in favour of a Central Bank."[91] Brownlee believed, however, that the situation was "more difficult than he had at first envisaged regarding the opposition of the bankers."[92] Whatever happened, Fisher reported that "there will be first-class row over the note issue and gold; the capitalizations and the board are two more difficult points."[93]

The chief commissioner, Lord Macmillan, was reported to favour a mid-step central authority that would eventually turn into a central bank down the road because it was "doubtful that a full Central Bank is politically possible, especially if it is to have a dividend yielding capital. There is a great deal of persuading still to be done."[94] Fisher implored Kershaw of the Bank of England to sail to Canada to persuade the commission on the question of the central bank. There was "quite a lot of support" in the hearings for a central bank, but a "great deal of misconceptions" about its functions."[95]

The Findings of the Royal Commission

The royal commission reported its findings in September 1933. Its first and most urgent recommendation was also the one that caused the most division: by a 3–2 margin, the commissioners called for the "immediate establishment of a central bank in Canada." The two British commissioners, Lord Macmillan and Sir Charles Addis, were strongly in favour, as was J.L. Brownlee. Sir Thomas White and Beaudry Leman were opposed.

The commission registered its "high praise" of the Canadian banking system for its "security, efficiency and convenience."[96] Yet the central bank was the key, central recommendation, not to say a foregone conclusion. The lack of a single banking authority to regulate the volume of credit and currency, for the maintenance of external stability of the currency, and for providing impartial and expert advice pointed to the necessity of a central bank. The commissioners also relied on the three major international monetary conferences held after the Great War that underlined the need for central banks, the most recent being the World Monetary and Economic Conference of 1933.[97] The commission majority argued that a central bank would be a logical outcome for any modern state working in an imperial and international environment. South Africa and Australia had central banks; India and New Zealand were on their way. Canada's Finance Act was insufficient as an instrument to control central banking facilities. So was the CBA's suggestion of an "Administrative Board" to deal with central bank-like matters. A central bank might not be able to fulfill all the expectations harboured in the public mind, but it would offer the present "undeveloped and anomalous system" a more rational and unified control over the credit structure of the country. A central bank would also provide a suitable instrument for the execution of national policy.[98]

The dissenters, Leman and White, objected to the establishment of the bank on the grounds of potential political interference and timing. In addition, White argued that a central bank would hamper, not help, "unfettered Governmental action" at a time when it is required.[99] He further suggested that the Finance Act was a sufficient instrument of financial policy and would not upset the financial machinery of the country. A central bank, in the direst of economic times, would be administered "by a necessarily untried and independent Board of Directors clothed with the power of controlling currency, credit and security issues" when the Dominion government required all the power and resources at its command to handle the economic emergency.[100] White also had little use for the views of international conferences. "History records no more tragic futilities than the deliberations and resolutions of these all too numerous gatherings from the treaty of Versailles to the present day."[101]

The bank proposed by the commission featured a shareholder-controlled corporation managed by a board, a governor, and subordinates. Directors would be chosen from "men of diversified occupations" (not bankers), along with other qualifications. The bank would have the sole right of note issue, issue limited dividends, manage the public debt, handle the buying and selling of gold, and so on.

The Fallout

The BOE's reaction to the report was primarily one of satisfaction over the majority recommendation of a central bank.[102] The dissent of White was described as "poor and anachronistic."[103] The British High Commission in Ottawa reported in November 1933 that the central bank proposal elicited the main interest, but it also cited the non-committal nature of the Toronto Conservative press to the proposal and the more openly negative attitude of Montreal newspapers. In particular, the Bank of Montreal-influenced *Montreal Gazette* and *Financial Post* were "frankly hostile to the institution of a central bank and give vehement expression to the apprehensions of the banking community."[104]

The demand for the Macmillan Commission report in London was strong, with multiple requests from the Canadian High Commission for large numbers of copies.[105] By contrast, the Liberal Party of Canada had committed itself to a central bank, but, even so, the Liberal press could "not be described as enthusiastic over the Royal Commission's Report."[106] Daniel Dafoe of the *Winnipeg Free Press* was supportive, and the farther left and west one went, the more support one found for the idea. Some of the more radical organs in the country suggested that the government should own the bank outright. Yet other sources were "filled with apprehension" that the proposed central bank would become an accessory to the Bank of England and especially its infamous governor, Sir Montagu Norman. Sources such as the *Financial Post* claimed in no uncertain terms that the British connection implied putting Canada under the thrall of Threadneedle Street.[107]

Indeed, one of controversies to emerge at the parliamentary committee hearings on the legislation concerned the selection of an English governor for the Bank of Canada. "Canada's new central bank will not be owned by the Canadian government," the *New York Times* quipped in May 1934, "and its governor apparently will be an Englishman."[108] Bennett objected strenuously to the inference of the Liberals that the new bank would be controlled by the Bank of England. In fact, when he consulted the BOE governor, Sir Montagu Norman, on the matter, the governor had been "fearful of giving any advice, so apprehensive was he that it might be misconstrued as implying interference by the Bank of England."[109] Considering the extent to which the Bank of England was involved in wire-pulling in Canada on the banking question, Norman's comment is breathtaking for its bald-faced effrontery. The Canadian banks also came in for some heavy criticism during the parliamentary committee hearings. One of the main charges was that they had "remained above water" by pushing Canadian industry "into the depths." The allegation was that the banks deflated "rapidly and cruelly," ruining prices and then reaping the reward. The banks, moreover, were said to control the bulk of Canadian industry through interlocking directorates.[110]

The Legislative Phase

On 22 February 1934 the Bennett government introduced legislation to create the Bank of Canada, following in almost every respect the recommendations of Lord Macmillan. The Bennett government had come a long way from its reluctance to propose such a measure, first calling the royal commission and now setting out a concrete plan for a central bank.[111] The Damascene conversion did not escape the notice of the wily Mackenzie King, who was determined that Bennett not get the credit, so to speak, for the creation of the institution.[112] "I am prepared to leave to the Prime Minister himself to make clear his own authorship of the idea. What, however, I do wish to refer to again, and to do so emphatically," King announced in the Commons, "is the failure of the Prime Minister, if he had [it] in his mind from September 1931 up to the time of the World Conference to establish a Central Bank in Canada[,] to impart that view to this House when it discussed the matter."[113]

The Bank of Canada Bill[114] was in some respects a compromise between the ideas of central bank proponents in the Canadian government and the Bank of England, on the one hand, and those of Canadian bankers, on the other. Deputy Minister of Finance W.C. Clark consulted very closely with his counterparts at the Bank of England,[115] which proposed several amendments through the winter of 1934 on wording and on more substantive matters such as power to make advances, competition with the chartered banks, foreign liabilities, Dominion note issues, and securities.[116] R.M. Kershaw, the chief economic adviser to the Bank of England, also exhorted Clark and the Ottawa mandarins to keep their nerve and override the banks' objections if the "Bank of Canada is intended to fulfill important objects set out in Preamble."[117] The Select Standing Committee on Banking and Commerce met throughout the winter and spring of 1934 and heard a wide range of testimony on how to treat the chartered banks, interlocking directories in the banking sector, the policy of the banks during the Depression, and even the banks' relations with the Canadian Pacific Railway.[118]

The bank would have its office in Ottawa, a capitalization of $5 million, be privately owned, and issue shares at a par value of $100 with a cumulative dividend of 6 per cent per annum. It would also have the power to establish branches and agencies throughout the Dominion.[119] The bank would become the exclusive reserve for gold, provide a rediscount function, and give chartered banks access to credit (as in the Finance Act). The chartered banks would be required to maintain deposits with the central bank equal to 5 per cent of the deposit liabilities in Canada.

The bank would have seven directors, to be British subjects and not members of Parliament (federal or provincial). Crucially, Finance Minister Edgar N. Rhodes remarked that the central bank was "not to be regarded as a break with the past ... We are not cutting away from the system which was served us so well. Rather the central bank is to be seen as but another stage in the natural evolution of our banking system."[120]

The Canadian Bankers Association was strategically quiet on many aspects of the bill, with one exception; the transfer of gold to the central bank. The government legislation directed the chartered banks to surrender the gold at a discounted price from the premium. Speaking for the CBA, Canadian Bank of Commerce General Manager S.H. Logan argued that it was "grossly unfair" that everybody would be paid the premium and the banks by contrast would receive only four-sevenths of the market value "because the gold happened to be in coin." Logan suggested that the "common man" would regard this as "unfair and unjust confiscation."[121] The banks, he stated, would be exposed to exchange losses because they would have no means to protect themselves in a situation where the gold had been sold at a deep discount and the premiums on sterling would be as much as 30 per cent.

The leader of the Official Opposition, William Lyon Mackenzie King, strongly advocated the establishment of a central bank for the purpose of credit control and to meet the specific challenges of the Depression.[122] As early as 1932, King and his key advisers – Daniel Dafoe, Vincent Massey, and Ernest Lapointe – had all converged on the idea that a national central bank of discount was required to "get low rate of interest on securities, credit available at low rate of interest on securities, credit available at low rate of interest, like Bank of Eng."[123] A central bank could be found in "practically any country of any financial importance."[124] The Liberal view would change somewhat, but only in the details. Originally, it also included the idea of leaving the issue of bank-note issue alone – there was to be no exclusivity of note issue for the proposed Bank of Canada in the early drafts.[125] As early as 1932, King had called for a commission of inquiry into banking and currency as well as underlining the necessity for a central bank.[126] Liberal MP N.M. Rogers had hoped that King would deal with the subject in the upcoming South Huron by-election.[127] In February 1933, King noted with satisfaction that "the Central Bank idea seemed to furnish the point of convergence of the many views [in caucus regarding currency, credit and banking]."[128]

The Liberal position on the bank was the subject of much internal dissent. An east-west split clearly formed in the Liberal caucus, with western progressives demanding strident action on the subject and easterners much more circumspect about the "socialisation" of banking. The leader of the left wing of the party, Ian Mackenzie, had, in the words of one observer, "embraced all the currency heresies that he has come across as yet and is no doubt prepared to welcome others as they come within his ken."[129] Mackenzie would be the author of a few amendments to the Bank of Canada bill that exhibited, in the words of the *New York Times*, "advanced monetary opinions." On the other side, there were right-wing Liberals who wanted nothing to do with a state-controlled central bank. Prime Minister Bennett took the opportunity of a speech before the Trades and Labour Congress of Canada (a supporter of nationalization) to declare: "When I realize what it could mean to have the Bank of Canada a political organization, I could not and would not do it."[130]

King's private diaries reveal the depth of the dissent in the Liberal caucus. On 1 March 1934 he reported that "member after member spoke in favour of a government-*owned* & controlled bank, a publicly owned bank. Several members notably Charlie Stewart Euler & others said that nothing would stop them advocating both, everyone was falling into their way of speaking." King wrote that "I had to strike out boldly, first on the politics of the thing, the folly of imagining this wd. be the issue in a campaign ... but [instead] forgotten (un fait accompli) save for our amendmts, re control." Government ownership and control would mean the "thin edge of the wedge to govt. *in business*" [emphasis in original].[131] King went on to tell the caucus that he could "not support state ownership of bank, knowing what it would mean in way of pressure by members & provinces on govts., etc." The party had a duty to remember how good the banking system was, and to be wary of the danger of "frightening capital, saving, etc." King reported that he carried most of the caucus with him, although "Euler was nasty in trying to have it appear I had "rid[sic] him out of the party" – because "I said those who favoured State Socialism ought to be with the C.C.F. I said our position was the middle of the road – with no quarter to Tories or State Socialists." King admitted that he disliked "fighting our own men, but the men themselves for the most part seemed to enjoy it & to feel the truth of what I was saying."[132] Three weeks later, King reversed himself on the wisdom of private ownership. The conversion came on the question of the power of the central bank. The idea that a central bank would have exclusive note issue and all the gold reserves and remain under private ownership was unsupportable. "It is one thing to continue privately owned institutions for private purposes[;] another to part with public property to private concerns without a predominating public control."[133]

In the Commons debates over the central bank in mid-1934, the Liberal position became clearer, with motions to nationalize the bank and also to have its three top posts reserved for qualified Canadians. "Is this bank going to be managed for the good of this country or is it going to be dominated by the Bank of England?" MP Maxime Raymond asked.[134] Prime Minister Bennett replied that the Canadian bankers themselves were of the opinion that "none among them was capable of taking control of a central bank."[135] For the Liberals, the issue boiled down to the sovereignty of Parliament, the supremacy of the "Political Power" represented by government versus the "Money Power" represented by the central bank.[136]

Elements of the farmer-labour left gathered around the leader of the CCF, James S. Woodsworth, who denounced the banks and called the debate over the Bank of Canada Bill the "last stand for democracy." The "sovereign state of credit" had been allowed to drift into the hands of a few. Specifically, Herbert Holt of the Royal, Sir Charles Gordon of the Bank of Montreal, and W.A. Black of the Commerce held a total of $9.6 million in bank stock. The Canadian financial oligarchy had to be stripped of the power of "practically determining the buying power of the dollar and of practically determining the price level since both were too important a function in the economy to be entrusted to the hands of private individuals."[137]

The rhetoric of left-wing members grew so heated that the Liberals, swallowing their own reservations, offered the governing Conservatives their aid in moving speedy passage of the legislation, forestalling more publicity on the question of complete government ownership of the bank and the nationalization and socialization of the credit function.[138] The bill passed in the autumn of 1934 with several amendments and came into effect on 1 January 1935. Bennett's New Year's message called the establishment of the Bank of Canada (BOC) the "fulfillment of a pre-confederation dream which will affect profoundly the mechanics of finance."[139] It was a dream for some, a nightmare or unfinished business for others.

The amendments to the legislation included some that softened the blow a little for the chartered banks by gradually reducing their note issue over a decade.[140] Other amendments were more worrisome in the area of lessening reserve quotas (a measure targeted at two or three of the smaller banks).[141] But the final legislation was to the banks' liking in that it configured the new institution as a private corporation with a capitalization of $5 million issued for popular subscription at a yield of 4.5 per cent.[142] The board was to be elected from seven of the shareholders.

The Bank of Canada would take over the entire stock of gold from the chartered banks. Its duties would focus on the regulation of internal credit and foreign exchange and to "mitigate fluctuations in trade employment and prices." The Bank would have sole right of note issue, but only after a transition period of ten years. In the meantime, however, the banks had to start conforming to the new smaller sizes of the currency mandated by the BOC.[143]

In September 1934 Graham F. Towers, the assistant general manager of the Royal Bank of Canada, was named the governor of the Bank of Canada. Towers was a McGill graduate and a Royal Banker from 1920 – his entire career (he was thirty-seven years of age).[144] The appointment of a highly qualified Canadian had gone some way to allay the fears that the "Mother Country Might Rule the Dominion's Finances"[145] – a fear in retrospect that was not without actual foundation. Bank of England official J.A.C. Osborne was appointed deputy governor.

Election of Directors

The directors of the first BOC board were elected in January 1935 from various defined categories – primary industry, commerce, and other occupations.[146] In all, sixty-nine persons had been nominated – among them one woman, the wife of Senator James Murdock.[147] The press noted that the "slate of directors proposed by the Chamber of Commerce carried the day, as every director elected was on the slate." Thomas Bradshaw was named executive director of the Bank.[148]

King called the election of the directors a scandal. The "Canadian Chamber of Commerce, aggregation of big business and finance, with headquarters in Montreal, selected a slate, circulated it throughout the country, conducted an electioneering campaign by letter and in the press. No other candidate had a chance. Every director elected was chosen by a group of financial men in Montreal and is indebted to that group for whatever honour, glory and emoluments go with the office."[149]

The Bank of Canada opened for business on 11 March 1935,[150] with total assets of $225 million in gold and securities and liabilities of the same amount. The discount rate would be around 2.5 per cent. "What more can a central bank do that the banking system itself has not done?" asked a Toronto bond house. "It ventures the opinion that the Bank of Canada will endeavour to reserve within the scope of monetary action certain of the recent developments and provide conditions favourable to the resumption of long and short term borrowing by industry and commerce on the one hand, and the reduction of Government borrowing on the other."[151]

One political move in March 1935 stands out as possibly connected to the central bank question: calls for the formation of a coalition government of Liberals and Conservatives. King learned on 13 March that "the magnates of Montreal" – Beatty of the CPR, Sir Charles Gordon of the Bank of Montreal, Molson, and others – had asked Thomas Ahearn, a Bank of Montreal director, to agree to "something of the kind." The Liberal caucus rejected the idea outright but decided to let the matter die quietly, in spite of the pro-coalition campaign being waged in some quarters of the Montreal press.[152]

The Gold Transfer

The issue of the compelled sale of gold reserves was a touchy one. The Bank of Canada Act required the transfer to the central bank of all the gold coin or bullion owned and held in Canada. Ottawa would profit when the banks would hand over the gold, at the expense of the banks.[153] Finally, in April 1935, the government concluded the transaction, receiving $37.8 million in gold from the chartered banks. The top two banks, the Canadian Bank of Commerce and the Bank of Montreal, each handed over a little over $13 million in gold reserves, representing about 70 per cent of the Canadian total[154] (see figure 12.2).

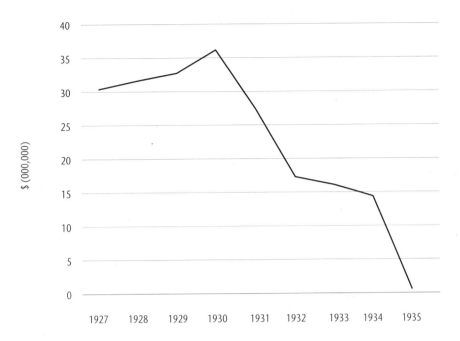

Figure 12.2 | Gold and subsidiary coin, Bank of Montreal, 1927–35

Source: Bank of Montreal Annual Reports, 1927–35.

"Bankers Are Realists"

Sir Charles Gordon, president of the Bank of Montreal, suggested that the effect of the banking legislation on the commercial banks will be to "lessen earning power by the curtailment of the note circulation privileges and by the operation of interest-limitation features." He also observed that any further move to curtail earnings would have a serious impact on the commercial banks. Indeed, some branches were beginning to close partly as result of the current restrictions – three weeks later, the Bank of Montreal branch at Wheatley, Ontario, was closed and the Bank of Canada was specifically cited as a reason. This action, the bank explained, was in accord with the policy being adopted whereby small centres were being turned over to the patronage of one bank. In this case, the Bank of Montreal ceded its accounts in Wheatley to the Royal.[155]

The banks in 1934 and 1935 were suffering, and not only in terms of falling earnings and stubborn expenses. As Gordon noted in his address to the annual meeting in October 1934, the situation in terms of commercial loans was steadily shrinking, and the rate of interest on securities was declining.[156]

The banks were, moreover, not popular with the public, and "perhaps more unpopular today than ever before," as one Bank of England commentator suggested. What was worse, Canadian public opinion was "infected badly" with crackpot US monetary theories that made for a more challenging environment of public opinion.[157]

Gordon reminded his audience that the Canadian banking system had served the country well. Its total assets were almost $3 billion; it had 4.7 million depositors, of whom the Bank of Montreal had over a million; in 1933 alone, $37 million of interest and $12 million in shareholder dividends were paid out.[158] The banks, moreover, had succeeded in placing branches and banking facilities within a reasonable distance of "nearly every point in the West where a farmer brings his grain to a country elevator."[159] W.A. Bog, the joint general manager of the Bank of Montreal, added that the Canadian banks' notes (which were about to be phased out over a decade) were particularly valuable for Canada since they prevented inflation of the currency. That was true since the bank notes were issued "only as business activity requires and when the immediate need is filled and the notes flow back to the banks and are redeemed."[160]

The coming of a central bank was not considered an indictment of the current Canadian banking system. One American expert, Benjamin H. Beckart, writing in the *Annalist*, suggested that "Canadian banking has adjusted itself on the whole admirably to the current requirement of the Dominion," and that there were certain features that could be followed in the United States as well.[161] Jackson Dodds aptly summed up the views of the Canadian chartered banks in September 1934. Of course, the new central bank would mean a sharp break in the evolution of Canadian banking, yet "there need be no fear Canadian bankers would not cooperate with the Bank of Canada." Since the Great War, Dodds argued, central banks had become very fashionable, and Canadians had been led into thinking that a central bank would be a chief factor in bringing a return to desired prosperity. "This advocacy of the central bank idea resulted in the Canadian public forgetting the record of Canadian banks in the past four or five years when they withstood the shock of depression with such firmness, as contrasted with the unprecedented upset in banking service and stability experienced in the United States with its Federal Reserve banking system functioning under central bank principles."[162] Dodds had a point, but the die had been cast. "Bankers are realists," he concluded ruefully. "They are ready to make the best possible use of the material in their hands, and when the central bank is established the bankers of Canada will cooperate with it in the interests of the country at large."[163]

Back in 1933, John P. Day of McGill University had written that "until the bankers are sincerely and whole-heartedly converted, the establishment of a Central Bank in Canada would be disappointment and a danger; any premature attempt would react to postpone the eventual successful accomplishment. Time must be given for the bankers' views to ripen and the natural course of events will push them towards thinking more and more of the banking system as a whole and less exclusively of the strength, progress and prosperity of their own particular bank."[164] Sensibly, Day suggested that "one does not want a committee of academic experts paid by the Government and disregarded by the Banks."[165]

The CBA did mount a public-relations campaign in 1935. Its annual meeting that year was widely covered, as was Jackson Dodds's presidential address. The *Ottawa Journal* reported the first event under the title, "SOUND AS THE ROCK OF GIBRALTAR," and lauded the four-cornerstone policy of Canada's chartered banks – protecting noteholders, safeguarding the deposits of citizens, mobilizing savings for the encouragement of agriculture and industry, and assisting in the development of external trade.[166] Dodds's speech as outgoing president in November 1935 was a comprehensive defence of a system of banking that was at once successful and under attack. He assailed "noxious" credit theories, especially those that led to the nationalization of banking.[167]

The Final Configuration

By 1935, the Liberals had made the nationalization of the Bank of Canada a key election issue. The main charge of the progressive left was that the Bank of Canada as it stood was iniquitous. King himself viewed the existing set-up of the bank as "of a fascist type: it is a private corporation with the volume of the country's credit."[168] "Until control of the issue of currency and credit is restored to the Government and recognized as its most conspicuous and sacred responsibility, all talk of the sovereignty of Parliament is futile. To regain for the nation what has thus been lost will continue to be the first objective of Liberal effort."[169] The Liberals did not make clear, however, how government control of currency and credit would be reasserted.[170] Instead, they just kept on the attack, arguing that the Bennett government had handed over gold reserves, securities, and property of the state to a private corporation – the Bank of Canada.[171] "The control of credit and currency is a public matter," King declared, "not of interest to bankers only, but of direct concern to every citizen."[172] "Do you realize," Mackenzie King told a rally in October 1935, "that the only party which voted against a privately owned bank and which sponsored a publicly owned bank was the Liberal party? The legislation setting up the private bank was introduced by the Conservatives, and Mr. Woodsworth, with the majority of his followers, supported it."[173]

King's other major concern was to ensure that the "Central Bank of Canada will in no way be in danger of becoming subordinated in the discharge of any of its functions to the banking institutions either of Great Britain or the United States or any other country."[174] The senior leadership and directors all ought to be British subjects as well as resident in Canada.

Once the Liberals won the October 1935 election, the new prime minister's exact intentions regarding the Bank of Canada were not known for some time. Speculation filled the gap. There was clearly a bias in favour of public ownership. The alternatives ranged from government control to continuing the present arrangement. The greatest fear was that the bank would slip under political control. The Bank of England's position was that the government should be made the sole owner of the shares, and the governor's autonomy, as well as the safeguards against possible control by large financial interests, should be left intact. In its view, the current personalities in place – Mackenzie King, Clark, Towers – provided a reassurance that reasonable solutions would be sought out and implemented. The issue certainly elicited much discussion and correspondence between the Bank of Canada officials and the Bank of England in 1935 as to what King would do and when he would do it.

Ultimately, in 1936, the King government introduced another Bank of Canada Act. The new act strengthened the position of the governor and augmented the powers of the Bank of Canada as the central bank of the country.[175] The Bank of Canada's shares were doubled to give the government a majority on the board of directors. In 1938 the bank was fully nationalized, with the government as the sole owner. The direct appointment of directors offered King an opportunity to connect further with regions of the country as interest groups made representations as to who should be on the board.[176]

A Complicated Battlefield

The struggle over the creation of the Bank of Canada sheds light on a period of transformational change in the Canadian banking system. As noted at the beginning of this chapter, the establishment of the Bank of Canada involved two distinct contests: a contest of politics, which determined the parameters of the debate and the possible outcomes; and a contest of elites.

The Contest of Politics

The conventional interpretation of the establishment of the Bank of Canada sees it as a political outcome as opposed to a financial necessity. The evidence presented here underscores the same conclusion. But that conclusion is obvious, given the urgency of the Depression and the search for financial instruments to respond to the crisis of credit, price instability, and unemployment.

The battle eventually became was not so much whether there was to be a central bank, but whether that bank was to be a private or public institution.

Between 1932 and 1934, this contest was played out in several arenas: within Parliament; within the Liberal Party caucus in particular, which struggled to develop a position that could accommodate both progressive members from western Canada and eastern MPs who were more comfortable with the current banking system; and within the Royal Commission on Banking and Currency, where a flood of economic actors both (mainly) for and (surprisingly often) against the idea of a central bank made their case – from investment dealers to farmers to chambers of commerce to retail associations.

The outcome of the battle was not inevitable, and the Canadian banks did not go without a fight. They offered strong arguments against the move to a central bank. The best argument in favour of the Canadian banks was their superior record of management when compared with American or European banks. The Canadian bankers fought hard to forestall the move to a centralized institution. When a central bank was seen to be an inevitability, the strategy of the banks switched to shaping the best possible outcome in the circumstances. That outcome, initially, was a privately run organization with a long sunset clause for the retiring of bank-note issues; this was first version of the Bank of Canada. The victory of the Mackenzie King Liberals in the October 1935 elections, however, ensured that the political wheel of fortune would make its final turn and produce a publicly owned central bank.

Given the context, forces, and circumstances facing them, the Canadian banks waged an uphill battle. The traditional reliance on elite accommodation to settle institutional arrangements could no longer apply. What is more, the traditional players – bank presidents, managers, ministers, and deputies – were joined by new players with very different conceptions of how a banking system should be run. The banks, therefore, were compelled to beat a strategic retreat from their preferred position of using the current system to maximum advantage; instead, once the die was cast, they tried to shape the central bank in such a way that their concerns would be addressed and their interests protected. The banks were remarkably successful at this, at least for a time.

The unprecedented airing of viewpoints and perspectives in the arena of the royal commission gave various groups the chance they needed to articulate what they saw as the place of banks in the Canadian economic, social, and political landscape. The reputation of financial institutions in Depression-era Canada, especially the west, could not be said to be high. Many complained about the frustrations of obtaining credit, branch closures, and other aspects of bank policy in the context of a brutal economic contraction. Others lamented the overreaching influence of the "Money Power" through interlocking directorates. The banks undoubtedly paid a reputational price. That is not surprising.

What is surprising, though, is the fact that by and large the Canadian banking system survived this period with its reputation for stability, probity, and managerial competence largely intact. Bankers knew that they would never be loved, but at least they would be respected, grudgingly or otherwise.

The eventual transformation of the Bank of Canada into a publicly owned institution revealed the limits of bankers' influence over broad policy decisions in the sector. The consensus in Canada around existing institutional arrangements in finance had been endorsed by the Finance Acts of 1914 and 1923. By the mid-1920s, however, that consensus had shown signs of weakening. International trends favoured greater central control; so did a growing chorus of academic economists – many of whom were at Queen's University in Kingston. In the 1930s, there would be no turning back to the old models or nostrums.

The Contest of Elites: Conspiracy and Choice

The establishment of the Bank of Canada was also, prominently, a contest of elites. Those elites were, on the one hand, the traditional "Money Power" in the colloquial parlance of the day – the Montreal and Toronto bankers of the most prominent banks: the Bank of Montreal, the Canadian Bank of Commerce, the Royal Bank of Canada, and the Bank of Nova Scotia. To varying degrees and in different ways, these bankers had long dominated the running of the Canadian financial system by virtue of their large and influential institutions. The Bank of Montreal was chief among them by virtue of its position as government banker and the depth of its capacities in London and New York. Sir Thomas White, a member of the Royal Commission on Banking and Currency, Sir Charles Gordon, president of the Bank of Montreal, Jackson Dodds, general manager of the Bank of Montreal, and J.M. McLeod of the Bank of Nova Scotia all exemplified this group, defending the status quo and the record of the Canadian banking system from an unmatched depth of experience.

A competing and formidable elite lined up to oppose these Canadian bankers over the central bank issue: a technocratic elite convinced of the inevitability and necessity of central coordination of currency and banking. This elite was most conspicuously represented by Bank of England bankers. The front men for this group were, naturally, Lord Macmillan and Sir Charles Addis, the two British members of the royal commission. Behind the scenes were the governor of the Bank of England, Sir Montagu Norman, and his coterie of banking experts – J.A.C. Osborne, J.L. Fisher, R.N. Kershaw, and others. The latter group kept in close touch with their Canadian fellow travellers – the most prominent of whom were W.C. Clark, the deputy minister of finance, and Graham Towers, the first governor of the Bank of Canada. The

BOE and its allies tirelessly advocated a central bank for Canada. As Peter Cain incisively points out, this "gentlemanly imperialism" had a consciously articulated objective: to pull Canada into the sterling area and to exploit New York's temporary financial relapse to steal back imperial supremacy.[177] The ties that bound were not only imperial but anti-American.[178] Imperial ties were further cemented by social affinities among this group. The powerful behind-the-scenes expertise of the Bank of England, the influence of like-minded Canadian technocrats, and the outstanding reputation of the British members of the royal commission made the success of the campaign to establish a central bank something that was not left to fortune, but was instead shaped forcefully by those convinced of their mission. Bank of England officials had ulterior motives that gave them additional incentives to press the case home: young central banks were "expected to behave very much like their parent who would supply them with advice and personnel."[179] Cain notes that the British contingent in Canada became "frankly conspiratorial" in their push for the proper outcome.[180] Once the Bank of Canada was established and running, however, the hopes for reorienting Canada to London were disappointed. Cain's conclusion on the matter is apt: "The Bank of England tried to use Canada's difficulties to promote its own agenda, but, in the event, it was Canadian politicians who succeeded in using the Bank's prestige and influence to serve their own domestic ends."[181] The fatal error of Macmillan, Norman, Addis, and others was to treat Canada with enormous condescension – an attitude that came naturally to the Bank of England's leadership.

Winners and Losers

The road to the Bank of Canada produced some clear winners and losers. Of course, any large policy transformation cannot be merely reduced to a win-loss column. Players can win a game and lose a season. Losses can be narrow or catastrophic.

In this case, the political winners were many. In the first instance, the Bennett Conservatives won applause for introducing the Bank of Canada, though in the longer term they were destined to lose power. The Mackenzie King Liberals were also winners, since their view of the Bank of Canada's constitution – the public nature of its ownership and mandate – prevailed. The greatest winners, though, were the technocratic financial elite. In the short term, this included the Bank of England's mandarins and especially the experts in the Canadian Department of Finance and the new BOC. In the long term, the Bank of England clearly lost in its bid to create a sterling area or reorient the Canadian lines of trade and finance to London from New York by any means necessary.

The defeated were, of course, the bankers, but not all the bankers equally. The greater the prominence, the greater the gold-reserve holdings, and the greater the note circulation, the greater the potential impact. If a bank was prominent in all those categories and also the official banker to the government of Canada, then the loss would be correspondingly greater. In this context, the Bank of Montreal had the most to lose. But, in fact, the creation of a central bank weakened the power not only of the Bank of Montreal but of Montreal capitalists generally. Montreal had shared increasing power and prestige with Toronto as the Toronto banks flourished. Now, Ottawa became an additional centre of power to be reckoned with.

There were other losers. The Canadian Bankers Association lost its coordinating role for credit expansion and contraction; henceforth, the institutions of central finance were the proper place for these public-policy decisions to be taken. Then there were the advocates of socialized banking. But to be fair, they never had a chance. By and large, this was a battle that was decided between elites, with a chorus of minor players exerting some sway but not determining the fundamental direction of policy.

In the long term, the surrender of reserves, note issue, and the status of official government banker went smoothly and the Canadian banking system profited from the establishment of a central reserve, however small or non-existent the money market in Canada was. The fundamental contours of the Canadian banking system did not change. There were gains and losses, but it was all in the family. As J.A.C. Osborne recalled in 1939, "it would have been only human, however, if the commercial banks did not exactly welcome the advent of the Bank of Canada: but they soon realised the essential difference between a central bank and a commercial bank. It meant coordination, not competition. Also perhaps some protection from the Government: if needed and justified."[182] The new central bank undertook the issue of all domestic loans for the Dominion government, with power to do so for provincial governments as well. The "easy money" policy of the BOC facilitated the refunding to a large amount of government debt at lower rates, and also the issue of fresh loans.[183]

At least in terms of profits, the Bank of Montreal had a bad year in 1934 but recovered; the Royal did poorly in 1935 (see figure 12.3). In terms of assets, here again the largest banks suffered the most to 1935, but by 1939 they were once again on solid footing (see figure 12.4)

One parting story. In September 1937 Prime Minister William Lyon Mackenzie King helped to lay the cornerstone on Wellington Street, Ottawa, of what was to become the new headquarters of the Bank of Canada. E.Y. Jackson wrote of the event to Bank of England Governor Sir Montagu Norman, describing it thus: "One of the great triumphs of the Bank of Canada,

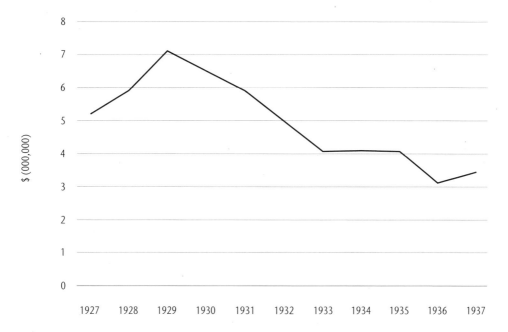

Figure 12.3 | Profits, Bank of Montreal, 1927–37
Source: Bank of Montreal Annual Reports, 1927–37.

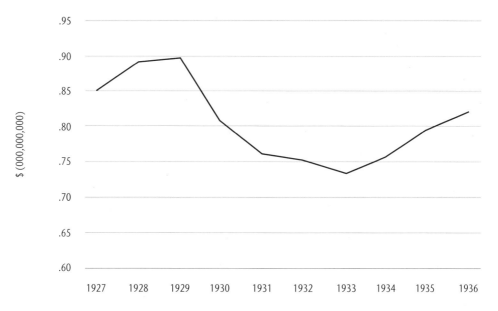

Figure 12.4 | Assets, Bank of Montreal, 1927–36
Source: Bank of Montreal Annual Reports, 1927–36.

to date, occurred when it successfully persuaded Mackenzie King to make a ten minute speech only, at the close of which he declared the corner stone well and truly laid; but I am privately informed that after the tumult and the shouting had died and all had gone, the workmen picked it up and laid it properly."[184] In a more than metaphorical sense, Mackenzie King had indeed laid the cornerstone for the Bank of Canada in the political and economic tumult of the 1930s. After the speeches were done, the more prosaic task of laying the proper foundations of the Canadian banking system would become the responsibility of Canada's chartered bankers, its new central bankers, and a new regulatory regime. When the Bank of Montreal handed over the reins of government banker to the newly established Bank of Canada, it could do so in the knowledge that the central bank would be responsible for the supervision and coordination of a solid, stable, and successful banking system.

CHAPTER THIRTEEN

Building Canada's Financial Arsenal

Canada declared war on Germany on 10 September 1939, following on Britain's declaration a week before. The outbreak of a second global conflict in the span of a quarter-century once again mobilized both Canadian state and enterprise to the coming war effort. The Bank of Montreal's role in this conflict would be somewhat different than in the previous one. Canada's new central bank would now coordinate the massive capital requirements for the Canadian government. Nonetheless, the Montreal Bank would prove to be a vital part of Canada's financial war effort through its financial network in the North Atlantic world. The relationships it offered and the expertise on which the Bank could draw were deep and extensive. The Bank of Montreal's leadership capacities as well its organizational capabilities would again be of great service to the state.

The Bank would face the Second World War without its long-time president, Sir Charles Blair Gordon, who died, suddenly, in July 1939. Gordon's Bank of Montreal had fought hard to maintain its balance-sheet health in the face of exceptionally difficult circumstances. Not only was Gordon compelled to navigate the institution through the turbulent waters of an unprecedented economic depression; he also had to begin to reorient the Bank as it transitioned away from its responsibilities as government banker, with the associated loss of status. The Bank's performance by the end of 1939 was in some measure an indication of how well Gordon's bank had performed: the Bank's assets then broke the $1-billion mark, the highest in its history.[1] The after-tax haul of the Bank in 1939 amounted to $3.462 million, a slight increase over the previous year.[2]

Gordon was succeeded by "quiet and kindly"[3] Huntly Redpath Drummond. Drummond's pedigree with the Bank extended to his grandfather (a former vice-president) and father (president). He was Gordon's vice-president during the latter's entire presidency. Drummond suffered from failing health and would serve only until 1942 (though he would live until age ninety-three in 1958). He was followed by G.W. Spinney, who would oversee the Bank's transition into the post-war world before his untimely death in 1948.

The Bank's wartime experience can be characterized by two overarching themes: mobilization for the war effort, and transformation into a new type of banking institution. This chapter outlines how the Bank of Montreal managed both tasks.

Canada's contribution to the war, as Bank of Montreal President Drummond remarked in 1939, was "to be largely as a source of supply to Great Britain." He proclaimed that the Bank's principal aim was to "assist to the limit of our abilities in the winning of the war."[4] Drummond knew that "in supplies of wheat, minerals and manufactured goods [Canada's] contribution toward the combined effort on the side of right in this war [would] far exceed what she was able to offer in the last; and there [was] abundant evidence in every province of the Dominion that Canada's contribution in men [would] be ample and of the type that in the last war brought ever-lasting glory to this country."[5]

At the same time, the Bank's leadership was concerned with avoiding some of the more dangerous consequences of an unbalanced or overheated post-war economy. "It remains for us to bring the full strength of a united Canada to the work of prosecuting the war to a successful conclusion," Drummond stated in 1939, but the Bank should also "[keep] our affairs so in hand that we may enter the readjustments of postwar conditions as free of inflation as possible, with debts at the minimum possible and with morale unimpaired. I am confident that just as we have entered as a unified Canada into the fiery ordeal of war, so we shall emerge, a nation one at heart but more mature in thought and aspiration, ready to go forward as a member of the British Commonwealth of Nations to the great destiny which undoubtedly awaits this country."[6]

Contributions to the national war effort went far beyond assisting the Dominion government. The Bank's 1939 annual report noted that "the outbreak of war caused the Bank to decide to suspend building operations, make proper provision for the protection of work already done, and postpone resumption of construction until conditions return to normal. This was considered a patriotic as well as a prudent course to take in the light of the responsibility resting on the Bank to hold itself in readiness to meet the additional needs of its customers in war time."[7] Furthermore, the Bank was restructured to better meet the needs of the country and the wartime economy. In 1942, in accordance with the policies of the Wartime Prices and Trade Board, the Bank curtailed all non-essential bank activities. The 1942 fiscal year saw the closure of twenty-five branches, sixteen of which were located in large cities with other branches nearby. The Bank also reduced three branches to sub-agency status.[8] The following year, a further fourteen branches were closed. To underscore its commitment to the war effort and the Canadian armed forces, however, the Bank of Montreal opened a new branch at Cornwallis, Nova Scotia, for the convenience of the officers and men of the Royal Canadian Navy.[9]

At the 124th annual shareholder's meeting in 1941, Drummond declared:

> Today, faced with the facts of total war, coupled with modern invention ... we have to discard old ideas. Airplanes, ships, submarines, radio and propaganda have abolished old limits. In such a war as this there are no longer fixed geographical frontiers to any country. As a Prime Minister of England has said, the frontier of England is on the Rhine, and today our frontier is in Europe. We are fighting an enemy whose whole energy has been devoted through years on end to world domination, and we have to meet that challenge. Democracy gives us great privileges but not for nothing; every privilege has its corresponding duty; to keep the privileges we must be prepared to sacrifice everything except ultimate freedom itself. Freedom is worth sacrificing everything else for.[10]

The intense convictions expressed by Drummond were almost certainly shared wholeheartedly by the management and directors of the Bank gathered in Montreal. This was an outlook strongly supportive of Canada's role in the defence of the realm. The ties that bound the Montreal Bank to London and the institutions of Empire were deeply wound around the Bank's history, experience, and legacy. Indeed, Bank of Montreal bankers were likely the most British of the Canadian bankers. Their connections to London and the Bank's intimate role as a Canadian point of reference in that city, not to mention ties of friendship, business, and affinity, all added up to a close identification with the trials of the mother country.

Patriotic fervour on the part of the Bank's most senior leadership extended to the support of conscription – the mandatory call-up of able-bodied males of military age. The issue had been deeply divisive in the First World War, tearing the Liberal Party of Sir Wilfrid Laurier in two and, more to the point, causing unprecedented political tension between an anti-conscription-minded French Canada and a pro-conscription English Canada.

In January 1942 the retired London branch manager, Dudley Oliver, wrote to Senator Arthur Meighen in support of conscription, which in itself may not have been a particular surprise. Oliver, however, enclosed a potentially explosive letter from General A.W. Currie dated long before, on 30 November 1917, in the midst of the Great War. In that letter, the commander of the Canadian Corps expressed some very definite views on the Military Service Act which would introduce conscription in Canada. "I believe that if its operation is interfered with, or even delayed, such a thing would be a catastrophe."[11] Currie continued, predicting that, without conscription, the "Canadian Corps as a fighting unit will practically disappear" and Canada will "not only have deserted the men here but will practically have deserted the Empire as well. The death struggle is fast approaching; the Empire must see it through; and if we do not play our part to the end it will mean almost that we do not care to remain a part of that Empire."[12] Currie told Oliver that he was considering sending such a message to Canada, even though he knew "it would mean that I would practically have to submit my resignation at the same time." He sought Oliver's advice about what the situation in Canada really was in November 1917, and what he should do about it.

Fast-forwarding to a quarter-century later, Oliver reasoned that if this confidential letter were made public, the reputation of Currie and the forcefulness of his views on conscription would sway the politicians in Ottawa engaged in the debate. Sending it to an old friend of the Bank, Sir Arthur Meighen (then a senator), might do the trick. In turn, Meighen consulted with Jackson Dodds, the general manager of the Bank, on the advisability of making the letter public. Calling the letter "the best I have ever seen" on the subject of conscription, Meighen suggested that it would be impossible to "justify withholding such a definite, direct and forceful presentation of the need for conscription in the last war as that made by Sir Arthur Currie in this letter." Meighen asked Dodds to "relieve Mr. Oliver of any restraint in allowing the use of the letter."[13]

Dodds's response is telling. The day after receiving Meighen's entreaty, Dodds replied that "I wonder if it's worthwhile introducing what a dead man said under conditions which do not parallel those of today." He suggested that, while Oliver was free to do what he wanted and Meighen could use the letter, he hoped that Meighen "would not bring the Bank's name into the matter because you will realize that there will immediately be a cry: 'St. James Street is behind this.'"[14] Dodds hastened to add that "all my friends on St. James Street are behind you in your endeavor to get conscription. I wish you had heard the speech of Mr. Crawford Crier, Headmaster of Bishop's College School, on the subject at the Canadian Club yesterday. I was present and applauded his all-out demands. I am 100% for what you want to do and it is not only as a General Manager of the Bank but as a friend and an admirer that I have written as I have."[15] Meighen acquiesced in Dodds's polite request, but not without lamenting the fact that General Currie's letter would have made a "tremendous impression on the people of Canada." He concluded by expressing his sincere "regret at not being able to use the letter."[16]

The Oliver-Currie affair offers a few insights into the Bank of Montreal experience in wartime. First, the Bank was anything but neutral in its views on how and to what extent Canada should pursue the war effort. Its leadership was not only supportive but, in the phrase of de Chateaubriand, "plus royaliste que le roi." Second, the war did not suspend the regular operations of politics and political relationships. The reference to St James Street and the apprehension felt by Jackson Dodds about having Montreal finance dragged into a political fight exposed the limits of Canadian political discourse. Finally, the affair made it clear that the Bank would channel its energies into building the financial arsenal of the Canadian war effort, where its efforts would truly pay off.

Bank of Montreal's Contribution

Between 1939 and 1945, the Bank's central concern was ensuring that the full financial and economic capacity of the institution and of its 6,347 employees[17] was put to maximum deployment for the war effort.[18] Its leadership also supported and indeed advocated for the imposition of significantly higher corporate and income taxes to pay for the war. There was no mistaking the drive and determination to mobilize the Bank of Montreal to the Allied cause. From late 1939, the Bank's leaders began to retool the organization into an institution aligned to meet the organizational, bureaucratic, and financial demands of wartime.

The Bank underwent a thorough bureaucratic retrofitting. "War measures" were implemented to reduce the volume of routine in the preparation of accounts. Additionally, scores of circulars were sent out across the country dealing with war orders, financing and lines of credit, and the legalities associated with the proper handling of these activities.[19] The circulars were the product of an extensive information network, with its central processing unit at the Montreal head office and thousands of nodes spread geographically and functionally across the organization from coast to coast. The head office issued thousands of orders, maintained rules and regulations, set out the rules of engagement on a wide range of activities, and offered advice on banking and a host of other matters – payments, loans, assessments, taxes, bonds, stocks, overseas remittances, discounts, overdrafts, credit reports, retention policies, business development, and much more. On 27 November

1941, for example, the Bank ordered managers and staff to cease reporting on loans if the outstanding balance was $100 or less or adequately secured by "first class bonds, high grade listed stocks or the cash surrender value of assigned life insurance in good order."[20] Circulars went out regarding the regular business of the bank through loans, fire insurance, and even loans for tires. Civil defence was also an important topic, including air-raid precautions for Montreal-area branches.[21] At war's end, the practical challenges of reintegrating veterans – re-establishing their credit and finding employment positions for them – were front and centre.

By 1943, the administrative burden had significantly expanded. "Transactions in cheques and deposits, Victory Bonds and relative coupons, pouring through our hands, have been immeasurably heavier than before the war," President Spinney reported that year. "We have already opened thousands of ration coupon accounts and handled coupons running literally into hundreds of millions."[22] In a sense, the expansion of banking facilities to a much broader public – beyond wealthy individuals and businesses – began just in this way.

Some of the major functions of the Bank in the First World War were assumed by the Bank of Canada in the Second. The raising of loans, the purchase of government debt, and the control of credit, prices, and wages were now the responsibility of the central bank. Alongside other chartered banks, the Bank of Montreal focused on providing credit to keep the machinery of war production going and on raising the massive capital required for the war effort through Victory Loan Bonds. These bonds were debt securities issued by the Dominion government to help finance the war effort. In all, nine Victory Bonds were floated during the war, raising $12 billion.[23] "The role of our managers," one Bank of Montreal circular suggested later in the war, "includes the attracting of new business and deposits and at the same time influencing their clients to invest a substantial portion of their surplus funds in new Victory Loans."[24]

The Victory Bonds were successful partly because of their effectiveness in reaching many small Canadian investors. By contrast, the first UK war loan did not aim at so widespread a response from the small investor, as Montagu Norman of the Bank of England confided to Bank of Canada Governor Graham Towers in March 1940.[25] "We feel that it is prudent, and will be advantageous, to till that field by our present methods for some time longer, – or at least until we want a much bigger harvest than our present circumstances demand."

Finance was not the only specialism the Bank offered the war effort. Leadership was also a prime export. Senior Bank of Montreal officers also assumed administrative and advisory roles in the government between 1939 and 1945, much as they had in the Great War. The most prominent example was Bank of Montreal General Manager (and later President) George Spinney, who played a key role in the success of the Victory Bonds in his capacity as head of the National War Finance Committee, the body in charge of the bonds' sale.[26] Spinney's value to the Dominion government is hard to underestimate. Prime Minister King strongly lobbied for Spinney to become Canadian finance minister in 1940 – a role that Spinney declined because of his obligations to the Bank and because the presidency of the Bank of Montreal, to which he was first in line after Huntly Drummond, would have been the culmination of a lifelong dream. The Second Victory Bond program, and the first under Spinney's chairmanship, was a notable success. The Bank's *Staff Magazine* wrote in 1942 that "preliminary returns at the time of writing indicate total subscriptions of over $979,000,000 but when all figures have been assembled and tabulated the figure may be in the vicinity of $1,000,000,000. This exceeds any of the Victory Loans of the last war and is the largest loan ever floated in Canada."[27] The huge success of the bond drive prompted a delighted Mackenzie King to remark that "in planning and in execution, the campaign has been a triumph of efficiency."[28] The following year, Mackenzie King wrote Spinney a letter expressing his "appreciation" for the "magnificent achievement represented by the Fourth Victory Loan."[29]

In a recognition of its international network and influence, the Bank of Montreal was also appointed as the authorized agent of the Foreign Exchange Control Board (FECB).[30] This board, created in September 1939 under the War Measures Act, was tasked with controlling foreign exchange to preserve the value of the Canadian dollar.[31] Here, too, the historical distance from these events dulls the perception of just how important the FECB was to the financial war effort. The foreign-exchange control policy would have not stood a chance, the *Globe* remarked in December 1943, "if it had not been that every bank had men who were trained experts in facilitating the complex operations of international trade."[32] The banks had saved Canadian taxpayers "very large amounts by taking on coupon banking in connection with the widespread rationing measure of the Wartime Prices and Trade Board and by helping finance millions of subscriptions to huge wartime borrowing campaigns of the Government."[33]

The war effort on the finance side was a complex one to wage. It involved questions of currency and foreign exchange, the relative value of the currency between the Canadian and US dollars and the UK sterling, and a myriad other issues. The balance of payments between allies in the North Atlantic world was also a significant challenge, as was the question of pegging values of the Canadian dollar to the sterling.[34] Canadian war finance also had to confront the massive need for US dollars. Canada's war production depended on an "enormous rise in her imports from the United States," one Bank of England memorandum explained. "These had to be paid for in American cash and there was no immediate prospect of a comparable increase in Canadian exports to the United States."[35] The Dominion government's imposition of extraordinary measures to ration supply and to impose massive defence taxes on income managed to stabilize the situation, though it did result in acute scarcity of commodities.[36] In the early part of the war, these policies "carried the main load of clearing the way, rather keeping the way open, for war production" by holding down civilian spending and imposing controls and very high taxation.

The Bank's wartime service had a deeply held patriotic purpose, to be sure. But that service served other purposes as well. The key role the banks played in the war effort served to blunt the argument that they ought to be nationalized and run by the state – an idea whose currency, if you will, was gaining some circulation among labour and progressive circles. The CCF had long held to the conviction that the banks ought to be nationalized in one form or another. Public ownership of the central bank was not enough. The CCF believed that "our financial institutions (banks, trust and loan companies, insurance companies) must be socialized and made an integral part of our democratic socialist planning. It is absolutely essential to recognize that in CCF policy socialization of finance and socialization of industry go together. You cannot have one without the other."[37] It was an article of faith for the CCF that "to secure a just and stable society we must also control the kind of investment into which the available funds go, and the spending of these funds. For these ends, nothing less than socialization of all the financial machinery, and of the main industries as well, will suffice. Socialization of finance is not a cure-all; but it is a necessary part of the prescription."[38] The chartered banks under a CCF government would become, in the words of the party's leader in Saskatchewan, T.C. Douglas, "branches of a government-owned and controlled Central Bank."[39] The CCF's position on banks and banking would continue to be a staple of its finance policy.[40] The position had been on the books since the mid-1930s, and few bankers paid serious attention. By 1943, however, a spectacular by-election victory in York South by J.W. Noseworthy of the CCF over Conservative leader and warhorse Arthur Meighen gave early signs of a possible political earthquake. The CCF's appeal to working-class voters in that contest was based on a commitment not only to "a full war effort" but to "social justice after the war."[41] On 4 August 1943, moreover, the CCF came in second in the Ontario provincial election, with 31.6 per cent of the popular vote and thirty-four seats in the ninety-seat legislature. Then, on 15 June 1944, Douglas led the CCF to a landslide victory in Saskatchewan, becoming the leader of the first socialist government in North America. By the end of 1944, the CCF formed government in one province and constituted the official opposition in four others west of the Ottawa River.[42] There was no mistaking the strong momentum for the CCF in 1943 and 1944 – a fact that was not lost governments and bankers alike.

In both 1943 and 1944, President Spinney was concerned enough to address the issue at two annual meetings. "If a Government monopoly were set up in Canada, the socialization of the rest of the economy would be scarcely more than a 'mopping-up operation.'"[43] Spinney suggested that this collectivist dystopia would end up putting all productive sectors of the Canadian economy under government control. In 1944 he redoubled his call to resist the temptation to "let government do everything," despite the great magnitude of post-war conversion problems, "unless we are content to go along the road Germany followed to Totalitarianism."[44]

Rallying to the Colours

Bank of Montreal employees across Canada contributed to the war effort in various and creative ways. In 1939 "some of the girls wished to knit for the Navy and wondered if some kind of club could be formed," the Bank of Montreal *Staff Magazine* noted in 1940. In early 1940, accordingly, the Bank of Montreal Toronto Staff War Service Committee was created with the intent of knitting for the benefit of the Canadian men in arms and to assist those suffering in Europe.[45] These efforts were not without results. On 27 June 1941 the committee shipped "direct to Lady Edith Curtis of Dorridge, near Birmingham, Eng., two hundred infant's wear articles for distribution to the 'bombed out' children in the Birmingham area."[46]

A similar initiative was started across the country in Vancouver, where employees organized the Bank of Montreal Service Club for the purpose of aiding the war effort. This group, too, was "busily engaged in sewing for refugees and knitting for the Air Force."[47] Likewise, at head office, staff formed the "War Service Unit," which after only three months had already knitted "41 scarves, 75 pairs of socks, 25 pairs of sea stockings, and 6 helmets. In addition to this, they [had] purchased four dozen turtle-neck sweaters for seamen." The *Staff Magazine* added that "the women in the Foreign Department who own their own knitting machine, have completed 35 pairs of socks for the Navy League, and a further group under Miss D. Johnston, since the beginning of the war, has knitted 75 pairs of socks and 15 sweaters for the Air Force."[48]

In 1941 the Bank of Montreal's British Columbia Service Club prepared Christmas parcels for those serving overseas. They also raised money for War Savings Bonds by selling raffle tickets and by sponsoring the production of a play, "Bunty Pulls the Strings," where at intermission they sold home-made candy. Their efforts "netted a nice sum."[49] In Winnipeg, meanwhile, the "Ladies Knitting Club" of the Bank of Montreal collected worn and discarded clothing to repair and to send to men in the Merchant Marine.[50]

Officers at Bank of Montreal branches in the United States likewise contributed. The Bank of Montreal's San Francisco office became the "depository for all activities" of the British War Relief Association of Central and Northern California.[51] Staff at that Bank of Montreal branch collected funds for the relief association by "supporting drives for funds through various mediums, selling buttons, etc."[52] Meanwhile, staff at the New York agency contributed by working as stenographers and accountants for the relief association after hours.[53] These instances are but a few of the many examples of how the people of the Bank of Montreal responded to Canada's wartime emergency far from the fighting.

Contributions in Europe: Waterloo Place

Many Bank of Montreal employees served on the front lines: eighty-four were killed. As Bank President B.C. Gardner (1948–52) noted in *Field of Honour*, a post-war Bank of Montreal publication created to commemorate those who had served during the Second World War: "In the years of conflict our men served the Canadian, British, and Allied forces on most of the world battle-fronts – on land, on sea and in the air. Our women too did their part in the auxiliary services[,] performing duties many of which were considered in the past the work of men. All acquitted themselves with distinction and left behind a proud record of service that will ever be gratefully remembered."[54] In total, nearly 1,500 Bank of Montreal employees served in the armed forces during the Second World War.[55] To put this number into perspective, that number amounted to almost a quarter of all Bank of Montreal employees. In 1940 the Bank's staff comprised 3,302 officers, 2,003 women employees, and 1,042 messengers and full- and part-time service employees, or a total of 6,347 persons.[56]

As it had in the Great War, the Bank of Montreal offices in London functioned as a hub for Canadians. A key difference from the 1914–18 period, however, was that the offices were now directly in the line of fire, under the relentless and intensive bombardment of German air power. All during the London Blitz, the Bank's offices carried on "accustomed banking facilities under actual bombardment." "In a very real sense," it was reported, "civilians in Great Britain have been fighting the enemy, not alone in refusing to abandon essential services, but in succoring the wounded, extinguishing fires and in performing the multifarious duties that fall to the Home Guard."[57]

The Bank was prepared for any eventuality. In 1939 it took the necessary preparations in the event of German bombardment or invasion. The detailed planning shed light on the powerful strengths of superior organization, as one remarkable testimony from the era notes:

Prior to the outbreak of war, measures were taken to provide Air Raid Shelters for the staffs and others who might be in the offices of our London and Waterloo Place branches ... Office rooms in the basement were strengthened with steel scaffolding and made gas proof. An emergency exit was provided in each case as well as medical supplies and other essential equipment. The staffs were drilled in the procedure to follow in the event of air raids, such as a fire, picketing, first aid, removal of books, cash and securities to vaults, etc. ...

Duplication of all essential records was completed and a method adopted to keep duplicates up-to-date so that in the event of loss of original records by enemy action duplicates would be available without delay. Duplicate records are stored in the basement at Farnborough, Kent and additional recorded films of security registers and ledgers were sent to Head Office. As a precaution, London rented three houses in Wimbledon, at 10 Grosvernor Hill, where the transfer department was moved, at 4 Lingfield Road, where sections of several other departments were moved and at 25 Homefield Road, which was held in reserve unoccupied. Thus the business was distributed among the three premises and only a small part of the staff remained at Threadneedle Street during the period of heavy air raids. During the Spring and Summer of 1942 a large part of the business which was being conducted at Wimbledon was returned to London.[58]

The Waterloo Place branch resumed its First World War role as a meeting place for Canadians abroad. The following passage from the 1944 *Staff Magazine* underlined the importance of Waterloo Place to Canadians in London:

It was Rudyard Kipling who said that if you wished to meet a fellow globetrotter you had only to wait long enough at one of three places – Singapore, Marseille or Charing Cross Station – and he would eventually turn up. To these three places has now been added a fourth, at least as far as Canadians are concerned – "No. 9, Waterloo Place." During the Great War of 1914–1918 our West End, London, branch was something more than a bank. It was a meeting place and information centre for men and women from every province of the Dominion. Men from the fighting front, the mud of Flanders still upon their clothing, made it their first call on reaching "Blighty." Many were the joyful reunions as these brothers-in-arms greeted fellow Canadians of whom they had not heard for months. Today, in World War II, "Waterloo Place" is still carrying on. Once more it is the rallying point of Canadians overseas, the meeting place of friends. Again its staff is serving loyally and unselfishly shouldering a great responsibility, helping to maintain that lifeline of service which links our boys abroad with those who wait for them at home.[59]

The Waterloo branch provided important services for Canadians serving abroad. It had served this role during the First World War, and the Bank of Montreal knew it would serve the same role again. In 1940, "prior to the arrival of the first contingent of the C.A.S.F. [Canadian Active Service Force, later simply the Canadian Army] in England, Waterloo Place branch made arrangements for the handling of a large number of officers' accounts and for the rendering of such services as they were called upon to provide in the previous war. The time of eighteen employees is fully employed in tending the accounts."[60] The office became so crowded that in 1943 the Bank was forced to rent office space from the French bank Crédit Lyonnais, located next door. As one Bank of Montreal employee observed, "this became necessary because the capacity of the present office [Waterloo Place] was taxed to the utmost, the office and public space was being congested. Furthermore the business of the branch [was] increasing steadily, mainly in accounts of members of the active service forces which have now reached important proportions."[61]

Sensitive to its role as a unique "Maple Leaf Lounge" in London, the Bank provided a taste of home abroad by circulating copies of its *Staff Magazine* to employees serving overseas. For the Bank employee turned soldier, the magazine was an important way of staying connected with Canada. Corporal D.H. Liang of the Bank's Calgary branch, serving with the 1st Battalion, Canadian Scottish Regiment, noted that "it is not very difficult to find a former B. of M. man and it only seems natural we talked 'Bank shop.' A copy of the *Staff Magazine* at times holds more interest than the progress of war, and on many a dull evening you can see former staff pouring over ... news and articles."[62] The staff magazine that began as a simple in-house organ for employee morale attained a popularity of which its contemporary counterparts can only dream.

On the Threshold of a Post-war World

When viewed from its St James Street headquarters, the "banker's war" was one where the leadership and people of the institution rallied to the cause of king and country. The Bank's leaders, as some of the country's most experienced bankers, offered their best efforts and experience to the Canadian war effort. The institution itself mobilized into a financial arsenal of Canadian democracy, deploying its services and expertise in personnel and organization where it would have the most effect. That mobilization demanded that the Bank itself temporarily halt many of its plans for building new branches and expanding services. The people of the Bank served both on the battlefront and on the home front, where they could make a difference. The Bank, in other words, rendered an important service to the Canadian war effort, and stepped up to the challenges that wartime had created for it.

The end of the war was also the end of a complex period in the Bank's experience. The quarter-century between the end of the First World War and the conclusion of the Second witnessed some remarkable transformations in the Bank's relationships, its functions, and its position in the banking system. From the struggles of the 1920s over mergers, acquisitions, and competitive position, to the radically changed public and market environment created in part by the Great Depression of the 1930s, to the remobilization of the Bank's resources and personnel for wartime emergency, the Bank of Montreal was compelled to respond to a series of major changes that would dramatically alter its operating context. Fortune, indeed, had been "changeful."

After the war, the Bank of Montreal would turn its attention toward personal banking. The 1944 decennial revision of the Bank Act facilitated that move. The act reduced the maximum interest rate from 7 per cent to 6 per cent. It also designated, finally, the Bank of Canada as the exclusive note-issuing agency in Canada, simplified procedures to widen the scope of lending to farmers and fishermen, and allowed banks to lend upon "the security of lien notes, sales contacts and other instruments or agreements respecting the sale of goods and merchandise or moneys payable thereunder."[63] To usher in its new post-war strategy, the Bank would later organize the "My Bank" campaign, which "signaled a conscious effort on the part of the bank not to appear solely interested in big business and government."[64]

In 1944 the Bank joined the country in looking to the post-war world. "It is quite obvious that there is emerging in Canada a deep and overwhelming conviction that after the pain and struggle of this war," commented G.W. Spinney, "there must come new opportunities for individual and social betterment in our time and for our children."[65] Banking had to keep pace with the new expectations of Canadians. By the following year, with the war's end in sight, the changes coursing through banking – a more liberal loan policy, a greater outreach to a broader audience, the development of a more person-focused banking – were already being felt. In the executive committee of the board in January 1945, a very large – $10 million – advance was being considered for

Lever Brothers. The explanation in the record is revealing: "The Committee[,] while noting that the making of term loans was a departure from ordinary banking practice[,] in keeping with changing times, approved the policy of making such loans under suitable safeguard, each application being dealt with on its own merits."[66]

The transition from war to peace, President Spinney suggested in 1945, "is the more difficult because in some respects there will still need to be wartime thinking for many months to come."[67] The most significant immediate economic danger was inflationary pressures which were "more intense and more fraught with potential danger than at any time during the years of actual conflict."[68] The post-war reconstruction plans of the Dominion and provincial governments were also very much on the radar of the Bank of Montreal administration. The Dominion-Provincial Conference on Reconstruction in the summer of 1945 attracted a great deal of attention in the Bank. The Bank's economic adviser, W.T.G. Hackett, prepared an analytical summary of the proceedings.[69] The conference proposed a vast overhaul of the financial foundations of government in Canada. Financial incentives were to be offered to the provinces for public-work programs. The Dominion government also proposed a "vastly extended program of social services," to be funded principally by the national government. This included a complete national-health program, an increase in and overhaul of the National Old Age Pension, an extension of unemployment insurance to cover all employed persons, and unemployment-assistance payments for "employables not eligible for Unemployment Insurance benefits."[70] In addition, the Dominion government proposed asserting its authority over corporation taxes at the same time as it implemented significant increases in these taxes to recoup and redouble the losses from the provinces.

Hackett calculated the probable cost of these new programs as running into the hundreds of millions of dollars. The expenditure for a national-health program, for example, would amount to $264 million – compared to the $43 million spent by public authorities in Canada for that purpose in 1944. The Old Age Pension proposals would cost an additional $165 million.[71] The full employment objectives of the King government, and the use of fiscal policy to control economic investment and consumer demand, were met with some skepticism.[72] Even so, the wholehearted embrace of Keynesian contra-cyclical financing and a vastly expanded role for the state was emerging as a permanent feature of financial life in Canada. The arrival of a measure of social security, the increased importance of crown corporations, the more interventionist philosophy of the Dominion government – all pointed to the arrival of a new era. The greatly expanded powers of the Dominion government may have been balanced on the pinhead of the War Measures Act at the beginning of the war, but by 1945 a massive legislative and programmatic foundation for state expansion had been laid.

The Bank's leadership had post-war plans of its own. New buildings and extensions had been put off until war's end. When the end came, the renovation program would be impressive: $5.8 million for upgrades, with a "reservation available of approximately $2 million," the major portion of which would go to the building of new Toronto offices. The Montreal head office itself was due for a major overhaul.[73] The post-war world posed huge challenges and generated massive opportunities for the Bank. Yet it could move into that world with an established record of endurance, achievement, and service to the country. The question was: Could the Bank translate that record into a sustained competitive advantage as the new day dawned?

NOTES

Abbreviations

BEA	Bank of England Archive
BMOA	Bank of Montreal Archives
DCB	*Dictionary of Canadian Biography* (www.biographi.ca; University of Toronto Press/Presses l'Université Laval, 2003–)
LAC	Library and Archives Canada
NAUK	National Archives of the United Kingdom
NSA	Nova Scotia Archives
PANL	Provincial Archives of Newfoundland and Labrador
PAS	Provincial Archives of Saskatchewan

General Introduction

1 The abbreviation "BMO" is used occasionally in this book as an editorial shorthand to reduce repetition of the institution's full name. It is not to be confused with the Bank of Montreal's formal adoption of that abbreviation as part of a rebranding exercise in the 1990s.

2 As of 31 October 2018. http://www.bmo.com/home/about/banking/corporate-information/about-us/bmo-financial-group (accessed 14 February 2019).

3 Duncan McDowall, *Quick to the Frontier: Canada's Royal Bank* (Toronto: McClelland and Stewart, 1993); James Darroch, *Canadian Banks and Global Competitiveness* (Montreal/Kingston: McGill-Queen's University Press, 2014).

4 Philip Scranton and Patrick Friedenson, *Reimagining Business History* (Oxford: Oxford University Press, 2013), 30, 32.

5 Ibid., 32.

6 William Deresiewicz, "Solitude and Leadership," *American Scholar* 790 (spring 2010): 24.

7 Scranton and Friedenson, *Reimagining Business History*, 114.

8 From the citation of Eliot's Nobel Prize for Literature (1948), cited in *Nobel Lectures Literature 1901–1967*, ed. Horst Frenz (Amsterdam: Elsevier Publishing Company, 1969).

9 T.S. Eliot, "Little Gidding," *Four Quartets* (San Diego: Harcourt Books, 1972), 59.

Chapter One

1 Adam Shortt, "Canadian Currency and Exchange under French rule," *Canadian Bankers' Association Journal* 5: 1057.

2 David Bergeron, "Funding the War of 1812," *Bank of Canada Museum Research Papers* (1 January 2012), 4.

3 Karen Campbell, "The Embargo Act of 1808," in *The Vermont Encyclopedia*, eds. John J. Duffy, Samuel B. Hand, and Ralph H. Orth (New Hampshire: University Press of New England, 2003), 114.

Contemporary reports suggest that the British Army received as much as one-third of its beef via smuggling from Vermont. When smugglers were arrested in the notorious "Black Snake Affair" of 1808, they initially resisted the revenue officers and killed two militiamen and an innocent bystander. Despite the efforts of the US Army and militia that patrolled the border, smuggling continued nearly unabated until the close of the War of 1812. See John Little, *Loyalties in Conflict: A Canadian Borderland in War and Rebellion, 1812–1840* (Toronto: University of Toronto Press, 2008). Little writes: "Western Vermont's natural trading links were along the Lake Champlain-Richelieu River corridor to Montreal. Consequently, Jefferson's Embargo failed to impede the traffic northward into Lower Canada, leading to a virtual rebellion in certain Vermont and New York communities. The outbreak of war with Britain in 1812 also did little to diminish that trade, despite the 170 seizures of smuggled goods in northern Vermont." See also Nicholas H. Muller, "Smuggling into Canada: How the Champlain Valley Defied Jefferson's Embargo," *Vermont History* 38, no. 1 (January 1970): 5–21. Muller suggests that 1808, the year of the embargo, saw an actual increase in trade by 31 per cent, to 140,000 pounds of goods.

4 Peter Andreas, *Smuggler Nation: How Illicit Trade Made America* (New York: Oxford University Press, 2013), 74–80. See also Louis Martin Sears, *Jefferson and the Embargo* (Durham, NC: Duke University Press 1927), reviewed by W.F. Galpin in *Georgia Historical Quarterly* 11, no. 4 (December 1927): 357–9; Jeffery A. Frankel, "The 1807–1809 Embargo against Great Britain," *Journal of Economic History* 42, no. 2 (June 1982): 291–308.

5 Bergeron, "Funding the War of 1812," 4.

6 Bray Hammond, *Banks and Politics in America from the Revolution to the Civil War* (Princeton, NJ: Princeton University Press, 1967), 641–3.

7 Merrill Denison, *Canada's First Bank: A History of the Bank of Montreal*, vol. 1 (Toronto: McClelland and Stewart, 1966), 62.

8 Bergeron, "Funding the War of 1812," 12.

9 Ibid., 5.

10 Ibid.

11 John R. Grodzinski, "Commissariat," in *The Encyclopedia of the War of 1812: A Political, Social, and Military History, Volume 1: A-K,* ed. Spencer C. Tucker (California: ABC-CLIO, 2012), 148–9.

12 Bergeron, "Funding the War of 1812," 9; G. Sheppard, *Plunders, Profit and Paroles: A Social History of the War of 1812 in Upper Canada* (Montreal/Kingston: McGill-Queen's University Press, 1994), 142; L.D. Bergeron, "Pretended Banking?: The Struggle for Banking Facilities in Kingston, Upper Canada, 1810–1837" (MA thesis, University of Ottawa, 2007), 72–4, cited in Bergeron, "Funding the War of 1812."

13 Bergeron, "Funding the War of 1812," 13; Sheppard, *Plunders, Profit and Paroles*, 104, 108, 122.

14 Bray Hammond, "Banking in Canada before Confederation, 1792–1867," in *Approaches to Canadian Economic History: A Selection of Essays,* eds. W.T. Easterbrook and M.H. Watkins (Toronto: McClelland and Stewart 1967), 127–8.

15 BMOA, The Founders (short biographies of), "Austin Cuvillier."

16 Jacques Monet and Gerald J.J. Tulchinsky, "Cuvillier, Austin," in DCB, vol. 7.

17 BMOA, The Founders, "Austin Cuvillier."

18 Ibid.

19 Monet and J.J. Tulchinsky, "Cuvillier, Austin."

20 BMOA, The Founders, "Horatio Gates."

21 Ibid.; BMOA, Writing of the Centenary of the Bank of Montreal, 1917, "Confidential Memorandum from Frederick Williams-Taylor to Mr. Vaughan," 14 May 1917.

22 Jean-Claude Robert, "Gates, Horatio," in DCB, vol. 6.

23 BMOA, "Horatio Gates"; ibid., "Confidential Memorandum from Frederick Williams-Taylor to Mr. Vaughan."

24 Robert, "Gates, Horatio."

25 Gerald J.J. Tulchinsky, "Garden, George," in DCB, vol. 6.

26 BMOA, The Founders, "George Garden"; BMOA, Centenary of the Bank of Montreal, 1917, "Confidential Memorandum from Frederick Williams-Taylor to Mr. Vaughan."

27 BMOA, The Founders, "John Richardson"; BMOA, *Centenary of the Bank of Montreal,* 1817, 8–2.

28 BMOA, The Founders, "John Richardson."

29 F. Murray Greenwood, "Richardson, John," in DCB, vol. 6.

30 Robert, "Gates, Horatio."

31 LAC, *Journal of the House of Assembly, Lower Canada* [1830 session] (Quebec: Neilson and Cowan, 1830), 212.

32 Ibid.

Part Two

1 BMOA, Writing of the Centenary of the Bank of Montreal, 1917, "Bank of Montreal, 1817–1917 – Vice-Presidents"; ibid., "Cashiers."

2 BMOA, New Stock Ledger, 1837–1845, shows Joseph Masson as the leading shareholder with 312 shares, John Molson with 205, and John Redpath with 100. This suggests a wide distribution of shares among the community.

3 BMOA, Bank Legislation, Board Minutes, 5 September 1817, 13 September 1817, 7 July 1818, 14 July 1818, 21 July 1818.

4 BMOA, *Statements of the Bank of Montreal as Required under the Act of the Provincial Parliament 11th Geo IV Chap VI for Amending and Continuing the Charter*, 1831.

Chapter Two

1 See Charles Fombrun, "The Building Blocks of Corporate Reputation: Definitions, Antecedents, Consequences," in *The Oxford Handbook of Corporate Reputation*, eds. Michael L. Barnett and Timothy G. Pollock (Oxford: Oxford University Press, 2014), 94–113 at 98–9.

2 Ibid.

3 Ibid., 99.

4 Rowena Olegario and Christopher McKenna, "Introduction: Corporate Reputation in Historical Perspective," *Business History Review* 87, no. 4 (Corporate Reputation) (2003): 643–54.

5 Ibid., 645.

6 Ibid.; Niall Ferguson, *The House of Rothschild*, vol. 1, *Money`s Prophets, 1798–1848* (London: Penguin, 2000); Niall Ferguson, *The World`s Banker: The History of the House of Rothschild* (London: Weidenfeld and Nicolson, 1998); Edwin J. Perkins, *Financing Anglo-American Trade: The House of Brown, 1800–1880* (Cambridge, MA: Harvard University Press, 1975); Susie Pak, *Gentlemen Bankers: The World of J.P. Morgan* (Cambridge, MA: Harvard University Press, 2014). For a more recent examination, see Johnathan Macey's discussion, quoted in Balleisen et al., "Corporate Reputation Roundtable," *Business History Review* 87, no. 4 (Corporate Reputation) (2003): 627–42. Macey examines J.P. Morgan and the Bankers Trust New York Corporation. He asks the question: "Does reputation carry the same weight in today's financial industry as it did thirty years ago?"

7 Susie Pak, "Reputation and Social Ties: J.P. Morgan & Co. and Private Investment Banking," *Business History Review* 87, no. 4 (Corporate Reputation) (2003): 703–28.

8 Ibid., 706.

9 Ibid., 727.

10 Christopher McKenna and Rowena Olegario, "Corporate Reputation and Regulation in Historical Perspective," in *The Oxford Handbook of Corporate Reputation*, 260–77 at 268.

11 Ibid., 269.

12 Pamela W. Laird, *Pull: Networking and Success since Benjamin Franklin* (Cambridge, MA: Harvard University Press, 2007); McKenna and Olegario, "Corporate Reputation and Regulation in Historical Perspective," 269.

13 McKenna and Olegario, "Corporate Reputation and Regulation in Historical Perspective," 272; J. Bradford DeLong, *Did J.P. Morgan's Men Add Value? An Economist's Perspective on Financial Capitalism* (Cambridge, MA: Harvard Institute of Economic Research, 1991), 205–36.

14 Robert Sweeny, "McGill, Peter," in *DCB*, vol. 8.

15 BMOA, *The Centenary of the Bank of Montreal, 1817–1917*, 43.

16 BMOA, Writing of the Centenary of the Bank of Montreal, 1917, "Confidential Memorandum from Frederick Williams-Taylor to Mr. Vaughan," 14 May 1917.

17 The Bank operated without a charter from 1817 to 1822, but it did transact business from its inception.

18 Edward P. Neufeld, *The Financial System of Canada: Its Growth and Development* (New York: St Martin's Press, 1972), 36.

19 Ibid., 39.

20 BMOA, *The Centenary of the Bank of Montreal 1817–1917*, 11.

21 BMOA, Board of Directors, Minutes, 10 October 1817, 2 June 1845, 27 February 1846, 1 September 1846.

22 Naomi Lamoreaux, *Insider Lending: Banks, Personal Connections and Economic Development in Industrial New England* (Cambridge, MA: Cambridge University Press, 1994).

23 Sweeny, "McGill, Peter."

24 Gerald Tulchinsky, "Moffatt, George," in *DCB*, vol. 9.

25 André Garon, "Leslie, James," in *DCB*, vol. 10; Jean-Claude Robert, "Gates, Horatio," in ibid., vol. 6.

26 BMOA, Board of Directors, Minutes, 27 August 1825.

27 BMOA, Resolve Books, July 1826.

28 BMOA, Board of Directors, Minutes, 7 June 1824, 12 January 1826, 13 June 1826, 23 June 1826, 27 June 1826, 4 October 1826, 3 November 1826, 7 November 1826, 8 November 1826, 12 December 1826.

29 BMOA, Articles of Association of Montreal Bank and Rules and Regulations of Montreal Bank, "Rules and Regulations adopted by the President and Directors of the Montreal Bank for Their Government and for Prescribing the Respective Duties of the President, Cashier, and Subordinate Officers of the Bank."

30 Sweeny, "McGill, Peter."

31 BMOA, *The Centenary of the Bank of Montreal 1817–1917*, 24–5.

32 See the *Journals of the Assembly of Lower Canada, 1829*, especially entries for 2 February 1829 and 5 February 1830.

33 BMOA, *The Centenary of the Bank of Montreal 1817–1917*, 26.

34 BMOA, Highlights of Board Minutes, 1837–1839, "Committee Report on Benjamin Holmes," 16 August 1837.

35 Lorne Ste Croix, "Holmes, Benjamin," in *DCB*, vol. 9.

36 BMOA, Highlights of Board Minutes, 1837–1839, "Committee Report on Benjamin Holmes," 16 August 1837.

37 *Kingston Chronicle*, 27 March 1830.

38 Anatole Browde, "Settling the Canadian Colonies: A Comparison of Two Nineteenth-Century Land Companies," *Business History Review* 76, no. 2 (2002): 299–335 at 319.

39 LAC, RG7 G12, vol. 50A, Gosford to Glenelg, 17 March 1836; Browde, "Settling the Canadian Colonies," 320.

40 Neufeld, *The Financial System of Canada*, 40.

41 BMOA, *The Centenary of the Bank of Montreal 1817–1917*, 28.

42 Ibid.

43 BMOA, Writing of the Centenary of the Bank of Montreal, 1917, "Bank of Montreal, 1817–1917 – Cashiers."

44 BMOA, Bank of Montreal Annual Report, 1845.

45 Violina P. Rindova and Charles J. Fombrun, "Constructing Competitive Advantage: The Role of Firm-Constituent Interactions," *Strategic Management Journal* 20, no. 8 (1999): 691–710.

Chapter Three

1 See, for example, Michael D. Bordo, Angela Redish, and Hugh Rockoff, "Why Didn't Canada Have a Banking Crisis in 2008 (or in 1930, or 1907, or...)?" *National Bureau of Economic Research Working Paper Series*, Working Paper 17312 (2011): 1–40.

2 Ibid.

3 "The Montreal Bank," *Daily National Intelligencer*, 13 December 1817.

4 LAC, *Journal of the House of Assembly, Lower Canada* [1828–29 session] (Quebec: Neilson and Cowan, 1829), 354.

5 David McKeagan, "Development of a Mature Securities Market in Montreal from 1817 to 1874," *Business History* 51, no. 1 (2009): 63. McKeagan further notes that there was an active market in bank shares supported by periodic advertisements in the *Montreal Herald* and *Montreal Gazette*. He examines very closely the movement of shares in the Bank, concluding that there was considerable activity, especially on the part of Bank officials "buying the shares and reselling them."

6 Ibid., 61.

7 Ranald C. Michie, "The Canadian Securities Market, 1850–1914," *Business History Review* 62, no. 1 (1988): 35–73, 81.

8 BMOA, Stock Ledger nos. 2 and 3.

9 McKeagan, "Development of a Mature Securities Market in Montreal from 1817 to 1874," 70.

10 Ibid., 60.

11 "Montreal Bank," *Times*, 3 April 1834.

12 Michie, "The Canadian Securities Market, 1850–1914," 35–73, 40.

13 Adam Shortt, "History of Canadian Currency, Banking and Exchange," *Journal of the Canadian Bankers' Association* 10 (January 1903): 35–9; Roeliff Morton Breckenridge, *The Canadian Banking System, 1817–1890* (New York: Macmillan, 1893), 121.

14 BMOA, Board of Directors, Minutes, 26 December 1845.

15 Ibid., 13 August 1847.

16 BMOA, "Proceedings at a General Meeting of the Stockholders of the Bank of Montreal, held at the Banking House on This Day," 5 June 1848.

17 Ibid.

18 Ibid.

19 *Journal of the Canadian Bankers' Association* 2 (September 1894–August 1895) (Toronto: Monetary Times Printing Company, 1895), 150.

20 Ibid., 174.

21 Ibid., 176.

22 BMOA, Bank of Montreal Annual Report, 1850; ibid., Bank of Montreal Annual Report, 1856.

Chapter Four

1 Adam Shortt, "The Early History of Canadian Banking: Canadian Currency and Exchange under French Rule, *Journal of the Canadian Bankers' Association* 5 (1898): 176.

2 See, for example, 18 Vic Cap 38–42.

3 *Montreal Gazette*, March 16, 1841.

4 Ibid.

5 NAUK, CO42/577, Records of the Lords of the Treasury, 20 February 1851.

6 Ibid.

7 Ibid.

8 Elinor Kyte Senior, "Routh, Sir Randolph Isham," in *DCB*, vol. 8.

9 Roeliff M. Breckenridge, "The Canadian Banking System 1817–1890," *Journal of the Canadian Bankers' Association*, 1894, 87.

10 Ibid., 51–3, 58, 59, 87–8.

11 Sessional Papers of the Legislature of United Canada, 1841, Select Committee on Banking and Currency, Appendix O, 10 Sept 1841.

12 Breckenridge, "The Canadian Banking System 1817–1890," 53.

13 Adam Shortt, "History of Canadian Currency, Banking and Exchange," *Journal of the Canadian Bankers' Association* 10 (1903): 35–9. 8, no. 3, 227.

14 NAUK, T1/3476, Treasury Department Order, 30 November 1832.

15 NAUK, T1/3476, bundle 63, no. 1599, 6 December 1832, Routh to James Stewart, in which Routh notes that he has received the instructions of "my Lords commissioners of His Majesty's Treasury [to] transfer the custody of the public money provided for the military expenditure in Canada to the Montreal and York banks."

16 NAUK, T1/3476 bundle 63, Routh to the Treasury, 20 November 1832.

17 NAUK, T1/3476 853/529/6, Benjamin Holmes to Routh, 27 June 1833.

18 NAUK, T1/3476, Long Papers, bundle 63, Banks Canada (British North America) 1790–1840, PO 42 Commissariat Canada, Quebec, Routh to the James Stewart, 15 November 1834, no. 2240

19 Ibid.

20 Ibid.

21 Ibid.

22 Ibid.

23 NAUK, T1/3476, Long Papers, bundle 63, Banks Canada (British North America) 1790–1840, PO 42 Commissariat Canada, Quebec, Routh to Assistant Commissary-General Price, 4 November 1834.

24 Ibid.

25 Ibid.

26 Ibid.

27 NAUK, T1/3476, Long Papers, bundle 63, Banks Canada (British North America) 1790–1840, PO 42 Commissariat Canada, Quebec, Routh to Price, 6 November 1834.

28 NAUK, T1/3476, Long Papers, bundle 63, Banks Canada (British North America) 1790–1840, PO 42 Commissariat Canada, Quebec, Routh to James Stewart, 15 November 1834.

29 Ibid.

30 NAUK, T1/3476, Long Papers, bundle 63, Banks Canada (British North America) 1790–1840, PO 42 Commissariat Canada, Quebec, Price to Routh, 6 November 1834.

31 Alasdair Roberts, *America's First Great Depression: Economic Crisis and Political Disorder after the Panic of 1837* (Ithaca, NY: Cornell University Press 2012).

32 For a first-hand account of the Panic of 1837 in a letter of a New York contemporary, see William H. Siles, ed., "Quiet Desperation: A Personal View of the Panic of 1837," in *New York History*, January 1986, 89–92. The Panic had a devastating effect on the lives of millions of Americans. See Jessica M. Lepler, *The Many Panics of 1837: People, Politics and the Creation of a Transatlantic Financial Crisis* (New York: Cambridge University Press, 2013); Jessica M. Lepler, "A Crisis of Interpretation: Prescursor to the Panic of 1837," *Financial History* 109 (2014): 30–3.

33 Lepler, "A Crisis of Interpretation," 32.

34 NAUK, T1/3476, Long Papers, bundle 63, Banks Canada (British North America) 1790–1840, PO 42 Commissariat Canada, Quebec, Benjamin Holmes to Routh, 18 May 1837.

35 Ibid.

36 NAUK, T1/3476, Long Papers, bundle 63, Banks Canada (British North America) 1790–1840, PO 42 Commissariat Canada, Quebec, Samuel Gerrard to Peter McGill, 15 May 1837.

37 Ibid.

38 NAUK, T1/3476, Routh to Deputy Commissary-General Coffin (Mexico), 18 May 1837.

39 Ibid.

40 Roeliff M. Breckenridge, *The Canadian Banking System, 1817–1890* (New York: Macmillan 1893), 61.

41 See, for example, NAUK, T1/3476/18279, Bank of Montreal Statements – Abstracts; T1/3476, General Statement of the Affairs of the Bank of Montreal on 1 February 1831, no. 5 enclosure, no. 39 dispatch.

42 NAUK, T1/3475, Long Papers, bundle 62, Banks: Canada (British North America) 1790–1840, n.d.

43 NAUK, T1/3476, "By the Right Honourable the Lords of the Committee of Council Appointed for the Administration of All Matters Relating to Trade and Foreign Plantations," 18 July 1830, at the Council Chamber, Whitehall.

44 NAUK, T1/3476, "Office of the Committee of the Privy Council for Trade at the Council Chamber, Whitehall, 16 July 1830, by the Right Honourable Lords of the Committee of Council Appointed for the Consideration of All Matters Relating to Trade and Foreign Plantations"; NAUK, T1/3476, Office of the Committee of the Privy Council for Trade, Whitehall, 1 July 1833, "Proposed Establishment of Banks in Canada."

45 Breckenridge, *The Canadian Banking System, 1817–1890*, 51–3, 58, 59.

46 See, for example, NAUK, CO42, T1/3476, no. 7286, 20 February 1833, Routh Dispatch 1679; Official Statement of the Bank of Montreal for 1832, no. 7286, Routh to James Stewart, 20 February 1833.

47 Ibid.

48 See, for example, NAUK, T1/3476, no. 3079, Commissariat Canada, Quebec, 22 September 1837, Routh to Attorney General Spearman, which attaches a letter from the cashier of the Bank of Montreal "with a view to place you in possession of the state of my account with that institution."

49 See also NAUK, CO42, T1/3476, no. 1352, Roth to James Stewart, 3 March 1832 (list of stockholders of the Montreal Bank); papers relating to the transfer of the money in the Military Chest to the banks in Canada, 11 January 1831 (Treasury Minute), 17 May 1831; Routh to Stewart, 29 June 1831; Mr Hay to E. Ellis, 19 July 1832; Treasury Minute – Routh, 6 December 1832; Routh (instructions to commanding officers); Routh to Benjamin Holmes, 11 January 1833; "General Statement of the Affairs of the Montreal Bank," 1 February 1831, no. 5 enclosure, no. 39 dispatch; NAUK, T1/1688, Lower Canada, Bank of Montreal, 3 May 1834, J. Fleming to Lt.-Col. Glegg.

50 NAUK, T1/1688, Routh to Fleming, 3 May 1831; Fleming to Routh, 3 May 1831.

51 Kyte Senior, "Routh, Sir Randolph Isham."

52 S.F. Wise, "Head, Sir Francis Bond," in *DCB*, vol. 10.

53 NAUK, T1/3476, 18279/37, Lt.-Gov. Bond Head to the Privy Council, 18 April 1837.

54 Ibid.

55 Ibid.

56 As Neufeld notes, there were other provisions such as the tax of 1 per cent on bank-note circulation, restriction of all debts excluding liabilities arising from the positive specie and government paper to three times the paid-up capital limitation of the bank-note circulation, and so on. E.P. Neufeld, *The Financial System of Canada* (Toronto: University of Toronto Press, 1972), 84.

57 Matthew Jaremski and Peter L. Rousseau, "Banks, Free Banks and US Economic Growth," *Economic Inquiry* 51, no. 2 (April 2013): 1606.

58 Ibid., 1607.

59 NAUK, CO42/576, C.E. Trevelyan to Treasury, 11 June 1851.

60 Ibid.

61 Ibid.

62 Ibid.

63 Ibid.

64 Ibid.

65 Ibid.

66 Ibid.

67 Ibid.

68 NAUK, CO42/576, Merivale to C.E. Trevelyan, 12 June 1851.

69 Jaremski and Rousseau, "Banks, Free Banks and US Economic Growth," 1608.

70 Neufeld, *The Financial System of Canada*, 76.

Chapter Five

1 BMOA, "Report of the Directors to the Stockholders at Their Fortieth Annual General Meeting Held 7th June 1858."

2 Ibid.

3 George Hague, "The Late Mr. E.H. King, Formerly President of the Bank of Montreal," *Journal of the Canadian Bankers' Association*, 9 (October 1896–July 1897): 21.

4 Merrill Denison, *Canada's First Bank: A History of the Bank of Montreal*, vol. 1 (Toronto: McClelland and Stewart, 1966), 60–70.

5 Ibid., 71.

6 BMOA, "Report of the Directors to the Stockholders at Their Forty-first Annual General Meeting Held 6th June 1859."

7 BMOA, "Report of the Directors to the Stockholders at their Forty-third Annual General Meeting Held 3rd June 1861."

8 *New York Times*, 24 December 1861, 7.

9 Ibid.

10 "Chicago," *Milwaukee Sentinel*, 25 October 1871.

11 Andrew Smith, "Continental Divide: The Canadian Banking and Currency Laws of 1871 in the Mirror of the United States," *Enterprise and Society* 13, no. 3 (September 2012): 455–503.

12 Charles W. Calomiris and Stephen H. Haber, *Fragile by Design: The Political Origins of Banking Crises and Scarce Credit* (Princeton, NJ: Princeton University Press, 2014), 303.

13 Philip Scranton and Patrick Friedenson, *Reimagining Business History* (Baltimore, MD: John Hopkins University Press, 2013), 30–1.

14 BMOA, Writing of the Centenary of the Bank of Montreal, 1917, "Bank of Montreal, 1817–1917 – Presidents"; ibid., "Vice-Presidents."

15 Gerald J.J. Tulchinsky and Alan R. Dever, "Ryan, Thomas," in *DCB*, vol. 11.

16 Ibid.

17 Gerald Tulchinsky, "Redpath, John," in *DCB*, vol. 9.

18 R.E. Rudin, "King, Edwin Henry," in *DCB*, vol. 12.

19 Denison, *Canada's First Bank*, vol. 1.

20 This was a favourite appellation of the *Toronto Globe*.

21 George Worts, Bank of Toronto, and John Rose, respectively.

22 Jean-Pierre Kesteman, "Galt, Sir Alexander Tilloch," in *DCB*, vol. 12.

23 David M.L. Farr, "Rose, Sir John," in *DCB*, vol. 11.

24 BMOA, Bank of Montreal, "Report of the Directors to the Stockholders at their Forty-sixth Annual General Meeting Held 6th June 1864."

25 BMOA, Bank of Montreal, "Report of the Directors to the Stockholders at their Forty-seventh Annual General Meeting Held 5th June 1865."

26 David McKeagan, "Development of a Mature Securities Market in Montreal from 1817 to 1874," *Business History* 51, no. 1 (January 2009): 62.

27 Ronald A. Shearer, "The Foreign Currency Business of Canadian Chartered Banks," *Canadian Journal of Economics and Political Science/Revue canadienne d'Economique et de Science politique* 31, no. 3 (August 1965): 331. Shearer's comment on the quality of call

loans deserves some attention. He notes that "in the eyes of a Canadian banker a call loan payable in New York City and secured by high class collateral is practically equivalent to cash on hand ... The call loans in Canada the bankers do not rely upon as in any way equivalent to or as a substitute for a cash reserve. Call loans in Canada are really not payable on demand. The securities put up as collateral cannot be quickly marketed without a sacrifice and bankers know very well that they cannot rely on such loans as a means for increasing their cash in an emergency." Quoted in J.F. Johnson, *The Canadian Banking System* (Washington, 1910), 73. See also, H.M.P. Eckhardt, "Modes of Carrying Cash Reserves," *Journal of the Canadian Bankers' Association* 16 (1909): 98–105; Roeliff M. Breckenridge, *The Canadian Banking System, 1817–1890* (New York: Macmillan, 1893), 343–5.

28 Bray Hammond, *Banks and Politics in America from the Revolution to the Civil War* (Princeton, NJ: Princeton University Press, 1967), 669–70.

29 Jay Sexton, "Transatlantic Financiers and the Civil War," *American Nineteenth Century History* 2, no. 3 (2001): 30.

30 Ibid.

31 See *The Centenary of the Bank of Montreal, 1817–1917* (Montreal, 1917). 49.

32 Hague, "The Late Mr. E.H. King," 23.

33 David F. Weiman and John A. James, "The Political Economy of the US Monetary Union: The Civil War Era as a Watershed," *American Economic Review* 97, no. 2 (2007): 271.

34 Ibid., 274. See also H. Bodenhorn, *A History of Banking in Antebellum America: Financial Markets and Economic Development in an Era of Nation-Building* (New York: Cambridge University Press, 2000).

35 Peter L. Rousseau, "The Market for Bank Stocks and the Rise of Deposit Banking in New York City, 1866, 1897," *Journal of Economic History* 71 (2011): 976.

36 Breckenridge, *The Canadian Banking System*, 185.

37 Denison, *Canada's First Bank*, vol. 1, 160.

38 *New York Times*, 22 February 1863.

39 Denison, *Canada's First Bank*, vol. 1, 132.

40 Rudin, "King, Edwin Henry."

41 Hague, "The Late Mr. E.H. King," 21.

42 "The Finances of Canada," *New York Times*, 13 March 1864.

43 Hague, "The Late Mr. E.H. King," 23.

44 As reported in "Provincial Parliament: Legislative Assembly," *Ottawa Citizen*, 8 August 1866.

45 Canada, Senate *Journal*, 1867–68, quotes the Select Committee report upon the "Causes of the Recent Financial Crisis in the Province of Ontario."

46 "The Late Canada Bank Failure," *New York Times*, 24 October 1867.

47 Ibid.

48 See a contemporary account of this period in Breckenridge, *The Canadian Banking System*, 128–9.

49 Ibid., 128.

50 Ibid., 135.

51 Ibid., 175.

52 R. Sylla, "Federal Policy, Banking Market Structure and Capital Mobilization in the United States, 1863–1913," *Journal of Economic History* 29, no. 4 (1969): 657.

53 Ibid., 659.

54 Ibid., 661.

55 Hague, "The Late Mr. E.H. King," 25.

56 Breckenridge, *The Canadian Banking System*, 185.

57 On the later war between the banks, see, for example, "The Banking System of Canada," *Globe*, 10 April 1869; "Bankers and Finance," *Globe*, 1 February 1872.

58 "The Galt-Howland Banking Scheme: Its Introduction Last Session; The Reception It Met With; Its Details," *Globe*, 30 October 1867.

59 "The Bank Crisis: Opinions of the Press," *Globe*, 30 October 1867.

60 "The Renewal of the Bank Charters," *Globe*, 23 November 1867.

61 "Bank of Montreal. From The Albion on Saturday." *New York Times*, 18 November 1867, 3. http://ezproxy.library.yorku.ca/login?url=https://search-proquest-com.ezproxy.library.yorku.ca/docview/92336443?accountid=15182. Accessed 15 December 2014.

62 *Globe*, 24 August 1869.

63 D.C. Masters, "Toronto vs. Montreal: The Struggle for Financial Hegemony, 1860–1875," *Canadian Historical Review* 22, no. 2 (1941): 140.

64 Ibid., 141.

65 See, for example, Matthew Jaremski, "National Banking's Role in US Industrialization, 1850–1900," *Journal of Economic History* 74, no. 1 (2014).

66 McKeagan, "Development of a Mature Securities Market in Montreal from 1817 to 1874," 70.

67 Lawrence L. Schembri and Jennifer A. Hawkins, "The Role of Canadian Chartered Banks in US Banking Crises: 1870–1914," *Business History* 34, no. 3 (1992).

68 Ibid., 138.

69 "Banking Review, 1871," *Monetary Times and Trade Review – Insurance Chronicle*, 2 February 1872.

70 "Bank Stocks," *Monetary Times and Trade Review*, January 1873.

Part Three

1 Nicolò Machiavelli, *The Prince*, translated by W.K. Marriott (Ballingslöv: Wisehouse Classics, 2015).

2 Arthur R. Lower, *Colony to Nation: A History of Canada* (Toronto: McClelland and Stewart 1981).

3 *Monetary Times and Trade Review* 6, no. 14 (4 October 1872): 271–2.

4 See Eric J. Hobsbawm's trilogy on the "long nineteenth century" (his term), all published in New York by Vintage: *The Age of Revolution, 1789–1848* (1962), *The Age of Capital, 1848–1875* (1975), and *The Age of Empire, 1875–1914* (1987).

5 The idea that the Depression of 1873–96 was not in fact a continuous depression but a period bookended by two distinct events was first suggested by H.L. Beales in his 1934 article "Revisions in Economic History: The Great Depression in Industry and Trade," *Economic History Review* 5, no. 1 (October 1934): 65–75. A similar argument is set out in S.B. Saul's *The Myth of the Great Depression, 1873–1896* (London: Macmillan, 1969).

6 Y Goo Park, "Depression and Capital Formation in the United Kingdom and Germany, 1873–1896," *Journal for European Economic History* 26, no. 3 (winter 1997): 511–34; A.E. Musson, "The Great Depression in Britain, 1873–1896: A Reappraisal," *Journal for European Economic History* 19, no. 2 (June 1959): 199–228.

7 R.T. Naylor, *The History of Canadian Business, 1867–1914, Volume One: The Banks and Finance Capital* (Montreal/Kingston: McGill-Queen's University Press 2006), 7–9.

8 Ibid., 10.

9 Ibid.

10 Michael Collins, "The Banking Crisis of 1878," *Economic History Review*, 2nd series, 42, no. 4 (1989): 504.

11 Ibid., 507.

12 Ibid., 525–6.

13 BMOA, Bank of Montreal Annual Report, 1898.

14 Ibid., 1899.

15 Ibid., 1900.

16 "Bank of Montreal: Largest Net Earnings on Record Shown in the Semi-Annual Statement," *Globe*, 14 November 1900.

17 Ibid.

18 "Bank of Montreal: Report Shows the Most Successful Year in Its History, *Globe*, 15 May 1901.

19 "The Canadian Banking System," *Globe*, 12 August 1901.

20 Naylor, *The History of Canadian Business, 1867–1914, Volume One, The Banks and Finance Capital*, 15.

21 Ibid., 10–11.

22 Gregory P. Marchildon, *Profits and Politics: Beaverbrook and the Gilded Age of Canadian Finance* (Toronto: University of Toronto Press, 1996), 10.

23 Ibid., 7–8.

24 Naylor, *The History of Canadian Business, 1867–1914, Volume One: The Banks and Finance Capital*, 7.

25 Ibid., 11.

26 Ibid.

27 Ibid.

28 Robert Bothwell, Ian Drummond, and John English, *Canada 1900–1945* (Toronto: University of Toronto Press, 1990), 71.

29 Ibid., 72.

30 Marchildon, *Profits and Politics*, 11.

Chapter Six

1 Frederick H. Armstrong, "Torrance, David," in DCB, vol. 10.

2 Ibid.

3 Ibid.

4 Alexander Reford, "Stephen, George, 1st Baron Mount Stephen," in DCB, vol. 15.

5 BMOA, Bank of Montreal Annual Report, 1884.

6 Alexander Reford, "Stephen, George, 1st Baron Mount Stephen," in DCB, vol. 15.

7 Merrill Denison, *Canada's First Bank: A History of the Bank of Montreal*, vol. 2 (Toronto: McClelland and Stewart, 1966), 410.

8 Alexander Reford, "Angus, Richard Bladworth" in DCB, vol. 15.

9 Ibid.

10 Ibid.

11 Carman Miller, "Clouston, Sir Edward Seaborne," in DCB, vol. 14.

12 Ibid.

13 BMOA, Bank of Montreal Annual Report, 1911, 1912.

14 Miller, "Clouston, Sir Edward Seaborne."

15 Ibid.

16 Ibid.

17 Ibid.

18 Alexander Reford, "Smith, Donald Alexander, 1st Baron Strathcona and Mount Royal," in DCB, vol. 14.

19 Ibid.

20 Ibid.

21 Ibid.

22 Ibid.

23 Ibid.

24 Michèle Brassard and Jean Hamelin, "Drummond, Sir George Alexander," in DCB, vol. 13.

25 "Sir G.A. Drummond Dies in Montreal: Prominent Financier and Leader in Good Works," *Globe*, 3 February 1910.

26 Brassard and Hamelin, "Drummond, Sir George Alexander."

27 Pierre Bisson, "Le Club Mont Royal," in *Les Chemins de la* Mémoire: Monuments et Sites Historiques du Quebec (Quebec: Commission des biens culturels, 2001).

28 William Fong, *J.W. McConnell: Financier, Philanthropist, Patriot* (Montreal/Kingston: McGill-Queen's University Press 2008), 280–1.

29 *Monetary Times and Trade Review* 7, no. 34 (20 February 1874): 829.

30 *Monetary Times and Trade Review* 7, no. 46 (15 May 1874): 1165.

31 *Monetary Times and Trade Review* 8, no. 23 (4 December 1874): 628.

32 BMOA, Bank of Montreal Annual Report, 1885.

33 BMOA, Board of Directors, Minutes, 13 May 1887.

34 BMOA, Bank of Montreal Annual Report, 1891.

35 BMOA, Bank of Montreal Annual Report, 1893.

36 BMOA, Bank of Montreal Annual Report, 1894.

37 BMOA, Ledger, 2007-094.

38 BMOA, Bank of Montreal Annual Report, 1894.

39 BMOA, Bank of Montreal Annual Report, 1892.

40 BMOA, Bank of Montreal Annual Report, 1893.

41 Ibid.

42 BMOA, Bank of Montreal Annual Report, 1895.

43 Ibid.

44 BMOA, Bank of Montreal Annual Report, 1896.

45 BMOA, Bank of Montreal Annual Report, 1897.

46 BMOA, Bank of Montreal Annual Report, 1899.

47 Ibid.

48 BMOA, Bank of Montreal Annual Report, 1905.

49 BMOA, Bank of Montreal Annual Report, 1908.

50 BMOA, Bank of Montreal Annual Report, 1913.

51 BMOA, Bank of Montreal Annual Report, 1914.

52 BMOA, Bank of Montreal Annual Report, 1916.

53 *Monetary Times and Trade Review* 5, no. 47 (31 May 1872): 947–8.

54 *Monetary Times and Trade Review* 9, no. 18 (29 October 1875): 493.

55 BMOA, Bank of Montreal Annual Report, 1882.

56 BMOA, Board of Directors, Minutes, 5 June 1871.

57 Neil Quigley, "The Chartered Banks and Foreign Direct Investment in Canada," *Studies in Political Economy* 19 (January 1986): 34–5.

58 BMOA, Bank of Montreal Annual Report, 1872.

59 *Monetary Times and Trade Review* 9, no. 46 (12 May 1876): 1294.

60 Ibid.

61 Ibid.

62 BMOA, Bank of Montreal Annual Report, 1876.

63 BMOA, Bank of Montreal Annual Report, 1879.

64 Ibid.

65 Ibid.

66 BMOA, Bank of Montreal Annual Report, 1881.

67 *Monetary Times and Trade Review* 16, no. 3 (21 July 1882): 67.

68 BMOA, Bank of Montreal Annual Report, 1883.

69 BMOA, Bank of Montreal Annual Report, 1885.

70 BMOA, Bank of Montreal Annual Report, 1889.

71 Denison, *Canada's First Bank*, vol. 2, 251.

72 BMOA, Bank of Montreal Annual Report, 1889.

73 BMOA, Character Book.

74 Ibid.

75 James C. Scott, *Seeing Like a State: How Certain Schemes to Improve the Human Condition Have Failed* (New Haven, CT: Yale University Press 1998), 2.

76 Andrew Smith, "Continental Divide: The Canadian Banking and Currency Laws of 1871 in the Mirror of the United States," *Enterprise & Society* 13, no. 3 (September 2012): 455–503 at 459.

77 Ibid., 476.

78 Lawrence L. Schembri and Jennifer A. Hawkins, "The Role of Canadian Chartered Banks in US Banking Crises: 1870–1914," *Business History* 34, no. 3 (1992): 122–52 at 124.

79 Smith, "Continental Divide," 455.

80 Lance E. Davis and Robert E. Gallman, *Evolving Financial Markets and International Capital Flows: Britain, the Americas, and Australia, 1870–1914* (Cambridge: Cambridge University Press, 2001), 416.

81 Schembri and Hawkins, "The Role of Canadian Chartered Banks in US Banking Crises," 130.

82 Smith, "Continental Divide," 457.

83 Ian M. Drummond, "Capital Markets in Australia and Canada" (PHD diss., Yale University 1974), 15. Cited in Davis and Gallman, *Evolving Financial Markets and International Capital Flows*, 414.

84 Denison, *Canada's First Bank*, vol. 2, 180.

85 Edward P. Neufeld, *The Financial System of Canada, Its Growth and Development* (New York: St Martin's Press, 1972), 101–2.

86 Denison, *Canada's First Bank*, vol. 2, 284.

87 Ibid., 270.

88 Ibid., 270–1.

89 Davis and Gallman, *Evolving Financial Markets and International Capital Flows*, 416.

90 Denison, *Canada's First Bank*, vol. 2, 255.

91 Kate Boyer, "'Miss Remington' Goes to Work: Gender, Space, and Technology at the Dawn of the Information Age," *Professional Geographer* 56, no. 2 (May 2004): 201–12 at 210.

92 BMOA, Bank of Montreal Annual Report, 1917, 1920: list of branches.

93 BMOA, Bank of Montreal Annual Report, 1925.

94 Denison, *Canada's First Bank*, vol. 2, 282.

95 Gregory Marchildon, "'Hands Across the Water': Canadian Industrial Financiers in the City of London, 1905–20," *Business History* 34, no. 3 (July 1992): 69–96 at 80.

96 Davis and Gallman, *Evolving Financial Markets and International Capital Flows*, 415.

Chapter Seven

1 Andrew Smith, "Continental Divide: The Canadian Banking and Currency Laws of 1871 in the Mirror of the United States," *Enterprise & Society* 13, no. 3 (September 2012): 456–7.

2 *Monetary Times and Trade Review* 5, no. 2 (14 July 1871): 29.

3 *Monetary Times and Trade Review* 6, no. 2 (1872): 614.

4 David McKeagan, "Development of a Mature Securities Market in Montreal from 1817 to 1874," *Business History* 51, no. 1 (January 2009): 70–1.

5 Ranald C. Michie, "The Canadian Securities Market, 1850–1914," *Business History Review* 62, no. 1 (spring 1988): 55.

6 Ibid., 52.

7 Ibid.

8 Ibid.

9 BMOA, Board of Directors, Minutes, 17 July 1874.

10 Ibid., 21 February 1879.

11 Ibid., 4 December 1891.

12 Merrill Denison, *Canada's First Bank: A History of the Bank of Montreal*, vol. 2 (Toronto: McClelland and Stewart, 1966), 243–5.

13 Carman Miller, "Clouston, Sir Edward Seaborne," in *DCB*, vol. 14.

14 LAC, Historical Statistics of Canada (11-516X), Section H: Government Finance, H35-51.

15 The first Bank Act of the Dominion of Canada received royal assent on 14 April 1871.

16 "The Financial Situation," *Globe*, 10 December 1910.

17 BMOA, William-Taylor-White Correspondence File, correspondence between BMO General Manager Sir Frederick Williams-Taylor and Sir Thomas White, minister of finance, 6 May 1915.

18 Ibid., 6 July 1915.

19 Michael D. Bordo, Angela Redish, and Hugh Rockoff, "Why Didn't Canada Have a Banking Crisis in 2008 (or in 1930, or 1907 or ...)" *NBER Working Paper Series* 17312 (2011): 11.

20 "The Canadian Banking System," *Financial News of London*, quoted in *Globe*, 12 August 1901.

21 "Bank of Montreal: Report of the Annual Meeting of the Shareholders," *Globe*, 4 June 1901.

22 Ibid.

23 BMOA, William-Taylor-White Correspondence File, correspondence between Sir Vincent Meredith, president, Bank of Montreal, and Sir Thomas White, minister of finance, 1915–19, 8 August 1918.

24 Ibid., 5 December 1918.

25 Ibid.

26 Ibid., 31 January 1919.

27 Harold A. Innis, *A History of the Canadian Pacific Railway* (Toronto: McClelland and Stewart, 1923), 97–8.

28 Ibid.

29 Ibid.

30 Ibid. 99.

31 BMOA, Board of Directors, Minutes, 28 September 1880.

32 Ibid., 10 March 1882.

33 Pierre Berton, *The National Dream: The Great Railway, 1871–1881* (Canada: Anchor Canada, 1970), 329–30.

34 BMOA, Board of Directors, Minutes, 21 November 1882.

35 Denison, *Canada's First Bank*, vol. 2, 216.

36 Ibid., 219.

37 BMOA, Board of Directors, Minutes, 5 May 1885.

38 Ibid., 6 February 1885.

39 Ibid., 18 September 1885.

40 Innis, *A History of the Canadian Pacific Railway*, 118.

41 BMOA, Bank of Montreal Annual Report, 1884.

42 BMOA, Bank of Montreal Annual Report, 1882.

43 BMOA, Bank of Montreal Annual Report, 1883.

44 BMOA, Bank of Montreal Annual Report, 1887.

45 BMOA, Bank of Montreal Annual Report, 1889.

46 Paul F. Sharp, *The Agrarian Revolt in Western Canada: A Survey Showing American Parallels* (Regina: Canadian Plains Research Centre, University of Regina, 1997), 16.

47 LAC, Historical Statistics of Canada (11-516X), Section F: Gross National Product, the Capital Stock, and Productivity, F179-182.

48 LAC, Historical Statistics of Canada (11-516X), Section J: Banking and Finance, J1-10.115.7 vs. 55.7-1935-9 is taken as the base value of 100.

49 LAC, Historical Statistics of Canada (11-516X), Section J: Banking and Finance, J481-494.115.7 vs. 55.7-1935-9 is taken as the base value of 100.

50 BMOA, Bank of Montreal Annual Report, 1902.

51 BMOA, Board of Directors, Minutes, 7 January 1903.

52 BMOA, Sweeny, Campbell Biofile, "From the First He 'Belonged' in B.C."

53 Ibid.

54 See, for example, *Globe*, 8 February 1904, 17 October 1905, 19 May 1909, 11 May 1911, and 23 July 1913.

55 BMOA, Correspondence of Campbell Sweeny, 1911–13; C.W. Parker, ed., *Who's Who and Why: A Biographical Dictionary of Men and Women of Canada and Newfoundland, especially compiled for Newspaper and Library Reference*, vols. 6 and 7, 1915–16 (Toronto: International Press 1914), 1050.

56 BMOA, Sweeny, Campbell Biofile.

57 Ibid.

58 "Coast Banker Dies," *Globe*, 3 December 1928.

59 BMOA, Bank of Montreal Annual Report, 1904.

60 BMOA, Bank of Montreal Annual Report, 1898.

61 BMOA, Bank of Montreal Annual Report, 1899.

62 *Financial Times*, 7 August 1915.

63 BMOA, Bank of Montreal Annual Report, 1908.

64 Joseph F. Johnson, "The Canadian Banking System and Its Operation under Stress," *Annals of the American Academy of Political and Social Science* 36, no. 3 (1910): 80.

65 Smith, "Continental Divide," 457.

66 George Rich, "Canadian Banks, Gold, and the Crisis of 1907," *Explorations in Economic History* 26 (1989): 138.

67 Ibid.

68 Johnson, "The Canadian Banking System and Its Operation under Stress," 80.

69 BMOA, Bank of Montreal Annual Report, 1908.

70 "Financial Storm Passing," *Globe*, 25 October 1907.

71 For more on the role of the Bank of Montreal and the Canadian banking system during the crisis of 1907, see: Christopher Armstrong, *Blue Skies and Boiler Rooms: Buying and*

Selling Securities in Canada, 1870–1940 (Toronto: University of Toronto Press, 1997); Johnson, "The Canadian Banking System and Its Operation under Stress"; Rich, "Canadian Banks, Gold, and the Crisis of 1907."

72 Lawrence L. Schembri and Jennifer A. Hawkins, "The Role of Canadian Chartered Banks in US Banking Crises: 1870–1914," *Business History* 34, no. 3 (1992): 137–8.

73 Ibid., 135.

74 Ibid., 128; Denison, *Canada's First Bank*, vol. 2, 260.

75 Schembri and Hawkins, "The Role of Canadian Chartered Banks in US Banking Crises," 134.

76 BMOA, Bank of Montreal Annual Report, 1908.

77 Ibid.

78 BMOA, Bank of Montreal Annual Report, 1909.

79 BMOA, Board of Directors, Minutes, 16 June 1912.

80 BMOA, Bank of Montreal Annual Report, 1914.

81 "A Wonderful Financial Record: Canada's Amazing Prosperity," *Globe*, 5 April 1911.

82 BMOA, Bank of Montreal Annual Report, 1910.

83 BMOA, Bank of Montreal Annual Report, 1913.

84 BMOA, Bank of Montreal Annual Report, 1914.

85 BMOA, Bank of Montreal Annual Report, 1915.

86 "Hundred Thousand from Bank of Montreal: Directors Authorize That Contribution to the Patriotic Fund," *Globe*, 22 August 1914.

87 BMOA, Board of Directors, Minutes, 2 October 1914, 27 October 1914.

88 Bank of Montreal Executives Hopeful," *Globe*, 8 December 1914

89 BMOA, William-Taylor-White Correspondence File, F. Williams-Taylor to T. White, 6 January 1915.

90 Ibid., 7 January 1915.

91 Ibid., 28 May 1915

92 BMOA, Bank of Montreal Annual Report, 1915.

93 Ibid.

94 Ibid.

95 BMOA, Bank of Montreal Annual Report, 1916.

96 "Bank of Montreal in Excellent Shape," *Globe*, 19 November 1919.

97 As of 31 October 1914, Bank of Montreal deposits were $197,200,000. Two years later, they stood at $299,200,000. BMOA, Bank of Montreal Annual Report, 1916.

98 "New High Record Set by Bank of Montreal," *Globe*, 20 November 1915.

99 BMOA, Bank of Montreal Annual Report, 1916.

100 "Bank of Montreal Assets Expand: Enormous Growth in Bank's Assets as Shown in Annual Statement," *Globe*, 22 November 1918.

101 "New Officers in Bank of Montreal: Executive Staff Enlarged by Appointment of Four Assistant General Managers," *Globe*, 23 November 1918.

102 BMOA, D.W. Oliver, "Reminiscences of Canadian Activities Overseas during the Great War, 1914–1918."

103 Ibid.

104 Ibid.

105 BMOA, War Letters: Bank of Montreal, 9 Waterloo Place, London, England, D.W. Oliver to Mr Parmelee, 11 January 1916.

106 Ibid., D.W. Oliver to Dr Matthews, 25 August 1916.

107 Ibid., D.W. Oliver to Mr Macpherson, 30 April 1915.

108 Ibid., D.W. Oliver to "Per S.S. St. Paul," 13 July 1916.

109 Ibid., D.W. Oliver to "My dear Bertie," 5 October 1917.

Chapter Eight

1 *Monetary Times and Trade Review* 5, no. 13 (29 September 1871): 244.

2 Ibid.

3 *Monetary Times and Trade Review* 5, no. 17 (27 October 1871): 207.

4 *Monetary Times and Trade Review* 5, no. 14 (6 October 1871): 266.

5 Ibid.

6 *Monetary Times and Trade Review* 7, no. 50 (12 June 1874): 1279.

7 Ibid., 1279–80.

8 Ibid., 1280.

9 Ibid.

10 Carman Miller, "Clouston, Sir Edward Seaborne," in DCB, vol. 14.

11 Christopher Armstrong and H.V. Nelles, "A Curious Capital Flow: Canadian Investment in Mexico, 1902–1910," *Business History Review* 58, no. 2 (summer 1984): 187.

12 Ronald A. Shearer, "The Foreign Currency Business of Canadian Chartered Banks," *Canadian Journal of Economics and Political Science / Revue canadienne d'Economique et de Science politique* 31, no. 3 (August 1965): 331–2.

13 Ibid.

14 Armstrong and Nelles, "A Curious Capital Flow," 178–9.

15 Ibid., 185.

16 BMOA, Mexico, Memos & Precis, 1926–1927, "Report on Accounts."

17 Ibid.

18 BMOA, Board of Directors, Minutes, 31 March 1905, 18 August 1905.

19 For more information about Drummond and Clouston's involvement with the Mexican Light and Power Company, see H.V. Nelles and Christopher Armstrong, *Southern Exposure: Canadian Promoters in Latin America and the Caribbean, 1896–1930* (Toronto: University of Toronto Press, 1988).

20 Miller, "Clouston, Sir Edward Seaborne."

21 Ibid.

22 BMOA, Bank of Montreal Annual Report, 1912.

23 BMOA, Mexico, Memos & Precis, 1926–1927, "Report on Accounts."

24 For a detailed account of this story, see Gregory P. Marchildon, *Profits and Politics: Beaverbrook and the Gilded Age of Canadian Finance* (Toronto: University of Toronto Press, 1996).

25 Miller, "Clouston, Sir Edward Seaborne."

26 BMOA, Bank of Montreal London Board Minutes, 16 July 1879. According to Merrill Denison, King joined the London committee in 1879, six years after his retirement from the Bank presidency. This information is corroborated by an entry in the Bank of Montreal's London board meeting minutes from 16 July 1879, which bore, for the first time, King's signature.

27 Ibid., 31 October 1888. On that day, E.H. King informed the London committee that he had withdrawn from the post of chairman.

28 Ibid., "Extract of Letter from the General Manager [Clouston]," 13 November 1893.

29 Ibid., 5 November 1879.

30 Ibid., 9 August 1906.

31 Ibid., 12 March 1908.

32 Ibid., 9 April 1908.

33 Lawrence Kryzanowski and Gordon S. Roberts, "Canadian Banking Solvency, 1922–1940," *Journal of Money, Credit and Banking* 25, no. 3, pt. 1 (August 1993): 364.

34 E.P. Neufeld *The Financial System of Canada* (Toronto: Macmillan, 1972), 81.

35 "Ontario Bank Absorbed by the Bank of Montreal," *Globe*, 13 October 1906.

36 "Strength of Our Banking System," *Globe*, 13 October 1906.

37 Ibid.

38 Ibid.

39 LAC, Sir Thomas White Papers, Meredith to White, 21 July 1915. See also BMOA, G.C. Cassels to Sir V. Meredith, 15 November 1917.

40 LAC, Sir Thomas White Papers, Meredith to White, 27 April 1917. The Beaverbrook strategy seemed to focus on the Colonial Bank, which he controlled, taking over the BBNA in anticipation of a merger of Canada and the West Indies.

41 Ibid.

42 LAC, Sir Thomas White Papers, Meredith to White, 28 April 1917.

43 LAC, Sir Thomas White Papers, White to Meredith, 10 October 1917.

44 LAC, Sir Thomas White Papers, Meredith to White, 11 October 1917.

45 LAC, Sir Thomas White Papers, Meredith to White, 12 October 1917.

46 Jack Carr, Frank Mathewson, and Neil Quigley, "Stability in the Absence of Deposit Insurance: The Canadian Banking System, 1908–1966," *Journal of Money, Credit and Banking* 27, no. 4, pt. 1 (November 1995).

47 Ibid.

48 Andrew W. Lo, *Adaptive Markets: Financial Evolution at the Speed of Thought* (Princeton, NJ: Princeton University Press, 2017), 8. For further elaborations on this topic, see Niall Ferguson, "An Evolutionary Approach to Financial History," *Cold Spring Harbor Symposia on Quantitative Biology*, 74 (2010): 449–54.

49 For a discussion on complexity, see Robert F. Weber, "Structural Regulation as Antidote to Complexity Capture," *American Business Law Journal* 49, no. 3 (2012).

50 BMOA, Frederick Williams-Taylor to Victor Ross, 31 August 1916.

51 BMOA, Frederick Williams-Taylor to Walter Vaughan, 28 April 1917.

52 BMOA, *The Centenary of the Bank of Montreal: 1817–1917* (Montreal, 1917), 5.

53 Ibid., 65.

54 Ibid.

55 Ibid.

56 Ibid., 65–6.

57 Ibid., 66.

Part Four

1 Laurence B. Mussio, *A Vision Greater than Themselves: The Making of the Bank of Montreal, 1817–2017* (Montreal/Kingston: McGill-Queen's University Press, 2016), 229.

2 BMOA, London Committee Board Minutes, 15 May 1919.

3 BMOA, Bank of Montreal Annual Report, 1918.

4 Mussio, *A Vision Greater than Themselves*, 201.

5 Maureen C. Miller, "Introduction: Material Culture and Catholic History," *Catholic Historical Review* 101, Centennial Issue 2015, no. 1.

6 Mussio, *A Vision Greater than Themselves*, 229.

7   H.V. Nelles, *The Art of Nation Building: Pageantry and Spectacle at Québec's Tercentary* (Toronto: University of Toronto Press, 2000), 317.

8   LAC, MG26-J13, Diaries of Prime Minister William Lyon Mackenzie King, 2 September 1921.

Chapter Nine

1   David J. Bercuson, *Confrontation at Winnipeg: Labour, Industrial Relations, and the General Strike* (Montreal/Kingston: McGill-Queen's University Press, 1990).

2   Merrill Denison, *Canada's First Bank: A History of the Bank of Montreal*, vol. 2, 341.

3   BMOA, Bank of Montreal Annual Report, 1920: list of branches.

4   BMOA, Bank of Montreal *Staff Magazine*, February 1946.

5   BMOA, Bank of Montreal Annual Report, 1920.

6   Ibid.

7   Ibid., 1923.

8   Ibid.

9   Duncan McDowall, "Meredith, Sir Henry Vincent," in DCB, vol. 15.

10 Ibid.

11 BMOA, Bank of Montreal *Staff Magazine*, October 1945, 5, 26.

12 BMOA, Reminiscence of George Lyness, 2 August 1982.

13 McDowall, "Meredith, Sir Henry Vincent."

14 LAC, MG26-J13, Diaries of Prime Minister William Lyon Mackenzie King (hereafter King Diaries), 4 November 1925.

15 Robert Craig Brown, "Gordon, Sir Charles Blair," in DCB, vol. 16.

16 Ibid.

17 Ibid.

18 Laurence B. Mussio, *A Vision Greater than Themselves: The Making of the Bank of Montreal, 1817–2017* (Montreal/Kingston: McGill-Queen's University Press, 2016), 21.

19 BMOA, Minutes of the Executive Committee of the Board, 5 Dec. 1927–13 Feb 1953, 11 December 1928; Brown, "Gordon, Sir Charles Blair"; Mussio, *A Vision Greater than Themselves*, 20.

20 "H.R. Drummond: Senior Bank Director Started out as Clerk," *Globe and Mail*, 11 December 1957.

21 BMOA, Clarkson-Coles, B21-4, box 1, #17, HR Record: Cockburn, Francis Jeffrey.

22 BMOA, Bank of Montreal *Staff Magazine*, February 1946.

23 Ibid.

24 BMOA, Bank of Montreal Business Summaries, 22 April 1926.

25 Ibid.

26 BMOA, Bank of Montreal Business Summaries, 23 January 1928.

27 BMOA, Bank of Montreal Annual Report, 1925.

28 Michael Bordo, Hugh Rockoff, and Angela Redish, "The U.S. Banking System from a Northern Exposure: Stability vs. Efficiency," *Journal of Economic History* 52, no. 2, 325–41 at 339.

29 "Bank of Montreal Profits $3,949,796" *Globe*, 22 November 1921.

30 BMOA, Minutes of the Executive Committee of the Board, 5 Dec. 1927–13 Feb 1953, 24 January 1928.

31 Ibid., 27 March 1928.

32 Ibid., 22 May 1928.

33 Ibid., 24 January 1928.

34 Ibid.

35 Ibid., 14 August 1928.

36 Ibid., 13 August 1929.

37 BEA, OV 58/1 430, "Office of the High Commissioner of Canada (Natural Resources and Industrial Information Bureau) Special Bulletin (J.L. Fisher)," 24 July 1929.

38 Ibid.

39 Ibid.

40 Ibid.

41 BMOA, Bank of Montreal Annual Report, 1923.

42 Ibid.

43 BMOA, Bank of Montreal Annual Report, 1926.

44 Ibid., 1924.

45 Ibid., 1928.

46 BMOA, Bank of Montreal Business Circulars, "Memorandum: Bank of Montreal Head Office to Managers (Quebec and Newfoundland District)," 10 January 1927.

47 Ibid.

48 BMOA, Bank of Montreal Business Circulars, "Confidential Memorandum: Bank of Montreal Head Office to Managers (Montreal Subsidiary Branches)," 2 June 1927.

49 BMOA, Bank of Montreal Annual Report, 1928.

50 "Bank of Montreal Capital Is Increased to $50,000,000," *Globe*, 4 December 1928.

51 BMOA, Minutes of the Executive Committee of the Board, 5 Dec. 1927–13 Feb 1953, 28 May 1929.

52 BMOA, "Treasury Board Documents and Correspondence relating to Bank of Montreal Increasing Its Capital at Various Times between 1903–1992, Secretary, Montreal Stock Exchange, to C.H. Cronyn," 7 June 1922.

53 Ibid., Treasury Board to Bank of Montreal General Manager, 3 January 1929.

54 BMOA, Bank of Montreal Business Summaries, 23 October 1929.

55 BMOA, "Mexico, Memos and Precis, 1926–1927"; "Mexico – Report on Accounts, Mexico, D.F. Managers – H.H. Davis – G.B. Howard," 11 May 1926.

56 Ibid.

57 BMOA, "Closure of Mexican Branches, J. Vera Estanol."

58 BMOA, "Closure of Mexican Branches, Memorandum for Mr. Spinney," 17 January 1946.

59 Ibid.

60 "Canadian Bank Back in Mexico," *Financial Post*, 12 September 1964.

61 "Principal Problems Ahead of Canada Dealt with at Annual Meeting of Bank of Montreal," *Globe*, 5 December 1918.

62 Ibid.

63 BMOA, Bank of Montreal London Board Minutes, June 17, 1920–October 25, 1923, 18 October 1923. See also 4 October 1923, where the Bank participates in the new Commonwealth of Australia loan.

64 BMOA, Bank of Montreal London Board Minutes, November 1, 1923–March 26, 1931, 6 October 1927, 15 December 1927, 12 January 1928, and 26 January 1928.

65 BMOA, Bank of Montreal London Board Minutes, October 23, 1913–June 10, 1920, 11 September 1919.

66 BMOA, Bank of Montreal London Board Minutes, November 1, 1923–March 26, 1931, 6 October 1927.

67 BMOA, Bank of Montreal London Board Minutes, October 23, 1913–June 10, 1920, 19 June 1919.

68 BMOA, Bank of Montreal London Board Minutes, June 17, 1920–October 25, 1923, 27 January 1921.

69 Historical Diary, Bank of Montreal, July 1936, "Expansion and Contraction, 1915–1936 – France."

70 BMOA, Bank of Montreal London Board Minutes, June 17, 1920–October 25, 1923, 4 May 1922.

71 Bank of Montreal London Board Minutes, April 9, 1931–November 4, 1937, 13 August 1931.

72 Historical Diary, Bank of Montreal, 15 April 1938, "Paris, France."

73 Historical Diary, Bank of Montreal, 9 October 1936, "Paris, France."

74 McDowall, "Meredith, Sir Henry Vincent"; Denison, *Canada's First Bank*, vol. 2, 348.

75 Jack Carr, Frank Mathewson, and Neil Quigley, "Stability in the Absence of Deposit Insurance: The Canadian Banking System, 1908–1966," *Journal of Money, Credit and Banking* 27, no. 4 (November 1995): 1137–58 at 1145.

76 For the US banking case, see: Lee J. Alston, Wayne A. Grove, and David C. Wheelock, "Why Do Banks Fail? Evidence from the 1920s," *Explorations in Economic History* (October 1994): 409–31; Kris. J. Mitchener, "Bank Supervision, Regulation, and Instability during the Great Depression," *Journal of Economic History* 65, no. 1 (March 2005): 152–85.

77 "Merchants Bank Now Absorbed by Bank of Montreal," *Globe*, 17 December 1921.

78 BMOA, "Merchants Bank of Canada Special Report Balance Sheet," 30 April 1921.

79 BMOA, "Agreement Made at Montreal This 10th Day of March 1922 between the Merchants Bank of Canada and the Bank of Montreal," 10 March 1922.

80 BMOA, "Certified Extract from the Minister of a Minister of the Treasury Board, Held on the 18th March 1922, approved by His Excellency the Governor General in Council on the 20th March 1922."

81 BMOA, "Memorandum for the Minister of Finance regarding the Internal Affairs of the Merchants Bank of Canada," 5 February 1923.

82 "The Merchants Bank Affair," *Globe*, 26 December 1921.

83 "Merchants Bank Now Absorbed by Bank of Montreal as Result of Disclosure of Heavy Losses," *Globe*, 17 December 1921.

84 James L. Darroch, *Canadian Banks and Global Competitiveness* (Montreal/Kingston: McGill-Queen's University Press, 2014), 43.

85 "Two Great Banks Raced for Leader," *Globe*, 17 December 1921, in Lawrence Kryzanowski and Gordon S. Roberts, "Canadian Banking Solvency, 1922–1940," *Journal of Money, Credit and Banking* 25, no. 3 (August 1993): 361–76 at 365.

86 Mussio, *A Vision Greater than Themselves*, 52.

87 "Bank of Montreal Effects Agreement to Acquire Molsons," *Globe*, 30 October 1924.

88 Ibid.

89 Ibid.

90 "Merger of Banks Makes Large Unit: Royal Bank Becomes Organization with Most Widespread Activities," *Globe*, 1 September 1925.

91 Carr, Mathewson, and Quigley, "Stability in the Absence of Deposit Insurance," 1150.

92 "The Home Bank Wreck," *Globe*, 13 October 1923.

93 A.B. Jamieson, *Chartered Banking in Canada* (Toronto: Ryerson Press, 1953), 65.

94 By contrast, Carr, Mathewson, and Quigley suggest that "claims that Canada had implicit deposit insurance must be reconciled with the fact that six of the failures, including the

last three, resulted in major losses to depositors." Carr, Mathewson, and Quigley, "Stability in the Absence of Deposit Insurance," 1138.

95 Ibid., 1143.

96 Ibid., 1151.

97 LAC, RG 19, file 488-61-232, "Memorandum on Canadian Banking System and the Home Bank Case," 3 March 1924.

98 Carr, Mathewson, and Quigley, "Stability in the Absence of Deposit Insurance," 1156.

99 BMOA, Bank of Montreal Business Summaries, 22 April 1926.

100 McDowall, "Meredith, Sir Henry Vincent."

101 Irving Brecher, "Canadian Monetary Thought and Policy in the 1920's," *Canadian Journal of Economics and Political Science* 21, no. 2 (May 1955): 154–73 at 154.

102 Ibid., 157.

103 J.H. Creighton, *Central Banking in Canada* (Vancouver: University of British Columbia, 1933), 169; Brecher, "Canadian Monetary Thought and Policy in the 1920's," 157.

104 Brecher, "Canadian Monetary Thought and Policy in the 1920's," 159.

105 Canada, House of Commons, "Proceedings (Revised) of the Select Standing Committee on Banking and Commerce of the House of Commons on Bill No. 83, An Act Respecting Banks and Banking and on the Resolution of Mr. Irvine, M.P. re Basis, Function and Control of Financial Credit, etc., 1923," 325.

106 Brecher, "Canadian Monetary Thought and Policy in the 1920's," 164.

107 Ibid.

108 Canada, House of Commons, House of Commons Select Standing Committee on Banking and Commerce, "Consideration of Improvement of the Banking System in Canada, Minutes of Evidence," 7 March 1928, 1.

109 BMOA, Vincent Meredith to Sir Thomas White, 5 December 1918.

110 BMOA, Meredith-White Correspondence, 1915, Thomas White to H.V. Meredith, 31 January 1919.

111 B.H. Higgins, *The War and Postwar Cycle in Canada, 1914–1923* (Ottawa: Advisory Committee on Reconstruction, 1943), 40; Brecher, "Canadian Monetary Thought and Policy in the 1920's," 171.

112 BMOA, Bank of Montreal Annual Reports, 1918–29, inclusive.

113 "Outstanding Figures Is Lost to Finance in Meredith's Death," *Globe*, 25 February 1929.

114 Stephen A. Otto, "Larkin, Peter Charles," in DCB, vol. 15.

115 LAC, King Diaries, 15 December 1921.

116 Ibid., 9 February 1922.

117 Canada's representation at the Genoa Conference was particularly important, since these international bodies were tasked with reparations in the post-war period and, generally, the avoidance of economic disaster in Europe. See, for example, LAC, MG26 H, Papers of Sir Robert L. Borden, vol. 433, "Financial Commission Minutes Feb-April 1919," 130; "Financial Commission – 1st Sub-Committee Procès Verbal no. 1," 15 March 1919.

118 LAC, King Diaries, 9 February 1922.

119 Ibid., 7 February 1922.

120 Ibid., 27 December 1921.

121 Ibid., 7 March 1922.

122 Ibid., 2 September 1921.

123 Ibid., 24 January 1922.

124 Ibid.

125 Ibid.

126 Ibid., 8 April 1922.

127 Ibid., 20 April 1922

128 Carman Miller, "Fielding, William Stevens," in DCB, vol. 15.

129 LAC, King Diaries, 17 September 1924.

130 Ibid.

131 LAC, King Diaries, 14 November 1927.

132 Ibid., 4 November 1925.

133 It was -3.9C that night. Government of Canada, Daily Data Report for November 1925.http://climate.weather.gc.ca/climate_data/daily_data_e.html?timeframe=2& Year=1925&Month=11&Day=4&hlyRange=%7C&dlyRange=1872-03-01%7C1935-03-31&mlyRange=1872-01-01%7C1935-12-01&StationID=4327&Prov=ON&urlExtension=_e.html&searchType=stnName&optLimit=specDate&StartYear=1840&EndYear=2018&selRowPerPage=25&Line=0&searchMethod=contains&txtStationName=ottawa.

134 LAC, King Diaries, 4 November 1925.

135 Ibid., 5 November 1925.

136 Ibid. See also William Fong, *J.W. McConnell: Financier, Philanthropist, Patriot* (Montreal/Kingston: McGill-Queen's University Press, 2008), 393–4.

Chapter Ten

1 BMOA, Bank of Montreal Annual Report, 1929.

2 Ibid.

3 Ibid.

4 "S.C. Mewburn," in *Who's Who in Canada 1938–1939*, ed. B.M. Greene (Toronto: University of Toronto Press, 1939), 848.

5 BMOA, Bank of Montreal *Staff Magazine*, December 1944.

6 BMOA, HR Records, File Blanchet-Bonthrow, W.A. Bog.

7 BMOA, Bank of Montreal *Staff Magazine*, December 1942.

8 "Prominent in Canadian Scouting, J. Dodds Dies," *Welland-Port Colborne Tribune*, 8 April 1961.

9 BMOA, Bank of Montreal *Staff Magazine*, April 1948.

10 LAC, MG26-J13, Diaries of Prime Minister William Lyon Mackenzie King (hereafter King Diaries), 23 June 1940.

11 Ibid.

12 Ibid., 26 June 1940.

13 Ibid.

14 A.E. Safarian, *The Canadian Economy in the Great Depression*, 3rd ed. (Montreal/Kingston: McGill-Queen's University Press, 2009), 72.

15 Ibid., 75, 194.

16 Ibid., 75.

17 Most of the failed US banks were "unit banks," rather than "branch banks," which were common in Canada. Richard S. Grossman, "The Shoe That Didn't Drop: Explaining Banking Stability during the Great Depression," *Journal of Economic History* 54, no. 3 (1994): 654–82 at 658.

18 For various interpretations of these factors, see: Donald J.S. Brean, Lawrence Kryzanowski, and Gordon S. Roberts, "Canada and the United States: Different Roots, Different Routes to Financial Sector Regulation," *Business History* 53, no. 2 (April 2011): 252; Lev Ratnovski and Rocco Huang, "Why Are Canadian Banks More Resilient?" *IMF Working*

Paper, WP 09/152; Charles W. Calomiris, "Bank Failures in Theory and History: The Great Depression and Other 'Contagious Events,'" working paper, National Bureau of Economic Research, 2007; Jack Carr, Frank Mathewson, and Neil Quigley, "Stability in the Absence of Deposit Insurance: The Canadian Banking System 1890–1966," *Journal of Money, Credit and Banking* 27, no. 4 (November 1995): 1137–58; Michael D. Bordo, Hugh Rockoff, and Angela Redish, "A Comparison of the United States and Canadian Banking Systems in the Twentieth Century: Stability vs. Efficiency?" Working Paper no. 4546, National Bureau of Economic Research, 1993; Lawrence Kryzanowski and Gordon S. Roberts, "Canadian Banking Solvency, 1922–1940," *Journal of Money, Credit and Banking* 25, no. 1 (August 1933); Ian Drummond, "Why Did Canadian Banks Not Collapse in the 1930's?" in *The Role of Banks in the Interwar Economy*, eds. Harold James, Hakan Lindgren, and Alice Teichova (Cambridge: Cambridge University Press, 1991), 232–50.

19 BMOA, Bank of Montreal Business Summaries, January 1930.

20 Ibid., March 1930.

21 BMOA, Bank of Montreal Annual Report, 1930.

22 Ibid., 1931.

23 BMOA, Bank of Montreal Business Summaries, June 1930.

24 BMOA, Bank of Montreal Annual Report, 1931.

25 Ibid.

26 BMOA, Bank of Montreal Annual Report, 1930.

27 Ibid., 1932.

28 Ibid.; BMOA, Board of Directors, Minutes, 24 November 1933.

29 BMOA, Bank of Montreal Annual Report, 1932.

30 BMOA, Bank of Montreal London Board Minutes, April 9, 1931–November 4, 1937, 5 May 1932, 19 May 1932.

31 Ibid., 4 May 1933.

32 Ibid., 10 October 1935.

33 BMOA, Bank of Montreal Annual Report, 1932.

34 Ibid.

35 BMOA, Bank of Montreal Business Circulars, "Confidential Memorandum (Not to Be Passed on to Managers), Bank of Montreal Head Office to Superintendents)," 10 May 1932.

36 BEA, OV 58/26 2056/3, D. Gordon to J.A.C. Osborne, 23 March 1939.

37 Ibid., D. Gordon to J.A.C. Osborne, 23 March 1939.

38 Ibid.

39 Ibid., General Manager to Governor, 15 May 1939.

40 Ibid., "Copy of Cable from Mr. Spinney, Head Office, to Bank of Montreal, London, Received 25 May 1939."

41 Ibid., "Confidential to the Governors Re: City of Montreal," 13 August 1941.

42 Ibid., "Draft Cable, Sir Montague Norman to Mr. Towers, Bank of Canada, Ottawa, SECRET, City of Montreal," 14 August 1941. The final cable was sent, in code, 16 August 1941.

43 Ibid., "Confidential to the Governors Re: City of Montreal," 13 August 1941.

44 Ibid.

45 Ibid., K.O.P. (K.O. Peppiatt) to D. Gordon, 9 March 1939.

46 Ibid.

47 Ibid., D. Gordon to J.A.C. Osborne, 23 March 1939.

48 Ibid., Cable, City of Montreal British Stockholders Committee to Braithwaite, 21 May 1943. See also ibid., City of Montreal British Stockholders Committee to C.F.

Cobbold, 18 April 1944. The plan of reorganization was to be sent out by the Bank of Montreal the following week.

49 BMOA, Executive Committee of the Board, Minutes, 5 Dec. 1927–13 Feb 1953, 28 October 1930.

50 Ibid.

51 Ibid., 17 December 1930.

52 Ibid.

53 Ibid.

54 Ibid., 23 February 1932.

55 Ibid., 6 October 1936.

56 Merrill Denison, *Canada's First Bank: A History of the Bank of Montreal*, vol. 2 (Toronto/Montreal: McClelland and Stewart, 1967), 377.

57 BMOA, Bank of Montreal Annual Report, 1932.

58 James L. Darroch, *Canadian Banks and Global Competitiveness* (Montreal/Kingston: McGill-Queen's University Press, 1994), 45.

59 BMOA, Bank of Montreal Annual Report, 1932.

60 Denison, *Canada's First Bank*, vol. 2, 380.

61 BMOA, Bank of Montreal Annual Report, 1931.

62 BMOA, Bank of Montreal Business Circulars, "Memorandum, Bank of Montreal Head Office to Superintendents," 4 September 1936.

63 BMOA, Bank of Montreal Annual Report, 1929, 1930.

64 Ibid., 1931.

65 NSA, MG2, vol. 1105 f 5, Sir Charles Gordon to R.B. Bennett, 4 March 1932, #47074-82.

66 Ibid.

67 A debt-management policy allowed an outstanding War Bond issue to be turned into a longer-term conversion bond, thus delaying the government's responsibility of paying it back. This was common after both the First and Second World Wars.

68 NSA, MG2, Sir Charles Gordon to R.B. Bennett, 4 March 1932.

69 NSA, MG2, vol. 1121 f 9, Charles Gordon to E.N. Rhodes, 3 May 1933, #52622-7.

70 BMOA, Bank of Montreal Annual Report, 1930, 1936, 1940.

71 PAS S-G2-1933-6, CCF Pamphlets, 1933, Regina Manifesto, July 1933.

72 Ibid.

73 Ibid.

74 Alvin Finkel, *The Social Credit Phenomenon in Alberta* (Toronto: University of Toronto Press, 1989), 22.

75 Ibid., 32.

76 Ibid., 56.

77 BEA, OV 58/4 430, "Chartered Banks," J.B.Loynes, 20 September 1940.

78 Ibid.

79 Ibid.

80 Ibid.

Chapter Eleven

1 Peter Neary, *Newfoundland in the North Atlantic World, 1929–1949* (Montreal/Kingston: McGill-Queen's University Press, 1996), 6.

2 Ibid.

3 PANL, MG955, box 7, file 2004 (17), Executive Council Newfoundland Memorandum, 26 March 1895.

4 PANL, GN2.5.582.3, 3 April–16 June 1933, Secret Memorandum.

5 Neary, *Newfoundland in the North Atlantic World*, 12.

6 Peter F. Neary, "'That Thin Red Cord of Sentiment and of Blood': Newfoundland in the Great Depression, 1929–34," draft, Center for Newfoundland Studies copy, courtesy of the author. 9–10.

7 Peter F. Neary, "With Great Regret and after the Most Anxious Consideration: Newfoundland's 1932 Plan to Reschedule Interest Payments," *Newfoundland Studies* 10 no. 2 (fall 1994): 250.

8 Neary, *Newfoundland in the North Atlantic World*, 14.

9 Neary, "With Great Regret and after the Most Anxious Consideration," 251.

10 LAC, MG26-K M893, External Affairs–Newfoundland–Bank of Montreal Correspondence, undated letter, 16940–2.

11 Ibid., R.B. Bennett to Jackson Dodds, 19 June 1931, 168943.

12 Ibid., Telegram from Dodds to Werlich, 20 June 1931, 168945.

13 PANL, GN.8.142, folder 1, Syndicate Bank Loans, various documents.

14 Neary, *Newfoundland in the North Atlantic World*, 14.

15 LAC, MG26-K M893, Dodds to Squires, 22 June 1931, 168949.

16 LAC, MG26-K M893, Dodds to Bennett, 7 October 1931, 168951.

17 BMOA, Executive Committee of the Board, Minutes, 5 Dec. 1927–13 Feb 1953, 24 November 1931.

18 LAC, MG26-K M893, C.B. Gordon to R.B. Bennett, 28 December 1931, 168952.

19 Ibid.

20 PANL, GN8.142, folder 2, Syndicate Bank Loans, A.A. Werlich to Richard Squires, 30 December 1931.

21 Neary, *Newfoundland in the North Atlantic World*, 14.

22 PANL, GN8.142, folder 2, Syndicate Bank Loans, telegram from J.H. Penson, rec'd. 25 December 1931.

23 LAC, MG26-K M893, Dodds to R.B. Bennett, 5 April 1932, 168961.

24 Peter Neary, "'Ebb and Flow': Citizenship in Newfoundland, 1929–1949," in *Belonging: The Future and Meaning of Canadian Citizenship*, ed. William Kaplan (Montreal/Kingston: McGill-Queen's University Press, 1993), 79–103 at 82.

25 LAC, MG26-K M893, Government of Newfoundland, 168956.

26 Ibid., R.B. Bennett to Mr. Creighton, 15 April 1932, 168966.

27 Neary, "With Great Regret and after the Most Anxious Consideration," 251.

28 Ibid., 251–2.

29 PANL, GN2.5.582.3, 3 April–16 June 1933, Secret Memorandum.

30 There are conflicting reports on this number. Other sources (PANL, GN2.5.582.3, 3 April–16 June 1933, "Secret Memorandum") say it raised only $350,000.

31 LAC, MG26-K M893, Jackson Dodds to R.B. Bennett, 16 September 1932, 169000; ibid., Dodds to Bennett, 168973.

32 Report of the Newfoundland Royal Commission, Appendix H, Treasury Control Act, 1932; Act for the Control of the Public Treasury, 256–.8

33 PANL, GN2.5.582.1 20, Sept.–15 Oct. 1932, A.A. Werlich to Alderdice, 21 September 1932.

34 BMOA, Executive Committee of the Board, Minutes, 5 Dec. 1927–13 Feb 1953, 13 September 1932.

35 PANL, GN2.5.582.3, 3 April–16 June 1933, Secret Memorandum.

36 PANL, GN2.5.582.1, 20 September–October 15, 1932, F.C. Alderdice to Jackson Dodds, 27 September 1932; See also: LAC, MG26-K M893, Alderdice to Dodds, 27 September 1932, 169019–20.

37 Ibid. See also LAC, MG26-K M893, Alderdice to Dodds, 27 September 1932, 169019–20.

38 PANL, GN2.5.582.1, 20 September–October 15, 1932, F.C. Alderdice to Jackson Dodds, 27 September 1932. See also LAC, MG26-K M893, F.C. Alderdice to Dodds, 27 September 1932, 169019–20.

39 LAC, MG26-K M893, Jackson Dodds to R.B. Bennett, 1 October 1932, 169018.

40 Ibid., R.B. Bennett to Dodds, 5 October 1932, 169022.

41 James K. Hiller and Michael F. Harrington, *Newfoundland National Convention, 1946–1948: Volume 1* (Montreal/Kingston: McGill/Queen's University Press, 1995), 546.

42 BMOA, HR Staff Ledger, Officers Book, S-T.

43 Gregory P. Marchildon, *Profits and Politics: Beaverbrook and the Gilded Age of Canadian Finance* (Toronto: University of Toronto Press, 1996), 232.

44 Ibid., 178. The Bank of Montreal trio headed by Clouston provided investment out of their own pockets for a bond-underwriting syndicate, in spite of the fact that the Bank was representing the takeover target, Western Canada Cement. That was not only a serious conflict of interest, since it combined the roles of bank manager, company promoter, and "stock market operator," but also put the Bank of Montreal at serious reputational risk because it resulted in the near-ruination of Sir Sandford Fleming.

45 LAC, MG26-K M893, Dodds to Bennett, 13 October 1932, 169044.

46 Ibid., "Report by Sir Percy Thompson on the Financial Circumstances of Newfoundland," 169029–42.

47 PANL, GN2.5.582.3 3 Apr.–16 June 1933, Newfoundland: Announcement by the Government.

48 LAC, MG26-K M893, Dodds to Bennett, 12 October 1932, 169026.

49 Ibid., Dodds to Bennett, 24 November 1932, 169080.

50 PANL, GN2.5.582.4, "Government Finances; Financial Acts: Amendments," 31 Mar.–24 Nov. 1933; Alderdice to Bennett, March 31, 1933.

51 PANL, GN2.5.582.1, 20 September–October 15, 1932, "Government of Newfoundland Announcement, n.d."

52 Report of the Newfoundland Royal Commission, Chapter IX – A Joint Plan of Reconstruction.

53 These recommendations are quoted directly from the royal commission's final report. A fully transcribed, text-searchable version of the report may be found here: www.heritage.nf.ca/articles/politics/amulree-report-introduction.php.

54 Neary, "'That Thin Red Cord of Sentiment and of Blood.'" The quote is from Harriet Irving Library, University of New Brunswick, R.B. Bennett Papers, Squires to Bennett, telegram, 168685.

Chapter Twelve

1 Dates of establishment of central banks: Bank of England, 1690; Banque de France, 1800; Reichsbank, 1876; Banca D'Italia, 1893; US Federal Reserve, 1907.

2 LAC, MG26, J MFMR, C-2475-A, Papers of William Lyon Mackenzie King (hereafter King Papers), "Central Bank – Prime Minister's Attitude and Representations Re. C108469."

3 LAC, RG33–17, vol. 4, file 11B (1), Records of the Royal Commission on Banking and Currency, "Memorandum by Mr. J.A. McLeod, President of the Canadian Bankers' Association on the Present Working of the Canadian Banking System," 7 August 1933.

4 BEA, OV 58/1-2049/1, "Canadian Banking," June 19, 1933.

5 LAC, RG33–17, vol. 7, file 12, Records of the Royal Commission on Banking and Currency, "Private Sitting Ottawa, 8 August 1933, copy of submission of Rt. Hon. R.B. Bennett, Prime Minister," 61.

6 Ibid., vol. 4, file 11B (1), Memorandum by Mr. J.A. McLeod.

7 Ibid., vol. 4, file 11B (3), Jackson Dodds, "Loans to Farmers," 1.

8 Ibid., vol. 6, nos. 36–7, "The Contribution of Canadian Finance toward the Solution of Canadian Problems," 14.

9 Ibid.

10 Ibid., 31.

11 LAC, RG33–17, vol. 4, file 11B (1), Records of the Royal Commission on Banking and Credit.

12 Ibid., "Memorandum by Mr. J.A. McLeod, President of the Canadian Bankers' Association."

13 Ibid., "The Extent of the Existing Control by the Banks of the Expansion and Restriction of Credit in Canada – the Means Available for Exercising Such Control. Their Efficacy and the Extent to Which They Are Utilized."

14 Ibid.

15 Ibid., "Memorandum by Mr. J.A. McLeod. President of the Canadian Bankers' Association."

16 BEA, OV OV 58/1-2049/1, "Note of an Interview with Mr. Pope, General Manager in London of the Bank of Montreal," 11 August 1933.

17 Ibid.

18 Ibid., Jackson Dodds to E.R. Peacock, 6 August 1933.

19 Ibid., "Canadian Banking," 19 June 1933; LAC, RG 33-17, vol. 4, file 11B(1), Records of the Royal Commission on Banking and Currency.

20 BEA, OV 58/1-2049/1, "Canadian Banking," 19 June 1933.

21 LAC, RG33–17, vol. 4, file 11B (1), "Memorandum by Mr. J.A. McLeod. President of the Canadian Bankers' Association."

22 BEA, OV 58/1-2049/1, "Memorandum on Canadian Currency Policy, T.E.G.," 10 October 1931.

23 Ibid.

24 Ibid.

25 Ibid., "Notes on the Monetary Situation."

26 Ibid.

27 Ibid., "Copy of a Letter from a Canadian Source to Mr. Peacock," 9 November 1932.

28 Ibid., "Depreciation of Canadian $," 2 February 1933.

29 Canada, House of Commons Debates, 19 May 1931, 1562; King Papers, "Re: Central Bank, etc."

30 LAC, RG25, vol. 1671, Records of the Department of External Affairs, PC 1562, 31 July 1933.

31 LAC, MG26K, Richard Bedford Bennett Papers, Clipping Series (hereafter Bennett Papers, Clipping Series), vol. 1048, John C. Reade, "Preparing for a Canadian New Deal," *Saturday Night*, 19 August 1933.

32 Ibid.

33 Ibid.

34 LAC, RG33–17, vol. 6, file 30-1/20-7, Records of the Royal Commission on Banking and Currency, "Difficulties Experienced by Canadian Firms in Export Trade due to the Exchange Situation," 2.

35 LAC, RG33–17, vol. 5, file 20-15/20-25, Records of the Royal Commission on Banking and Currency, "Retail Merchants Association of Canada Memorandum Submitted to the Royal Commission on Banking in Canada," 18 August 1933.

36 King Papers, "British Columbia Bond Dealers Association to the Royal Commission," September 1933.

37 Ibid.

38 BEA, OV 58/1 2049/1, J.L. Fisher to Kershaw, 5 September 1933.

39 LAC, Bennett Papers, Clipping Series, vol. 1048, "Blame Banking System for Difficult Economic Conditions in Alberta," *Saskatoon Star Phoenix*, 19 August 1933. See also "Alberta Farmer Problems before Commission: Economic Burdens Laid at Door of Banking System," *Edmonton Bulletin*, 19 August 1933.

40 LAC, Bennett Papers, Clipping Series, vol. 1048, "Central Bank Controlled by Bankers Not Enough Is Declaration of Farmers," *Lethbridge Herald*, 18 August 1933.

41 LAC, MG26, Series 5, vol. 149, Papers of Arthur Meighen (hereafter Meighen Papers), Copy of letter, W.M. Southam to Sen. Arthur Meighen, 22 May 1933.

42 Ibid., "Economic Reform Association: The Proposed Central Bank for Canada," February 1934.

43 Ibid., W. Robertson to Sen. A. Meighen, 5 June 1934.

44 "The Banking Inquiry: Questions Not Yet Asked," *Globe*, 15 May 1934.

45 LAC, MG26 I, M1096, Papers of Richard Bedford Bennett (hereafter Bennett Papers), D.M. Carmichael, assistant manager, Bank of Montreal, to general manager, Bank of Montreal, 8 March 1934.

46 LAC, RG33–17, vol. 6, no. 30-1/20-7, Records of the Royal Commission on Banking and Currency, "Memorandum Presented by the League for Social Reconstruction to the Royal Commission on Banking and Currency," 2.

47 Ibid., vol. 4, file 11B (1), Records of the Royal Commission on Banking and Currency, H.J. Coon, Bank of Nova Scotia, 14.

48 Ibid.; LAC, Bennett Papers, Clipping Series, vol. 1048, "Bank Managers Attack Central Bank Proposals," *Ottawa Morning Citizen*, 15 September 1933.

49 LAC, RG33–17, vol. 4, file 11B (1), Records of the Royal Commission on Banking and Currency, H.J. Coon, Bank of Nova Scotia, 14.

50 LAC, King Papers, "Resolution No 124 of the Commission on Public Finance, Adopted Unanimously by the International Financial Conference, Brussels," 1920.

51 LAC, RG33-17, vol. 4, file 11B (1), Records of the Royal Commission on Banking and Currency, H.J. Coon, Bank of Nova Scotia, 14.

52 LAC, Bennett Papers, vol. 1047, "WA Pope, HANDS OFF THE BANKS! Bank Act Must Not Become Target of Political Argument or Subject of Hasty Consideration or Experiment," *Saturday Night*," 29 October 1932.

53 LAC, Bennett Papers, "Personal Memorandum to the Rt. Hon R.B. Bennett, Canadian Bankers' Association: Is It Desirable to Establish a Central Bank in Canada? Additional Conversations, from one of the Members Referred to in Mr. J.A. McLeod's Letter of the 3rd October 1932 in Reference to the Above," 3.

54 Ibid., 6.

55 LAC, RG33–17, vol. 4, file 11B (1), Records of the Royal Commission on Banking and Currency, H.J. Coon, Bank of Nova Scotia, 14.

56 Ibid., 16.

57 Ibid., 23.

58 Ibid., 25.

59 LAC, Bennett Papers, "Personal Memorandum to the Rt. Hon R.B. Bennett, Canadian Bankers' Association: Is It desirable to Establish a Central Bank in Canada?" 1.

60 LAC, RG33–17, vol. 4, file 11B (1), Records of the Royal Commission on Banking and Currency, H.J. Coon, Bank of Nova Scotia, 30.

61 On this point, Bennett himself had doubts. On his copy of J.P Day's book *A Central Bank in Canada*, Bennett wrote on the margin next to a passage about bankers' claim that they had no power over the control of credit in respect to inflation and deflation: "Fundamental Liars!" LAC, Meighen Papers, John Percival Day, *A Central Bank in Canada* (McGill University/Macmillan Canada, 1933), 51.

62 LAC, RG33–17, vol. 7, file 12, Records of the Royal Commission on Banking and Currency, "Private Sitting Ottawa, August 8, 1933, Copy of Rt. Hon. R.B. Bennett, Prime Minister," 9. Those present included the commissioners themselves; B.J. Roberts, secretary; A.F.W. Plumptre, assistant secretary; J.A. McLeod, president of the Canadian Bankers Association; H.B. Henwood, Bank of Toronto; Jackson Dodds, Bank of Montreal; S.H. Logan, Canadian Bank of Commerce; M.W. Wilson, Royal Bank of Canada; Henry T. Ross, secretary, Canadian Bankers Association; A.W. Rogers, assistant secretary, Canadian Bankers Association; Professor Gilbert Jackson, adviser; and W.C. Clark, deputy minister of finance.

63 LAC, RG33–17, vol. 7, file 12, Records of the Royal Commission on Banking and Currency, "Private Sitting Ottawa, August 8, 1933," 10.

64 Ibid., 11.

65 Ibid.

66 Ibid.

67 Ibid., 31 (J. Dodds).

68 Ibid., 27 (S.H. Logan).

69 Ibid., 37.

70 Ibid., 44.

71 Ibid., 53.

72 Ibid., 54.

73 Ibid., 60.

74 LAC, Bennett Papers, Strom Board of Trade to G.D. Robertson, minister of labour (forwarded to Prime Minister's Office), 22 October 1930.

75 LAC, RG33–17, vol. 7, file 12, Records of the Royal Commission on Banking and Currency, "Private Sitting Ottawa, August 9, 1933 (Day 2), Copy of [Remarks of] Rt. Hon. R.B. Bennett, Prime Minister," 12.

76 Ibid., 109.

77 BEA, OV 58/14 2053/1, E.A. Peacock to J.A.C. Osborne, 27 September 1933; "Memorandum: A Central Bank for Canada" (CBA, 29 June 1933/17 July 1933).

78 Ibid.

79 Ibid.

80 BEA, OV 58/14 2053/1, E.A. Peacock to J.A.C. Osborne, 27 September 1933.

81 Ibid.; "Memorandum: A Central Bank for Canada," 2.

82 Ibid.

83 Ibid., "Memorandum 'Gold.'" Notation says: "Given privately to Clark in Ottawa September 1933, RK." Clark was the deputy minister of finance.

84 Ibid., E.A. Peacock to J.A.C. Osborne, 27 September 1933; "Memorandum: A Central Bank for Canada," 18.

85 Ibid., J.A.C. Osborne to E.R. Peacock, 2 October 1933.

86 LAC, MG26-J13, Diaries of Prime Minister William Lyon Mackenzie King (hereafter King Diaries), 27 September 1933.

87 LAC, RG33–17, vol. 4, file 11B (3), Records of the Royal Commission on Banking and Currency, Jackson Dodds, "Royal Commission on Banking and Currency, Matters of General Policy."

88 BEA, OV 58/1 2049/1, J.L. Fisher to Kershaw, 14 August 1933.

89 Ibid.

90 Ibid.

91 Ibid.

92 Ibid.

93 Ibid.; see also ibid., "Memorandum Royal Commission on Banking and Currency of Some Points to Be Discussed with Representatives of the Canadian Banking Association at Meetings to Be Held at Ottawa on 13 September 1933, and Following Days."

94 Ibid., J.L. Fisher to Kershaw, 13 August 1933.

95 Ibid.

96 LAC, RG33–17, vol. 7, file 1, Records of the Royal Commission on Banking and Currency, "Press Release – Report of the Royal Commission on Banking and Currency," 1.

97 Ibid., 2–3.

98 Ibid., 5.

99 Ibid., 7.

100 LAC, RG33–17, vol. 7, Records of the Royal Commission on Banking and Currency, Report, 88–9.

101 Ibid., 90.

102 BEA, OV 58/14 2053/1, Royal Commission on Banking and Currency in Canada.

103 Ibid., 5. One BOE memo, however, cited other "interesting" facts that included Canada's turn from Great Britain to the United States for private placement of issues.

104 Ibid., Office of the High Commissioner for the United Kingdom to Rt. Hon. J.H. Thomas, secretary of state for Dominion affairs, London, 23 November 1933.

105 LAC, RG25, vol. 1671, Records of the Department of External Affairs, O.D. Skelton to Col. Vanier, 21 December 1933; O.D. Skelton to W.C. Clark, 15 November 1933; telegraph no. 155, high commissioner to deputy minister of finance, 15 November 1933.

106 BEA, OV 58/14 2053/1, Office of the High Commissioner for the United Kingdom to J.H. Thomas, 23 November 1933.

107 Ibid.

108 "Canada to Borrow Central Banker," New York Times, 18 May 1934.

109 Ibid.

110 Ibid.

111 LAC, King Papers, "Central Bank. Prime Minister's Attitude and Representations re: C108463."

112 Ibid., "Attitude of Government towards Central Bank," C108748. There are scores of pages setting out in great detail the evolving positions of the prime minister on the matter.

113 Ibid., "Central Bank," 9, quoted from Hansard, n.d.

114 Canada, Fifth Session, 17th Parliament, 24 Geo V. 1934, An Act to Incorporate the Bank of Canada – Bill 19, 22 February 1934.

115 BEA, OV 58/14 2053/1, W.C. Clark to R.M. Kershaw, 24 February 1934; see also R.M. Kershaw to Governor Norman, 26 April 1934; Canadian High Commissioner G.H. Ferguson to R.M. Kershaw, 25 April 1934.

116 Ibid., "Bank of Canada Bill," 26 April 1934.

117 Ibid., Kershaw to Clark via G.H. Ferguson, high commissioner, 2 May 1934.

118 Ibid., "Central Bank Bill 25/2/34, Kershaw."

119 "Canada To Have Central Bank," *New York Times*, 23 February 1934.

120 Quoted in ibid. See also "The Bank of Canada," *Globe*, 23 February 1934.

121 "Transfer of Gold at Former Price Strongly Opposed," *Globe*, 1 June 1934.

122 LAC, King Papers, "RE: Central Bank."

123 LAC, King Diaries, 8 September 1932.

124 LAC, King Papers, "RE: Central Bank."

125 Ibid.

126 Ibid., N.M. Rogers to William Lyon Mackenzie King, 26 September 1932.

127 Ibid.

128 LAC, King Diaries, 8 February 1933.

129 BEA, OV 58/31, "Canada. Banking and Currency Legislation, Overseas and Foreign Department, Notes on the Proposed Nationalisation of the Bank of Canada," 15 November 1935.

130 "Bank of Canada Stays As It Is, Labor Is Told," *Globe*, 7 February 1935.

131 LAC, King Diaries, 1 March 1934.

132 Ibid.

133 Ibid., 21 March 1934.

134 "Bans Public Control over Bank of Canada – Commons at Ottawa Defeats Motion to Nationalize New Central Institution," *New York Times*, June 22, 1934.

135 Ibid.

136 LAC, King Papers, "Central Bank 108534."

137 "Strong Opposition for Banking Bill by Western Group: Labor and Progressive Members Lambaste Amendments: Dictatorship Charted: Committee Told Small Group Controls Dominion's Finances," *Globe*, 2 March 1934.

138 "Fight Is Started by Radical Group against Bank Act. Amendment Calling for Government Ownership Is Moved. Liberals Offer Aid. Right Hon. WLM King Agrees to Expedite Passage of Bill," *Globe*, 9 March 1934.

139 "Mr. Bennett's Message," *Globe*, 1 January 1935.

140 BEA, OV 58/14 2053/1, "Overseas and Foreign Dept., Canada. Memorandum Chartered Banks' Cash Reserves," 6 July 1934.

141 Ibid., Personal and Confidential, R.M. Kershaw to W.C. Clark, 13 July 1934.

142 "Central Bank Plans Are Fully Achieved: Shares Are Offered," *Globe*, 17 September 1934.

143 "Banks to Reduce Size of Currency," *Globe*, 24 September 1934.

144 BEA, OV 58/14 2053/1, "Copy. Telegram from the High Commissioner in Canada for His Majesty's Government in the United Kingdom to the Secretary of State for Dominion Affairs, September 7, 1934 Received 10.20 pm. 7 September 1934, No. 153"; "Young Canadian Named Central Bank Governor," *Globe*, 7 September 1934.

145 "Canada Picks Head for Central Bank," *New York Times*, 7 September 1934.

146 "Primary Industries to Provide Directors for Bank of Canada," *Globe*, 5 October 1934.

147 "Sixty-Nine Names for Bank Board: Wife of Senator James Murdock Included in Nominations," *Globe*, 13 December 1934.

148 "Bradshaw Is Named Executive Director of Bank of Canada," *Globe*, 31 January 1935.

149 LAC, King Papers, "Criticism of Private Ownership (cont'd) C108599."

150 "Bank of Canada Handles Millions on Opening Day: Branches throughout Country Start Business without Ceremony," *Globe*, 11 March 1935.

151 "The Bank of Canada Opens," *Globe*, 11 March 1935.

152 LAC, King Diaries, 13 March 1935.

153 "Ottawa to Profit When Banks Hand over Gold," *Globe*, 23 February 1934.

154 BEA, OV 58/31, "Canada. Banking and Currency Legislation, Copy. Privy Council Order in Council PC, 1110," 1; "Chartered Banks Held 40 Per Cent of Gold Reserves," *Globe*, 6 June 1935.

155 "Bank of Montreal Branch at Wheatley Being Closed," *Globe*, 27 December 1934.

156 BEA, OV 58/1 2049/1, "Overseas Dept., Canada, Memorandum, Sir Charles Gordon's Picture...," n.d.

157 Ibid.

158 "Bank of Montreal Annual General Meeting Held 3rd December 1934," *Globe*, 6 December 1934.

159 Ibid.

160 Ibid.

161 "Canada Well Served by Banking System: High Standards of Dominion's Institutions Lauded," *Globe*, 26 December 1934.

162 "Central Bank Destined to End Present Trend but Cooperation of Canadian Banks Praised by Dodds," *Globe*, 9 November 1934.

163 Ibid.

164 LAC, Meighen Papers, vol. 149, "John Percival Day, 'A Central Bank in Canada,'" 43.

165 Ibid., 44.

166 LAC, Bennett Papers, Clipping Service, vol. 1047.

167 Ibid., "Jackson Dodds Attacks 'Noxious' Credit Theories," *Toronto Star*, 14 November 1935.

168 BEA, OV 58/31 "Canada. Banking and Currency Legislation, Overseas and Foreign Department, Nationalisation of Bank of Canada," 20 August 1935.

169 Ibid.

170 LAC, King Papers, "Currency Credit and Banking," C108441.

171 Ibid., C108443.

172 Ibid., "Credit and Banking – Mackenzie King," 108464.

173 Ibid., "Currency Credit and Banking," C108443.

174 Ibid., King Papers, "Rt. Hon Mackenzie King, Speaking at Windsor," 7 October 1935, C108359.

175 BEA, OV 58/31. "Canada. Banking and Currency Legislation. Memorandum: Control," 29 July 1936.

176 LAC, King Papers, Correspondence Primary Series, Norman Priestley to Prime Minister Mackenzie King, 4 September 1936.

177 P.J. Cain, "Gentlemanly Imperialism at Work: The Bank of England, Canada, and the Sterling Area, 1932–1936," *Economic History Review*, vol. 49, no. 2 (May 1996): 336–57.

178 Ibid., 352.

179 Ibid., 342.

180 Ibid., 348.

181 Ibid., 354.

182 BEA, OV 58/14 2053/1, "Notes for Mr. Osborne's Speech to the '39 Club,'" February 1939.

183 Ibid.

184 Ibid., "EY Jackson to the Governor of the Bank of England," 6 September 1937.

Chapter Thirteen

1 BMOA, Bank of Montreal Annual Report, 1939. The onset of the Second World War was, in part, responsible for the upsurge as governments began a massive borrowing program to begin to finance the war effort.

2 Ibid.

3 BMOA, Bank of Montreal *Staff Magazine*, October 1945, February 1958.

4 BMOA, Bank of Montreal Annual Report, 1939.

5 Ibid.

6 "Huntly Drummond Sees Canada United, Strong in Emergency," *Globe and Mail*, 1 December 1939.

7 BMOA, Bank of Montreal Annual Report, 1939.

8 Ibid., 1942.

9 Ibid., 1943.

10 Ibid., 1941.

11 BMOA, B35-5, box 2, file 21, 2012-216-76, #631, A.W. Currie to D. Oliver, 30 November 1917.

12 Ibid.

13 Ibid., Sen. Sir Arthur Meighen to J. Dodds, 12 January 1942.

14 Ibid., J. Dodds to A. Meighen, 13 January 1942.

15 Ibid.

16 Ibid., Meighen to Dodds, 14 January 1942.

17 BMOA, Bank of Montreal Annual Report, 1941.

18 Ibid., 1940.

19 BMOA, Bank of Montreal Business Circulars, "Memorandum, Bank of Montreal Head Office to Superintendents," 5 November 1941.

20 BMOA, Bank of Montreal Business Circulars, "Memorandum, Bank of Montreal Office of the Superintendent to Managers (Montreal District Branches)," 27 November 1941.

21 BMOA, Bank of Montreal Business Circulars, "Memorandum, Bank of Montreal Head Office to Superintendents," 27 March 1943.

22 BMOA, Bank of Montreal Annual Report, 1943.

23 Norman Hillmer, "Victory Loans," in *The Canadian Encyclopedia* (Historica Canada, 2006), www.thecanadianencyclopedia.ca/en/article/victory-loans.

24 BMOA, Bank of Montreal Business Circulars, "Memorandum, Bank of Montreal Head Office to Superintendents," 13 January 1945.

25 BEA, OV 58/4-430, Sir Montagu Norman to G.F. Towers, 5 March 1940.

26 BMOA, Bank of Montreal Annual Report, 1942.

27 BMOA, Bank of Montreal *Staff Magazine*, April 1942. See also ibid., "Excerpts from Speech by Mr. G.W. Spinney about Ninth Victory Bond," October 1945.

28 Ibid., April 1942, 23.

29 Laurence B. Mussio, *A Vision Greater than Themselves: The Making of the Bank of Montreal, 1817–2017* (Montreal/Kingston: McGill-Queen's University Press, 2016), 33.

30 James Darroch, *Canadian Banks and Global Competitiveness* (Montreal/Kingston: McGill-Queen's University Press, 1994), 45.

31 Alan O. Gibbons, "Foreign Exchange Control in Canada, 1939–51," *Canadian Journal of Economics and Political Science / Revue canadienne d'Economique et de Science Politique*, 19, no. 1 (February 1953): 35–54.

32 "Finance at Large," *Globe and Mail*, 9 December 1943.

33 Ibid.

34 BEA, OV 58/4 430, "Canada. 'Should the Canadian $ be Pegged to Sterling?'" (enclosure to letter 28.2.40). See also ibid., 58/4, "Foreign Exchange Control in Canada: Purposes and Methods," by Louis Rasminsky.

35 BEA, OV 58/4, "Canada's Economic War Policies," autumn 1941.

36 Ibid.

37 See, for example, PAS, G1, 1944.21, "The CCF Policy on MONEY" (Saskatchewan CCF, 1944).

38 Ibid.

39 PAS, S-G1, 1944, 23, "Where's the Money Coming From?" Radio broadcast by T.C. Douglas, MP, 3–9 February 1944.

40 CCF, "Security for All," in *Canadian Party Platforms, 1867–1968*, ed. D. Owen Carrigan (Toronto: Copp Clark Publishing 1968), 168–78.

41 Larry A. Glassford, "Meighen, Arthur," in *DCB*, vol. 18.

42 Keith Archer, *Political Choices and Electoral Consequences: A Study of Organized Labour and the New Democratic Party* (Montreal/Kingston: McGill-Queen's University Press, 1990), 17–19.

43 "Banking Monopoly in Canada Opposed," *New York Times*, 7 December 1943; "Montreal Bank Head Calls for Initiative," *New York Times*, 5 December 1944.

44 "Montreal Bank Head Calls for Initiative," *New York Times*, 5 December 1944.

45 BMOA, Bank of Montreal *Staff Magazine*, "Toronto Staff War Service Committee," April 1940.

46 BMOA, Bank of Montreal *Staff Magazine*, October 1941.

47 Ibid., August 1940.

48 Ibid., October 1940.

49 Ibid., April 1942.

50 Ibid., June 1942.

51 Ibid., February 1941.

52 Ibid.

53 Ibid., August 1941.

54 BMOA, Bank of Montreal, *Field of Honour: The Second World War, 1939–1945* (Montreal: Bank of Montreal 1950).

55 Ibid.

56 BMOA, Bank of Montreal Annual Report, 1940.

57 Ibid.

58 BMOA, "Historical Diary, Bank of Montreal," 1 September 1939.

59 BMOA, Bank of Montreal *Staff Magazine*, "Waterloo Place," August 1944.

60 BMOA, "Historical Diary, Bank of Montreal," 16 February 1940.

61 Ibid., 9 February 1943.

62 BMOA, Bank of Montreal *Staff Magazine*, "Gleanings from Letters of Members of the Staff Now Overseas," April 1944.

63 BMOA, Bank of Montreal Annual Report, 1944.

64 Darroch, *Canadian Banks and Global Competitiveness*, 47.

65 Ibid.

66 BMOA, Executive Committee of the Board Minutes, 5 Dec. 1927–13 Feb. 1953, 4 January 1945.

67 BMOA, Bank of Montreal Annual Report, 1945.

68 Ibid.

69 BMOA, Bank of Montreal Business Circulars, "An Analytical Summary of the Dominion-Provincial Conference, Ottawa, Prepared for the Confidential Information of the Directors by our Economic Advisor Mr. W.T.G. Hackett, Montreal," August 1945.

70 Ibid.

71 Ibid.

72 Ibid.

73 BMOA, Executive Committee of the Board Minutes, 5 Dec. 1927–13 Feb. 1953, 4 January 1945.